HOLLYWOOD FROM VIETNAM TO REAGAN ...AND BEYOND

Expanded and Revised Edition

Robin Wood

Columbia University Press
New York

Columbia University Press
Publishers Since 1893
New York   Chichester, West Sussex
Copyright © 1986, 2003 Columbia University Press

Library of Congress Cataloging-in-Publication Data
Wood, Robin, 1931–
Hollywood from Vietnam to Reagan—and beyond /
Robin Wood. —Expanded and rev. ed.
p. cm.
Rev. ed. of: Hollywood from Vietnam to Reagan, 1986.
Includes bibliographical references and index.
ISBN 0–231–12966–1 (alk. paper)
ISBN 0–231–12967–X (paper : alk. paper)
1. Motion pictures—United States—History.
2. Motion pictures—Political aspects.
I. Wood, Robin, 1931– Hollywood from Vietnam to Reagan.
II. Title.

PN1993.5.U6W64   2003
791.43'0973—dc21   2003043514

Printed in the United States of America
Designed by Audrey Smith
c 10 9 8 7 6 5 4 3 2 1
p 10 9 8 7 6 5 4 3 2 1

For Richard
WITH MY LOVE

CONTENTS

ACKNOWLEDGMENTS (1986)

Some of the material in this book has appeared in various publications, though in most cases the essays have been revised and in some cases considerably extended. The essays on Altman, *Raging Bull*, and *Heaven's Gate*, and the section of the Brian De Palma essay on *Sisters* appeared in *Movie*, as did "The Incoherent Text." The chapter on the 70s horror film has been assembled from a number of articles published in *Film Comment*. The third section of chapter 8 ("Returning the Look") appeared in *American Film* under the editorially imposed title "Beauty Bests the Beast." The remarks on John Badham's *Dracula* in the third section of chapter 5 ("Testing the Limits") are taken from a long essay entitled "The Use and Obsolescence of Count Dracula" published in the Canadian literary journal *Mosaic*. All these are reprinted with the editors' permission. Brief sketches for certain sections appeared in *Canadian Forum*, for which I write a regular film column, and sketches for the section on *Making Love* and *Victor, Victoria*, co-written with Richard Lippe, appeared in *Body Politic*.

Two writers who are also my close friends—Andrew Britton and Varda Burstyn—have had a major influence on this book and indeed on the whole direction of my thought over the past few years. They are given specific acknowledgment in the text, but their influence is far more pervasive than such local recognition suggests.

Two of my ex-students, now my colleagues, who wrote M.A. theses under my supervision, have certainly taught me at least as much as I taught them. Florence Jacobowitz and Lori Spring will doubtless detect the traces of our collaboration in these pages, although I am not conscious of specific borrowing.

I cannot claim direct influence (our paths have been too divergent), but I would like to say hello here to two film critics and theorists whose work I have come greatly to admire: Stephen Heath and Noel Burch. I have learned a lot from their writings, and have found in them a most important stimulus to the more precise definition of my own approach. And although I lack their subtlety and their daunting grasp of complex theoretical issues, we share at least a radical position.

I want to thank Arthur Penn for his kindness in reading the essay on *The Chase* and for correcting certain misapprehensions concerning his involvement in that film—and also for his generosity and encouragement over many years.

I come now to a very problematic and cloudy area. Virtually everything I write originates as lectures for my classes; innumerable minor modifications and clarifications have resulted from classroom discussions or from my reading of students' work. The kind of debt involved is impossible to detail. If any of my students read this, however, I would like to say to them that they probably never realized the importance to me of their encouragement and enthusiasm. Their attitudes, their openness, their readiness to explore and discover, and—in the case of those who have allowed me glimpses into their personal lives—their recognition of the need to rethink human relationships have frequently rekindled my faith in a culture whose dominant movement tends to extinguish it.

Finally, I want to acknowledge the contribution to this book of its dedicatee, Richard Lippe, my lover since 1977. Richard has read every sentence of the text and has made many suggestions that I have incorporated. Without his support, most of it would never have been written in the first place.

I think lots of people know perfectly well they're being cheated and betrayed, but most people are too scared or too comfortable to say anything. It doesn't help to protest or complain, either, because the people in power don't pay any attention.

—Rebecka Lind in *The Terrorists* (by Maj Sjöwall and Per Wahlöö, p. 269)

Recently—no, for as long as I can remember—large and powerful nations within the capitalist bloc have been ruled by people who according to accepted legal norms are simply criminals, who from a lust for power and financial gain have led their peoples into an abyss of egoism, self-indulgence and a view of life based entirely on materialism and ruthlessness toward their fellow human beings. Only in very few cases are such politicians punished, but the punishments are token and the guilty persons' successors are guided by the same motives.

—Rebecka's defending counsel (p. 286)

My turn to start? Then I say X— —X as in Marx. (p. 347)

Prologue (2003)
Our Culture, Our Cinema
FOR A REPOLITICIZED CRITICISM

For Nicholas Gee-Ming Chin Wood

THEORISTS, SCHOLARS, CRITICS

I am a critic. As such, I see my work as in many respects set apart from that of theorists and scholars (though it is of course frequently dependent upon them). The
theorist and the scholar are unburdened of any necessity to engage intimately and
on a personal basis with any specific work; they can hide behind their screens of
theory and scholarship, they are not compelled to expose the personal nature of
their work because they deal in facts, abstract ideas, and data. Any *critic* who is honest, however, is committed to self-exposure, a kind of public striptease: s/he must
make clear that any authentic response to a work of art or entertainment is
grounded not only in the work itself but in the critic's psychological makeup, personal history, values, prejudices, obsessions. Criticism arises out of an intense and
intimate personal relationship between work and critic. If it is the critic's duty to
strive for "objectivity" (in the negative sense of avoiding distortions), s/he knows
that it is an objectivity that can never be fully achieved, because even when one is
convinced that one "sees the work as it is," the relationship to it has still to be established. I have not the right to say, for example, "David Lynch makes bad movies":
many people for whom I have great respect admire them, and they can certainly be
defended on grounds of imagination, accomplishment, originality, strong personal
commitment. I *do*, however, have the right to say, "I find Lynch's films extremely
distasteful; my sense of value repudiates them."

The critic, it follows, must never set him- or herself up as some kind of infallible oracle. The relationship between critic and reader must always be one of debate.

One might invoke here F. R. Leavis's famous definition of the ideal critical exchange: "This is so, isn't it?" / "Yes, but . . . " All interesting criticism is founded in the critic's beliefs and values, political position, background, influences, and these should be made explicit or so clearly implied as to leave no room for ambiguity. The theorist and the scholar can (up to a point) conceal any personal commitment behind a cloak of objectivity. The personal element will always be there (in such matters as choice of material to be pursued and analyzed, choice of premise from which to work), but it can only be exposed with precisely that "reading between the lines" that the apparent perfect objectivity is there to deflect.

This will sound to many presumptuous in the extreme, but I feel the need to assert that, in the hierarchy, criticism occupies (or *should* occupy) the highest position, simply because the critic is the only one centrally and explicitly concerned with the question of value, which is the most important—the *ultimate*—question. For the theorist and the scholar, almost by definition, the question of value does not exist or is brought in as an afterthought: their tasks are, respectively, to develop and produce *ideas* about what cinema is, and to examine and catalogue data. But my claim requires two important qualifications:

1. In our present age, with criticism virtually expelled from the higher reaches of intellectual/academic activity, it has become thoroughly debased, the preserve of "popular" journalism; there is almost no "criticism" any more, as F. R. Leavis envisioned it.

2. In a sense critics are parasites, very much dependent on the work of theorists and scholars, which they ignore at their peril. Theory and scholarship supply materials upon which critics can build, applying the theories relevant to their work, using the data for accuracy and factual support.

Hollywood from Vietnam to Reagan: THE BACKGROUND

In the preface to the recent revised edition of *Hitchcock's Films Revisited* (2002), I attempted to expose the relationship between the various stages of my work and the events in my personal and professional life. Here, to avoid repetition, I shall make reference only to what seems essential. I want also to provide a double context within which this book might be read today—that within which it was written, and that within which we find ourselves now. The latter will include some commentary on developments in the Hollywood cinema since the 80s, discussing its relationship to the wider sociopolitical arena within which it operates and to which—in devious ways, never explicitly—it refers: the cinema, one might say, that the current cultural situation deserves and gets.

Hollywood from Vietnam to Reagan was first published in 1986, but it had gestated gradually over the previous decade, when some of its material was written (the earliest was the chapter on Altman, the most recent that on *Heaven's Gate*). It belongs, then, to a particular period of my life and the particular historical decade in which it was lived: the period of my growing politicization, under the influence of radical feminism, gay liberation, black power, the logical swing to the political left that accompanied such developments. It was also the period in which my marriage finally broke down, I left my wife and children, and "came out" as gay—the period, then, for me, of the greatest upheaval, the greatest pain, the greatest exhilaration, the most radical change, the construction (in my usual messy and blundering way) of a new life. The most potent individual influence on me was Andrew Britton, officially my student but swiftly my mentor, who still (a decade after his death) seems to me the finest film critic in the English language, and who helped me discover that it was possible to become political without having to enroll in the semiotics movement.

Feminism initially terrified me (I had to rethink all my previous relationships with women—my mother, my sisters, my wife, numerous friends) and then sustained me during my "coming out" period. In my blinkered state I didn't catch up with the women's movement until then: I'd absorbed no more than distant rumors of its existence and, in my role of "happily married bourgeois family man," I felt no impulse to take an interest. But, when I stepped outside that role, the connection seemed (and still seems) so obvious: women and gays had been oppressed, throughout the centuries, by the heterosexual male hegemony, so it followed that they were natural allies in the war for liberation. And during that period they were. In the background of my book (too far in the background, I now feel—I wish it had been more radical, and more challenging, and more defiant, than it was) was the pervasive sense of excitement, of wonderful new possibilities, a new, reformed world to be created, a transformed civilization built—after all the existing one's power/domination structures had been demolished—upon cooperation and a *true* democracy that would have little in common with the false one in which we still live: a democracy based upon values other than money.

Today all that has evaporated. The radical movements of the 60s and 70s have been effectively co-opted and emasculated in an archetypal movement of assimilation/rejection, that vast and insatiable octopus the Dominant Ideology drawing into its ugly belly what it can comfortably digest without fundamental change and spewing out what it can't. Women can now (within limits) attain the kind of power that was previously the prerogative of men; gays are now widely (provisionally?) accepted (at least within our major cities); blacks and other persons of color have become partially, reluctantly integrated, to the extent that Toronto (where I live), for example, now feels able to pride itself on its multiculturalism. One cannot of course regret that these improvements have occurred (though "concessions" might be the more accurate term): many women, gays, and nonwhites now feel themselves accepted and, to a certain degree, empowered. But at what cost?

All real power (wealth) remains overwhelmingly in the hands of white heterosexual males; a few women can attain senior positions in the big companies and corporations, provided they play the male game and are untainted by feminism; in our multicultural Toronto there are very few wealthy and powerful blacks and Asians (persons of color can be seen riding the subway in large numbers, but very few have limousines); there are many smug and prosperous gay men visible in the gay neighborhoods of our major cities, mostly running their own businesses and without a single political thought in their well-groomed heads. As I write this, Gay Pride Week is once again upon us, with the Pride Day march a few days away. When I moved here twenty-five years ago it was a great event, essentially a political protest; now it gives the overall impression of a vast advertising campaign, with many of the floats supplied by companies cashing in on its newfound trendiness to promote their products. They ignored us when we were an oppressed and vilified minority: there was no money in it. Now that the march is "popular," and thousands line the streets to cheer, the companies are "gay-friendly," and go out of their way to show it. "Fair-weather friends" indeed: the moment a backlash started (and it could at any time), the floats would vanish overnight. The "empowerment" of women and minorities is in reality their conscription and assimilation into the still dominant masculinist order, within which "the business woman" and "the affluent gay male" are easily recognizable types.

Today I feel more politically motivated than ever; as a result, I also feel somewhat stranded. Contemporary reactions to my work (though they are generally polite and intended to be encouraging) depress me. People praise my book on Hitchcock, but it usually turns out that the sections they admire are those written for the original little book in the very early 60s, when I had no political awareness whatever; a close friend told me recently that he values my work solely for its analyses of films, finding the sociopolitical views superfluous; one of the very few reviews (it appeared on the Internet) of *Sexual Politics and Narrative Film* (which I consider my best work) insisted upon a sharp division between the (apparently) insightful analyses and my beliefs, the writer rejecting the latter contemptuously. This seemingly common reaction bewilders me: everything I have written from *Hollywood from Vietnam to Reagan* onwards seems to me characterized and structured by my political position, so that it should be impossible to separate the aesthetics from the politics (in which I include of course sexual politics), the analyses from the radical attitude that animates and pervades them: if you accept one, you accept the other. Perhaps I should be humble and attribute this to my shortcomings as a political thinker (I lay no claim to profundity or originality); I prefer to attribute it to the present climate of political apathy and disenchantment, perhaps underpinned by an unadmitted despair and (understandable) sense of helplessness. Today we need political struggle, protest, and feminism more than ever before, but the enemy now seems dauntingly pervasive and omnipotent. My aim in this prologue is to do everything in my extremely limited power to reactivate the revolutionary ideas and ideals of the 60s and 70s and to develop them further, within the context of a world that, at its increasing peril, appears to regard them as redundant.

If I have achieved no more of value than a few allegedly illuminating interpretations of films, then my life, professionally at least, has been wasted.

A QUESTIONNAIRE (FOR THE READER)

1. Are you aware that *men* are responsible for at least 90 percent of the evils and suffering in the world that are not caused by natural disasters?
2. How many wars, throughout human history, can you name that were started and conducted by women? (No, the Trojan War is not even a partial answer. It was not even provoked by Helen but by the arrogant possessiveness of males.)
3. Did women invent and develop the atomic bomb, and were women responsible, directly or indirectly, for dropping the bombs on Hiroshima and Nagasaki at a time when those cities were known to be populated predominantly by women, children, and the aged?
4. What proportion of acts of violence throughout the world would you guess are initiated and perpetrated by women?
5. What proportion of rapes?
6. What proportion of acts of domestic violence?
7. How many of the major corporations currently responsible for pollution, deforestation—hence, for global warming and the possible end of life on our planet—are effectively dominated by women?
8. How many of the world's major governments are dominated and led by feminists (male or female)?

The questions are, of course, rhetorical, and I see no reason to supply statistics even if I could, the answers being obvious.

You will note that in the final question I have substituted "feminists" for "women." There are or have been female leaders, of whom Margaret Thatcher is probably the most notorious instance in the West, but, politically, Mrs. Thatcher was simply a man in drag. I must add here also that the opposite of "feminism"—"masculinism"—is in politics taken for granted: it is very unlikely that many of our "democratic" male leaders consciously think of themselves as "masculinist." If you position yourself outside the dominant ideology, you are forced to define and name yourself; if you're within it, you aren't. A feminist must declare him- or herself; a masculinist simply *is*. And one must further note a not-too-subtle distinction between the meanings of the two terms: "feminism" is a demand for women's *equality*; "masculinism" is an assumption of the rightness—the *naturalness*—of male *dominance*.

I would like to forestall at this point a possible objection: "He's got his nerve—

a man telling women what they should be doing." But I am addressing this equally to my fellow men, straight or gay—to those who care about life, both its quality and its continuation. When what is at stake is no less than the survival of life on this planet, we are in a no-holds-barred situation. This should be the concern of every human individual, irrespective of gender, color, race, nationality, sexual orientation, class position, who is able to think clearly about our predicament above the constant and ubiquitous "noise" of the capitalist media, and to see beyond the willful and irresponsible blindness of our appointed leaders. Many today appear to assume that the emancipation of women has happened and is now complete. In my opinion it has barely begun, and it won't be completed until men are ready to accept and embrace their own femininity, granting women their share of the "masculine."

I have occasionally been told by women that, as I am (as Marlene Dietrich so memorably described Hank Quinlan) "some kind of a man," I cannot call myself a feminist, because only a woman can understand what being a woman feels like; but I have never accepted this. Because I am white, can I not declare myself anti-racist? Or can I not proclaim my commitment to animal rights because I am not a cat? Obviously, yes, I cannot experience quite "what it feels like to be a woman." Yet one can surely align oneself with a movement *on principle*? And surely there are important connections between the woman's experience and the gay experience under patriarchy? They are not, of course, the same, but there are sufficient overlaps, both being oppressed, belittled, and marginalized groups. The difference might be summed up thus: it is still not difficult (though perhaps within some limited cultural groups not quite as easy as it used to be) for a man to declare himself "anti-gay"; it would be far more difficult for him to declare himself "anti-women."

MASCULINITY, JANÁČEK, AND LIBERATION

"Masculinism" is still frequently confused by many with "masculinity." The two are of course related but they are certainly not synonymous. The term "masculinism" might be defined as "the *cult* of masculinity," the claim that men have a natural right to power and domination, the belief that the "masculine" is intrinsically superior to the "feminine." Many men (and, apparently, and even more unfortunately, many women) still appear to believe this masculinist myth.

There is no reason to believe that what have traditionally been regarded as the "masculine" virtues (strength, courage, activeness, energy, . . .) are the exclusive property of men, or that what have been regarded (especially, and conveniently, by men) as the "feminine" virtues (gentleness, tenderness, nurturing qualities, supportiveness, passivity, . . .) are exclusive to women. The ideal human being would combine the two sets of virtues in balance. My own perfect embodiment of this is the music of Mozart, the supreme musical genius of Western culture, in which the "masculine" and "feminine" coexist in harmony and fusion; in his five greatest operas the identification we can deduce from the music is fairly equally and impartially distributed among the male and female characters. I want here, however, for reasons that will become clear, to celebrate a composer of more immediate and direct relevance to our current predicament.

I am coming increasingly to the belief that Janáček's music deserves to stand, in relation to the twentieth century and beyond, in an equivalent position to that generally accorded Beethoven's in the nineteenth. The obstacle to such recognition is clear and has nothing to do with the music's quality or meaning: the core of his achievement is the eight operas;[1] they are composed to Czech texts, and the composer was quite explicit about the organic relationship of his music to the rhythms and accents of the Czech language; hence, they defy translation. Given the problems involved (one might assume them to be insuperable)—the training of soloists and choruses in a fluent and idiomatic grasp of a language far removed from English, French, Italian, or German—it is surprising what advances have been made. Today, most major opera houses have more than one Janáček opera in their repertoire; all the last seven ought to be.

Beethoven and Janáček have certain features in common. Both were revolutionaries, in the aesthetic sense (developing radically new and original idioms, extending the boundaries of musical thought), but also in the political. Both, in their later years, became visionaries (one might compare the *Choral* Symphony to the *Glagolitic Mass*, though the latter seems to me the more completely successful of the two works). Finally, both were essentially "masculine" composers, far removed from the Mozartian ideal, their music exhibiting to an extreme degree the allegedly "masculine" virtues outlined above. The degree is even more extreme in Janáček: his music is characterized by tremendous energy, forcefulness, passion, dynamism. Yet with Janáček this untrammeled masculinity is placed unhesitatingly in the service of liberation and the overthrow of power/domination in all its forms, accompanied by an overwhelming compassion for its victims. The energy and force, far from serving domination, are diverted into furious protest against it. One of the marks of great genius is the courage to "go all the way," never to rein in the creative imagination or hold back in the interest of "rules" and conventions (one might relevantly evoke here William Blake, whose poetry has much in common with Janáček's music). Many of Janáček's most startling audacities of har-

---

1. Strictly speaking, there are nine: the second opera, *Romance*, has apparently never been performed, although the score survives. One continues to hope that some Janáček scholar will resurrect it and there will be a recording. Even if it is a failure, any work of Janáček's demands to be made available.

mony, rhythm, scoring were long regarded even in his own country as errors to be corrected (the great conductor Vaclav Talich repeatedly "touched up" the scores when performing them, ironing out the idiosyncrasies, making them "safe"). But there is nothing naive or clumsy about the apparent uncouthness; it is quite simply the expression of a mind driven on by its own irresistible and irrepressible energy, an aspect of the "masculinity." (We are fortunate today to have seven of the operas—all restored to their original form—available in recordings, under Charles Mackerras, that may well prove unsurpassable.)

The peak of Janáček's achievement is represented by seven late works: his last four operas (*Katya Kabanová*, *The Cunning Little Vixen*, *The Makropoulos Case*, *From the House of the Dead*), two orchestral masterpieces—*Taras Bulba* and the *Sinfonietta*—and the *Glagolitic Mass*, arguably his supreme statement. They divide neatly into two pairs and a trio. *The Cunning Little Vixen* (a misleading title—the heroine's name, *Liška Bystrouška*, means literally "the vixen Sharpears," and his animal heroine has none of the negative overtones of "cunning") and *The Makropoulos Case* are both concerned with the celebration of earthly life and the natural cycle of life/death/rebirth, the *Vixen* positively, the *Case* its negative complement (the heroine has discovered the elixir of life and is several hundred years old, clinging on to a life that has become barren, emotionless, and empty; in the ironically "happy" ending she chooses death). *Katya* and *From the House of the Dead* are both "protest" operas, denunciations of oppression: women's oppression in the former, where the women have internalized the monstrous demands of patriarchy and the sense of inevitable punishment for transgression; the horrors of the prison camp in the latter. The two orchestral works and the *Glagolitic Mass* are visionary embodiments of revolution, liberation, and transcendence. Considered altogether, the seven works amount to a coherent and immensely powerful, fully committed statement about the potentiality of human life, the horrors of the forces of oppression (internal and external), and faith in the possibility of realizing the former and triumphing over the latter: precisely the vision we need today. In Janáček's music, the political and the spiritual fuse and become inseparable.

The sense of a coherent vision is intensified by certain thematic overlaps. Witness, for example, the hilarious scene in *Liška Bystrouška* where the vixen attempts to rouse the hens to revolution, preaching Marxist feminism and the overthrow of the Cock (whom she proceeds to slaughter); or the moments in *From the House of the Dead* of a tender and tentative homosexual love between the political prisoner Goryanchikov and the boy Aljeja ("Did you ever have a sister? . . . I'm sure she was a beauty if she was like you"), their intimacy suddenly transcending the pervasive atmosphere of misery, oppression, breakdown, the collapse of identity and hope. In presenting Janáček here, in this way, my intention is to hold him up as a model of what masculinity today should be animated and driven by—the masculine energies of both men and women, straights and gays, whites and persons of color: the urgent necessity to work for the dismantling of all forms of domination and oppression, and the realization of the vision of the Transfigured City that was Janáček's inspiration for his *Sinfonietta*.

TECHNOLOGY AND SCIENCE

I am no Luddite; I am not "against" technology and its development. To be so would be both useless and stupid. It is true that I resisted owning a computer for many years after everyone else seemed to have one, and that, when I at last capitulated, I continued to express my (partly unconscious) resistance by making ridiculous errors, erasing whole articles "by accident." But today I have not the slightest desire to return to that laborious process of writing everything by hand, then typing it up, then revising and changing, then having to retype the whole thing from scratch. (I still, however, work out every article I write by hand in rough, with headings and more or less elaborate notes, frequently sitting in a pub or a cafe with a bottle of wine or a pint of beer within reach . . . my liquid inspiration, increasingly necessary given the current world situation.)

With the astonishing—and astonishingly swift—scientific and technological advances made in our own lifetimes, it is at least conceivable that famine, pestilence, and disease could now be banished from the earth, that the millions of people all over the globe who are at this minute dying of disease or starvation could be saved—could *already have been* saved. This, of course, has not happened, and despite numerous pious statements of intent it seems unlikely to happen in the near future (as I write, we have just had the G-8 summit, where President George W. Bush has made clear his lack of interest in "saving" Africa from AIDS). The *primary* function of technology today is not to feed starving peoples and combat disease; it's to make very rich people richer. The world is in the process—it seems inexorable, a veritable juggernaut—of being taken over by the big corporations and conglomerates, especially those centered in the United States, which throw their money behind right-wing governments (whether they call themselves "Democrat" or "Republican" still matters a little, but not much). Under capitalism, wealth equals power; power is already largely in the hands of the corporations, supported by the right-wing governments which they in turn support; this includes power over technology and all scientific development, which in turn includes, today, the power over life and death. The first aim of the revolution I now see as our only remaining hope (preferably peaceful—see below: I am not bloodthirsty, I have no desire to see heads rolling down the steps from guillotines; I think our millionaires should be treated decently and humanely, allowed a reasonable monthly income and given life-sustaining jobs on the assembly line) must be to dismantle all privatization and hand over technology to the people (if they have not already been so corrupted by the capitalist hegemony that they won't know what to do with it; one must hope—a desperate hope—that they will at least know to elect governments that will).

GLOBAL WARMING

What has become of the many (and devastating) scientific "doomsday" predictions, not least that, if global warming, pollution, depletion of the ozone layer, and so on continue at the present rate, the planet may not be able to sustain life (*any* life, not only human) within a hundred or two hundred years? One still reads of them occasionally, a couple of short paragraphs buried away in the inner pages of our newspapers. They are not, apparently, considered important enough (or, perhaps, imminent enough) to make the front pages, where one might reasonably expect to find such items. There also seem to be fewer of them, which may explain why there is no sense of urgency in the general population. But one has only to consider the alarming changes in our weather to feel that perhaps these prognostications are being fulfilled rather rapidly. Can it be that our scientists (or all but a very few honest and conscientious ones) have been bought up, are actually *afraid* to speak out for fear of losing their jobs? None, as far as I know, has come forward to tell us that predictions of global warming or catastrophic climate change were incorrect. Or are such warnings simply not being reported, our media also being under the control of corporate capitalism? In any case, their success in preserving the mystification of the public they are supposed to serve seems considerable, to judge from the number of times, when I meet my neighbors, I am greeted with "Isn't this weather *marvelous?*" Even as I write this there are floods all over much of Europe and the Middle East, and we have been enduring a prolonged period of suffocating heat, with record-breaking temperatures, extreme humidity, daily smog warnings, but no official account seems ready to point out that this may be the beginning of the end of life on this planet and that no government is doing anything effective about it. When some troublesome account *does* make it to the inner pages, our bolder scientists are continuing to tell us that, "If something is not done at once . . . ," and even that "It may already be too late." But nothing is being done. President Bush even refuses to sign the Kyoto agreement, itself long regarded as insufficient and inadequate.

As I write this, my son and daughter-in-law are expecting daily the birth of their first child, my fifth grandchild. He (science has told us his gender) does not have a name yet, but he will have one before I finish writing and I am dedicating this preface to him. I wonder what world he will grow up in? One must assume that our millionaires and billionaires don't care in the least about *their* grandchildren, so long as, when they die, they have amassed the wealth that they have not lived to spend. Today, money, and not even what it can buy, is clearly in itself the Grand Phallus, completely useless beyond a certain point of accumulation, but Power is Power . . . The image our millionaires, billionaires, tycoons, heads of corporations belching pollution over our environment evoke is that of the Gadarene swine, possessed, rushing headlong toward their destruction . . . and unfortunately everyone else's. In a certain sense, of course, "they know not what they do": people believe what it is necessary for them to believe, or "don't know" what it is necessary not to know, in order to continue along their chosen path—like colonialists believing that the subjugated races were somehow inferior, not fully human, or masculinists who believe that it is women's true destiny to be docile and serve them. It isn't necessarily stupidity, just willful and convenient blindness, indispensable to their sense of security: culpable ignorance.

DISTRACTION

Meanwhile, so few people appear to care, and one must ask: Why not? The necessary information is, after all, available (if not given much prominence), and one has only to look for it. For many, of course, with the steadily rising gulf between rich and poor, the worries of daily life are distraction enough: how to earn enough for the basic necessities and a few pleasures, how to pay one's credit card debts . . . But *distraction*, when one looks around, seems the operative principle that makes the continuance of corporate capitalism possible (combined with the almost complete suppression, within North American culture, of any strong left-wing voice). Contemporary mainstream Hollywood cinema plays an important role in the "distraction principle," and I discuss this below in a separate section; it is not by any means the only factor.

"New Is Good"   An advertisement, currently prominent on our Toronto subway system (it runs half the length of a carriage) for a local rock station actually culminates in this pronouncement (with its understood corollary, "Old Is Bad"). Does anyone, today, care about the death of the Past? When discussing recently Michael Haneke's first masterpiece *The Seventh Continent* with an allegedly advanced film class, I attempted to elucidate his use of Bach and Berg in a scene crucial to the film's meaning, and I watched the eyes glaze over (they had presumably, at least, *heard* of Bach, but the name was clearly synonymous with Boring): one could almost see attention dispersing in the theater air. But it is not just Bach in particular or classical music in general. On another recent occasion with another advanced film class, I discovered that almost no one in an audience of around fifty students had even heard of Brecht (he was, after all, a Marxist, and we all know that Marxism has been discredited and is no longer relevant), and instead of the scheduled discussion of

Lang's *M* I had to devote the time to an explication of Brechtian theory. It has happened more than once, at the end of a screening on the first night of a new class, that a student has come to me and said, "Will you be showing a *lot* of black-and-white movies in the course? I never watch them." Many registered film students appear never to have seen a film made before (at latest) the seventies. The current DVD market is of great significance here. Every week the stores are flooded with new releases, of which the overwhelming majority are recent movies mostly of minimal value (including numerous films that were considered unreleasable and so went "direct to video"). Presumably these sell, though it is difficult to imagine anyone looking at most of them twice, or even lasting through a first screening. But they are "new," "the latest," what we must have now, this minute, to keep us happy and "with it." Meanwhile, a vast number of masterpieces from the Classical Hollywood period (not to mention thousands of foreign movies, new and old) languish in limbo, many unavailable in any form: one thinks of *Man of the West, Bigger Than Life, Rally 'Round the Flag, Boys!, The Tarnished Angels, Make Way for Tomorrow, The Big Sky, The Reckless Moment* . . . In the words of the distinguished Canadian director William Macgillivray, "If we lose the past, we lose the future," and today we have been essentially disinherited by corporate capitalism. It teaches us that all that is important is making money: *enough* money if you're poor, *more* money if you're rich. The enormously rich (in senses beyond the financial) legacy of the past can teach us so many different ways, not merely of *thinking*, but of *feeling*. It can reveal attitudes, complexities, emotions that today have been rendered either inconvenient or irrelevant. We no longer need Mozart's music to give us an emblem of the fully human because we can go off to the nearest supermarket and buy whatever has just come in, whether food, clothing, rock music, candy bars, "improved" popcorn, and this will make us feel really good . . . for a few minutes. "Comfort food," or its equivalent in other commodities, has become a principle of life.

The real point of keeping our minds on today and "the latest" is to prevent us from giving so much as a single thought to our children and grandchildren—not to mention the world's animal and wild life. We are supposed not to care, so long as we are happy (a word that has become totally degraded, beyond serious use any more), "with it," and/or have pots of money in the bank (which somehow makes us better than the homeless person lifting up his cap on the street—if we have it, we must deserve it). And the rapidly increasing numbers of homeless people in Toronto, including whole families (an enormous leap over the last few years, under our Conservative government, for which people must have voted quite knowing what they doing) don't count: they have no addresses, so they won't even get ballot papers. "Democracy"?

Noise Silence used to be considered golden; today it's forbidden, at least in our cities. The almost continuous noise that surrounds us is a marvelous deterrent to thought. Street noise at least has a certain validity in the shape of transportation, though it could be lessened and minimized without causing undue suffering, as can be seen from those rare enlightened cities—Denver comes to mind—that have turned their centers into pleasant malls, with gardens, benches, and play areas. When we escape from street noise we are assailed by music, in every store, every shopping mall, and almost every restaurant, the *type* of music and its volume apparently selected according to the class status, age, and supposed tastes of the expected clientele. We are no longer permitted to eat or converse with our friends without a background. Most such backgrounds I have learned to ignore, unless they are very loud indeed and I am sitting near a loudspeaker: it has become just "noise." I am far more angered by the use (in the more "up-scale" restaurants) of classical music. If I want to listen to (say) the Mozart clarinet quintet, I want to be allowed to *listen*, at the proper volume, from beginning to end, surrounded by silence, not fragmented, reduced to semi-audibility, while I am trying to engage in discussion with a friend. To treat the quintet (or, I would have thought, *any* piece of music of any merit, in whatever genre, jazz, rock, folk . . .) in this way shows a total lack of respect for its composer. But the great amount of music being churned out today seems to have been *intended* as background; once again, people appear to have become complicit with the powers that be in *wanting* the partial distraction, the filling in of silences, the distraction from thinking that is a necessity for the system's continuance. Something of the kind I mean is, while I write this, droning out from a loudspeaker in a tree on the patio of the pub in which I am sitting with my "pint." Which makes me wonder if "distract" is after all quite the word, as I am not especially distracted (I would be if it was Mozart). Perhaps "soothe" or "lull" is the more appropriate term: I can see that it might operate as a kind of mild drug, with its group of singers, its indistinguishable (at this volume level) words, its endlessly repetitive rhythmic accompaniment, its ritualistically recurring refrain.

"Dumbing Down"   This appears to have become a recognized social phenomenon in which our cinema has played—is playing—a major role (from which the high school comedies, discussed in the new chapter 16 for this expanded edition, are not by any means exempt): one reads about it in one's daily newspaper, where it is treated with an ambiguous, unstable half-seriousness, as if one should perhaps see it just as a joke. But "dumbing down" is a reality, and absolutely necessary to the current processes of what some people still refer to quite seriously as "democracy." As such, it is especially terrifying as it is happening within the country that seems set on dominating, and spreading its "values" over, the entire globe. I do not of course wish to be taken as suggesting that this process is part of some articulated, coordinated, deliberate, diabolical plot. The direct control our governments have over the film, television, and entertainment industries is relatively slight, expressed mainly in official censorship. Rather, the process must be seen in terms of evolving, interacting, mutually sup-

portive structures. And "dumbing down" is only possible within a civilization whose inhabitants *want* to be dumbed down, are willing and complicit victims.

"Permissiveness" President Bush may continue to drone on about "families" (by which he means only one of many possible models of family—the patriarchal, biological, nuclear one, of all available models the most oppressive, neurosis-breeding, and insular, the enemy of true community). Given his intransigence on this subject, and the recent threat to deprive women of their right to abortion, it is a little surprising that he hasn't yet said or done more to combat "permissiveness," which today threatens the traditional family on all sides. Perhaps the attempt to recriminalize abortion is merely a first step and will be followed by others even more drastic. (Parenthetically, I should say here that my own belief is that we should be thinking in terms, not of families, but of communities, and that children should be raised communally, choosing whenever practicable the adults to whom they wish to relate. I would like to start a "Children's Rights" movement—why should kids have to remain tied to parents whom they dislike and who abuse them in various ways both legal and illegal, frequently "for their own good"?).

One of the most positive signs of recent years has been the widespread (and apparently quite sudden) acceptance of homosexuals,[2] at least within the middle- and upper-class circles of large cities (let's not get carried away!). But it seems clear that that acceptance (which we should still consider provisional rather than permanent) has only become possible with the growth of sexual permissiveness generally. Since what we used to (and many still do) call "cheating" has become taken for granted among heterosexuals (not always openly, old bad habits lingering on), it became harder to deny homosexuals their right to the same—indeed, their (relative) freedom and refusal of guilt in such matters was probably envied, becoming a kind of surreptitious guideline. If our right-wing politicians decide to do something about permissiveness (in defense of "family values"), homosexuality will be the first target, because the most obvious.

There are reasons to believe, however, that this may not happen. In the present phase of cultural evolution, sexual freedom still carries a definite charge of danger, excitement, daring. It is important to stress here that the current obsession with "getting laid" (the immediate result of our "sexual liberation," which seems to me anything but—rather, a move from one kind of imprisonment to another) is by no means restricted to the gay population. One has only to consider the 90s cycle of American high school comedies (see chapter 16), which are strictly heterosexualized. The ideal of "sexual liberation" has degenerated into the pursuit of sex for the sake of sex, the thrill of the chase and conquest becoming a major preoccupation,

---

2. I use the term here to cover both genders. Many still seem not to have grasped that "homo-" derives, not from the Latin for "man," but from the Greek for "same."

or in other words, yet another distraction—hence, invaluable to the continuance and development of the current progression toward extinction: if we can have sex with, say, six people a week on average, why worry about global warming? (It is of course doubtful that our politicians, so upright and moralistic except when it comes to financial matters, think such devious thoughts consciously, but that doesn't mean they are not present somewhere just below that "moral majority" surface). Isn't this why we now have the "permissive" society? You can be homosexual, you can screw around all you want, you can do drugs if you're discreet about it (so many do that it seems improbable that police surveyance is even intended to be effective). You can do anything that will distract you from asking serious questions.

Co-option   Which brings us back to a topic I have touched on above but which is again relevant here. The Great White Heterosexual Male is still (within the corporate capitalist Establishment) the rightful Lord of the Universe, and women and minorities are distrusted. They are, however, today, granted some rights, though grudgingly and provisionally. Since Hitler, concentration camps have lost something of their popular appeal (most people have at some time seen the films); therefore, camps for feminists might be a problem, and besides, there's all that messy cleaning up. So the safest method is incorporation. But no more than necessary—*that* would be overdoing it. No, just enough so that governments and the media they control (and are to some extent controlled by, in an obscene performance of mutual masturbation) can say, Look, we're liberal now, we *accept* these people, we even *like* these people. And besides, we *need* them: we need all the votes we can get. Of course, such sentiments can be trusted about as far as a goat can trust a python that is crawling toward it to devour it for its dinner—on the apparent assumption that, when the python has devoured you, digested you, and passed you out through its anus you will in sheer gratitude vote conservative for the rest of your life.

DESPAIR

Despair is perhaps today our most dangerous enemy, and the most difficult to combat. The odds seem so hopeless, the chips stacked so heavily against us. Money is power, and it is overwhelmingly in the hands of our potential destroyers, who are supported by the governments so many of us have helped to elect. I have a voice somewhere inside me that says, all too frequently, "Give up, shut up; *really* retire; do all the things you want to do, read your books, listen to your music, watch your movies, it's already a lost war, leave it all alone." But then those books, that music, those films, tell me the exact opposite: "You *must* fight, you *must* speak. If you stop, what happens to your self-respect?"

I put it in this personal way because that's how I experience it, but I think the tendency to despair today may be widespread, may in fact underlie people's apparent *willingness* to be distracted, to be lulled, to be duped: If thought is inevitably depressing, who wants to think?—especially with children to raise, money to earn, fatigue to combat, the sense of overwhelming odds and personal helplessness. Better to succumb, enjoy what you can, let it all happen—it's not, after all, *your* fault: "I am not responsible" (as the concentration camp guards said at the trials after World War II) . . . But we are all responsible: to say nothing, to sink into weary passivity, to allow despair to numb the intelligence, is to share in the responsibility.

HOPE

Even as I write this (and who knows, given the speed at which things happen nowadays, what developments there may have been by the time it is published?), the U.S. administration appears to be reaching its nadir of respectability, and what masqueraded as moral probity looks increasingly like total moral bankruptcy. From the viewpoint of this prologue, the current daily exposures of corporate financial shenanigans offer grounds, not for increased despair, but for fresh hope: how long will the American people, however duped and doped out, however encircled by distractions, tolerate such a government? It is surely time for change, for *drastic* change. But whether a majority of the American people will begin to see through the fog of fear and secrecy that is the Bush administration's modus operandi remains to be seen.

Still, the current and increasing surges of protest—directed so far primarily (and rightly) at the Free Trade Agreement and "globalization" (which, realistically, means world domination by the United States), but seeming constantly on the verge of widening to a virtually all-encompassing disillusionment and rage—are at once an acknowledgment that all is not yet lost and an encouragement to stronger and more widespread hope. Protest is crucial, but it is not in itself enough. The Establishment can get away with not taking it seriously, seeing it as "hooliganism" and criminalizing it. Above all, we need the creation and development of a strong (and eventually international) party—a party of the humane radical left that could at some stage (early or subsequently) incorporate the existing Green Party and its relevant concerns. The next stage would be gaining its election (against all the currently existing odds) by passionate yet thoroughly rational and thereby effective campaigning.

The practical problem is obvious: to form such a party and develop it to the point where it can conduct effective campaigns and get members elected to our parliaments requires money, and (despite idealistic—or are they just increasingly cynical?—notions about "democracy" and everyone having the right to vote) the overwhelming economic advantage today is solidly in the corrupt hands of what I can only call, albeit melodramatically, the forces of evil. Yet it is becoming a matter of the greatest urgency that the attempt be made. The world desperately needs leaders—not mere demogogues, but enlightened, educated, committed leaders, idealistic yet schooled in the actualities of political theory, thought, and action.

In the United States today no such party, and no such leaders, exist as effective public presences. The Green Party's agenda remains too restricted and insufficiently radical to become politically effective (though it might, perhaps, provide the necessary organizational nucleus). In Canada we have a nominally leftist party (the NDP, or New Democrats), but, at time of writing, it appears to have lost whatever energy, passion, or conviction it once had, and its policies place it only marginally to the left of the currently reigning liberals (roughly the equivalent of the Democrats in the United States).

As this party acquires power, its initial platform and duties would be:

1. To take over all the major corporations, demolish their present antidemocratic structures, and rebuild them so that profits go to the benefits of humanity at large (depending upon needs), irrespective of race, nationality, creed. This would be accompanied by
2. The drastic curtailment of all methods of production that threaten the future of life and welfare on our planet.

I am quite aware that this proposal will be rejected by many (most?) readers as hopelessly naive and idealistic, and they will be swift to point out that I offer no practical account of *how* such an agenda (which may, in the present cultural context, appear as realizable as flying over the rainbow) is to be realized. But I never laid claim to being a political theorist. My knowledge of what is happening to us goes little beyond reading the headlines in our daily papers (we are privileged, where I live in Toronto, to have one which is at least marginally to the left of center). What I am presenting appears to me the only viable alternative to outright and universal disaster. If anyone has a better, more practical solution, let's hear it. Prayer (if you're religious) is all that comes to mind, and that seems to me infinitely more naive and impotent than my admittedly simplistic blueprint. The first aim is to persuade people of the desperateness of our situation, without which no solution is even thinkable. It is also obvious that this must happen, first and foremost, within the United States, its clear primary agenda, already on the way toward fulfillment, being no less than world domination. While its various administrations (Republican or Democrat) remain firmly behind (not to mention dependent upon) corporate capitalism, there is no hope.

THE CINEMA WE DESERVE

The cultural situation outlined above finds its reflection, almost point by point, in the Hollywood cinema of the past decade; it can be analyzed under many of the same headings. It is above all a cinema of distraction, of unreality, designed not to encourage thinking but to dull it into extinction. It is the era above all of the "teen pic," the wooing of the "youth market," it being especially important that those just growing into full man- or womanhood be indoctrinated with the generalized sense that "life is fun and nothing else matters."

Notoriously, Hollywood is now largely run by corporations—Coca-Cola, Sony, etc. It used to be common among intellectuals to deplore the fact that Hollywood films were produced, ultimately, by the moguls—men like Louis B. Mayer or Samuel Goldwyn or Harry Cohn, with minimal intellectual interests and unrefined tastes. But at least they were men who loved making movies, delighted in and were proud of their own products, the stars and directors in their own "stables." One has the sense today that the majority of Hollywood products materialize because a group of businessmen sit around a table asking each other, "Well, what made the most money last year?"—then planning an imitation or a sequel, trying to "go a little further" in thrills, yucks, or special effects, putting together a "package." And, unfortunately, in most cases the "youth market" laps it up: they know that "New Is Good." How many Hollywood films in the past ten years can you name that seem addressed to an adult intelligence, or to any but a thoroughly coarsened and petrified sensibility? What films disturb us—rather than titillate or dull our senses?

TECHNOLOGY

The great technological advances have affected our cinema in obvious ways, many of them clearly positive: better sound, stronger definition, new potentials to add to the possible range of expression. We must welcome, in principle, any developments that add to the artist's means of realizing his/her vision. Most strikingly and pervasively, however, they have been used quite irresponsibly to create what I see as a kind of magical unreality that seeks to impose itself as a new and better "realism." This is most obvious in science fiction movies, but it also, today, pervades the action film, which, typically (after perhaps an initial half hour establishing the characters), degenerates into a series of car chases, smash-ups, explosions, fights, "suspense" (both literal and metaphorical) with the hero improbably dangling from, falling from, escaping from ledges, rooftops, drainpipes . . . , all largely created by computerization. Enjoyment of this is perhaps quite complex, on various interacting levels. We know it's all impossible, yet it *looks* so real, so we can thrill to it and at the same time laugh knowingly; the fundamental level is the enjoyment of spectacle as the creation of technology, the knowing "Wow! That's *brilliant*, man," the sense that technology has now developed to the point where it can create the world, saving us the trouble of having to do it ourselves. Classical Hollywood, though far removed from, say, the ideals of Italian neorealism, never entirely lost touch with human problems, human emotions, and human actions, its genres rooted firmly in the culture's ideological contradictions, its works frequently arousing passionate discussion. Today, what audiences seem to want is this "real" unreality, voluntarily losing themselves in what they know to be absurd. *The Bourne Identity* can stand as example. As much "thriller" as "action movie," it is not especially spectacular, but two sequences make my point eloquently. As preface, I should mention that, when I screen Classical Hollywood action movies for my classes, there is often laughter during the fight scenes: the actors appear to be landing and receiving punches that would knock anyone cold instantly, yet the fight continues. The students have a point of course: one could not expect John Wayne and Randolph Scott (not to mention the producers) to accept a lengthy spell in hospital in the interests of "realism." However, at least here one can see the actors "acting" a fight. Cut to the fight scene in *The Bourne Identity*, when one of the bad guys invades Matt Damon's apartment. No shot lasts more than a second or two; we never see even the semblance of a punch actually landing, though most of them look violent enough to appear lethal. It is, in fact, almost impossible to make out what the two men are physically doing to each other—we are just allowed a very generalized sense of extremely violent movement. At the end, if I recall correctly, Damon has somehow managed to emerge without so much as a nosebleed. Yet, here, no one laughs: the fight appears to be taken by the audience as authentic, "realistic," whereas all the actors seem to have been called on to do is strike gestures, then "Cut!" to the next shot. The fakery is so transparent that the readiness of spectators to accept it as "real" shows a quite extraordinary eagerness to "believe." (It is possible that the scene was shot that way because Matt Damon can't do "action." The film's solitary and perfunctory love scene suggests that he can't do that either.)

The film's climactic action sequence is even more remarkable. Damon is trapped at the top of an immense spiral stairway, about ten floors up in a large ornate building; the stairs are blocked by bad guys; how can he escape (escape he must, not because of anything intrinsic in the plot but because he is "the Hero" and this is a contemporary action movie)? Well, there is a convenient corpse (a bad guy already disposed of by Our Hero), with its convenient head poking conveniently between the banister railings. Damon gives it a good shove, the railings part, and the body falls—not head first, as an unimaginative person like myself might expect, but horizontally. Then Matt: 1. Hurls himself upon it, using it as a kind of magic carpet to fall ten floors or so to safety (I thought of Sabu on *his* magic carpet in *The Thief of Baghdad*, but that is signaled as "fantasy"); 2. Finds time on the way down to turn his head and shoot one of the worst of the bad guys halfway up the stairs, and 3. Lands without even being winded. Is this what the term "magic realism" means? No one in the audience seemed to find it as hilarious as I did; a few applauded. Today, it seems, anyone will believe anything; the whole distinction between "reality" and "fantasy" (always somewhat precarious in Hollywood movies) has become completely eroded, the impossible has become "real": perfect training for life in today's culture. Compared to what we have now, the practices of Classical Hollywood seem actually to merge with Italian neorealism. (The only thing positive I took away from this stupid, empty movie was some moments of Franka Potente, who at least preserves a certain dignity and sense of distinction; but it is sad to see the vibrant star of *Run, Lola, Run* wasting her time in such drivel.)

One recent film stands out in this context (though my claims for it are fairly minimal): John Frankenheimer's *Ronin*. Frankenheimer insisted (and the film's promoters made a point of this, as an audience attraction) that the many car chases and crashes be for real: no faking, no technological "assistance." The car chases are indeed, as a result, quite thrilling, but the film failed at the box office. Today the "real" is old-fashioned; only the computerized unreal is *really* "real." It's possible though, that the film failed commercially because it didn't have Matt Damon, only Robert De Niro . . .

LOST CAREERS

Directors

My choice of *The Bourne Identity*, in most respects arbitrary, was made partly because it was directed (if one can be said to "direct" such a film, and in what direction?—the material and the technology end up directing *you*) by Doug Liman, a director in whom I had become very interested. His first film, *Swingers*, showed intelligence, a gift for sly satire, a critical stance toward his characters; his second, *Go*, is a *tour de force* of considerable brilliance—I have seen it several times without in the least tiring of it, a rare experience with today's Hollywood cinema. But intelligence and brilliance no longer draw in the "youth market" (a typically brutal blanket catchphrase to describe a group of human beings), and that despite the fact that *Go* is a "youth" movie which deserved a far greater commercial success than it received (a number of intelligent students I know admired it). The message: that you can succeed in Hollywood today only if you are willing to prostitute yourself by churning out assembly-line "action" films, "dumbed down" teen flicks, or "grossout" horror/comedies. (The ideal Hollywood filmmakers today are apparently those too stupid even to realize that they *are* prostituting themselves.) I understand that two sequels to *The Bourne Identity* (a big commercial hit) are planned and that Liman has committed himself to them.

A close parallel: in recent years Sam Raimi has made two intelligent and distinguished films (*A Simple Plan*, *The Gift*). The latter, despite its astonishing central performance by Cate Blanchett, was a box office disaster. Raimi's latest movie is *Spiderman*. This is better, at least, than *The Bourne Identity* (thanks as much to

Tobey Maguire as to Raimi): it has a few (technology-free) strong scenes. Again, a series of sequels is planned, though it is not clear as yet whether Raimi will be directing. There is even a rumor that David Fincher is going to direct *Mission Impossible 3*. None of this is certain at time of writing, yet the very fact of likelihood suggests an inescapable pattern. I would like to believe that the only reason these directors accept such assignments is to enable them to make other, more personal films on smaller budgets. "Watch the skies." It appears to be almost impossible for a relatively new director to sustain a career in Hollywood today if he is unwilling to prostitute himself.

An interesting and daring alternative direction (so far moderately successful) has been taken by Paul Thomas Anderson. I still think his first film, *Hard Eight*, made independently, is by far his finest, with the kind of distinction (economy, precision, and "personal" in the best sense, the sense in which Anthony Mann's early *films noir* are personal) found in certain now-legendary Classical Hollywood "B" movies. But he has had the audacity to present himself, within the contemporary Hollywood system, as a kind of European "arthouse" *auteur*, and has even managed to impose himself as such. Still . . . I wanted so much to admire *Boogie Nights* and *Magnolia*, but the former seemed to me self-indulgent and fundamentally uninteresting, the latter pretentious and ultimately empty. *Magnolia* did, however, impose itself (rather like the early films of Ingmar Bergman) as the work of someone who might be worth watching. It seems doubtful whether such a description corresponds at all closely to how Anderson sees his work, *Magnolia* continuously giving the impression of declaring itself a masterpiece. But how can anyone hope to develop within a milieu and a system that understand nothing except "making money"—not merely "getting back your investment" but making millions in profits? *Punch-Drunk Love* is interesting but seems desperately in need of a further rewrite; the Emily Watson character in particular makes no sense.

The number of clearly talented new directors who (since the 80s) have made one (or two) intelligent and distinguished films and then either vanished from sight or moved into other work is remarkable: think of Michael Tolkin (*The Rapture*, *The New Age*) or David Koepp (*The Trigger Effect*), both of whom seem to have turned to scriptwriting; or Greg Mottola, who, since *The Daytrippers* (which would be on my list of the ten best American films of the 90s), has had nothing released, although there have been vague rumors of a second film in various stages of development or completion. One would have thought that the (richly deserved) success of *My Best Friend's Wedding* would have been sufficient to establish the credentials of P. J. Hogan, yet even he appears to have been unable to set up a film since, despite various attempts. The Hollywood directors of the past could work securely within genres but continue to "be themselves"; today this seems to be becoming increasingly difficult. Any of these films would have secured for their directors a five-film contract in the "classical" period.

What has become of David O. Russell, one of the very few contemporary American filmmakers who has shown any ambition to create an oppositional cinema? *Spanking the Monkey* remains perhaps unique among "teen" movies in concerning itself, not with the satisfactions of "getting laid," but with the pleasures and frustrations of masturbation (which may well be more relevant to the lives of most teenagers today). *Flirting with Disaster* dared hilariously to question our culture's strange obsession with biological parentage. *Three Kings* (definitely an "un-American activity") gave us a view of the Gulf War and the U.S. involvement that was, to say the least, jaundiced. The first got made because it was "independent" and "low budget," the second because it was "just a comedy." the third (presumably) because it was an "action movie." Three years have passed, and I have found no information that Russell has made or is making another movie.

(Parenthetically, I should make explicit here the dangers in writing a prologue like this that, in examining the present, must also to a certain degree foresee the future. No one will be more delighted than I if, by the time this book is published, Tolkin, Koepp, Mottola, and Russell have all had new and distinguished films released.)

Genres

It will be clear already that I think the most useful and relevant touchstone against which contemporary Hollywood should be judged is not the European (or, today, the Asian or Iranian) cinema, but the Classical Hollywood of the period approximately from 1930 to 1960, which represents one of the richest "movements" in twentieth-century art. A full account of the conditions that made it possible (at the same time defining its limitations) is beyond the capacity of the present volume, but certain specific comparisons are illuminating.

Consider, first, the issue of genre itself. Classical Hollywood was (notoriously?) a genre cinema and, as such, looked down upon by intellectuals (who might, one would have thought, have spared a moment to reflect that all the plays of Shakespeare belong to genres). In the new chapter on 90s high school comedies I develop the notion of the importance of genre within a communal art (in which the artist, instead of living and working in isolation, feels a part of a community, with common concerns and a shared creativity). The major genres—western, musical, gangster film, *film noir*, screwball comedy, romantic comedy, domestic melodrama, horror film, etc.—offered a potential range of material, expression, and interaction for which there is no comparable equivalent today, where the only genres with any kind of spurious vitality are the action movie, sci-fi, and grossout comedy (one might add, today, the war movie, as an offshoot of the action film, and, I suppose, that emptiest of genres the "spoof" movie). One of the few recent Hollywood films of any distinction, *The Deep End*, provides an illuminating instance of the decline of

genre, partly because no one seemed to recognize it as belonging to one: it was simply a drama about people. It is, in fact, a close remake of one of the great Classical
Hollywood genre movies, Max Ophuls' *The Reckless Moment* (1949). The far greater
richness of the earlier film is attributable not only to the intelligence of one of the
world's greatest film directors (though Ophuls' presence is palpable throughout)
but to the collision of two immediately identifiable, clearly defined, and usually
quite distinct genres, the domestic melodrama and *film noir*, both bringing with
them the resonances of a developed tradition.

I don't think anyone who sees *The Deep End* registers anything of this, even
unconsciously, because these genres no longer operate as recognized phenomena.
(Occasional attempts at contemporary *film noir*—broadly becoming known as
"neo-noir"—come across as self-conscious pastiche.) A whole dimension of expression and meaning has been lost.

Genre has traditionally been seen as essentially conservative (since it merely reproduces the same patterns, the same trajectories, the same "happy endings"). Yet far
more challenging and radical work was produced during the Classical Hollywood
period than appears to be possible today. Indeed, it is difficult to think of a period in
the Hollywood cinema of the past in which so little can be read as oppositional to the
dominant forces. *The Reckless Moment* offers, in effect, a remarkably caustic yet com-
passionate analysis of the values (and oppressiveness) of American bourgeois family
life, centered upon the entrapment of the wife/mother. Today we have only an *American Beauty* to gesticulate messily, crudely, and impotently about the sufferings of men
burdened with stupid, racalcitrant wives. We have no *Bigger Than Life* to articulate
(despite its copout ending) a sense of the impossible constraints of bourgeois existence, no *Man of the West* to reveal the impossible contradictions at the very basis of
American ideology, no *Rally 'Round the Flag, Boys!* to offer us a wish-fulfillment fantasy that America had never existed. To be "daring" or "audacious" today means
merely to "go a little further," to titillate without disturbance, playing straight into the
hands of the dominant culture and the distractions its continuance demands.

Stars

During the classsical period directors were mostly under contract, expected to make
a certain number of films during a certain period of time. The great directors
became associated with particular genres with which they felt an affinity (or, in the
case of Hawks, a particular style of filmmaking) and were able to develop distinguished careers within or around the generic limits; lesser directors were more likely
to be treated as employees and handed assignments. The system was obviously not
ideal but it allowed a balance of freedom and discipline, and the richness of the
period is in part due to it. Much the same was true of stars: they were typically

under contract, they were "groomed" for certain types of roles, they were guaranteed a certain number of films over a certain number of years. The concept of the "star vehicle" developed naturally out of this. When the studio/genre/star system collapsed during the 60s and 70s, many actors rejoiced in their newfound "freedom": they could now choose their roles freely, move about from studio to studio, negotiate (through their agents) increasingly lucrative contracts for individual films. It has worked for some (Jack Nicholson, Harrison Ford, Mel Gibson, Al Pacino, Eddie Murphy, Tom Cruise, Mike Myers, Julia Roberts), either because they are widely recognized as great actors, or because they have committed themselves to one or other of the contemporary genres. It is not exactly an accident that most of the names on that list are male.

The women's movement produced in Hollywood a backlash of hysterical masculinity of which the only surprise is that it did not erupt sooner: the "key" year is 1982, the year of the release of *Conan the Barbarian* and *First Blood*, which, respectively, made Schwarzenegger a major (i.e., "bankable") star almost overnight and pumped new blood into Stallone's career after one or two too many punch-drunk *Rocky* sequels. With the collapse of radical feminism and the co-option of what was left of it into mainstream male-dominated culture, the hysteria died out but the overemphasis on ultra-macho masculinity did not: the 90s has merely substituted a kinder, less blatant, less parodic, and less downright silly form of it. The credibility of the Stallone/Schwarzenegger model may collapse, but Harrison Ford and Mel Gibson (and, more recently, Ben Affleck and Matt Damon) are on hand to offer a more emotional, more vulnerable, more *human* image of maleness. The cost of this (for them) is that they (and even, sadly, Tobey Maguire) are forced into the "action," fantasy, or sci-fi genres. (I remember that, when I saw Harrison Ford in *Witness*, I compared him to the young Cary Grant. I don't any more—nor even to the older Cary Grant.)

During the classical period, furthermore, the great female stars were able to develop and sustain careers well into middle age and sometimes beyond. This is so obvious that it seems unnecessary to mention names. But that was when there existed genres that were centered on women's problems within the constraints of the culture. The contemporary myth has it that women are no longer trapped in domesticity, marriage, and family, so films like *Blonde Venus*, *Beyond the Forest*, *The Reckless Moment* are no longer relevant, and films about women's rebellion and its consequences like (to follow the same trajectory of directors) *The Devil Is a Woman*, *Ruby Gentry*, *Letter from an Unknown Woman* are now totally redundant. Today (in the official version) women have everything they've fought for: they are happy, and if they're not, they ought to be. So why bother making films about them any more? All those old problems of inequality have been solved long ago, so now we can concentrate on the male audience (most specifically, the male teen audience). They're the ones who pay for the tickets.

Over the past decade I have developed a great attachment to a number of female stars, whether as actors or as "presences," and I have watched their careers steadily dwindle. The most spectacular case is that of Mimi Rogers, who, in *The Rapture*, gave one of the greatest performances in the history of the Hollywood cinema. The film was not sufficiently respectable for either it or its star to be nominated for an Academy Award, and Rogers' career went roughly the same way as its director's. It is amazing that it got made at all—a film in which a woman refuses, at its climactic moment, to be taken up into Heaven because she has grasped the monstrousness and cruelty of the God of the so-called "Christian" religion. Rogers might have become the Barbara Stanwyck of modern Hollywood cinema; she is now reduced to playing grotesque mothers in *Cruel Intentions 2* and the Canadian horror movie *Ginger Snaps*. She is the most extreme instance of the predicament of the female star in a cinema that has no place for strong, passionate women, but one has only to consider the careers, in the 90s, of Sigourney Weaver, Sharon Stone, Michelle Pfeiffer, Meryl Streep, Jessica Lange . . . to grasp the humiliating situation of mature women in contemporary Hollywood, where only "bimbos" or "chicks" need apply. (It is possible that Pfeiffer's decline may be her own fault, that the dreadful movies in which she has appeared recently were her own bad choices; they might have looked promising on paper.) In this context, Julia Roberts is (in my opinion deservedly) something of a phenomenon, though one wonders how long her success can continue. Our culture's resentment of strong older women (i.e., any who can no longer be classified as "chicks") comes out repeatedly in the obsessively sneering and ungenerous comments of reviewers even when they cannot withhold praise of her performances, and this phenomenon (trivial in itself) speaks volumes about the dominant masculinist attitude to women who dare become powerful.[4]

✳ ✳ ✳

This, then, is roughly how I view the culture in which I live and the mainstream cinema that is at once its product and support. As in the culture, so in the cinema: there are hostile and dissonant rumblings, but they are seldom allowed to enter the mainstream. In the new last chapters of this expanded edition, I do examine one instance of (marginal) progress (the acceptance of gays and gay-related subject matter into mainstream comedy), one instance of a generic cycle that is at least lively

---

4. Since this was written, *The Hours*, with its three superb leading performances, has proven that a great "woman's picture" can still be made, though it may turn out to be an isolated phenomenon. One also watches, with great interest, the developing career of Julianne Moore.

and intermittently engaging (the high school movies), and two filmmakers who have attempted to introduce a note of dissonance (Jim Jarmusch and David Fincher—though Jarmusch, for all the availability of his films, can scarcely be called "mainstream" and would I'm sure regard it as an insult, and Fincher compromised himself disastrously with *The Game*).

Finally, a few words about this book today. Looking through it somewhat cursorily (I hate reading my own work), I find that I stand by most of its judgments. The weakest chapter seems to me, ironically, the one that has been most frequently reprinted (one gets the impression that one can't open a critical anthology without coming upon at least an excerpt): the chapter on the horror film. Its thesis applies to only one branch of the genre (though it still seems to me the most important), and it fails to discriminate sufficiently in terms of value, lumping together major works and the relatively trivial simply because they reveal the same generic patterns—a common failing of "theoretical" criticism. I hope the addition of a chapter on *Day of the Dead*, the extraordinary culmination of Romero's trilogy which, in its completion, represents one of the great achievements of the period, will do something toward correcting this. And I stand by my celebration of *Heaven's Gate*: if there has been a greater Hollywood film since its disastrous first appearance, I haven't seen it, and it is if anything more important and relevant today, in the contemporary political context, than when it was made.

I have become aware of one striking omission: there is no chapter on Kubrick, and I still don't feel ready to add one. My relationship with his films has been one of startling ups and downs. With the partial exception of *Paths of Glory* I found it difficult to make contact with the early films, intellectually or emotionally. Then, when I saw *A Clockwork Orange*, I made a solemn vow never to see another. I managed to hold to this for several years, despite the urgings of my friends to see *Barry Lyndon*. Finally, one of them trapped me in his New York apartment, sat me down in front of his television set, and told me I couldn't leave until I watched it. My attitude to Kubrick changed instantly, and I became a great admirer of *The Shining* also. Subsequently, I was so overwhelmed by *Full Metal Jacket* that I couldn't speak for half an hour after emerging from it—an experience shared with my colleagues Richard Lippe and Andrew Britton (I remember us walking together in silence around the streets of Toronto, not liking to meet each other's eyes). I have not yet plucked up the courage to watch it again. *Eyes Wide Shut* I have also seen only once, for the different reason that it left me feeling somewhat blank. But one of my many projects now is to watch all Kubrick's films again (yes, even *A Clockwork Orange!*) in chronological order. I have no doubt of his major status, but I have no firm grasp of his career as a whole.

Just as I am aware of Kubrick as a major absence in the original book, so am I aware of the absence of Steven Soderbergh from the new additions. He is another

The Shining: Patriarch (Jack Nicholson) on the rampage, wife (Shelley Duvall) on the defense director of obvious significance, though of exactly what kind I remain uncertain. I cannot seem to get a firm grasp on his films. My experience of them has been curious: I admire the surface, the polish, the sheer crafsmanship and virtuosity, the feeling for elaborate structures: everything relates to everything and everything seems to work, just as it should in the work of a major artist. But, invariably, I come away with a sense of emptiness, realizing that, while I have admired, I have never become emotionally involved. And it *is* a sensation of emptiness, not of distancing. One can talk of distancing in the work of many great directors over a very wide range of achievement: Ozu, Ophuls, Preminger at his intermittent best (from *Laura* to *Advise and Consent*), Kiarostami, Hou, Tsai, Denis, Haneke . . . But "distancing" there (taking many different forms) has the function of allowing a certain critical detachment that never precludes a simultaneous emotional involvement: if we are made to feel very strongly for Joan Bennett's predicament in *The Reckless Moment*, we remain extremely critical of her, aware of her limitations, the entrapment in domesticity she is incapable of recognizing for herself. For me, at least, the pleasure of watching a Soderbergh movie is rather like a child's pleasure in a perfect clockwork toy. Perhaps that is why the Soderbergh movie I have most enjoyed is *Ocean's Eleven*, a perfectly empty work in which form and content are almost perfectly integrated: the perfect heist, the perfect movie, everything going like clockwork, the only divergence being that there are moments when the heist, but not the movie, doesn't. Perhaps it is this sense of emptiness that makes Soderbergh the ideal "serious" director for the early 2000s, the artist who can fascinate, even dazzle, us while giving us, actually, so little. I don't see him (as I now see Kubrick) as a major artist. More a brilliant conjuror, or even, in less charitable moments, a superior con artist. To put it another way: I feel (perhaps quite mistakenly) that I "know" Ozu, Ophuls, Kiarostami, Hou, Tsai, even the elusive Preminger, as human beings. But I don't know Soderbergh at all: I don't know what's there, he gives nothing away. I maintain the right to change my mind. I am intrigued by the fact that his most elaborately "distanced," "intellectual," "clockwork toy" movie, *The Limey*, is also the one where some kind of powerful emotional disturbance seems dangerously close to the surface. One day, perhaps, we shall bear witness to an explosion, though with *Full Frontal*, supposedly the "small," "personal" film he "really wanted to make," I don't detect even a distant rumble.

But there is a far more important absence than that of Soderbergh, and I realize it demands explanation, though it leads me into somewhat personal territory. My failure to write about Spike Lee is a matter partly of respect, partly of cowardice, partly of a past hurt. *Do the Right Thing* is a great movie (among the most important in the American cinema since *Heaven's Gate*), a fully achieved work of great intelligence and integrity, and everything Lee does must be seen by anyone with a serious interest in film and/or American culture. But I suffer from a prototypical white person's inhibition: the black experience is so integral to Lee's work, and,

Do the Right Thing: Racial tensions (Spike Lee, Danny Aiello)

although his films are by no means inaccessible to whites, I am not sure that a white person can write about them with the necessary inwardness, or without embarrassing blunders.

As I earlier claimed the right to call myself a feminist without being a woman, this reluctance to deal with black issues may see inconsistent and perhaps irrational, but underlying it is a somewhat painful personal experience. Almost ten years ago I contributed an article to an issue of *CineAction* (no. 32) devoted to race, and it brought down the wrath of the righteous upon my head, this being at the peak of "political correctness" at its strictest. I committed two major crimes. At this time a production of *Show Boat* (the musical) was about to be mounted in a Toronto auditorium, and there had been a great public outcry, a number of professed leftists going so far as to demand that it be banned by the local authorities. This strikes me as a frightening microcosmic expression of how easily Marxism can degenerate into Stalinism, with freedom of expression flung out the window (would not organized protests outside the theater be sufficient to draw the public's attention to possible objections?). I defended *Show Boat*, both Edna Ferber's novel and James Whale's film (and George Sidney's remake seems harmless enough, simply—the indestructible Ava Gardner aside—a bad and boring movie), claiming both as, for all their shortcomings and insufficiencies, powerfully antiracist. My other crime was much worse: I suggested that black persons be called brown and white persons pink, on grounds not merely of greater accuracy. One of the strongest underpinnings of racism, it seems to me, has always been the close association of "black" with evil and "white" with good. To quote myself: "I'm sure white supremacists have a commitment to exactly such an association of ideas, and play upon it surreptitiously: they would hate to have to think of themselves as 'pinkish-beige.' " (I was, and remain, fully aware of the importance of "black" as a political weapon.) This still seems to me harmless at worst, but it provoked an outpouring of abuse. One leading North American leftist film critic actually demanded, when he sent in his subscription renewal, that all articles by "the racist Robin Wood" be removed from his subsequent copies (a request with which we failed to comply, not wishing to deprive the gentleman of the satisfaction of tearing them out himself). I shall be interested to discover whether the repetition of these ideas here provokes similar outrage today. I suspect it won't. But something of the pain lingers. If it did not prevent me from writing at length on *Mandingo* (in my *Sexual Politics and Narrative Film*), that is perhaps because the film is set in the past, the issue of slavery distancing it from contemporary concerns. I hope to write about Spike Lee's films at some time in the future; for now, I shall simply express my admiration.

I might well have saved the last two essays (on *Before Sunrise* and *The Doom Generation*) in *Sexual Politics and Narrative Film* for inclusion here if I had known there would be a new edition. Araki's film especially belongs to this prologue and this period, and its remarkable force remains undimmed by the subsequent collapse

Do the Right Thing: Images of Mookie (Spike Lee)

(temporary one hopes) of his career. Few American films since 1990 have greater claims to "classical" status. Its rage and desperation—the inevitable corollary, today, of its life-affirmative passion—is, as with *Heaven's Gate*, more relevant than ever. Yet the film now appears to have become totally marginalized, an obvious necessary sacrifice on the altar of corporate capitalism and the "patriotism" that celebrates it.

Which brings me to my major gripe about contemporary criticism, a gripe both personal and more-than-personal. I bitterly resent the collapse, today, of critical debate. It is of course consistent with (indeed, the product of) the general movement of critical discourse in cinema: theory and scholarship dominate, the *value* of the individual work is no longer an issue, it "doesn't matter." But it matters to me.

In recent years, in this book and its successor, I have built what I believe to be irrefutable cases for several generally despised films, notably *Heaven's Gate*, *Mandingo*, and *The Doom Generation*, claiming them as major works and important statements (on a lower level of achievement I could add *Cruising*). As far as any kind of response in print is concerned, it's as if these defenses—celebrations—never existed. In the wide general view, the first film remains a "fiasco," the second "disgusting exploitation," the third . . . well, has anyone but myself even bothered to examine it seriously?. And gay critics still find it necessary to vilify *Cruising* without any acknowledgment that another gay critic has at least attempted a defense of it. If I am wrong about these films, why have my analyses not been refuted? Where is the stimulating engagement one might—or should—expect from other serious movie critics? Are these films really so silly that reasoned refutation would be superfluous? I thought I was issuing a challenge, but I have to assume that the challenge was either unanswerable or totally insignificant. Leavis's "This is so, isn't it?" is no longer answered by "Yes, but . . . " but by "Why bother?" (I should add that, on the individual level, a number of professors in film studies have at various times congratulated me on my treatment of these films and assured me that they now use them in their classes, together with my writings on them. I am of course delighted that this is so, but it doesn't appear, so far, to have affected in the least the films' "official" status within film culture.)

* * *

A week ago, for the first time, I held in my arms my tiny grandson, Nicholas Gee-Ming (the names acknowledging his British father and Chinese-Canadian mother). My head was full of Schubert's late string quartets, which I had been listening to somewhat obsessively, especially the A minor. The two experiences merged, the music expressing so eloquently the beauty, the joy, the pain, the despair, of human existence, the new life in my arms so innocent (but is any of us born innocent?), so fragile, so impossibly tiny, so trusting . . . I cannot help wondering how he will fare in a world now controlled by the forces of domination and greed.

✳ ✳ ✳

I must here acknowledge an important influence: Varda Burstyn's magnificent book *The Rites of Men: Manhood, Politics, and the Culture of Sport* (University of Toronto Press, 1999). Although her move to another city has put us out of touch, Varda, whom I have known for many years both professionally and as a personal friend (we taught film classes together), gave me a copy of the book some years ago and it rested, unread, on my shelves, my reluctance due to my own total lack of interest in professional sport. (I think games should be played for fun and exercise, and no one should care especially who wins.) I don't know what mysterious instinct induced me to take it down and read it just as I started work on this prologue, but I certainly would not have written as I have without it. It acted as a necessary release of my beliefs and commitments, and gave me the courage I so often lack. It seems to me one of the indispensable books for anyone interested in the issues I have tried, in my clumsy, blundering way, to raise. Meticulously researched, it is a shining example of the amalgamation of theory, scholarship, and criticism so that they become indistinguishable.

Finally, I thank my intelligent editor, Roy Thomas, for his creative suggestions and occasional contributions.

Hollywood from Vietnam to Reagan
... and Beyond

I.

Cards on the Table

This book is not a survey: it does not pretend to cover every trend, every genre, every cycle—let alone every film—in the period (roughly 1970–1984) with which it is concerned. It is not, in the usual sense, a history, though the ordering of the chapters is generally chronological, with occasional flashbacks: the reader will find little of the factual information of which our histories are typically composed. It is not exactly a thesis (though it contains one): the argument is not clearly linear, starting from "This is what I shall prove" and progressing to "This is what has been proven." But neither is it a collection of miscellaneous, unconnected essays, though each chapter is more or less self-sufficient: the cross-references are intricate (often, more so than I realized while writing it), so that, in the last resort, everything relates to everything. It is my hope that the openness of the structure, the refusal of a step-by-step linearity of argument, will allow the reader a sense of her/his own space and the possibility of making other connections and developing ideas in other directions. The book contains a number of embryonic books, each with its own potential thesis: studies of Scorsese, Cimino, De Palma; a book on the relationship (part rupture, part continuity) between "Classical" and "modern" Hollywood; a book on the "incoherent texts" of the 70s; a book on the attempted recuperations of the 80s (but that would be very tedious both to write and to read); a book on the Hollywood cinema's response (or lack of it) to feminism; above all, perhaps, a book on the traces, both manifest and hidden, within our popular cinema, of that innate bisexuality the repression of which Freud saw as necessary for the construction of "socialized" men and women in our culture. But what interests me is the interconnectedness of these phenomena, and it is this that I have tried to catch. I have also wanted to make more accessible some of the major concerns of contemporary film theory: perhaps, in attempting to clarify, I have simplified and falsified, but the risk seems to me worth taking.

The book's unifying principle is the attempt to grasp, in all its complexity, a decisive "moment," an ideological shift, in Hollywood cinema and (by implication) in

American culture. The *degree* of decisiveness can only be judged from some future vantage point, and what happens in the cinema will clearly depend upon what happens in American society and politics. Side by side with this is the attempt to examine and evaluate some of the work that has been produced, distinguishing between different kinds and different levels of significance and achievement. These two impulses do not seem to me cleanly separable. On the one hand, I have never felt great interest in an approach to cinema that was merely sociological, that reduced films to so many examples of this or that tendency; on the other, I have become increasingly aware of the importance of seeing works in the context of their culture, as living ideological entities, rather than as sanctified exhibits floating in the void of an invisible museum. The true distinction of a great film lies in its relation to its time, the relation being frequently (today, necessarily) one of opposition. Paradoxically perhaps, the works that prove to have lasting significance are usually those most intricately and complexly involved in the cultural moment that produced them, but of which they are not mere products.

Sociological criticism is often vitiated by an over-reliance on "reflection theory": the overall movement of cinema reflects the overall movement of society. So long as one stresses the word "overall," I see no reason to quarrel with this, and a reflection of this kind will be acknowledged in this book. As soon as one gets down to specifics, however, it proves far too simple: cinema is never monolithic, within the overall movement there appear cracks, disruptions, countercurrents. From the viewpoint of this book the works that embody these oppositional tendencies (opposing to the dominant tendencies not so much a coherent radical position as a stubbornly obsessional and intuitive refusal of submission to ideological norms) are of greater interest (and infinitely greater artistic significance) than those that merely reflect—hence what will seem to many the disproportionate space devoted to De Palma, Cimino, and Scorsese as against, say, Lucas and Spielberg (though the latter have no cause to feel neglected).

Although I never intended to cover everything, I am aware of certain glaring omissions. Among individual filmmakers, the most obvious is Francis Ford Coppola. I must admit to finding it very difficult to make any meaningful contact with Coppola's work. On the level of intention and ambition it obviously looms large within this period, yet I find most of the films (the *Godfather* movies being partial, but only partial, exceptions) compounded of a daunting mixture of the pretentious and the banal, in roughly equal measure. A chapter on Coppola would approximately parallel the essay on Altman, taking up similar themes: the self-consciousness of the self-proclaimed auteur, the desire to produce the equivalent of the European "art" movie within the alien environment of the Hollywood industry, the gulf between ambition and achievement, the sense that the interest of the films is primarily symptomatic, exemplifying certain problems of "the artist" in contemporary Hollywood.

✳ ✳ ✳

My ambition in writing this book can be put negatively, in a phrase that will sound more modest than it is: to avoid triviality. Most contemporary film criticism, and virtually all journalist criticism, seems to me trivial (which is why I read less and less, and more and more selectively). Another way of saying this is that, while this book is concerned with the analysis of films, I wish it nevertheless to be *political*, in a sense at once wide and precise. To be political is today the only way to avoid the trivial. The cogency of this should be obvious enough, on various levels. For a start, we face the possibility of imminent extinction: the end of our civilization, the end of the human race. In such a situation, to quibble over which film is better acted, better photographed, or more entertaining, which director is the more skillful technician, and whether a or b has the better special effects, seems trivial indeed, though the exercise—the distraction—is still practiced all around us, and not just in the daily newspapers. Beyond that level, even if you believe that "everything will be all right" (if you "don't look," like the American protagonists of *Raiders of the Lost Ark*), there is the inescapable, enormous, and pervasive disturbance in the everyday realm of human relationships, especially male-female relationships—the realm to which, since the "naturalness" of the relative positions of men and women began to be challenged, we have given the name "sexual politics." Beyond that, again, is the steadily growing force of the gay liberation movement, no longer content with a plea for the tolerance of homosexuals, but (in close alliance with radical feminism) calling into question the very *construction* of sexuality within our culture. Though superficially they may appear quite distinct, these levels finally all come together and cohere: it is because of the way in which our civilization has constructed "masculinity" upon the repression of constitutional bisexuality (the masculinity on the possession of which the director of *Conan the Barbarian* and *Red Dawn* so proudly congratulates himself, making manifest its direct connection to Fascism) that all our lives are in jeopardy today.

To write politically about film means, basically, to write from an awareness of how individual films dramatize, as they inevitably must, the conflicts that characterize our culture: conflicts centered on class/wealth, gender, race, sexual orientation. For me, it is to commit oneself to the struggle for liberation that arises from those conflicts, the winning of which (that is, the victory of socialism and feminism) will be the only possible guarantee of our survival. The urgency of the situation—the need for every individual, working in whatever sphere, to decide what side he/she is on—was suggested by Norman O. Brown in a book published in 1959: *Life Against Death: The Psychoanalytical Meaning of History*. Brown's thesis is that the history of the human race is the history of the struggle between repression and liberation, and that in our own century that struggle has entered its climactic phase: we have to choose, quite simply, between the creation of a liberated society and the extinction of the human race. I quote from his concluding chapter:

The path of sublimation, which mankind has religiously followed at least since the foundation of the first cities, is no way out of the human neurosis, but, on the contrary, leads to its aggravation. Psychoanalytical theory and the bitter facts of contemporary history suggest that mankind is reaching the end of this road. Psychoanalytical theory declares that the end of the road is the dominion of death-in-life. History has brought mankind to that pinnacle on which the total obliteration of mankind is at last a practical possibility. At this moment of history the friends of the life instinct must warn that the victory of death is by no means impossible; the malignant death instinct can unleash those hydrogen bombs. For if we discard our fond illusion that the human race has a privileged or providential status in the life of the universe, it seems plain that the malignant death instinct is a built-in guarantee that the human experiment, if it fails to attain its possible perfection, will cancel itself out, as the dinosaur experiment canceled itself out. But jeremiads are useless unless we can point to a better way. Therefore the question confronting mankind is the abolition of repression.   (p. 269)

The urgency has scarcely lessened in the twenty-five years since the book's publication: indeed, our newspapers confirm daily the validity of Brown's thesis and the necessity, for those who believe in life, to commit themselves to opposing, on every front and every level, the dominant movement of our culture.

In relation to the ambition I have defined, I must here frankly admit to certain limitations. I have never systematically studied political science; though I try to think and feel film politically, I cannot claim to be a political thinker outside my chosen field, and certainly not an original one. Although my work has aligned itself with Marxist approaches to art, increasingly throughout the last decade, I still hesitate to call myself a Marxist. If I must have a label, I would prefer a less specific designation such as "free-lance radical": with the proviso that any form of radicalism that wishes to have any substance or force must necessarily, given the available choices, gravitate toward Marxism (but *which* Marxism?—there are today as many Marxes as there are Freuds). The reluctance to commit myself less equivocally is motivated less by doubt than by an awareness of the insufficiency of my knowledge, together with a suspicion that many Marxists might resent my adoption of that title. I would like to think that Marxists will find my work sympathetic and, in its attempts to define a radical approach to mainstream cinema, not incompatible with their own more precisely defined commitments. I do not, however, write primarily for Marxists: they already know more than I do. I would like to reach as wide and disparate an audience as possible. As a gay, I want to talk to heterosexuals; as a feminist, to those who have not given too much thought to the question of gender roles and the oppression of women; as a free-lance radical, to those who may feel, for a multitude of reasons, debarred from giving the Marxist position serious consideration.

It seems important to confront, directly and at the outset, the problem suggested in that last statement. Most people in our society would presumably concede that Marxism is the most formidable, and perhaps the only, alternative to capitalism. For most, however, it is automatically, axiomatically, not an *acceptable* alternative; it doesn't need to be seriously considered, can indeed be rejected without any careful inquiry into what, in fact, it might amount to. I am alluding here to the widespread suppression—in a culture that calls itself democratic and advertises itself as based on principles of freedom of thought, freedom of speech—not only of Marxist theory but of all coherent radical positions. The chief means of this suppression is simple but efficient: it consists of the assumption that Marxism is either identical with, or inevitably results in, Stalinism—which is rather like blaming Christ for the Spanish Inquisition. Within my own experience, one form this has taken, on several occasions when I have expressed Marxist interests, is the question (either incredulously serious or, more often, satirical-ironic), "Do you mean you'd rather be living in Russia?" Of Stalin's many heinous crimes perhaps the worst—because the most far-reaching in its consequences—has been to provide the West with a ready-made myth of Marxism which it can use as an automatic bogeyman.

The other common response has more semblance of plausibility: the objection that, to date, no Marxist or quasi-Marxist revolution has succeeded in developing the liberated society that most modern Marxists postulate as Marxism's true aim. The answer is twofold. First, every Marxist revolution to date has taken place in countries where theoretical principles have come to take second place to the most pressing economic needs: the struggle against starvation, poverty, illiteracy. This by no means excuses the failure (the Stalinist argument); it merely explains why it has become so easy for the ever-present forces of reaction to become dominant and distort or actually reverse the less directly material revolutionary impulses. It is common knowledge that the Russian Revolution in its early phase made ideological and legislative advances (the liberation of women, the repeal of laws against homosexuality, the displacement of the family as central social value) that still leave the Western democracies far behind—all of which Stalinism reversed. Second, every Marxist revolution to date has been too simple in its premises: Marx alone is not enough. It should be understood here that the term "Marx," like the term "Freud," refers to a body of theory that is in no way final or sacrosanct (dogma) but, on the contrary, is in need of constant modification, development, and reinterpretation in the light of cultural/historical experience. "Marx" offers no *adequate* account of sexuality, of the construction of the subject in ideology, or of the oppression of women. Every Marxist revolution so far has had to function within circumstances (economic, ideological) that have encouraged reaction and compromise in areas it has been ill equipped to deal with: in Cuba, for example, the strong tradition of machismo has proved stubbornly resistant to feminist overthrow, and the persecution of gays is an entirely logical corollary of this. The formidable nature of "the enemy" is only now becoming widely recognized: not just capitalism, but patriarchy.

This view is confirmed most eloquently by Varda Burstyn—one of the great Marxist-feminist thinkers of our time—in a characteristically lucid and forceful article, "Masculine Dominance and the State":

> The path to socialism can only travel through gender relations as well as economic relations, if social relations really are to lose their character as matrices of domination.

> But, and this is why so many feminists are engaged in this debate with Marxist men, Marxism is also the most radical of the world views to come out of the male-dominated epoch of human history, and many of us still think it carries within it the possibility for the correction of its internal omissions and distortions, and the practical transcendence of its internal weaknesses. The commitment to a human society free from domination and the implacable opposition to ideological mystification put Marxism as a theory and a movement in a qualitatively different position *vis-à-vis* feminism than any other male-stream social theories.
>
> (*The Socialist Register*, 1983, p. 81)

The article concludes on a note one may indeed call inspirational (no one more than Burstyn is able to communicate the sense that the struggle of "Life against Death" is still worth fighting, despite the discouraging conditions within which we all live):

> And insofar as Marxist theory *per se* has a useful role to play in the longer and larger process of social transformation, Marxist men must begin to engage as seriously with feminist political theory as feminists have done with Marxist political theory. If we really do want to constitute forms of public coordination and cooperation which maximise the creative potential in both individuals and collectivities, Marxist men really must engage with feminism at all levels, to see what can be learned and changed, so that we can go forward together towards human liberation.

When we have a Marxist revolution that is also, equally, a feminist revolution, and is built upon those theories of the cultural construction of sexual difference developed within the Freudian tradition by thinkers such as Marcuse and Gad Horowitz—then we shall see. Until then, the verdict must remain open.

Meanwhile The "Marxist-Freudian synthesis" (the subtitle of Michael Schneider's valuable book *Neurosis and Civilization*) is obviously the most hopeful, positive and vital development in contemporary thinking about culture, and, indeed, about the future of the human race. It has provided us all, if we care to use them, with the theories for an understanding of our culture and the tools with which to dismantle and rebuild it. If the present book emphasizes the Freudian side of that synthesis above the Marxist, that is partly because I feel more comfortable with it and partly because the Hollywood cinema has always been more accessible to analysis—more candidly profuse in its proliferation of material—on the level of sexual politics than on that of class politics. The explanation of this phenomenon is obvious: on the level of sexual politics, there has been no defined alternative to the status quo that can be presented as a bogeyman; consequently the taboo on deviant or subversive thought, while still very potent, has not been institutionalized and is much easier to evade. It is difficult to imagine, within the Hollywood system, the equivalent of a Hitchcock or a Sternberg operating on the level of *class* politics: both those directors, of course, repeatedly touch on it, but it is the level of sexual politics that is foregrounded and dominant.

It is necessary to confront at this point the standard opposition between the "free world" and the world of totalitarianism; an opposition usually centered on the notion of freedom of speech. Yes, of course there is a difference. Doubtless, if I lived in Russia it would be impossible for me to publish the equivalent of this book (since it expresses strong antagonism to the existing social system and the entire structure of our cultural organization); if it were published, it could not be distributed; if it were distributed, the author, the publishers, and the distributors would all be subject to terrible penalties. Yes, I am grateful that I live and work in the free world. *Ungratefully*, however, I want here to consider the limits of that freedom: for the "free world" of capitalism has its own methods of coercion and suppression, so that it does not yet have to resort to direct state intervention (that it is always ready to do so is obvious from the ease with which advanced capitalism has repeatedly escalated into Fascism).

The chief method is a complicated process of marginalization: the exclusion of radical positions from the popular media and their relegation to universities and precarious and generally short-lived counterculture periodicals. The operation has two functions: to prove that our culture permits freedom of speech, including dissident speech; to ensure that dissident speech remains ineffectual. The formidable challenge should clearly come from the universities, but they are being systematically eroded both from without and within, converted into career-training institutions. One watches the gulf between F. R. Leavis' formulation of what the university should be (the "creative center of civilization") and the actuality widening daily. The media have their own way of marginalizing academics—most typically, simply by applying that term. To be labeled an academic in the popular press is almost as automatically discrediting as to be labeled a Marxist: the connotations are less sinister, of course, suggesting irrelevance rather than menace. The term also offers a convenient alibi for the dismissal of any serious attempts to argue a radical position: the attempt is not dismissed because of the radical position (we have, after all, "freedom of speech"), but because it is written in an "academic style." It is certainly valid on occasion to use the term "academic" in a pejorative sense: the universities are not lacking in academics teaching courses that are totally out of touch with the exigencies of contemporary reality. In the press, however, the phrase "academic style" has come to cover any attempt to discuss serious and complex issues seriously and complexly, so that what is being (effectively) suppressed is, ultimately, seriousness and complexity. When we are told that something is written in an academic style, what we are really being told in the great majority of cases is "You will find this difficult, and neither reassuring nor entertaining. Why worry?"

(It will be noted that I have annexed, in a manner that may seem surreptitious, "seriousness" to "radicalism." I have to admit that for me the two are becoming increasingly inseparable. I suppose there *is* such a thing as an intelligent and defensible conservative position, though I haven't encountered one, and wonder what it will look like when, if we are unfortunate enough to survive the nuclear holocaust, we sit dying amid the ruins of everything we have striven to build.)

The media have a further alibi, the really foolproof one: their function is to give people what they want, and radicalism isn't popular. Or, to put it more bluntly, radicalism doesn't sell. The media have created a vicious circle: they teach people what to want, then thrive on supplying it, carefully nurturing the desire for more (since what is given never really satisfies, merely fosters the illusion of satisfaction, leaving intact the desire for the *next* illusion, Indiana Jones Part 3: "Trust him," as the advertisements exhort with a knowing cynicism in which the public is assumed to be knowingly complicit). Thus capitalism has its own methods, apparently spontaneous and "natural," of suppressing undesirable positions without needing to resort to state intervention—at least, so long as radical ideas remain unpopular and uncommercial, and can be kept that way by the media's steady barrage of distractions, flatteries, commodities, entertainments. If your life is unsatisfying, there's always a new shampoo to try, a new Spielberg movie to see, the next installment of a TV sit-com, the chance of winning a lottery.

Our educationalists, politicians, authorities, ecclesiastics, and parents are often heard helplessly bemoaning the fact that young people today are so cynical, disillusioned, apathetic or negatively anti-social. What else are they supposed to be, given that they believe they are going to die soon in a variety of horrible ways, and that the educational establishment, together with the entire social/ideological structure that sustains it, systematically deprives them of the only possible means by which they might develop hope for the future?—the notion that it is within the bounds of the human imagination radically to transform and restructure our culture. Conceal that notion, or hold it up to ridicule, or brush it aside as hopelessly utopian, and what can you expect, given the contemporary realities, but cynicism, disillusionment, apathy? Our young are being destroyed by the very people that set themselves up as their protectors, and the protection is the means of destruction.

This book is for students of all ages.

2.

The Chase

FLASHBACK, 1965

This essay constitutes a flashback in two senses. The minor sense: I wrote a chapter on *The Chase* in a little book on Arthur Penn published about fifteen years ago, in the days of my critical innocence (or culpable ignorance, as you will)—innocence, above all, of concepts of ideology, and of any clearly defined political position. The major sense: the film was released some years before the period with which this book is concerned. My evaluation of *The Chase* has not changed, but my sense of the *kind* of importance to be attributed to it has changed somewhat: I now see it as a seminal work, anticipating many of the major developments that took place in the Hollywood cinema during the decade following its production, hence a fitting starting point for this investigation. The present account will differ from the earlier, not only in approach but in ambition. There the aim (within the framework of an uncomplicatedly auteurist study) was to provide an appreciation of *The Chase* as "an Arthur Penn film," despite the obviously collaborative nature of the project and despite its auteur's own explicit reservations, marking a phase in a personal development. Here, while reaffirming my admiration for the film (and for Penn's work in general—*Night Moves* is among the finest Hollywood films of the 70s), I use it partly as a pretext for a number of more widespread concerns that are basic to this book: to establish a far more complex attitude toward the auteur theory; to introduce certain critical/theoretical concepts fundamental to my present position, which will reflect in particular on assumptions about "realism" and the "realistic"; to initiate a discussion of the differences (specifically, the ideological differences, though of course all differences are in a looser sense ideological) between the Classical and modern Hollywood cinema (one can take 1960 as a convenient, though to some degree arbitrary, point of demarcation).

We may begin with Penn's own attitude to the film and with the bourgeois myth of "the artist" that would have us attach a definitive importance to it: the myth of the artist as a superior being, donating to the world works which are the result of his conscious intentions and over which (at least if they are successful) he is assumed to have control. It may appear superfluous, after two decades of structuralism, semiotics, and psychoanalysis, to attack the "intentionalist fallacy" yet again; but it dies hard, as anyone involved in film education will be aware. If the director says his film is bad, how can the critic assert that it is good? If the director claims total unawareness of certain layers of meaning in his work, then how can those layers of meaning exist outside the critic's imagination? If the director ("the artist") says he had no control over a given film, then how can that film be worth defending? One of the major concerns of twentieth-century aesthetics has been progressively to answer, and in effect dismiss, such questions: first, through the "primitive" use of psychoanalysis (the artist is not aware of his own unconscious impulses), a use that proved perfectly compatible with, and assimilable into, traditional aesthetics; then, through Marxist concepts of ideology (where traditional and modern aesthetics part company), revealing a whole range of cultural assumptions, tensions, and contradictions operating through codes, conventions, and genres, largely beyond the artist's control; finally, through the sophisticated use of psychoanalytical theory that seeks to explain, not merely the individual "case," but ideology itself, the construction of the subject within it, the relationship between subject and spectacle.

Yet an important sense remains in which the production of a work is an intentional act—(the intentions of several or many may of course be involved)—and the discernible presence of authorial "fingerprints," "signature," "touch," etc., remains one of the clearest tokens of the specificity of a particular text. The error of primitive auteurism lay in its reduction of the potential interest of a film to its authorial signature, so that a film was worth examination only in so far as it could be shown to be characteristic (stylistically, thematically) of Ray, Mann, or Hawks, for instance: the rest was "interference," "an intractable scenario," attributable to the imposition of unsuitable projects or the misguided commercialism of producers. In discussing Hollywood movies now, I prefer to speak of the "intervention" of a director in a given project (even if the project was of his choice, even if he also wrote the screenplay), seeing him as more catalyst than creator. There is a level on which *The Chase* is palpably "an Arthur Penn film": the level of performance. The core of Penn's work, the source of its energy, has always been his work with actors, and the surface aliveness of the film, and much of its emotional intensity and complexity, derives from the responsiveness to his intervention of a magnificent cast.[1] I

---

1. The format of this essay makes it awkward to incorporate the names of the actors in the text (the practice elsewhere in this book). The characters referred to are played as follows: Sheriff Calder: Marlon Brando; Ruby Calder: Angie Dickinson; Anna Reeves: Jane Fonda; Bubber Reeves: Robert Redford; Val Rogers: E. G. Marshall; Jake Rogers: James Fox; Edwin Stuart: Robert Duvall; Emily Stuart: Janice Rule; Damon Fuller: Richard Bradford; Mary Fuller: Martha Hyer; Mrs. Reeves: Miriam Hopkins; Mr. Reeves: Malcolm Atterbury; Mrs. Briggs: Jocelyn Brando; Mr. Briggs: Henry Hull; Mrs. Henderson: Nydia Westman.

acknowledge this at the outset because it is not a level with which the present discussion will be explicitly concerned, yet it must certainly affect any reading of the film in ways that may be too oblique to be precisely defined. Suffice it to say that if *The Chase* had been directed by a Michael Winner or a J. Lee Thompson, it is probable that, however resonant the project, it would never have caught my attention.

As for Penn's partial rejection of *The Chase*, the critic's perspective on a film is likely to be very different from the filmmaker's. Penn worked on the elaboration of the scenario in close collaboration, first with Lillian Hellman, then with Horton Foote; he established and retained a marvelous rapport with the actors. What made the experience of the film unpleasant to the extent that he is still almost traumatized by the memory of it is the fact that he was denied the right to edit. He attaches a definitive importance to editing—the process of "extracting" the film from the "raw material." From his viewpoint, to deny him the right to edit is effectively to destroy the film, to make it no longer truly his: it becomes, in his own words, "a film that I cannot embrace." He has two specific complaints: To begin with, in the first takes the actors followed the script; then, getting into their roles, they became freer and more spontaneous and (especially in the case of Marlon Brando) began to improvise, so that later takes were far more developed, Brando in particular giving an apparently extraordinary performance. The editor (acting presumably on instructions from Sam Spiegel, the producer) in most cases returned to the script and the earlier takes, jettisoning the rest (though some of Brando's impromptus remain in the final cut). Second, the intended effect of the ending was destroyed by the editor's reversal of the last two scenes: the scene in which Anna (Jane Fonda), waiting outside the hospital, is told of her lover's death was meant to precede the scene in which Calder (Brando) and his wife Ruby (Angie Dickinson) drive away.

I shall return later to the question of the ending. As for the first complaint, *The Chase* as we have it is above all an ensemble film; if Brando's role stands out from the rest, it is because of the character's position within the diegesis (his authority and his isolation as sheriff). Brando's performance in the discarded takes was doubtless remarkable, but Brando's performances tend often to be so remarkable that they seriously unbalance the film. This happens, in my opinion, in *Last Tango in Paris* and in Penn's own *The Missouri Breaks*; though Penn disagrees, I think it might have happened in *The Chase*. More generally, Penn complains that the editor chose inferior takes throughout: "It is not the verbal content of the improvisations that I so sorely miss but the quality of performance that was present in the more loosely performed 'improvised' takes. The failure in the editor's choices is not with his adherence to the text—written by at least three and perhaps four people—it is with his blind and heavy choice of the most conventional take against those which are eccentric, antic and unorthodox." As the material Penn shot is inaccessible (and perhaps no longer in existence) I cannot comment on this, beyond saying that the film as we have it demonstrates effectively that Penn's worst, "most conventional" takes are ten times as exciting as most directors' best.

One should also take into account Penn's attitude to Hollywood. A New York intellectual with one eye on Europe, he shows little positive interest in the Hollywood genres for their own sake: they are at best vehicles for making "significant statements," at worst obstructions to be attacked and destroyed. He shows little sense that the genres—western, melodrama, horror film—are inherently rich in potential meaning. His remark that *The Chase* is "a Hollywood film, not a Penn film" was obviously intended to be derogatory. I think it says far more than he intended—that the layers of meaning of which Penn appears to be unaware in the film are intricately bound up with, determined by, its place in the evolution of genres and the ideological shifts that evolution enacts. It is as a Hollywood film that I shall discuss *The Chase* here.

In order to gain the kind of perspective on films that is impossible (or at least highly improbable) for their makers, I want to introduce concepts drawn from the work of two diverse but variously influential aestheticians.

In *Art and Illusion* E. H. Gombrich offers one of the classic statements about representation—about the relationship between reality and art. He quotes, with qualified approval, Zola's definition of a work of art as "a corner of nature seen through a temperament," and goes on to "probe it further." It is insufficient to treat representation as reality mediated simply by the individual artist: many other factors contribute to the mediation. Basic is the choice of tools and materials. Two landscape artists, trying faithfully to reproduce the same scene, one using a hard pencil, one working in oils, will offer two very different versions of the reality in front of them; their different media will influence them to see it differently, the former seeing everything in terms of line and shape, the latter in terms of mass and color. It is easy to extend this to the cinema and its available technology. The reality the screen so seductively offers is at all points mediated by the choice of camera, lens and focus; the argument can be developed to include editing and camera movement. Nor is this simply a matter of availability: also important are the conventions dominant within a given period. Even at the level of technology and shooting/editing method, *The Deer Hunter* cannot be *My Darling Clementine*; try to make a classical Hollywood film in black and white in the 70s and the overall impression will be affectation (*The Last Picture Show*).

But what most concerns me here, for its bearing on Hollywood genres, character types, and narrative conventions, is Gombrich's perception of the extent to which art is dependent upon the availability of "schemata" (established patterns, formulas, stereotypes), and the degree to which the nature of the particular work is determined by the particular schemata at the artist's disposal. Gombrich offers numerous examples from art history, from which I shall select two:

Perhaps the earliest instance of this kind dates back more than three thousand years, to the beginnings of the New Kingdom in Egypt, when the Pharaoh Thutmose included in his picture chronicle of the Syrian campaign a record of plants he had brought back to Egypt. The inscription, though somewhat muti- lated, tells us that Pharaoh pronounces these pictures to be "the truth." Yet botanists have found it hard to agree on what plants may have been meant by these renderings. The schematic shapes are not sufficiently differentiated to allow secure identification. (p. 67)

The implication is that the illustrations, while intentionally drawn from life, were heavily influenced by the schemata of plant drawings available.

When Dürer published his famous woodcut of a rhinoceros, he had to rely on second-hand evidence which he filled in from his own imagination, colored, no doubt, by what he had learned of the most famous of exotic beasts, the dragon with its armoured body. Yet it has been shown that this half-invented creature served as a model for all renderings of the rhinoceros, even in natural history books, up to the eighteenth century. (pp. 70–71)

Gombrich goes on to quote James Bruce's claim that his 1789 illustration of a rhinoceros, "designed from the life," contrasts with Dürer's ("wonderfully ill-exe- cuted in all its parts"), and to show that Bruce's picture still, nonetheless, derives from the Dürer tradition rather than from "nature." Gombrich concludes that "the familiar will always remain the starting-point for the rendering of the unfamiliar. . . . Without some starting-point, some initial schema, we could never get hold of the flux of experience. Without categories, we could not sort out our impressions" (p. 76).

The usefulness of this—suitably modified and extended to encompass move- ment and narrative, the term "schemata" covering characters and narrative patterns with terms such as "genres" and "cycles" substituted for Gombrich's "categories"— in exploring a traditional art like the Hollywood cinema should be clear. Crucially, it offers an invaluable corrective to all those naive notions of "the realistic" (whether merely descriptive or, as is almost invariably the case, evaluative) that still obsti- nately linger on. Whenever filmmakers or critics lay claim to a new realism, we would do well to remember Mr. Bruce's rhinoceros, adopt a certain skepticism, and examine the work in question in relation to the available schemata. An acquain- tance (not a casual moviegoer, but a person in a position of responsibility in film culture) once informed me confidently that *Mandingo* must be a bad film because it showed a southern plantation and mansion in a state of decay, and "in reality" they were extremely well maintained. Leaving aside the assumption of an absolute- ness that allows for no exceptions (*all* southern mansions?), such a comment naively

confuses the highly conventionalized genre of melodrama (only in relation to
which can the film be properly understood) with some vague notion of documentary reconstruction, assuming, with equal naiveté, the superiority of the latter
mode. The decaying mansion of *Mandingo* relates to one of the most important
and enduring schemata of American culture, the "terrible house," whose line of
descent can be traced from Poe (*The Fall of the House of Usher*) to Hooper (*The Texas
Chainsaw Massacre*). (For a more comprehensive treatment, see Andrew Britton's
analysis of *Mandingo* in *Movie 22*.) The TV movie *The Day After* represents an
immediately topical instance of this misconception at time of writing. It has been
widely advertised, and generally received, as offering a "realistic" depiction of the
aftermath of nuclear war. It may be accurate enough (though surely reprehensibly
understated) in the information it offers as to the physical effects of nuclear attack;
as a narrative, however, it relies extensively on the disaster movies of the 70s, both
in overall structure and in specific, detailed narrative strategies. Critics who have
noticed this see it as invalidating the film, in my opinion quite unjustifiably: "the
familiar will always remain the starting point for the rendering of the unfamiliar."
The Chase itself was savagely mauled by the majority of critics on its release because
of its alleged exaggerations: "Texas isn't really like that"—a perception as misguided
as it is irrelevant.

I shall at this point list some of the traditional schemata that structure *The
Chase*, using as a convenient touchstone Ford's *Young Mr. Lincoln*—convenient
because it is likely to be familiar to readers, because it shares so many of the later
film's schemata, and because there is obviously no question of any direct link
between the two films, the notion of schemata going far beyond any question of
influence.

1. "The Law," embodied in a male authority figure, the superior, charismatic
   individual (Lincoln; Sheriff Calder).
2. Woman as the hero's support and inspiration (Ann Rutledge; Ruby).
3. The innocent young, accused of murder, in need of the authority figure's
   protection and defense (the Clay brothers; Bubber Reeves).
4. The lynch mob—townspeople, normally "respectable citizens"—who
   attempt to break into the jail.
5. The mother of the accused (Mrs. Clay; Mrs. Reeves) and her anxiety for the
   safety of her son(s).
6. The young wife of the accused (Hannah; Anna), also concerned for his
   safety.
7. Religion (Lincoln's appeal to the bible in the lynching scene; Miss Henderson and her reiterated "I'm praying for you").
8. Phallic imagery linking violence with sexuality (the lynch party's battering
   ram; the repeated, explicit play on the connotations of pistols—"With all

those pistols you've got there, Emily, I don't think there'd be room for mine").

9. Books and learning as emblems of progress (Lincoln's Blackstone; the university model presented to Val Rogers on his birthday).

10. The emblem of a lost happiness/innocence (the memory of Ann Rutledge; *The Chase*'s ruined building. As the parallel here is somewhat weak and inexact, I shall adduce two examples from outside *Young Mr. Lincoln*: the "Rosebud" of *Citizen Kane* and "the river" of *Written on the Wind*).

It becomes clear at this point that Gombrich is not enough. Before examining in detail the implications of the recurrence of these schemata over a quarter of a century (they can be traced back, of course, to earlier times and forward to the present), we must pass beyond him, exposing his limitations. They could perhaps be said to expose themselves, in the passage following directly on from the last sentence I quoted: "Without categories, we could not sort out our impressions. Paradoxically, it has turned out that it matters relatively little what these first categories are."

If the absence here of any political dimension, of any concept of ideology and of schemata as its concrete embodiment, is not immediately obvious, this is because Gombrich restricts his examples entirely to flora and fauna; had he included examples from representations of the human form (the nude, for instance), the absence could not have been so easily covered by the assumption of neutrality. For Gombrich, apparently, the schemata are without important inherent meaning, abstract counters the artist can use as he pleases. The untenability of such a position becomes even more obvious when one applies it to the larger narrative forms such as the novel and the cinema. Gombrich's tendency, in fact, is generally to depoliticize art and aesthetics. He ends the chapter I have been drawing upon ("Truth and the Stereotype") by remarking that "the form of a representation cannot be divorced from its purpose and the requirements of the society in which the given visual language gains currency," but he never effectively follows through the implications of such a perception. It is time to turn to Roland Barthes, the Barthes of *Mythologies*.

Barthes' concept of "myth" can be defined by means of the famous example he offers. In a barber's shop, at the time of the Algerian Uprisings and attempted suppressions, he picked up a copy of *Paris-Match*; on the cover a black soldier in uniform, was looking up, presumably at the French flag, and giving the salute. A simple image conveying, on the surface, a simple statement: here is a black soldier saluting the flag. But beyond the simple statement (the level of denotation), this simple signifier carries a wealth of surreptitious meaning (the level of connotation): the blacks are proud to serve the mother country, France; they are dignified and ennobled, and their lives are given meaning, by this service; imperialism is justified, indeed admirable, as it brings order, civilization, and discipline (embodied in the uniform) to the lives of the subject races ("natives" being by definition lax, unruly

The Chase

(right)
Marlon Brando as
Sheriff Calder

(below)
Jane Fonda and
James Fox in the
wrecked-car dump

and childlike). In other words, the simple, seemingly innocent and "real" image (black soldiers do, after all, salute the flag of the country they serve) insidiously communicates at unconscious levels a political (here deeply reactionary) statement.

To Gombrich's invaluable concept of schemata, then, it is necessary to add Barthes' concept of myth—roughly speaking, schemata with their political dimension restored, the image as purveyor of ideology. Applying the notion of myth to the recurrent schemata of the Hollywood cinema, one recognizes the full significance of the obvious point that no direct connection exists between *Young Mr. Lincoln* and *The Chase*. What is involved is far greater than a specific resemblance based on chance or influence between two films made about twenty-five years apart: the schemata belong to the culture and carry cultural meanings which the two films variously inflect, the inflections determined not merely by two auteurs but by the complex cultural-historical network within which they function.

We can now consider the ten schemata, starting from the position that both films (vehicles of myth from the Classical and post-Classical periods respectively) are centrally concerned with America.

1. The male authority figure, the symbolic Father, repository and dispenser of the Law, combines myths of individualism and male supremacy that are central to capitalist democracy, enacting the functions of control and containment. In Ford's film, Lincoln quells the lynch mob (that doesn't break in to the jail), subsequently solves the crime and saves the lives of the Clay brothers, restores the family, and walks out of the film to become President of the United States. In *The Chase*, Calder fails to control the mob (the unruly respectable citizens break into the jail and beat him to a pulp), fails to save the young man's life, and drives out of the town defeated on all fronts. Lincoln from the outset knows by some kind of Divine Grace that he will succeed, confidently presenting himself (despite his total inexperience) to Mrs. Clay as "your lawyer; Ma'am"; all Calder's assertions of confidence prove unfounded (for example, his assuring Lester of the safety of the jail, where "we won't have any of our citizens bothering you": Lester is savagely beaten in his cell by the town's supreme citizen, Val Rogers). Lincoln, above all, maintains his control over *himself*; Calder loses even that, succumbing finally to the all-pervasive hysteria and violence in his beating of the man who shoots Bubber Reeves. The collapse of confidence in patriarchal authority is also variously inflected in the presentation of Val Rogers and Mr. Reeves, whose ineffectual, last-minute attempt to make contact with his son by addressing him as "Charlie" provides one of the film's most poignant moments.

2. In *Young Mr. Lincoln* Ann Rutledge dies but lives on as the protagonist's spiritual support (it is "her" decision—the stick falling toward the grave—that sends him to study law). The myth of woman as man's supporter/inspiration/redeemer is of course long-standing; *The Chase* does not explicitly challenge it, presenting Ruby as intelligent, sympathetic and (above all, and sufficiently) a wife. Yet the myth

makes sense only in relation to the myth of the patriarch: if the hero's charismatic and legal authority becomes invalid or ineffectual, the myth of woman-as-supporter collapses with it. Hence the emphasis on Ruby's helplessness: locked out of the cell in which Val Rogers beats up Lester, she is subsequently locked out of the room in which the respectable citizens beat up her husband, and is finally unable to restrain Calder when he surrenders to the epidemic of useless violence. Where Lincoln leaves the film under Ann's spiritual guidance to become President, Calder leaves the town under Ruby's supervision ("Calder . . . let's go") to drive—nowhere. Ruby's last line itself relates significantly to an obstinately recurring motif of the American cinema, the line (invariably spoken by the man to the woman) "Let's go home" (or variations on it: "I'll take you home," "We can go home," etc.) Here, the man no longer has the authority to utter it, and there is no home left to go to.

3. In *Young Mr. Lincoln* the innocence of the young accused is unambiguous: the brothers, representing simple "manly" virtues, are central to Ford's idealization of the family, the celebration of family life being central to the film. Bubber's innocence is far more equivocal: if he escapes the pervasive ugliness and corruption of the society, his chief characteristic is confusion on all levels, as shown by Emily's describing his stare "like everything's going wrong and he just can't figure out why." If Matt Clay represents a confidence in the values of the American pioneer past, Bubber, though among the film's more positive characters, represents an uncertainty about the values of any possible American future.

4. Ford presents the lynch mob as essentially good citizens whose energies (finding release, initially, in the Independence Day celebrations) get temporarily out of control. They need to be reminded of what is "right"—of a fixed and absolute set of values ratified by biblical text—whereupon their basic soundness is reaffirmed. Their violence is taken as given, a fact of nature that demands no explanation, as unquestionable as the morality that subdues it. Such simple dualism has become impossible in *The Chase*: the violence is merely the logical eruption of the corruption, frustration and entrapment of the society. The citizens can no longer be told, effectively, to go home to bed (they would scarcely know which bed to go to); there are no texts, no absolute morality, to which appeal can be made. Further, the constitution of the mob is now quite different. In *Lincoln* it is composed of on earthy, vigorous proletariat still in close spiritual touch with the original cabin-raisers; in *The Chase* it is composed of the dominant classes, the affluent upper-middle and upwardly mobile middle, the wealthy patriarch Val Rogers (who virtually owns the town) in their midst. Calder's own position, unlike Lincoln's, is itself compromised: he owes his appointment as sheriff to Rogers and, however he may struggle to preserve his personal integrity, is never allowed to forget the fact.

5. Ford's idealization of motherhood is central to *Young Mr. Lincoln* and to the ideology it embodies. The mother is reverenced as the rock on which the family, hence civilization, is built, and she never has to ask herself, like Mrs. Reeves,

"Where did I go wrong?" At the same time she has no voice, no potency, in the male-dominated world of money, law, authority. Her simplicity (the guarantee of her sanctity and moral strength) is repeatedly stressed: she can't read or write. By the time of *The Chase*, confidence in this central, supportive role has crumbled away. It is remarkable that, given the very large number of characters of all ages in the film, there is only one mother: Mrs. Reeves, hysterical, ineffectual, consistently wrongheaded, ultimately rejected by her son. This collapse of confidence in the figure of the Mother (for Ford, the spiritual core of civilization) points directly to a collapse of confidence in the family structure and, beyond that, in traditional sexual relationships generally.

6. It follows from Ford's veneration of the mother that nothing in *Young Mr. Lincoln* questions the rightness and sanctity of marriage: Hannah, waiting anxiously, dutifully and passively for the outcome of the trial, is simply the Abigail Clay of the next generation. Against this we may set Anna Reeves and the uncertainty about traditional marriage ties introduced through her relationship with both Bubber and Jake Rogers. Her eventual commitment to Bubber carries considerable moral force (as does her active and forceful participation in events), but it has nothing to do with the sanctity of the marriage tie: she realizes that it is Bubber who really needs her.

7. In *Young Mr. Lincoln* the bible (and its later substitute, the *Farmer's Almanack*—God and Nature conceived of as one) is the ultimate sanction, and Lincoln's authority is seen as God-given; in *The Chase*, religion is reduced to the helpless, absurd and annoying mumblings of Miss Henderson, who is represented as mad. It no longer underpins and validates the system; it has become marginal to the point of irrelevancy.

8. The link between violence and male sexuality, which is implicit and probably unconscious in *Young Mr. Lincoln*, is fully explicit in *The Chase*. Ford's work is consistently preoccupied with the ways in which "excess" energies can be safely contained (communal work, communal dances and celebrations, communal comic brawls), much of its complexity arising from the fact that both the energy and the forms of containment are highly valued. By the time of *The Chase*, all sense of the worth of the culture in whose name the containment is enforced has been undermined, and the energies themselves are seen as corrupted. Against Ford's dances—celebration of energy and community—set *The Chase*'s three parties, which culminate and coalesce in the destructive chaos of the fireworks display in a wrecked car junkyard: sexual games, erupting into games of violence, which escalate in turn into real violence ending in total and irreparable breakdown.

9. Lincoln's progress in Ford's film is stimulated by his learning from the books passed on to him by the Clay family: he is guided toward his destiny as President by Ann Rutledge and Blackstone's *Commentaries*, by women and nature, law and learning. In *The Chase* the concept of progress through learning has been debased

to status-seeking display (the competitive money grants for the university) and hypocrisy (the remark that "only through learning is progress possible" delivered as an empty platitude).

10. Hollywood's emblems for a lost innocence/happiness suggest a steady descent into disillusionment. Ann Rutledge, though dead, becomes the spiritual support of Lincoln's career; Kane's "Rosebud" epitomizes not only a lost childhood but an alternative, perhaps more fulfilling life uncorrupted by power. By 1956 "the river" of *Written on the Wind* represents only the illusion of past happiness (even as children, the characters were never really happy). In *The Chase*, the emblem of a nostalgically viewed childhood innocence has become an irreparably ruined, skeletal shed.

❋ ❋ ❋

The Chase amounts to one of the most complete, all-encompassing statements of the breakdown of ideological confidence that characterizes American culture throughout the Vietnam period and becomes a major defining factor of Hollywood cinema in the late 60s and 70s. It achieves this *as a Hollywood film*: the ideological shift registered in the use of the ten schemata I have presented goes far beyond any overt social-political comments (on the position of blacks, etc.), which, like Penn, I find somewhat crude and obvious (though they make their contribution to the overall structure). It is the first "American apocalypse" movie, the first film in which the disintegration of American society and the ideology that supports it (represented in microcosm by the town) is presented as total and final, beyond hope of reconstruction. The ideological force of all the available schemata taken up by Ford in *Young Mr. Lincoln* (and therein celebrated as myths) is here definitively undermined.

Yet the work of the film is not merely negative: out of the collapse, a new positive movement, though extremely vulnerable and tentative, begins to manifest itself. One sees this most plainly in the attitude the film defines toward sexuality and sexual organization. The question "Do you believe in the sexual revolution?" is explicitly raised in the dialogue, and it seems fitting to conclude a discussion of *The Chase* by attempting to define the answer the film provides.

Three attitudes to sexual relationships are dramatized in *The Chase*, two of which are defined very clearly, the third remaining tentative and somewhat confused.

1. Traditional patriarchal monogamy: the Calders, Mr. and Mrs. Briggs, Mr. and Mrs. Reeves. The Calder relationship *seems* to be endorsed by the film—it is presented as strong, stable, and mutually supportive. Yet if patriarchal authority is overthrown, the ideological strength of the relationship logically falls with it. The film sets up fascinating parallels between the Calders and the Briggses: the

monogamy of both relationships is emphasized, along with the subordination of the woman to the man; the barrenness of both is made explicit (Ruby wonders if they should have adopted children, Mrs. Briggs wonders whether having children or not having children is worse); Calder and Briggs are the only two who respect the law (Calder's caustic "That makes two of us"). The Calders are presented positively, the Briggses negatively—opposite poles of the film's value structure. This makes even more interesting the sense that the latter are a dark reflection of the former. There is a marvelous moment when the two main sexual worlds of the film make passing contact, the moment when Briggs (his wife as usual in tow, hanging on his arm) comments to Emily outside her house on the "permissive" behavior at her party ("Changing partners?"), and adds "But my wife and I, we're old-fashioned." As he says it, Mrs. Briggs stares at him with a look bordering on pathological hatred: it brilliantly epitomizes the repressiveness of patriarchal monogamy and the frustrations of women within it. The Reeves couple appears to offer the inverse of this with the woman as dominant partner, but is more accurately a variation on it: all Mrs. Reeves' emotional energy has been displaced on to her male child, hence her hysteria when he "goes wrong." If the Calders are viewed as heroic, the overall sense of the film reveals them as defending a system that has become obsolete. Finally, all they can do is drive away from the ruins.

2. Permissiveness: the 'sexual revolution' as understood by the Fullers, Stuarts, etc., taking the form of squalid and furtive adulterous intrigue undertaken for its own sake, out of boredom, frustration or a desire to get even with one's spouse, with a strong insistence on phallocentrism (Edwin "doesn't have a pistol," Damon obviously does). If the film implicitly undercuts traditional monogamy, it openly attacks this permissiveness as purely destructive and motivated by destructiveness, rather than by any impulses of concern, tenderness or generosity. Yet permissiveness is clearly but the other side of the coin (suggested by the Briggs/Emily exchange referred to earlier)—the logical result of the collapse of repressive and artificial proscriptions.

3. The attitude dramatized in the Bubber-Anna-Jake triangle. During the episode in the junkyard the three try to work out what is potentially a new morality (it is significant that the film roughly coincides with the growth of the hippy movement): a genuine new morality, as against the *im*morality fostered ("permitted") by the old morality. Central to it is Anna's recognition that she is able to love two men at once, her relative autonomy of choice, decision and action (unique among the women of the film), and Bubber's acceptance of her and Jake (his wife and best friend) as lovers. This goes against both traditional monogamy, by rejecting its artificially imposed, legalized repressiveness, and permissiveness, by rejecting its egotistic heartlessness and phallocentrism. Monogamy and permissiveness are both based upon an obsession with sexuality (the one with its containment, the other with its supposedly free expression): within both arrangements, sex becomes

the central criterion by which behavior is judged, the notion of fidelity or infidelity restricted to the simple act of intercourse. The Bubber-Anna-Jake story enacts the tentative dethronement of the sexual act, without at all diminishing the importance of sexuality as human communication. It suggests that sexuality is not incompatible with friendship, with sharing, with an unrestricted human concern. Significant in relation to this is the older generation's total inability to understand or predict the behavior and motivation of the younger characters. Hence Val Rogers assumes without hesitation that Bubber will kill Jake when he finds out that he and Anna are lovers; hence Mrs. Reeves can find no word for Anna but "whore." Anna—her activeness, her autonomy, her refusal to allow herself to be defined by a relationship with a man—is at the heart of the film's tentative, uncertain positive movement.

Herein lies the appropriateness of the ending as it stands, albeit unsanctioned by the film's director, an appropriateness both within and outside the fiction. The Calders drive away, defeated. The film abandons them to end on Anna Reeves, the character, still able to learn, reflect, develop, and Jane Fonda, the actress, walking toward her problematic future career, both cinematic and political. Like young Mr. Lincoln, she walks out of the frame, leaving behind a film and a society that can no longer comfortably contain her.

3.

Smart-Ass and Cutie-Pie

NOTES TOWARD THE EVALUATION
OF ALTMAN (1975)

Obviously, Altman is "in." Highly favorable articles on his work proliferate on both sides of the Atlantic, from Pauline Kael's premature ecstasies over *Nashville* in the *New Yorker* to Jonathan Rosenbaum's more modest assessment in *Sight and Sound* that Altman, while "he really cannot be considered in the same league at all" as Rivette or the Tati of *Playtime* has "opened up the American illusionist cinema to a few of the *possibilities* inherent in this sort of game:" the game being, apparently, "the notion that artist and audience conspire to create the work in its living form." It is a conspiracy in which I have so far failed to participate, finding works either created or not, as the case may be. If the film isn't up there on the screen "in its living form," I don't feel there is much I can do about it. I view Altman with mixed feelings, finding most of the films interesting and a very small number very good. *Nashville*—an enormously ambitious work, a kind of *War and Peace* of country and western— may well prove the decisive film of his career, a watershed like Losey's *Eve*, a definitive statement of artistic identity from which there is no turning back. As with *Eve*, its unpleasantness casts a certain retrospective shadow over the films that preceded it, highlighting features to which one has not previously attributed great importance. It seems likely to be hailed as a masterpiece, and Altman's films are already on the way to that fashionable acceptance where criticism ceases to ask questions and lapses into a celebration of excellences. With the release of *Nashville*, it seems the right moment to take stock of Altman's achievement so far, to attempt to sort out strengths and weaknesses, and to ask how they relate to each other.

The particular interest of Altman's work derives from a complex of attributes, central to which, of course, is the intrinsic quality of his best films. He is already clearly identifiable as an auteur, with certain themes, structures, attitudes, and stylistic features (not to mention his familiar stock company of actors and collaborators) recurring across a wide range of genres and subject matter. Michael Dempsey provides a good definition of Altman's auteurship in an article called "The Empty Staircase and the Chinese Princess" in *Film Comment* (September-October 1974), and I am in almost complete agreement with his relative evaluation of the films (I think he is too generous to *Images* and too hasty in his dismissal of *California Split*). Counterpointing this sense of auteurist consistency, in fact, is one's sense of the extreme unevenness of Altman's work—unevenness that can't be accounted for neatly in terms of the external excuses the commercial cinema traditionally provides (studio interference, imposed projects, incongruous casting, etc.), because the worst films are just as personal as the best and because Altman's control over his work (at least in the material sense) seems always to have been more or less total. He seems to me to have been responsible for some of the best (*McCabe and Mrs. Miller, The Long Goodbye*) and some of the worst (*M.A.S.H., Images*) films by American directors in the past decade, his other films covering the full range of intermediate success and failure between these.

Most important of all is the centrality of Altman's work to the development of the modern American cinema. Because of its distinction, because of the presence of a clearly defined creative personality, it brings to a sharp focus most of the features that characterize that development: the growing sense of disorientation and confusion of values, with the consequent sapping of any possibilities for affirmation; attitudes to the Hollywood of the past and its traditional genres; awareness of the modern European cinema and the desire to assimilate its techniques; the change (also influenced by Europe) in the role and status of the director, from studio employee to (at least in theory) all-determining artist. An attempt to define Altman's work in thematic terms will inevitably spill over into an exploration of the dominant themes of the American cinema today. During a discussion in *Movie 20*, Victor Perkins remarked that a thematic description of Nicholas Ray would closely resemble one of Kazan. The same could be said now of (to name but three of the most distinguished contemporary figures) Penn, Altman and Schatzberg. Close parallels can be drawn, for example, between *Puzzle of a Downfall Child* and *Images*, and between *Scarecrow* and *California Split*. In both cases—in the former decisively—the comparison would be, in my opinion, to Altman's disadvantage, but my point is that, for all the changed status (more perhaps an appearance than a reality, but not entirely illusory) of the director as artist-expressing-himself, one cannot sensibly discuss any of these films without placing them in a wider context, that of the movement of the American cinema and, beyond it, American society.

Since the early 60s, the central theme of the American cinema has been, increasingly, disintegration and breakdown. On the most obvious and vulgar level, it is expressed in the recent cycle of disaster movies in which the threat of total destruction is faced by a microcosm of bourgeois-capitalist society (the working classes and the student population scarcely, if at all, represented: a most significant suppression, the disaster standing in for social revolution). Being expensive super-productions, producers' rather than directors' movies, studio-dominated with a minimal intervention of individual creativity (which is almost invariably disruptive to some degree), the films are very strongly determined by status quo ideology, hence are as much survival pictures as disaster pictures, concerned to demonstrate capitalist society's ability to come through. Even their expensiveness is a comforting assertion of the stability of the capitalist system. Yet the necessity for this not very convincing insistence on survival is itself eloquent. Meanwhile, various genres have reached their apocalyptic phase, most significantly that reliable barometer of America's image of herself, the western—a development instigated by *The Wild Bunch* and confirmed by Eastwood's crude but remarkable *High Plains Drifter* wherein the Lone Hero rides in from the Wilderness not to defend the Growing Community but to reveal it as rotten at its very foundations before annihilating it. In the discussion in *Movie 20*, somebody asked what had become of the American Family Picture. I suggested *Night of the Living Dead* and *The Exorcist*. I might have added *Rosemary's Baby*, which seems to occupy the place in the development of the American horror film that *The Wild Bunch* occupies in the development of the western—they appeared in the same year. Most opportunely, the release of *It's Alive*, in which the Ideal American Family itself gives birth to a destructive monster, adds vivid confirmation.

The sensation of imminent or actual breakdown, of rottenness at the ideological core of capitalist society, presented with such irrefutable pervasiveness by the popular cinema, is explored more consciously and intellectually in the work of directors like Penn, Schatzberg and Altman. *Nashville* is, in fact, the supreme example of the spiritual-intellectual disaster movie, with that multi-plot, multi-character structure essential to the genre, Nashville itself being, like the ship of *The Poseidon Adventure*, the plane of *Airport 1975*, the skyscraper of *The Towering Inferno* or the Los Angeles of *Earthquake*, an image of America, though much more pessimistically conceived, with the notion of survival (as epitomized in the crowd's final mindless chanting of "It don't worry me") become bitterly ironic. The process of disintegration provides the characteristic movement of the films of all three directors, whether it is located within a single disturbed personality (*Mickey One*, *Puzzle of a Downfall Child, Images*), a social milieu or community (*The Chase, Alice's Restaurant, Nashville*), or a personal relationship (*Night Moves, Panic in Needle Park, Scarecrow, California Split*).

Consider the cases of *Scarecrow* and *California Split*. Both belong firmly within that most curious and characteristic of contemporary subgenres, the "male duo" movie, a phenomenon that has yet to be sufficiently explained. Though there are of course antecedents (notably in Hawks), the cycle was decisively inaugurated by *Easy Rider* and *Midnight Cowboy*, and has proved strikingly prolific and generally popular (*Butch Cassidy and the Sundance Kid, Little Fauss and Big Halsey, Bad Company, When the Legends Die, Thunderbolt and Lightfoot,* etc.) It can be regarded as a response to certain social developments centered on the emancipation of women and the resultant undermining of the home. The implicit attitude is "You see, we can get on pretty well without you, anyway—except as occasional sex objects." Certainly, women play very peripheral roles in the films, most of which have homosexual overtones, usually suppressed or ambiguous. The surface emphasis is always on the camaraderie between the two men, the detailed, high-spirited give and take, offering opportunities for improvisatory acting and self-expression to two gifted players. But the seductive charm of the surface play invariably conceals absences. The films take the form of journeys with complicated, rambling, usually aimless itineraries—journeys to nowhere, searches in which the real object of the search remains undefined or uncertain. In both *Scarecrow* and *California Split* one of the protagonists is linked, albeit tenuously, with a home: in Schatzberg's movie, Al Pacino clings tenaciously to the illusion that he can return whenever he wishes, after years at sea, to the wife and child he has abandoned; in Altman's, George Segal's disorientation and rootlessness have for background a recently broken marriage. Both films move toward a point where the characters become aware of the sense of loss—a culmination movingly realized in *Scarecrow,* lightly touched on in *California Split,* where Segal, having won a fortune gambling, abruptly grasps that it means nothing to him and announces that he's going "home." The understated poignancy of the ending derives from our awareness that he no longer has a home to go to.

The difference between the two films lies in the much greater emphasis on surface charm in Altman's: where Schatzberg is committed to exploring his characters and their predicament (and seems to care much more about them), Altman is more interested in playing improvisatory games with his actors. *California Split* is the more immediately appealing movie, *Scarecrow* the more substantial. Altman's tendency to allow himself to be seduced by surface play, and to use it to seduce audiences, is one aspect of the strategies of evasion that characterize his work. The distinction, however, is also bound up with certain issues in the realism/antirealism debate, In *Scarecrow* we think primarily of the actors as characters; in *California Split* we are much more aware of them as Themselves (especially the irrepressible Elliott Gould). I shall return later to the antirealist elements in Altman's work, which represent its most obviously problematic aspect.

This sense of collapsed or discredited values is reinforced if one juxtaposes *Thieves Like Us* with *They Live by Night,* Ray's 1948 version of the same novel. One's immediate impression is that the Farley Granger/Cathy O'Donnell couple represents a much more bourgeois-romantic concept than that embodied in the casting and direction of Keith Carradine and Shelley Duvall. Ray was still able to half believe in certain bourgeois values of stability, home, family (see also *The James Brothers*). Behind the riven bourgeois families of *Rebel Without a Cause* and *Bigger than Life* there hovers a traditional norm of the healthy family, which is reaffirmed (necessarily without carrying full conviction) at the ends of the films. In Altman, Schatzberg, recent Penn, this has largely disappeared (in *Bonnie and Clyde* it had already become a pale ghost, little more than a pathetic illusion, an idea expressed visually in the scene of the reunion with Bonnie's mother). The broad changes in the way in which the American cinema interprets the American past might also be adduced: in 1940 the Joads could still trek through the Depression to at least a hypothetical Promised Land; the aimless itinerary through the Depression of *Thieves Like Us* leads only to the empty staircase justly emphasized by the title of Michael Dempsey's article. *They Live by Night* gains from its basis in traditional values (however qualified by Ray's critical irony), not because the values were "true," but because they provided a tension that *Thieves Like Us* lacks; for all the intelligence at work in individual scenes, the overall effect is curiously empty and lacking in dynamism, an almost academic demonstration of futility.

The most persistent recurrent pattern in Altman's films—their basic auteurist structure—constitutes a personal inflection of the general thematic of the contemporary American cinema. The protagonist embarks on an undertaking he is confident he can control; the sense of control is progressively revealed as illusory; the protagonist is trapped in a course of events that culminate in disaster (frequently death). The pattern is already embryonically present in the astronaut of *Countdown* (James Caan)—though there the film has a last-minute, ideologically obligatory happy ending. It is expounded fully in *That Cold Day in the Park*: a spinster (Sandy Dennis) takes in a hippy (Michael Burns) whom she sees from her apartment window, huddled on a park bench in the rain; each believes him/herself to be in control of the situation that develops, she by adopting an attitude of maternal but pseudo-permissive protectiveness that conceals her sexual drives, he by totally withholding speech, hence remaining mysterious (the audience is uncertain until about a third through the film whether he can speak or not). In fact, their sense of control (over each other, over the relationship, over themselves) is dependent on very limited awareness; they are mutually involved in a process that culminates in breakdown and murder. The loss of control is epitomized in the moment when Sandy Dennis drives a carving knife into the heaving bedclothes, not knowing whether she is stabbing the boy or the whore with whom she has provided him.

The Altman protagonist characteristically has, whatever his age, an adolescent quality, a combination of arrogance and vulnerability: McCabe, Marlowe in *The Long Goodbye*, Bowie in *Thieves Like Us*, Elliott Gould in *California Split*, Keith Carradine and the young assassin of *Nashville* are all obvious examples. The archetype is Brewster McCloud (Bud Cort), the boy who believes he will be able to fly. From the point of view of the audience, the character's assumption of control is undermined from the outset, the product of immaturity and ignorance. This partly accounts for the relative lack of dynamic tension in Altman's films, both in overall structure and in the detail of individual scenes—relative, that is, if one compares not only *Thieves Like Us* with *They Live by Night*, but *The Long Goodbye* with *Night Moves*, or, again, *California Split* with *Scarecrow*. *M.A.S.H.*, while it in some ways reverses the Altman pattern (the heroes survive and come out on top), displays this characteristic lack of dynamic tension to an extreme degree: its heroes' resilience is purchased at the price of a total and unquestioning acceptance (theirs and Altman's) of their own arrested adolescence, which the film seeks to justify by an equally unquestioning and glib acceptance of a sort of debased existential absurdism.

While the personal basis of Altman's choice of protagonist can scarcely be doubted (it is too consistent through the films and too consonant with their general attitudes), it may also be partly determined by the more general quandary of the antiestablishment director in the American commercial cinema: only certain types of protagonists are available to him. Figures such as Penn, Peckinpah, Schatzberg and Altman are in somewhat the same position as Godard up to *Pierrot le fou*: rejecting the established society in which they live but having no constructive social/political alternative to offer, their logical gravitation is to the outsider, the outcast, the criminal. By inhibiting the growth of a social dimension in their work, this in turn, places inevitable barriers in the way of development and makes it difficult to sustain the affirmative impulse so essential to a flourishing creativity. To this can be partly attributed the increasing desperation, perfunctoriness and self-parody of Peckinpah's work since *Junior Bonner*, the recourse to the ineffectual adolescent hero in Altman's, the long hiatuses in Penn's (though he alone of these directors, with much the strongest sense of social responsibility, has consistently tried to explore alternative concepts—the hippies of *Alice Restaurant*, the Cheyenne of *Little Big Man*). The path taken (for better or for worse) by Godard since *Pierrot le fou* is by definition closed to anyone who wishes to continue working in the commercial cinema, and would in any case be particularly difficult to follow in America. *The Longest Yard* (*The Mean Machine*) is probably the closest the American commercial movie can get to a genuine revolutionary cinema—which to say, scarcely closer than *Z*. Its subversiveness is qualified by characteristically Fascist overtones (the People turn out to be helpless without their Leader), but Aldrich has certain useful negative prerequisites for the development of a revolutionary mentality—a natural coarseness of sensibility combined with a total lack of interest in the cultural tradition.

It is doubtless this question of temperament that makes it possible for the revolutionary critical fraternity to continue to take an interest in emotional barbarians like Aldrich and Fuller while showing almost none at all in Penn, Schatzberg and Altman, all of whom are hampered, from this viewpoint, by a comparatively civilized sensibility. One aspect of this is their evident attraction to the European cinema, with its concept of film as a personal art, its enthronement of the director as artist, its encouragement of artistic consciousness (or self-consciousness) The debt of *Bonnie and Clyde* to the New Wave, for example, has become critical commonplace; that of *Puz-*

zle of a Downfall Child to Bergman, Resnais, and Fellini (not to mention Welles) is even more obvious—or would be if anyone had the chance to see Schatzberg's remarkable first film, which is so much better than an account of its derivations suggests. The richness of Altman's best films, as well as the meretriciousness of his worst, derives partly from his cultural schizophrenia: obsessed with America and with being American, he casts continual longing looks to Europe. At its worst, his hankering for European models expresses itself in cheap opportunistic borrowings that deprive the originals of all their complexity: the "Last Supper" pose in *M.A.S.H.*, the Makavejev effects (notably René Auberjonois' recurrently intercut bird lecture) in *Brewster McCloud*, the use of *Romeo and Juliet* to accompany and counterpoint the love-making in *Thieves Like Us* (surely traceable to the English lesson in *Bande à Part*). What is interesting here is not the effect Altman achieves but the relative resourcefulness of the gleanings—Buñuel, Makavejev, and Godard, instead of the usual Fellini (though he turns up too in the circus finale of *Brewster McCloud*).

But the European influence in Altman's work is more interesting, more pervasive, less direct, than this suggests. His worst films, interestingly, represent the polar extremes of his work: the purely American, TV-style *M.A.S.H.*, the imitation European art movie *Images*. His best films are hybrids, products of a fusion of "European" aspirations with American genres. *The Long Goodbye* has more in common with *Blow Up* than with *The Big Sleep*, but nevertheless draws sustenance from the genre Altman supposed himself to be satirizing. The sophisticated visual style of *McCabe and Mrs. Miller* repeatedly invites comparison with painting (the Degas-like scene of the whores' bath, for instance), and the use of Leonard Cohen's songs, more as counterpoint than accompaniment, has a complexity and sophistication beyond what one is accustomed to in western scores. But the film has its place in the mainstream of the development of the genre. It offers particularly suggestive points of comparison with *My Darling Clementine*, the opportunistic entrepreneur McCabe replacing the ideologically committed Earp, Mrs. Miller replacing Clementine as the "girl from the East," the whorehouse replacing the church as the center of the growing community, the melancholy shoot-out in the snow replacing the gunfight at the OK Corral.

The elaboration of an immediately recognizable, self-assertive personal style seems no more common in the American cinema today than it was in the heyday of the studio system: style, that is, has become much more assertive but no more personal. Both the technical means (e.g., the zoom lens) and the stylistic determinants (e.g., television and commercials) have changed, but the average film is no less anonymous than it used to be. It is beyond the scope of the present chapter to account satisfactorily for the complex of factors—ideological, economic, technological—determining the general stylistic features of the modern American cinema (the sort of work one hopes to see done in *Screen*). What most interests me (and it is a development to which, again, Altman's work is central) is the way in which the movement toward that particular variety of realism associated with deep focus photography has been reversed. Deep focus offered the spectator the illusion of natural perspective, the effect (always qualified in Welles by the disorientating rhetoric of Expressionist angles and ostentatious camera movement, but much cultivated by the arch-bourgeois Wyler) of a stable world of real spatial relationships. Today space is habitually flattened by the telephoto lens, and perspectives are no longer stable: focus pulling and the use of the zoom have become permissible, indeed, standard, overt devices.

The overtness is the point. Such devices as focus pulling were not alien to the Hollywood cinema of the past, provided they were cunningly concealed, effectively invisible. As Madame Constantin descends the stairs toward Ingrid Bergman in a long held subjective shot in *Notorious*, the background gradually goes out of focus as she approaches the camera, and a long shot becomes a close-up, but the audience, intent, like Ingrid Bergman, on attempting to read the woman's face, is quite unaware of this. Compare any of those moments to which we are now so habituated (Sandy Dennis's awareness of Michael Burns from her apartment window as she entertains guests to lunch at the beginning of *That Cold Day in the Park* is a good example) in which the audience's focus of attention is deliberately shifted by a shift of focus within a shot.

The implications of such changes cannot be formulated simply. They are clearly bound up with what Victor Perkins called "the death of *mise-en-scéne*," a remark dependent on a definition of *mise-en-scéne* that would stress the relative invisibility of the director and of technique, the strict subordination of style to the action. The changed status of the director is also relevant: a Kubrick, a Peckinpah, an Altman is encouraged to assert his presence in the film—or at least has to fight for his right to do so against less unfavorable odds than was the case for von Sternberg or Welles. Most fundamentally, however, and closely connected with this, the stylistic changes in the American cinema imply a tacit recognition that the "objective reality" of the technically invisible Hollywood cinema was always a pretense, a carefully fostered illusion—an admission that all artistic reality is subjective. For all the stylization of the action and the very particularized Hawksian world, it was still possible to watch *Rio Bravo* as if one were looking through a window at the world: nothing overtly intervenes between the spectator and the action. *The Long Goodbye* is "a film by Robert Altman"—we cannot escape the director's omnipresent consciousness. The implicit statement is no longer "This is the way things happen," but "This is how I see the world." Yet if all reality is subjective, all certitude is impossible.

Though he is less obviously in the forefront, Altman (within the context of the American commercial cinema) bears something of the same relationship to the zoom/telephoto lens as Welles to deep focus and Ray to CinemaScope: he didn't invent it, but his peculiar genius has enabled him to grasp and realize its expressive potentialities. The zoom is central to the change in the relationship of audience to film. Its significance lies in its obtrusiveness: directors who use the zoom "tactfully," trying to make a zoom-in indistinguishable from a tracking shot, are not really using it at all, but are trying to suppress its particular properties. For Altman, the zoom is at once his means of guiding the audience's consciousness and of asserting his own presence in the film; but he has also grasped its potential for dissolving space and undermining our sense of physical reality. Frequently associated with his use of it is the most immediately striking phenomenon of his style, the obsession with glass surfaces, windows, mirrors. This again is scarcely new in the American cinema: it is a feature of a certain "baroque" tradition (one thinks of von Sternberg, Welles, Sirk, Losey). Yet in Altman it is given a new dimension of stylistic assertion. One can sit through *Written on the Wind* or *Imitation of Life* "for the story," without necessarily becoming conscious of the mirror shots as such, because they are always integrated in the action, a part of *mise-en-scène* before it died; the same could scarcely be said of *That Cold Day in the Park* (where Altman repeatedly zooms in to glass cabinets and glass shelves that have no immediate bearing on what is happening) or *The Long Goodbye* (in one scene of which spatial reality is dissolved in a bewildering ambiguity of reflecting surfaces).[1] The difference is important: in the Sirk films, the audience is invited to contemplate a world (which is presented in clear images with analytical precision) in which characters are uncertain of their own reality; in *The Long Goodbye*, the uncertainty is assumed to be shared by the director and by the audience; it has become part of the method and texture of the film as well as its subject matter.

One can reinforce the point, and suggest its wider significance in terms of the development of the American cinema and American society, by comparing *The Long Goodbye* and *Night Moves* (and one might add, among other films, *The Conversation*) with their forerunners, the private eye movies of the 40s. Altman and Penn leave areas of unresolved doubt as to the various degrees of guilt and the precise motivation of certain of their characters: the tendency is more extreme in *Night Moves* than in *The Long Goodbye*, but after repeated viewings I am still uncertain as to the precise nature of Eileen Wade's involvement in the intrigue and the extent of her culpability. In *The Conversation* Coppola seems to play at one point on the assumption that the spectator will doubt the evidence of his own ears as much as the undermined protagonist—the shift in emphasis, in a crucial sentence on the tape, from "He'd *kill* us if he got the chance" to "*He'd* kill *us* if he got the chance." A central point of the films has become the misguidedness or inadequacy of the investigator (who nonetheless remains our primary identification figure): Hawks' Marlowe was not infallible, but Altman's is infallibly *wrong*. With this goes, in both Penn's film and Altman's, a carefully cultivated and preserved *moral* uncer-

1. Richard Lippe has drawn my attention to the very striking anticipation of this in the scene of James Mason's suicide in Cukor's 1954 version of *A Star Is Born*.

tainty: it is not simply that the protagonist's assumptions and decisions are called into question—the spectator too is prevented from forming secure judgments. Whatever we may deduce about Eileen Wade's motivation and guilt, there is no longer any coherent moral position established in the film from which she might be judged. If she and her husband remain the film's most moving characters, it is purely because they have the greatest capacity for suffering. We may occasionally, in the 40s have remained in some uncertainty as to the chain of events (*The Big Sleep*), but never as to what to think of the characters; one might contrast Bogart/Spade's definitive dismissal of Brigid O'Shaughnessy in *The Maltese Falcon* with the equivocal *Third Man* ending (Altman's analogy) of *The Long Goodbye*.

I suggested earlier that *The Long Goodbye* has more in common with Antonioni than with Hawks (the dope-taking, yoga-practicing nude girls who live across the way from Marlowe would be quite at home in *Blow Up*), and I have been struck by a similarity in the way Altman and Antonioni talk about their films. The theme they stress is the problem of adapting to the changed conditions of modern life, and they speak as if their protagonists were to be criticized for their failure to adjust ("Rip van Marlowe"). Yet the films never satisfactorily answer the unspoken question of what adjustment would entail: the world of ephemerality and promiscuity of *L'Avventura*, the dehumanized technological world of *Red Desert*, and the moral and emotional quicksands of *The Long Goodbye* offer little of a positive nature that could make adjustment seem desirable from any viewpoint but that of mere survival. The effect in *The Long Goodbye* is curious: one has the feeling that Altman despises "Rip van Marlowe" yet is very close to him—closer, perhaps, than he would wish to acknowledge. *Red Desert* gives the impression that Antonioni wanted to make a film that would place Giuliana's inadequacies in a context, show her failure in relation to positive social possibilities, but that he was in fact so close to Giuliana that he was able to show the context only from the viewpoint of her inadequacies, colored (literally, at moments) by her neurosis. So with Altman and Marlowe. Marlowe, a child in a world of corrupt and dangerous adults, is incapable of making sense of anything and his every decision is wrong. Yet Altman can give the audience nothing else to latch on to except the experience of pain (the Wades): Marlowe, ultimately, is where he's at. In both Antonioni and Altman, the gestures toward a progressive viewpoint thinly conceal despair and a sense of helplessness.

✳ ✳ ✳

I have so far concentrated on Altman's centrality to the development of the American cinema, though in doing so I have demonstrated inadvertently how description inevitably shades into evaluation. It remains to try to define more precisely the

Marriage in 1970s *Film Noir*

(left)
Nina van Pallandt and
Sterling Hayden in
The Long Goodbye

(below)
Gene Hackman and Susan Clark
in *Night Moves*

nature and quality of the sensibility expressed in Altman's films. During the sequence in *The Long Goodbye* in which Marlowe is interrogated at the police station, there is a running discussion as to whether he is a "smart-ass" or a "cutie-pie." The distinction between the two is less than clear-cut: presumably the "smart-ass" antagonizes while the "cutie-pie" seeks to disarm, but both use slickness or cleverness as a defense and an evasion. They express at once an assertion that one is in control and an inadvertent admission (because of their transparent inadequacy) that one is not. They are Marlowe's means of evading not only the questions of the police but the need to try to understand things, to make sense of life. Smart-ass and Cutie-pie are both prominent in the artistic personality projected in Altman's films. *M.A.S.H.* is dominated by them exclusively. If Aldrich and Fuller are emotional barbarians, *M.A.S.H.* makes one realize how preferable barbarism is to smart-ass sophistication, the barbarian being open to at least some of the tensions and complexities that the smart-ass of *M.A.S.H.* ruthlessly represses: neither Aldrich nor Fuller would ever descend to the way Altman treats the Robert Duvall and Sally Kellerman characters in that film. Apparently at the other extreme, *Images* in its trendy esoteric way is almost as dominated by this side of Altman: what could be more cutie-pie than the way all the actors exchange names (René Auberjonois as Hugh, Hugh Millais as Marcel, Marcel Bozzuffi as René, Susannah York as Cathryn, Cathryn Harrison as Susannah)? And the "surprise" ending (Cathryn thinks she has knocked her alter ego over the waterfall, but it turns out to be her husband) is just a cheap gimmick quite ungrounded in any realized psychological significance. It is striking that the film that seems most directly personal in its material (schizophrenia, and the dissolution of the sense of objective reality) should be the one (after *M.A.S.H.*) most dominated by Altman's smart-ass defense mechanisms. *Brewster McCloud* provides ample evidence of the pervasiveness of Smart-ass and Cutie-pie, and of Altman's readiness to surrender to them. The film has a kind of reckless inventiveness that is both endearing and maddening—really an inability to define a level of seriousness or engagement, so that one's final impression, for all the film's thematic richness and the intelligence intermittently at work, is of a glorified TV revue.

Smart-ass and Cutie-pie also intervene disconcertingly at moments in Altman's better films. They are a constant threat in *The Long Goodbye* (in the use, for example, of the all-pervading theme song that even turns up as the chimes on Eileen Wade's doorbell), but are just sufficiently "placed" by the pain and sense of confusion the film so impressively communicates. The most startling single eruption is in the lovemaking sequence of *Thieves Like Us*. Altman's conception of the scene courts disaster: as Victor Perkins points out, the decor (song sheets plastered all over the walls) is in its obtrusiveness and insistence more distracting than expressive; the use of *Romeo and Juliet* on the radio is perilously obvious. Yet Altman almost makes it work, partly because his actors are so good, partly because the heavily ironic use of the play is made somewhat more complex by its radio vulgarization (complete with Tchaikovsky), so that it both evokes the original's concept of absolute romantic love and is convincingly a part of the lovers' debased environment. But Altman can't leave well alone: he seems terrified that someone might still suspect him of being "romantic." So, not once but three times, every time the lovers copulate, he has the radio announcer proclaim "Thus did Romeo and Juliet consummate their first interview by falling madly in love with each other."

What is revealing about this is that the Bowie-Keechie relationship in *Thieves Like Us* is the only instance in Altman's work so far of a successful sexual union (successful, that is, in terms of a developing mutual commitment). Everywhere else, sex is presented as either trivial or destructive or, occasionally, disgusting (the offensive use of lesbians in a scene in *That Cold Day in the Park* to elicit a stock response that rebounds, very simply, on Altman). The sexual relationships in Altman's films that are movingly treated are either frustrated (McCabe and Mrs. Miller, Allen Garfield's attachment to Ronee Blakley in *Nashville*) or embittered and mutually destructive (the Wades in *The Long Goodbye*). Significantly Brewster McCloud is destroyed by sex, which undermines his ability to fly. And Marlowe, of course, has only his cat (and loses that): his general impotence, though not made explicitly sexual, is repeatedly given sexual connotations through his helplessness in situations involving women (Joanne, Eileen Wade) and in contrast with the brutally sexual Terry Lennox.

The antirealist tendencies in Altman seem inextricably bound up with the Smart-ass elements. If one ignores matters of tone, devices like the interchange of names in *Images* or the use of the radio announcer in *Thieves Like Us* can be theoretically justified on antirealist lines, the former blurring the distinction between characters and actors, the latter disrupting our involvement in the fictional reality. Yet one has only to evoke Godard to recognize how spurious such justifications are. Consider, as a simple example, certain of the non-diegetic elements in *Le Mépris*— the shots of Brigitte Bardot in nude *Playboy*-style poses inserted into the long central dialogue in the apartment. The film's fictional narrative is centered on the theme of prostitution (in the wide, Godardian sense): the inserted nude shots fulfill the truly Brechtian function of extending the audience's awareness outside the diegesis, but without loss of thematic relevance, to take in Bardot's public image, the "sexist" image of Woman, the producers' demand that Bardot appear naked in the film, the spectator's own demand to see her naked, the ambiguity of Godard's position as "commercial" filmmaker. Altman's antirealist devices, on the other hand, seem merely his defense against a too intense involvement in the fiction, the Smart-ass shrugging off of the responsibilities of engagement. They are part of a psychological-aesthetic complex of which the distrust of sexual involvement, the fascination with drugs (a motif in most of the films) and gambling (*California Split*), and the fondness for turning filmmaking into self-indulgent play with friends, at once disarming and evasive, are all aspects.

Only *M.A.S.H.*, however, is completely dominated by Smart-ass and Cutie-pie, just as only in one film are they successfully dominated. Altman's positive qualities are dependent on the precariousness of the defense-mechanisms. All his finest work is centered on the revelation of vulnerability and the experience of pain. His films are successful in direct ratio to the degree to which the Smart-ass element is assimilated and placed within the narrative structure, dramatized in the leading character (McCabe, Marlowe) and revealed as the inadequate defense of a very vulnerable man. Only in *McCabe and Mrs. Miller* (which is fed also by the richest of all American genres) are the conditions completely met. *The Long Goodbye* contains perhaps the finest scenes in Altman to date (those involving the Wades and, outstandingly, the scene of Roger Wade's suicide, a *locus classicus* of resurrected zoom lens *mise-en-scène*), but in the last resort the film suffers from the fact that Gould's Marlowe is simply too silly, too juvenile, to give the film the dynamic moral/emotional tension that makes *McCabe and Mrs. Miller* so far unique in Altman's work: Marlowe's smugness, unlike McCabe's, is incorrigible. I have hinted that Marlowe is one of the characters to whom Altman seems closest—which may explain why he finds it necessary to express such contempt for his stupidity (the same thing happens, more extremely and disastrously, with the Geraldine Chaplin character of *Nashville*). Comparison with *Night Moves* is illuminating: the decisions and deductions of Penn's hero are just as misguided as Marlowe's, yet they are the mistakes of a confused adult rather than an arrested adolescent. Penn doesn't feel it necessary always to be insisting on his own superiority to his protagonist.

Everything in Altman so far—the good and the bad—comes together in *Nashville*. Its great scenes—Gwen Welles' enforced striptease, Ronee Blakley's onstage breakdown, everything involving Lily Tomlin—are all centered on the characters' exposed vulnerability and realized with painful intensity. At the other extreme are the embarrassingly Cutie-pie uncredited guest appearances of Elliott Gould and Julie Christie as Themselves. But *Nashville*'s central failure lies in the Geraldine Chaplin figure ("In a way, she's me in the film," Altman remarked in a rather startling moment during an interview on the set of the film, in *Positif 166*). The character is central to the film's structure: as Altman says, she "serves as liaison between the characters." More important, as outsider-interviewer she is the only character in the film with the distance that might make possible an understanding of the moral and emotional confusion in which everyone else is trapped, and who might, as potential identification figure, provide the possibility of such distancing for the audience. Altman's reaction (and I'm afraid it is a profoundly characteristic one) is to make her as idiotic as he can. The film's total effect—for all the marvelous local successes—is to engulf the spectator in its movement of disintegration, making intellectual distance impossible. The ironic force of the ending, with the crowd confronting catastrophe by singing "It don't worry me," a communal refusal to think, is weakened not simply by the inability to offer any constructive alternative but by a perverse rejection of the possibility. A movie that left Pauline Kael feeling "elated" ("I've never before seen a movie I loved in quite this way") left me feeling somewhat sick and depressed, for all my admiration for its scope and audacity.

⁂

The old Hollywood, with its very strong traditional framework of conventions, rules, and expectations, provided many of the necessary conditions wherein minor artists like Tourneur and Borzage could intermittently produce outstanding work. The predicament of Altman (whose best films are scarcely superior to *I Walked with a Zombie* or *Out of the Past*—though to me that is sufficiently high praise) strikes me as that of the minor artist forced by circumstances into a position where he must be a major artist, a self-sufficient genius, the "star" director: after *Nashville*, everyone is going to be looking for the next masterpiece. Those who can resist the very strong pulls of fashionability will watch his development with great interest and great anxiety.

POSTSCRIPT

This essay was written in 1975, during a transitional period in my work. There are things in it I would not say now, or would say differently: I am not happy with the description of Aldrich and Fuller as "emotional barbarians" (at least without careful qualification), and I regret the disparaging reference to the "revolutionary critical fraternity," to which I now aspire to belong. But I said them, and would not care now to pretend I didn't (I am opposed on principle to the rewriting of work one has in some respects passed beyond in order to conceal formerly held views). The essay is included here because it is central to the development of this book's thematic concerns, and because I see no reason whatever to retract or substantially modify its argument: the account of Altman I offered ten years ago has received nothing but repeated confirmation from his subsequent work.

Hence, I see no point in discussing that work in detail: the diagnosis stands, and the prognosis is scarcely more favorable now than it was in 1975. The *M.A.S.H./Images* opposition is reproduced in the relationship of *A Wedding* (1978) to *Three Women* (1977). The former is, in its smug superiority to and contempt for its characters and in its unquestioning assumption of the audience's complicity, one of Altman's most unwatchable and embarrassing films. *Three Women* expresses a similar contempt, adding to it "European" pretensions of Significance, the model this time being *Persona*. The thesis that women conditioned by our culture, however seemingly independent, might not be able to escape entrapment in familial roles and structures is not unpromising (though perhaps hazardous for a *man* to propose). Unfortunately, Altman is totally unequipped to analyze cultural conditioning; the women emerge as victims, yes, but primarily of their own innate stupidity. *Quintet*, with its mean distinction, has its importance for an auteurist reading of Altman, as it presents his view of human existence in its most naked and schematic form: life as one-upmanship.

Only one of the later films transcends the oppressive limitations of Altman's insistently reiterated "view"—*Come Back to the Five-and-Dime, Jimmy Dean, Jimmy Dean*. The success of the film (arguably, after *McCabe and Mrs. Miller*, Altman's finest) depends upon a complex of factors inherent in the material. On the one hand its affinity with Altman's recurrent preoccupations is sufficient to ensure his wholehearted involvement in the project: the play is about women and, specifically, their suffering and humiliation (significantly, the only redeeming scene in *A Wedding*, the one crack in the Smart-ass armature, was centered on Nina van Pallandt and the agony of drug addiction); much of its action takes the form of games of one-upmanship. But here, the "three women," unlike their predecessors, are placed firmly within a defined and realized social context, their various humiliations seen in relation to the pressures of patriarchal (or heterosexual male) domination and oppression. Further, through the successive revelations of terrible secrets and exposures of the women's pretenses and pretensions, they are permitted to reach both self-awareness and mutual supportiveness and acceptance, however qualified.

Obviously, Altman's identification with a female (never feminist) position is extremely problematic: it is limited almost exclusively to the notion of woman-as-victim, to sensations of pain, humiliation and breakdown. If one reads it as the expression of Altman's own "femininity," then it is centered upon masochism and self-punishment; if one reads it as an effort to understand how actual women within patriarchal culture *feel*, then the masochism begins to look suspiciously like its counterpart, sadism. What is especially interesting about *Come Back to the Five-and-Dime* is the connection it makes between the oppression of women and patriarchy's dread of sexual deviation and gender ambiguity. Joe (the only male character to appear in the film, in flashback) is clearly (and sympathetically) presented as feminine (as opposed to the stereotypically effeminate), woman-identified, and gay; as Don Short has perceptively shown,[2] the film implies that he has become a transsexual (superbly played by Karen Black—but all the performances are extraordinary) because his society had no place for a gay male. Joanne, having seen more of the world, regrets her sex change; from there, the film goes on to establish her sense of solidarity with the other women, only Mona (Sandy Dennis), as the one least able to relinquish her compensatory fantasies, expressing an insurmountable resistance.

2. In an article that remains unpublished at time of writing.

Paul Newman in *Quintet*

Warren Beatty in *McCabe and Mrs. Miller*

The ending (the final credits, as the camera moves over the now empty and derelict store) remains unresolvably ambiguous: it can be read either as a symbolic gesture of despair ("This is all it amounted to, anyway") or as a statement that, having learned to understand themselves, their oppression, and each other, the women have been able to leave their prison and move on. People I have consulted tend categorically to affirm one or the other reading as "correct," those favoring the former alternative being, in general, those more familiar with Altman's work. But I don't think anything within the film compels one to accept the auteur-consistent reading; indeed, the second alternative follows more logically from the progress of the action.

Altman's other recent piece of filmed theater, *Streamers* (intended, presumably, as an all-male counterpart to *Come Back to the Five-and-Dime*) is far more confused and problematic. It is also far more hysterical, and it is debatable whether the hysteria resides in the material or in Altman's response to it. In any case, the parallels between the oppression of blacks and the oppression of gays are much less resonant than those between the oppression of gays and the oppression of women. However, it is clear that the new-found interest in sex- and gender-ambiguity is (as in, on a higher level of achievement, the recent work of Ingmar Bergman—see *From the Life of the Marionettes* and the Ishmael sequence of *Fanny and Alexander*) the most promising sign in Altman's work of profitable new development.

4.

The Incoherent Text
NARRATIVE IN THE 70s

COHERENCE / INCOHERENCE

All traditional art (and for that matter most avant-garde art) has as its goal the ordering of experience, the striving for coherence; yet all art reveals, if one pursues the matter relentlessly enough, areas or levels of incoherence. Let us consider the coherence first. The drive to understand and, by understanding, to dominate experience must always represent one of the deepest human needs. (This does not necessarily involve dominating other people but rather managing to control one's *experience* of them—though one of the recurrent drives in Western art has been domination through objectification and the denial of otherness, a tendency greatly encouraged by bourgeois capitalism with its emphasis on possession.) The artist's perception of experience may be that it is incoherent, chaotic, absurd, meaningless; he may, alternatively, be battling against what he perceives as false experience (enslavement by the illusory order of the dominant ideology) and may deliberately produce texts that are fractured and fragmentary. In such cases the fragmentation—the consciously motivated incoherence—becomes a structuring principle, resulting in works that reveal themselves as perfectly coherent once one has mastered their rules. The dividing line between coherent works that register incoherence and works that are incoherent within themselves may not always be clear; furthermore, they may well be produced by the same set of cultural conditions.

I want to make it clear from the outset that in referring to "incoherent texts" I am not proposing to discuss (again) *Weekend* and *Wind from the East*, films which become as coherent as any when one grasps their mode of functioning. Rather, I am concerned with films that don't wish to be, or to appear, incoherent but are so nonetheless, works in which the drive toward the ordering of experience has been visibly defeated. I am not, therefore, going to argue that *Taxi Driver, Looking for Mr. Goodbar*, and *Cruising* are great works, merely that they are very interesting ones, and that their interest lies partly in their incoherence. The "partly" is important: there are countless movies floating around which are incoherent because totally inept. The three films I have chosen all seem to me to achieve a certain level of distinction, to have a discernible intelligence (or intelligences) at work in them and to exhibit a high degree of involvement on the part of their makers. They are neither successful nor negligible. It is also of their nature that if they were *more* successful (at least in realizing what are generally perceived to be their conscious projects), they would be proportionately less interesting. Ultimately, they are works that do not know what they want to say.

The reason why any work of art will reveal—somewhere—areas or levels of incoherence is that so many things feed into it which are beyond the artist's conscious control—not only his personal unconscious (the possible presence of which even the most traditional criticism has been ready to acknowledge), but the cultural assumptions of his society. Those cultural assumptions themselves have a long history (from the immediate social-political realities back through the entire history of humanity) and will themselves contain, with difficulty, accumulated strains, tensions, and contradictions. Relevant here is Freud's scarcely disputable contention that civilization is built on repression, which accounts for the fundamental dualism of all art: the urge to reaffirm and justify that repression, and the urge of rebellion, the desire to subvert, combat, overthrow. Further, Marcuse, following Freud, has suggested that repression itself operates on two levels: basic repression (universal, necessary to *any* form of civilization) and surplus repression (specific to each culture, varying enormously in degree from one culture to another), the two levels being continuous and interactive rather than discrete. The revolt against repression may then be valid or invalid, a legitimate protest against specific oppressions or a useless protest against the conditions necessary for society to exist at all, the two not being easily or cleanly distinguishable.

One can say that in periods, usually those designated Classical, when the artist is at one with at least the finest values of his culture—able, like Alexander Pope and Jane Austen, to criticize society for falling short of a set of commonly understood and approved moral codes—the degree of incoherence is likely to be lowest; though one might alternatively argue that in such periods it is simply most deeply buried. There is also the phenomenon of Mozart's music (created at the precise point of poise or transition between the Classical and the Romantic), which remains for me emblematic of what the ideal Marcusean civilization might be like: art in which work becomes play, in which everything is eroticized, in which freedom and order are proved, after all, perfectly compatible.

CLASSICAL HOLLYWOOD

It would be foolish to imply any strict correlation between Classicism and repression, Romanticism and liberation; nature, after all, has its own order, without which it couldn't exist, and, at the other extreme, Fascism (the most artificial and repressive imposition of order) is the logical extension of a certain kind of Romanticism. The available theoretical polarities, however, can help give some definition to the way in which the "Classical" Hollywood cinema deserves its title—a Classicism as far as possible removed from anything one might call Mozartian. The American cinema has always celebrated energy, a tendency one normally associates with the Romantic; the energy, however, can only be celebrated when it has undergone a very thorough process of repression, revision, sublimation, displacement. The Classicism of Hollywood was always to a great degree artificially imposed and repressive, the forcing of often extremely recalcitrant drives into the mold of a dominant ideology typified at its simplest and crudest, but most clarified and regulated, by the Hays Office Code. The need for the code (negatively denouncing sexuality in all but its most patriarchally orthodox, procreative form—and displays of it even then—positively upholding marriage, the family, and the status quo) testifies eloquently, of course, to the strength and persistence of the forces it was designed to check: its requirements, passively accepted by studios and audiences, corresponded neither to the films people wanted to make nor to the films people wanted to see. Insofar as Classicism stands for control and Romanticism for release, the Hollywood cinema expresses in virtually all its products, but with widely varying emphases, the most extraordinary tension between the Classical and the Romantic that can be imagined. No wonder that the analysis of Classical Hollywood movies in recent years has laid the primary stress on "contradictions," "gaps," "strains," "dislocations."

Readers scarcely need to have recapitulated for them the story of what happened to Hollywood in the 50s and 60s—the process that was well under way when *Movie* first appeared to celebrate a cinema that was already disappearing: television came, the Hays code went, and the studio/star/genre system partly disintegrated. The containing framework of Hollywood Classicism largely ceased to exist. The films made by John Ford after *The Man Who Shot Liberty Valance*, by Howard Hawks after *Hatari!*, and by Alfred Hitchcock after *Marnie* all have interest (a few, like *Seven Women* and *Red Line 7000*, a very special interest), but they have in common a loss of authority and confidence, an uncertainty as to the tone they wish to adopt. By the mid 60s, the circumstances that had made possible (in *Liberty Valance*, in

Rio Bravo, in *Psycho*) the transmutation of ideological conflict, such as necessarily exists in any Hollywood movie, into a significantly realized thematic no longer existed.

THE 70s

Although Classical Hollywood had already been dealt a series of death-blows, it might have taken a much longer time dying had it not been for the major eruptions in American culture from the mid-60s and into the 70s: overwhelmingly, of course, Vietnam, but subsequently Watergate, and part counterpoint, part consequence, the growing force and cogency of radical protest and liberation movements—black militancy, feminism, gay liberation.

There are two keys to understanding the development of the Hollywood cinema in the 70s: the impingement of Vietnam on the national consciousness and the unconscious, and the astonishing evolution of the horror film. One must avoid any simple suggestion of cause-and-effect—the modern American horror film evolves out of *Psycho*; feminism and gay liberation were not products of the war; the history of black militancy extends back for generations. What one can attribute to Vietnam is the sudden confidence and assertiveness of these movements, as if they could suddenly believe, not merely in the rightness of their causes, but in the possibility of their realization. The obvious monstrousness of the war definitively undermined the credibility of "the system"—the system that had hitherto retained sufficiently daunting authority and impressiveness to withstand the theoretical onslaughts of Marx and Freud, the province only of dubious intellectuals. Protest became popular, the essential precondition to valid revolution.

Psychically, the consequences of this reached out far beyond outrage at an unjust war. The questioning of authority spread logically to a questioning of the entire social structure that validated it, and ultimately to patriarchy itself: social institutions, the family, the symbolic figure of the Father in all its manifestations, the Father interiorized as superego. The possibility suddenly opened up that the whole world might have to be recreated.

Yet this generalized crisis in ideological confidence never issued in revolution. No coherent social/economic program emerged, the taboo on socialism remaining virtually unshaken. Society appeared to be in a state of advanced disintegration, yet there was no serious possibility of the emergence of a coherent and comprehensive alternative. This quandary—habitually rendered, of course, in terms of personal drama and individual interaction, and not necessarily consciously registered—can be felt to underlie most of the important American films of the late 60s and 70s. It is central to the three I am discussing here, largely accounting for their richness, their confusion, and their ultimate nihilism. Here, incoherence is no longer hidden and esoteric: the films seem to crack open before our eyes. Among the most obvious manifestations of this are the notoriously problematic endings of both *Taxi Driver* and *Cruising*. In the former, there seems to be little agreement as to the attitude and tone of the final sequence—as to what the film is trying to say, conclusively, about its protagonist; in the latter, the uncertainty rises up to the surface of the narrative—the film's relative commercial failure seems partly attributable to audiences' exasperated bewilderment over who has done what.

I discuss the significance of the horror film in the 70s at length in the next chapter. Here I simply signal the fact of the infiltration of its major themes and motifs into every area of 70s cinema. All three films discussed here could be regarded, without undue distortion, as horror movies, taking up the genre's major preoccupations: the monster-as-human-psychopath, who is a product of "normality" (*Taxi Driver*); the notion of descent-into-hell (*Looking for Mr. Goodbar*); the doppelgänger, about which *Cruising* is obsessive to the point of delirium.

TAXI DRIVER

Central to the incoherence of *Taxi Driver* is a relatively clear-cut conflict of auteurs, though one should not be blinded by this to the ideological conflicts that underlie, and are to some extent dramatized in, the Scorsese/Schrader collision.

Martin Scorsese, with his Catholic Italian immigrant background, his fascination with the Hollywood tradition, and his comparatively open responsiveness to contemporary issues, seems to me a difficult figure to characterize simply; his future development is not easy to prophesy. His films operate within a liberal humanist tradition whose boundaries and limitations remain only hazily defined. *Alice Doesn't Live Here Anymore* seems to me in crucial respects a more challenging movie, as well as being altogether richer and more complexly pleasurable, than *An Unmarried Woman* (whose structure it anticipated in some detail). *New York, New York* is, as Godard recently observed, "un vrai film" about contemporary "rapports" that has been much harmed by being perceived as "un film rétro."

The position implicit in Paul Schrader's work, on the other hand, can be quite simply characterized as quasi-Fascist. This may not be immediately obvious when one considers each film individually, but adding them together (including the screenplays directed by others) makes it clear. There is the put-down of unionization (*Blue Collar*), the put-down of feminism "in the Name of the Father" (*Old Boyfriends*), the denunciation of alternatives to the Family by defining them in terms of degeneracy and pornography (*Hard Core*), the implicit denigration of gays (*American Gigolo*, to which I shall return later) and, crucial in its sinister relation to all this, the glorification of the dehumanized hero as efficient killing-machine (unambiguous in *Rolling Thunder*, confused—I believe by Scorsese's presence as director—in *Taxi Driver*). It is true that this fundamental position is clouded within individual films by the spurious interest in Existentialism and Bressonian spiritual transcendence, and more would need to be said about, particularly, *Blue Collar* (the least unpleasant of his movies); but I think this defines the essential viciousness of Schrader's work.

Although some clash of artistic personalities and ideologies lies at the heart of *Taxi Driver*, I do not see any possibility, even were it desirable, of sorting through the film to assign individual praise and blame. Instead, I offer a series of annotations designed to indicate the major concerns of the film and its unresolved contradictions.

1. The Excremental City   *Taxi Driver* represents the culmination of the obsession with dirt/cleanliness that recurs throughout the history of the American cinema—together, of course, with its metaphorical derivatives, corruption/purity, animalism/spirituality, sexuality/repression. In the vision of Travis Bickle (Robert De Niro), which is neither identical with nor clearly distinguishable from the vision of the film, the filth kept at bay through so many generations of movies by the traditional values of monogamy/family/home has risen up and flooded the entire city. Travis becomes obsessed with the mission of washing the scum from the streets—the scum being both literal and human flotsam. The outcome of this obsession is the massacre in the brothel and the rescue of Iris (Jodie Foster) in order to restore her to her parents and a small-town education, the act that establishes Travis as a hero in the eyes of society and the popular press.

2. The Angel   Luther saw heaven while sitting on the lavatory. Travis' vision is of Betsy (Cybill Shepherd) as an "angel" floating above the excrement of the city. The film progressively exposes (for Travis—it is always obvious enough to the viewer and might be argued to be implicit in the casting) the illusoriness of this: she is an ideological construct, a figure of almost total vacuity whose only discernible character trait is opportunism. The imagery of the last scene enacts all this beautifully, reducing her to a disembodied head floating in Travis' rearview mirror.

3. The Commune in Vermont   The city is filth, the angel an illusion; what is left? During Travis' conversation with Iris, he asks her if there is anywhere she wants to go to escape the squalor of her current existence as a thirteen-year-old prostitute. She replies tentatively that she has heard about "a commune in Vermont." This, mentioned in passing, given no concrete realization, parallel or further reference anywhere in the film, is the nearest it ever comes to proposing a constructive alternative, a life that might resolve the dirt/repression quandary. Travis dismisses it immediately: he once saw a picture of a commune in a magazine and it "didn't look clean."

4. The "Scar" Scene   The relationship of *Taxi Driver* (and *Hard Core*) to *The Searchers* has been widely recognized. Scorsese and Schrader were fully aware of it and refer to the brief scene between Iris and her pimp/lover Sport (Harvey Keitel) as the "Scar" scene—the equivalent of a "missing" (and arguably essential) scene in *The Searchers* defining Debbie's relationship to Scar and Comanche life. It is a scene Ford could not conceivably have filmed, and Scorsese and Schrader are quite right in implying (I presume) that its absence definitively highlights the cheating, evasion, and confusion that characterize the last third of his film (itself an archetypal incoherent text). It is certainly to their credit that the "Scar" scene exists in *Taxi Driver* (significantly, it is the only substantial sequence that takes place beyond Travis' consciousness); it is less certain that it represents any sort of valid equivalent (to equate life with the Comanches to life in a brothel may strike one as dubious on several counts) or that its existence helps clarify what the film is saying. It provides the movie with its solitary moment of tenderness, suggesting that Sport loves Iris as well as exploiting her, hence by implication opening up the question of what exactly "love" might be, beyond the societal norms of Travis' romantic idealization of Betsy and Iris' parents' concern for her. Already in *The Searchers*, the ideological weight of the notion of "home" was pretty thoroughly undermined, but it retained sufficient force for the "happy ending" of Debbie's return (supported by the film's suppressions and distortions) to come across as slightly more than a mockery. In *Taxi Driver*, "home" is reduced to a photograph on a wall and a letter read aloud on the sound track. The function of the "Scar" scene seems to be, in opposition to this, to call into question any easy assumption we might have that *anything* would be preferable (for a thirteen-year-old girl) to prostitution: with Sport, Iris shares an equivocal tenderness, whereas there is no indication that "home" offers her anything at all.

5. The Hero   As with *The Searchers*, the central incoherence of *Taxi Driver* lies in the failure to establish a consistent, and adequately rigorous, attitude to the protagonist. We can see the film in relation to both the western and the horror film. With the former, Travis is the gunfighter-hero whose traditional function has always been to clean up the town; with the latter, he is the psychopath-monster produced by an indefensible society. The latter option appears fairly unambiguously dominant through most of the film, but the former is never totally eclipsed. The film cannot believe in the traditional figure of the charismatic individualist hero, but it also cannot relinquish it, because it has nothing to put in its place. Travis' behavior is presented as increasingly pathological (culminating in his acquisition of a Mohawk Indian haircut), with his ambitions increasingly monstrous (the assassination of a politician no worse than most) and his achievements useless, unless one has an automatic commitment to the family (the city will go on as before, excremental as ever). Yet the film can neither clearly reject him (he remains, somehow, The Hero, like Ethan Edwards) nor structure a complex but coherent attitude to him (such as Cimino partially achieves in *The Deerhunter*).

6. *Chingachgook Meets Geronimo*   A tantalizing addendum to this is provided by the fascinating confrontation between Travis (his head shaved like a Mohawk) and Sport (with the long hair and head-band of an Apache). No moment in the American cinema dramatizes more succinctly the famous fundamental ambivalence in the American attitude to the Virgin Land (Garden of Eden/Savage Wilderness) and the Indian (Noble Savage/Ignoble Heathen Devil). Further, the Mohawk is traditionally associated with the cleanness of forests and lakes, the Apache with the dirt of the prairie. Yet what the scene ultimately testifies to is the Hollywood cinema's (America's) continuing inability to resolve its dichotomies. The Mohawk/Apache, Garden/Wilderness opposition becomes (within the context of the Excremental City) a sterile dialectic that appears at once archaic and unresolvable, the image of the Noble Savage reduced to the rhetorical gesture of a psychopath, the revolutionary rage of the Ignoble Savage to the attempted self-vindication of a pimp.

7. *The Ending*   No one is likely to suggest that the ending of the film (the scenes following the point where most people, at first viewing, expect it to end—the massacre and Travis' finger-to-forehead gesture of mock suicide) can be read quite unironically, yet the irony seems curiously unfocused, its aim uncertain (the ending of *Fort Apache* offers a very close parallel). The effect is of a kind of paralysis. Being unable to achieve any clear, definitive statement about the hero, either as individual character or, beyond that, as the dominant mythic figure of patriarchal culture, the film retreats into enigma. Travis becomes a public hero (ironic), feels satisfaction at what he has done for Iris and her parents (arguably ironic), and reaches some personal serenity and satisfaction with himself (doubtfully ironic); he is now able to see through and reject his angel, and, mission accomplished, retreats into the streets rather as Ethan Edwards retreats into the wilderness. *Rather* like but not *quite* like, as Ethan is going nowhere and Travis is back in the heart of the Excremental City. The individual spectator can think (according to personal predilection) either that the hero will continue to cleanse the city of its filth, or that the psychopath-monster will explode again in another useless bloodbath. There is a third alternative, which comes closest to rendering the action and images intelligible—the notion that Travis, while achieving nothing for an obviously beyond-help society, has achieved through his actions some kind of personal grace or existential self-definition, and that this is really all that matters, since civilization is demonstrably unredeemable. This is very Schrader (*American Gigolo* moves to an identical conclusion) and not at all Scorsese. I find it morally indefensible, pernicious, and irresponsible: it implies that one's existential self-definition can validly be bought at the cost of no matter what other human beings. It also represents a debased and simplistic (again,

quasi-Fascist) version of Existentialism, restricting it to a matter of the Chosen Superior Individual and depriving it of all social force. It could only work in the film (as it does, if "work" just means "make sense," in the spiritually and emotionally poverty-stricken *American Gigolo*) if the audience were identified with a single ego and all the other characters reduced to puppet-like subordination. It seems to me that at the end of *Taxi Driver* we are (thanks to Scorsese and Jodie Foster) more concerned about Iris than about Travis, who has long since moved outside the bounds of any reasonable human sympathy or identification.

LOOKING FOR MR. GOODBAR

Looking for Mr. Goodbar has been widely perceived as an ultra right-wing, reactionary movie. Liberals were quick to heap abuse on it; some feminists saw it as an assault on women's liberation and as tending to encourage violence against women; gay activists saw it as strengthening the popular myth that associates homosexuality with neurosis. A Canadian minister wrote a eulogy of the film as a Lesson to Us All, claiming it to be an account of its heroine's descent into Hell (her face disappearing into blackness at the end) as rightful punishment for promiscuity and a neglect of the Good Old Values. I am not going to argue that these responses are totally misguided or that they answer to nothing in the film; in terms of immediate general impression, they are probably partly correct. But they are certainly very partial, leaving out of account many elements and implications that would qualify and contradict them.

1. The theme of descent—or progressive dissolution—is certainly strong in the movie, signaled especially by the care Richard Brooks has taken, from sequence to sequence, to trace the deterioration of Teresa's apartment. Yet it is highly questionable whether the tone is moralistic, at least so far as Teresa (Diane Keaton) is concerned, and whether the notion of self-righteous satisfaction at watching a woman receive just punishment for sexual freedom, drug-taking, and rebellion against traditional values sufficiently (or even at all) accounts for our experience of the movie. For one thing, the punishment (even if we are thorough-going puritans) isn't just: like Marion Crane in *Psycho*, Teresa has firmly decided to reform her life just before she is killed; she picks up her murderer, not because she wants sex, but as a means of deflecting the attentions of an unwanted but persistent suitor. More important, however, are matters of casting and identification. Keaton (with Brooks' obvious encouragement—there are no signs of a clash of intentions between director and star) brings an infectious zest and vitality to the role; though her sexual experiences are not presented as deeply satisfying, they retain a sense of enjoyment, resilience, and sheer fun. I find no suggestion in the scenes in singles bars, for example, that we are supposed to be shocked.

The question of identification is obviously very complicated, with the constant possibility of the intrusion of personal bias (my own experiences have at certain periods of my life been very close to Teresa's—short, so far, of getting murdered—and I have always felt grateful to the film for reflecting them in what strikes me as a very *un*puritanical way). Much valuable work has been done by feminists, such as John Berger and Laura Mulvey, on the objectification of women in Western culture and the resulting position (ownership, domination) of the (by implication) male spectator. But some of this work (e.g., Mulvey on Sternberg) can lead to dangerous over-simplification, by failing to take into account either the complexity of narrative structures or the large areas of experience—and ways of experiencing—common to both sexes. Virtually all of *Goodbar* is given us via Teresa's consciousness; the fantasy sequences allow us privileged access to her mind, a dimension denied the male characters (it is they, here, whom we look *at*, from Teresa's viewpoint). The characterization and the narrative procedures combine to transcend any sexual division in identification. I doubt very much whether any man (short of an advanced sadist) simply takes pleasure in the violence inflicted on Teresa at the end; he is far more likely to empathize with her terror.

2. The descent-into-hell structure would depend, for its validity and effectiveness, on the presence within the film of a realized concept of the "normal" as yardstick, and this simply does not exist. The characters who might embody a traditional normality are consistently undermined. The university professor (Teresa's first great love) cheats on his wife and exploits his female students for sex; the unity and solidarity of Teresa's own family is shown as a desperate and repressive illusion sustained by the father, and depends on a refusal to recognize unpleasant truths (in the nostalgically venerated past as well as the "decadent" present). Patriarchal authority is nowhere endorsed as providing adequate judgment on Teresa's life.

Crucial here is the most significant change Brooks made from Judith Rossner's novel—the transformation of the character of James, the lawyer in the novel, who becomes the film's social worker (William Atherton). In the book, James does represent a possible "normality," a settled and stable life, which Teresa could theoretically choose; he doesn't excite her (especially sexually), but he is safe, reliable, and loving, everything a good girl is supposed to need. The film makes him just as neurotic and potentially dangerous as everyone else. Teresa's murder is, in fact, anticipated in two key scenes that set up both her suitors as potential killers: Tony's (Richard Gere) dance with the phallic, luminous switchblade (where Teresa thinks he is going to attack her), and James's story (which he later tells her was a fantasy, thereby increasing rather than diminishing its sinister application to himself) about how his father beat his mother into a bloody pulp when she laughed at him for being impotent (precisely the reason Teresa is killed—though the laughter is only in the killer's mind). The points established seem to be that "normality" is an ideological construct, not a reality; that violence is inherent in sexual relationships under patriarchy; and that it doesn't ultimately matter who kills Teresa—any of the men in her life could have, and the killing arises more out of a cultural situation than individual responsibility. All three points strikingly anticipate *Cruising*.

3. Other changes and emphases in Brooks' adaptation of the novel, however, push the film in exactly the opposite direction.

He places far more emphasis than Rossner on Teresa's work, changing its nature and idealizing it as the "positive" side of her life. In the book, she is just a school-teacher, and not much is made of it; in the film, she teaches *deaf* children. The change allows Brooks to give Teresa's work incontrovertible value, while at the same time enabling him to evade (and the audience to forget) the fact that the children will grow up in the same world that confuses and finally destroys Teresa. We never think of them as inheriting *her* moral and emotional problems, because they have to cope with a highly specific, practical one; Teresa is helping them lead a normal life in a sense that gives a very limited definition to the word. The scene in which the children express violent resentment at Teresa for arriving late one day seems to me both implausible (they don't even wait to find out whether she is ill or has been in an accident) and overstated: it depends purely on the *audience's* knowledge that she has overslept after taking drugs, and exists exclusively to add to our sense of her guilt and degeneration.

Brooks also strongly underlines the probability that Teresa's childhood disease is hereditary, and thus seriously weakens and confuses the film. He seems to want to say that Teresa is representative of the problems, disturbances and confusions of stepping outside a stable social/moral structure; that such a move is, however, legit-imate; that in any case the stable order (if it ever *was* stable) has crumbled, and was always repressive. This would involve him in defending the right of physically and psychologically healthy women to express their sexuality with any partners they wish. He can't quite do this (though he comes surprisingly close), so he has to say that Teresa is a special case, crippled, unable to bear children for fear of passing on a hereditary disease. Her sexual freedom can now be explained, implicitly, as the result of her being excluded from a normal life; the explanation has to remain implicit (though very close to the surface), because the concept of normality is clearly rejected by the film.

4. This confusion (evasion?) is paralleled in the presentation of the film's gay characters. If one had only the closing scene to deal with, it could be argued that the treatment of gayness is both intelligent and enlightened. Brooks makes it clear that the young man murders Teresa, not because he is gay, but because he can't accept that he is gay: instead of associating homosexuality with neurosis, the film here associates self-oppression with neurosis, an entirely different matter. There is another significant change here from the novel: in the book, the murderer is not really gay, but at most bisexual (he has been exploiting a gay man in order to be fed and housed in a strange city); his pregnant wife is given the verification of doc-

umentary third-person narration; he successfully has sex with Teresa. In the film, we assume (having only his word for it) that he is inventing the wife and baby as a way of asserting his "normality" and "manhood"; he kills Teresa because his inability to get an erection with her forces on him the truth about himself. Like Teresa, then, he is the victim of a society that assigns people fixed roles, imposing on them notions of what a real man or real woman should be. One might even obliquely infer from the ending a *negative* statement of the links between feminism and gay liberation, since the catastrophe arises out of the characters' failure to grasp them.

Any such reading, however, is offset by the previous treatment of gay characters. The gay bar, though not in itself presented offensively, seems clearly meant to mark a stage in Teresa's descent; the murderer's lover is a shamelessly offered stereotype, hysterical, self-hating, sniveling. It's as if the film wants to say both that homosexuals would be all right if society let them accept themselves and that homosexuals are inherently sick and degenerate.

Of the three films, *Goodbar* seems to me ultimately the most unreadable, the farthest from resolving—perhaps from recognizing—its contradictions, or organizing them into a significant dialectic.

Cruising

To do some kind of justice to *Cruising* (it has received none so far),[1] it needs to be placed in two contexts: the sudden outcrop of movies either centrally or peripherally concerned with gayness that have emerged at the tail end of the 70s, and the social issues raised by the gay liberation movement, the theoretical program it implies.

"Emerged" may not be quite the word: of the four main relevant films, one has not yet been released and another has already sunk without a trace. Yet the fact that the films got made testifies to some (however muddled and hostile) awareness that the gay movement was somehow there and posed some kind of threat; their existence marks a point where gays can no longer be represented surreptitiously, without overt reference to sexuality, whether as comic-relief interior decorators or shifty-eyed *film noir* henchmen. And, although it came rather late, I think the recognition of gayness belongs very clearly to the 70s, the reactionary 80s so far marking a

1. Since this essay was written in 1980, I have discovered two reviews of *Cruising*, written independently and around the same time, published in the Australian magazine *Cinema Papers*, October-November 1980. The reviews, by Tom Ryan and Adrian Martin, substantially confirm my own findings while adding interesting insights of their own.

happy return to the mindless and clandestine (as in *Can't Stop the Music*), as if nothing had happened.[2]

The chief interest of *New York After Midnight* (aside from the fact that it was coscripted by Louisa Rose and that tantalizing thematic echoes of *Sisters* can be glimpsed among its ruins) lies in its remarkable sociological insight that if a woman goes into a gay disco, the men will immediately stop dancing with each other and try to rape her; as the film may never surface, one need say no more. *Windows*, in which Elizabeth Ashley believes that, if she pays a man to rape Talia Shire, the latter will instantly be converted to lesbianism and return her unrequited passion, mindlessly reproduces the familiar stereotype of lesbians as sick and predatory. So few people went to see it that its social impact is negligible; one is only sad that an intelligent actress (Elizabeth Ashley) consented to appear in it.

The key film here (*Cruising* apart) is one in which gayness appears peripheral, the film's homophobia being so muted as to have passed largely unnoticed (with the honorable exception of Stuart Byron in the *Village Voice*). Nonetheless, homophobia is central to *American Gigolo*. It was playing without protest in the same Toronto theater complex where gay activists were picketing *Cruising*; I find it incomparably the more offensive of the two films, and would argue that its social effect is probably far more harmful, being covert and insidious (in addition to the fact of the film's trendy commercial success). The entire progress of the protagonist, Julian (Richard Gere), is posited on the simple identification of gayness with degradation. Julian, the gigolo of the title, is accorded the status of Existential Hero because he takes pride in bringing frustrated middle-aged women to orgasm (for suitable monetary compensation). He is trying to forget a past when he used to "trick with fags," and is threatened with having to return to it, coerced by a black homosexual pimp and criminal. As Julian is not supposed to get pleasure from his sexual experiences with older women but likes to give *them* pleasure, as well as get paid, the implication is presumably that "fags" don't even deserve pleasure. The film traces Julian's progress toward salvation, in the form of a heterosexual relationship, viewed with true Fascist sentimentality (and direct plagiarism from Bresson) as uplifting and redemptive. The fact that the ultimate Schrader villain is both black and homosexual can scarcely be regarded, in the general context of his work, as coincidental.

Hollywood has adopted somewhat different strategies in dealing with, and putting in their patriarchal place, the women's movement and the gay movement. To an astonishing degree it has managed to ignore both (it never acknowledges them as movements, except derogatively). Its method with feminism has been generously to admit that, yes, a woman has every right to be independent and autonomous,

---

2. Subsequent 80s films on gay themes, released after this essay was originally written (1980), are dealt with in chapter 11; they qualify but do not seriously contradict the account offered here.

before going on to suggest that she will then be able to use her freedom of choice to commit herself to a burly, bearded patriarch like Kris Kristofferson or Alan Bates. With the gay movement, in the context of a generally homophobic culture, it can safely resort to simple vilification.

In contradistinction to all this, and pointing ahead to a discussion of *Cruising*, one may briefly suggest the issues one would hope to see acknowledged in a contemporary movie about gayness.

1. The oppression/exploitation of gays in our culture.
2. The repression of bisexuality, a commonplace of psychoanalytical theory. Here, bisexuality is posited as the natural state of the "polymorphously perverse" infant, whose social/ideological construction (fulfilling the accepted norms of masculinity and femininity, a major aspect of "surplus repression" within our culture) involves the systematic denial of its natural homosexual impulses. The failure of this process of socialization results in *exclusive* homosexuality—which one can therefore logically accept as a perversion, provided this description is accepted of exclusive heterosexuality as well. This gives rise to
3. The acknowledgment that gayness is not a thing apart—that everyone is potentially gay or has potential gay proclivities, and also
4. Homophobia: the irrational hatred of homosexuals. The theory of the repression of bisexuality offers the only plausible explanation of this unfortunate maladjustment: what is repressed is not destroyed but continues to exist in the unconscious as a constant threat; what the homophobe hates is the gay within himself.
5. The assault on patriarchy and the "Law of the Father," with the heterosexual male as the ideologically privileged figure of our culture.
6. The critique of heterosexual relations under patriarchy (as based on inequality and domination, i.e., the subordination of women): the family, monogamy, romantic love.
7. Attempts to construct new ways of relating, hence, necessarily, new forms of social organization.
8. The need to project strong positive images of gay life to offset the prevalent homophobia.
9. The recognition of gay liberation as a subversive political movement with defined theories, aims and principles.
10. The strong connections between gay liberation and the women's movement.

Gay activists have demonstrated against *Cruising* at all stages, attempting to disrupt the filming and attacking it in the gay press. In terms of its probable immediate social impact, they may be quite correct (and in any case the campaign against the film after its release, involving the picketing of cinemas and the distribution of leaflets, is exemplary in suggesting, within a democratic society, a constructive alternative to censorship). Yet *Cruising* opens up (not necessarily from a positive viewpoint) the first six of the above issues, as I shall show. For the rest, within the international commercial cinema only Ettore Scola's *A Special Day* broaches the last, and the other three have yet to be raised or even hinted at. A useful comparison is provided by *The Consequence*, a German film widely regarded by gay activists as "positive," which raises only the first of my ten issues and proceeds to labor it far beyond the point of overkill in a tone of whining self-pity, at the same time whole-heartedly reinforcing the good old heterosexual values of romantic monogamy and placing its pair of doomed and idealized gay lovers in a world of heterosexuals characterized as exclusively evil, manipulative and vindictive. I shall argue that the negativity of *Cruising* offers far more that can be *used*: that, whatever he may have intended (which remains, to me, largely mysterious), William Friedkin's film is by far the more radical and subversive of the two.

i. On one level, the incoherence of *Cruising* is of a different order from that of *Taxi Driver* and *Goodbar*: its surface is deliberately fractured, the progress of the narrative obscured, in a way that one must recognize as extremely audacious within the Hollywood context (though not necessarily artistically successful). In one respect, indeed, it presents its narrative as strictly impossible, providing cinematic statements that are not only contradictory but mutually exclusive. I find it very hard to be sure just what Friedkin had in mind here—to judge the level of sophistication on which the film seeks to operate. In style, it is as little "Brechtian" as one can imagine, yet it seems to want its viewers to question the "realist" experience of narrative itself. One can begin at the end:

a. Who committed the last murder (the brutal stabbing of Ted Bailey/Don Scardino, the most sympathetic of all the film's gay characters)? Friedkin makes it impossible to know, whereas in Gerald Walker's novel it is perfectly clear. There are strong signals that it may be the protagonist Steve Burns (Al Pacino), the cop who has assumed the identity of the killer he has tracked down, and who is continuing the killer's destruction of gay men who arouse him sexually (Pacino's final look in the mirror; Detective Edelson's very emphasized "Jesus Christ!" when he learns that Burns lived next door to the victim). Yet the film provides no evidence for this assumption, and, indeed, does provide contradictory suggestions that Ted may have been murdered by his lover (last seen brandishing a knife identical to the murder weapon).

b. But: who committed all the other murders? The film culminates in a confrontation and an arrest (played out in meticulous doppelgänger fashion between policeman and suspect). The "killer," on his hospital bed, denies that he has ever killed anyone. The only legal evidence is his fingerprint on a coin attested to by Edelson, who—though presented as more humane and concerned than most of his colleagues—has been shown to be less than perfect, and who is under great pressure to produce a murderer or lose his job. There is also one indisputable piece of cine-matic evidence—but this is precisely where the narrative impossibility comes in. We see the killer, Stuart Richards (Richard Cox), entering the park to talk to his father in a sequence strongly signified as "fantasy" by being overexposed (we learn subsequently that the father had died ten years ago); during this conversation, Friedkin cuts in "memory" flashbacks of the first two killings shown in the film, to which only the murderer could have access. There should be, then, no doubt that Stuart Richards is the killer—except that the killer in the first pick-up/murder scene is very clearly played by a different actor. If a central point in the narrative is proved impossible, then presumably the whole film loses its "realist" intimidation: every-thing becomes a matter of "if," "maybe," "let's pretend," rather than "*this* is what happened."

c. The film does not suggest that Burns could have been responsible for all the killings, but it clearly links him with more than the last one. After the murder of the clothes designer in the porno peep show, Friedkin cuts directly to Burns arriv-ing home, appearing haggard, disturbed and weary—as if he had just performed the murder. When he confronts his doppelgänger in the park at the climax, he repeats the killer's ritual baby talk which precedes each murder (obviously a father/child game): "Who's here? *I'm* here . . . " The only way he could possibly know about this is from the garbled account of the male transvestite who reports it (to another policeman) as something a friend of his overheard—except that the transvestite misquotes it, and Burns gets it right.

The film suggests then: that there are at least two killers and could be several; that we don't have to feel we know who the killer is, because it could be anyone; and that the violence has to be blamed on the culture, not on the individual. One of the strongest complaints of gay activists has been that the film associates the violence specifically with *homosexual* culture, and shows both as somehow contagious ("the vampire theory of homosexual contagion" as Robin Hardy says in *Body Politic*). It is quite possible that this is the overall impression the film makes on general audi-ences, the imagery of violence and leather bars being so insistent. It is not, however, what the film actually *says* or certainly not all it says.

2. The near-beginning of *Cruising* (after a prologue showing the finding of a half-decomposed arm in the river) succinctly takes up the excremental city theme of *Taxi Driver* and seems to apply it specifically to the homosexual subculture: "They're all scumbags," says a cop in a patrol car, introducing a point-of-view shot of a nocturnal street populated exclusively by cruising gays. This simple vision, which presumably typifies the kind of thing against which gay activists were protesting, is very strongly qualified by three facts. First, the cop in question is given unmistakable signifiers (physical appearance, expression, body language, intona-tion) indicating "This is a very unpleasant, uptight, potentially violent person." Second, a couple of screen minutes later he is compelling a male transvestite to suck

him off. Third, his fellow patrolman has just been indulging in a diatribe against his wife to the tune of "I'll get that bitch"—the film's first intimation of violence is established within the context of "normal" heterosexual relationships, with strong connotations of patriarchal domination and brutality, before any gays have appeared.

This introduction concisely states the theme of the interchangeability of the police force and the leather bars—the film's most comprehensive extension of the doppelgänger motif. When the transvestite protests to Detective Edelson (Paul Sorvino) against his exploitation by the patrolmen, Edelson asks, half cynically, "How did you know they were cops?" It is clearly his way out and establishes his complicity in the film's exploitation/corruption patterns. Yet, subsequently, the remark is given some ironic force when we are taken inside an S/M bar in which *all* the clientele are dressed in police uniforms. (The irony becomes particularly convoluted when Burns is accused by the proprietor of being a cop and turned out—because he is out of uniform.) Further, the married cop of the opening (or, given the narrative games Friedkin plays, his double, played by the same actor) turns up twice in the context of the gay subculture, cruising Burns once in a bar (where he is closely juxtaposed with Stuart Richards) and once in Central Park. (He is also in charge of the investigation into the final murder, before Edelson takes over.) The film never explains this: we cannot imagine that in the cruising scenes he is another decoy, because the decoy has to have the physical build and general appearance of Al Pacino. Finally, the grotesque scene in which both Burns and the innocent suspect are beaten up at police headquarters by an immense black policeman dressed only in a cow-boy hat and jockstrap has only the vaguest narrative plausibility, and seems to be there primarily to underline the connection between the two worlds.

All of this certainly affects our reading of the development of Steve Burns into the actual or potential killer of Ted Bailey: yes, he can be seen as brutalized by his experience of the S/M sub-culture, but equally his brutalization can be attributed to the contamination of police work. Both dominant culture and sub-culture are revealed as built on, and hopelessly corrupted by, power relationships.

The two moments in the film where the imagery seems most insistently to link violence with homosexual behavior are both specifically concerned with domination: the murder of the clothes designer in the porno peep show, culminating in blood splashing over the images of homosexual lovemaking on the screen; the increasingly frantic intercutting of Burns drawn into disco-dancing with another man and progressively enjoying it with a) a man being publicly fist-fucked and b) the aloof silent figure of a leather-masked executioner. The film clearly presents pornography (domination through objectification) and public fist-fucking in terms of degradation (a view I feel no great desire to challenge). Whether we are meant to view Burns' enjoyment of gay disco-dancing in the same light seems to me uncertain. The images *can* be given that meaning; yet montage carries inherent ambiguities (comparison or contrast?—"attraction" or "collision"?). The alternative is to read the scene, not as an attack on the evils of gay disco-dancing, but as an acknowledgment of the contamination of everything in our culture (even a pleasurable dance) by the domination/subjection drive. If Burns at the end of the film has taken over the identity of homophobic killer, then this scene (the arousal in him of homosexual desire) becomes crucial.

3. The film presents no positive images of gay culture, but then it offers no positive alternatives of any kind to the corrupt and disintegrating society it depicts— certainly not a return to any possible traditional "normality," which (insofar as it is even hinted at) takes the form of a cop saying of his wife "I'll get that bitch." A film depicting the warmth, generosity and openness I have found in gay life—qualities vitally connected to sexual freedom, to the partial undermining within gay culture of the possession/domination/submission syndrome—has yet to be made. Only the admission to the film of some such dimension could have resolved *Cruising*'s knot of contradictions. In its absence, one should note two (admittedly subordinate) aspects that somewhat mitigate the overall suggestion of the leather sub-culture as the epitome of a domination-and-violence, inherently sadomasochistic culture. One is that, with the exception of Ted Bailey's lover, all the individual gay characters (the suspect and the victims, including Ted himself) are presented quite sympathetically, with no sense that we are meant to be shocked at their sexual orientation. (The novel from which the movie was adapted, on the other hand, can scarcely contain its disgust for homosexuals; its thesis that the only thing more loathsome than a homosexual is a person who hates homosexuals involves its author in quite inextricable knots.) The other arises from Friedkin's use of gay extras in the bar scenes in the pursuit of authenticity, many of whom look irrepressibly happy and energetic, especially in contrast to the haggard face of Al Pacino: we may ask ourselves how, if this is hell, so many people appear to be enjoying themselves in it.

4. The issue of homophobia is at the thematic heart of the film, in its revelation of the reasons why the murders are being committed. If its narrative obscurities have the effect of removing blame from any individual killer, this is to define it the more clearly on the thematic level. Stuart Richards is told (believes he is told) to commit the murders by a father who would otherwise despise him: the killings are his way of proving himself the "man" his father wanted him to be. By killing gays, that is, he is symbolically destroying the gay within himself "in the Name of the Father"—a long-dead father interiorized as superego. Taking Stuart as the killer throughout (which the film both asserts and denies), one can trace a logical progression through the murders: the first victim we know of was Stuart's Columbia University professor (psychologically a particular aggravation in combining father figure and sexual object/seducer); the second is the actor (the first murder shown in the film), the only victim with whom we know the killer had intercourse; from there on, presumably, arousal without performance is enough to trigger off the

Doubles in *Cruising*

Al Pacino in a gay bar

Al Pacino and Richard Cox

mechanism. Further, all the victims (plus Burns, plus various extras, including an Al Pacino clone who turns up a couple of times in the bar scenes) are Stuart's doubles—i.e., the tangible embodiments of his repressed gay self: the killings are the projection of an internal violence directed against himself. Somewhat explicitly but more by implication, the film's real villain is revealed as patriarchal domination, the "Law of the Father" that demands the rigid structuring of the subject and the repression of all conflicting or superfluous realities—the denial of the Other, both internal and external. The implications of this are enormous: taken symbolically, it was Stuart's father who demanded the Vietnam war. His demands (and their impossibility) are enacted in the brutality and corruption of the police, and parodied in the sadomasochism of the leather bars. It is a remarkable paradox that a film almost universally perceived as antigay should produce at its center one of the fundamental social/psychoanalytic insights on which the case for gay liberation rests. (For an unambiguously antigay movie, compare the Dutch *Dear Boys*, by Paul de Lussanet, which presents all its gay characters as mean-spirited predators.)

5. It remains to consider the development of the Pacino character, his relationship with his lover Nancy (Karen Allen), and the film's extremely enigmatic ending. It is here that *Cruising* seems at its most tentative and evasive: uncertain what it wants to say (what it dare say?), it moves into a kind of paralyzed neutrality. To start almost at the end, if we assume that Burns has murdered Ted Bailey, the only possible motivation is an extension of the previous killer's homophobia. The film seems deliberately evasive as to whether Burns actually has sex with men in the pursuit of his duties, but it is clear that his confidence in his heterosexuality becomes progressively undermined, and the possibility that a sexual relationship with Bailey might develop is strongly suggested: he murders Bailey because he is sexually aroused by him. Looking back from that, we can trace the undermining of his patriarchal sexual identity, his involvement in the sub-culture systematically counterpointed with scenes showing the deterioration of his relationship with Nancy, his lovemaking vacillating between (compensatory or sadistic?) aggression and passivity. Part of the problem in reading the film is that the relationship is given no clear definition at the outset; it certainly carries no positive charge, both characters seeming physically pallid and drained of energy (energy fills the leather "underworld"). Nancy, until the end of the film, remains a colorless, neutral figure with no defined position beyond that of offering Burns ineffectual support.

How to read their final scene? Burns, the assignment officially over (but with Bailey's unsolved murder in the immediate background), has asked to come back to her, and is shaving in her bathroom (symbolically cleansing himself?); he nicks his throat; his face continues to look haggard and disturbed. Meanwhile, Nancy finds the SS uniform he has worn in leather bars discarded on a chair, and automatically puts it on. Cut back to Burns' face in the mirror. We (and he) hear the clinking of metal approaching the bathroom door. Slow dissolve from his face to the river and

tug-boats—has the film come full circle to its opening images, implying the finding of another corpse or severed limb? One can read this in two ways (again, playing the film's game of "perhaps"): Burns, now irremediably disturbed, is about to
murder Nancy when he sees her dressed in leather; *her* body will be found in the
river. Or, less specifically, though one murderer has been caught, this resolves nothing; while the culture continues as it is, the patterns of violence will continue,
spreading everywhere. What is interesting is that it is *Nancy* who dons the uniform:
the "contagion" theory becomes strained to breaking point if we have to assume
that she has now contracted the "disease" from Burns. Rather, it seems logical to
take the ending as answering the cop's words about his wife at the beginning. It then
becomes a reminder that sadomasochism, far from being the preserve of leather-
clad-homosexuals, pervades the entire culture and is inherent in its fundamental
relationship patterns (parent-child, husband-wife), all of which are centered on
domination/submission: Nancy is simply reversing the traditional male/female role
and becoming the dominator.

One could certainly accuse Friedkin of not having grasped the positive, radical
implications of gay liberation (but how could he, given the overwhelming suppression of gay voices within the dominant culture?): he uses gay culture to epito-
mize domination relationships, whereas at its best it transcends them. (Even gay
S/M seems usually to carry strong connotations of play and parody—i.e., it turns
the domination/submission patterns of traditional relationships into a game, with
the roles often interchangeable.) He hasn't fully confronted the fact that the central
inequality of our culture is male/female, and that same-sex relationships offer at
least the possibility of escaping this. Yet the confusion of *Cruising* seems to me infinitely preferable to the self-indulgent romanticism of *The Consequence* or the gay
self-contempt of *Dear Boys*.

CONCLUSION

What, finally, do I wish to assert about these films?

First, that they offer more complex experiences than have generally been recognized: they have occasioned me a great deal of pleasure and disturbance, in roughly
equal measure.

Second, that the only way in which the incoherence of these movies (the result,
every time, of a blockage of thought) could be resolved would be through the adoption of a radical attitude: in *Taxi Driver*, the *consistent* critique of the patriarchal
hero; in *Goodbar*, a commitment to feminism; in *Cruising*, to gay liberation; in all
three, a commitment to social/sexual revolution. No possibility of this yet exists
within the Hollywood context: the radical alternatives remain taboo. Yet the films'
incoherence—the proof that the issues and conflicts they dramatize can no longer

even appear to be resolvable within the system, within the dominant ideology—testifies eloquently to the logical necessity for radicalism.

Third, that any promise of a radical vision they may seem to hold will have to be stored away for the future. *Cruising*, shot in 1979, already seemed an anachronism when it was released in 1980: in the midst of the parade of demoralizingly "moral" reactionary movies heralded in the late 70s by *Rocky* and *Star Wars*, it sticks out like a sore thumb. In the age of *Star Trek*, *Serial*, *Bronco Billy*, *Urban Cowboy*, and *Honeysuckle Rose*, when even progressive liberals like Jerry Schatzberg and James Bridges are succumbing without apparent protest to the tide of reaction, recuperation, and reassurance, we can already look back to Hollywood in the 70s as the period when the dominant ideology *almost* disintegrated.

5.

The American Nightmare

HORROR IN THE 70s

To describe the 70s as the Golden Age of the American horror film will seem to many dubious: it was the period in which the evolution of the genre produced films more gruesome, more violent, more disgusting, and perhaps more confused, than ever before in its history. They tended also to be more disturbed and more disturbing, and this disturbance (shared by filmmaker and audience) is, from the point of view of this study, crucial. If many are "incoherent texts," and if, overall, the genre itself moves characteristically toward an unresolvable and usually unrecognized dilemma, both the incoherence and the dilemma become in themselves eloquent, speaking for the quandary of a civilization. In fact, the flowering of the genre in the 70s can be seen in retrospect to be entirely logical, even inevitable (as can its decline—worse, the hideous perversion of its essential meaning—in the 80s). In order to make this clear, it is necessary to outline a general theory of the horror film.

In the previous chapter I briefly introduced the distinction between basic and surplus repression, developed out of Freud by Marcuse, and given definitive expression in a book that should be far better known than it is: *Repression*, by Gad Horowitz. The book's subtitle is "Basic and Surplus Repression in Psychoanalytic Theory: Freud, Reich, Marcuse"; it is dense, often difficult, very closely and cogently argued, and the account offered here is necessarily bald and simplified.

Basic repression is universal, necessary, and inescapable. It is what makes possible our development from an uncoordinated animal capable of little beyond screaming and convulsions into a human being; it is bound up with the ability to accept the postponement of gratification, with the development of our thought and memory processes, of our capacity for self-control, and of our recognition of and consideration for other people. Surplus repression, on the other hand, is specific to a particular culture and is the process whereby people are conditioned from earliest infancy to take on predetermined roles within that culture. In terms of our own culture, then: *basic* repression makes us distinctively human, capable of directing our own lives and co-existing with others; *surplus* repression makes us into monogamous heterosexual bourgeois patriarchal capitalists ("bourgeois" even if we are born into the proletariat, for we are talking here of ideological norms rather than material status)—that is, *if* it works. If it doesn't, the result is either a neurotic or a revolutionary (or both), and if revolutionaries account for a very small proportion of the population, neurotics account for a very large one. Hardly surprising. All known existing societies are to some degree surplus-repressive, but the degree varies enormously, from the trivial to the overwhelming. Freud saw long ago that our own civilization had reached a point where the burden of repression was becoming all but insupportable, an insight Horowitz (following Marcuse) brilliantly relates to Marx's theory of alienated labor. The most immediately obvious characteristics of life in our culture are frustration, dissatisfaction, anxiety, greed, possessiveness, jealousy, neuroticism: no more than what psychoanalytic theory shows to be the logical product of patriarchal capitalism. What needs to be stressed is that the challenges now being made to the system—and the perceptions and recognitions that structure those challenges and give them impetus—become possible (become in the literal sense thinkable) only in the circumstances of the system's imminent disintegration. While the system retained sufficient conviction, credibility and show of coherence to suppress them, it did so. The struggle for liberation is not utopian, but a practical necessity.

Given that our culture offers an extreme example of surplus repressiveness, one can ask what, exactly, in the interests of alienated labor and the patriarchal family, is repressed. One needs here both to distinguish between the concepts of *re*pression and *op*pression and to suggest the continuity between them. In psychoanalytic terms, what is repressed is not accessible to the conscious mind (except through analysis or, if one can penetrate their disguises, in dreams). We may also not be conscious of ways in which we are oppressed, but it is much easier to become so: we are oppressed by something "out there." One might perhaps define repression as fully internalized oppression (while reminding ourselves that all the groundwork of repression is laid in infancy), thereby suggesting both the difference and the connection. A specific example may make this clearer: our social structure demands the repression of the bisexuality that psychoanalysis shows to be the natural heritage of every human individual and the oppression of homosexuals: obviously the two phenomena are not identical, but equally obviously they are closely connected. What escapes repression has to be dealt with by oppression.

What, then, is repressed in our culture? First, sexual energy itself, together with its possible successful sublimation into non-sexual creativity—sexuality being the source of creative energy in general. The "ideal" inhabitant of our culture is the individual whose sexuality is sufficiently fulfilled by the monogamous heterosexual union necessary for the reproduction of future ideal inhabitants, and whose sublimated sexuality (creativity) is sufficiently fulfilled in the totally non-creative and non-fulfilling labor (whether in factory or office) to which our society dooms the overwhelming majority of its members. The ideal, in other words, is as close as possible to an automaton in whom both sexual and intellectual energy has been reduced to a minimum. Otherwise, the ideal is a contradiction in terms and a logical impossibility—hence the necessary frustration, anxiety and neuroticism of our culture.

Second, bisexuality—which should be understood both literally (in terms of possible sexual orientation and practice) and in a more general sense. Bisexuality represents the most obvious and direct affront to the principle of monogamy and its supportive romantic myth of "the one right person"; the homosexual impulse in both men and women represents the most obvious threat to the norm of sexuality as reproductive and restricted by the ideal of family. But more generally we confront here the whole edifice of clear-cut sexual differentiation that bourgeois-capitalist ideology erects on the flimsy and dubious foundations of biological difference: the social norms of masculinity and femininity, the social definitions of manliness and womanliness, the whole vast apparatus of oppressive male/female myths, and the systematic repression from infancy ("blue for a boy") of the man's femininity and the woman's masculinity, in the interests of forming human beings for specific predetermined social roles.

Third, the particularly severe repression of female sexuality/creativity, the attribution to the female of passivity, and her preparation for her subordinate, dependent role in our culture. Clearly, a crucial aspect of the repression of bisexuality is the denial to women of drives culturally associated with masculinity: activeness, aggression, self-assertion, organizational power, creativity itself.

Fourth, and fundamentally, the repression of the sexuality of children, taking different forms from infancy, through 'latency' and puberty, and into adolescence—the process moving, indeed, from repression to oppression, from the denial of the infant's nature as sexual being to the veto on the expression of sexuality before marriage.

None of these forms of repression is necessary for the existence of civilization in some form (i.e., none is "basic")—for the development of our human-ness. Indeed, they impose limitations and restrictions on that development, stunting human potential. All are the outcome of the requirements of the particular surplus-repressive civilization in which we live.

Closely linked to the concept of repression—indeed, truly inseparable from it— is another concept necessary to an understanding of ideology on which psychoanalysis throws much light, the concept of "the Other." Otherness represents that which bourgeois ideology cannot recognize or accept but must deal with (as Barthes suggests in *Mythologies*) in one of two ways: either by rejecting and if possible annihilating it, or by rendering it safe and assimilating it, converting it as far as possible into a replica of itself. The concept of Otherness can be theorized in many ways and on many levels. Its psychoanalytic significance resides in the fact that it functions not simply as something external to the culture or to the self, but also as what is repressed (though never destroyed) in the self and projected outward in order to be hated and disowned. A particularly vivid example—and one that throws light on a great many classical westerns—is the relationship of the Puritan settlers to the Indians in the early days of America. The Puritans rejected any perception that the Indians had a culture, a civilization, of their own; they perceived them not merely as savage but, literally, as devils or the spawn of the Devil; and, since the Devil and sexuality were inextricably linked in the Puritan consciousness, they perceived them as sexually promiscuous, creatures of unbridled libido. The connection between this view of the Indian and Puritan repression is obvious: a classic and extreme case of the projection on to the Other of what is repressed within the Self in order that it can be discredited, disowned, and if possible annihilated. It is repression, in other words, that makes impossible the healthy alternative—the full recognition and acceptance of the Other's autonomy and right to exist.

Some versions follow of the figure of the Other as it operates within our culture, of its relation to repression and oppression, and of how it is characteristically dealt with:

1. *Quite simply, other people.* It is logical and probable that under capitalism all human relations will be characterized by power, dominance, possessiveness, manipulation: the extension into relationships of the property principle. Given the subordinate and dependent position of women, this is especially true of the culture's central relationship, the male/female, and explains why marriage as we have it is characteristically a kind of mutual imperialism/colonization, an exchange of different forms of possession and dependence, both economic and emotional. In theory, relations between people of the same sex stand more chance of evading this contamination, but in practice most gay and lesbian relationships tend to rely on heterosexual models. The otherness and the autonomy of the partner as well as her/his right to freedom and independence of being are perceived as a threat to the possession/dependence principle and are denied.

2. *Woman.* In a male-dominated culture, where power, money, law, and social institutions are controlled by past, present, and future patriarchs, woman as the Other assumes particular significance. The dominant images of women in our culture are entirely male created and male controlled. Woman's autonomy and independence are denied; on to women men project their own innate, repressed femininity in order to disown it as inferior (to be called "unmanly"—i.e., like a woman—is the supreme insult).

3. *The proletariat*—insofar as it still has any autonomous existence and has escaped its colonization by bourgeois ideology. It remains, at least, a conveniently

available object for projection: the bourgeois obsession with cleanliness, which psychoanalysis shows to be an outward symptom closely associated with sexual repression, and bourgeois sexual repression itself, find their inverse reflections in the myths of working-class squalor and sexuality.

4. *Other cultures.* If they are sufficiently remote, no problem arises: they can be simultaneously deprived of their true character and exoticized (e.g., Polynesian cultures as embodied by Dorothy Lamour). If they are inconveniently close, another approach predominates, of which what happened to the American Indian is a prime example. The procedure is very precisely represented in Ford's *Drums Along the Mohawk*, with its double vision of the Indians as "sons of Belial" fit only for extermination and as the Christianized, domesticated, servile, and (hopefully) comic Blueback.

5. *Ethnic groups within the culture.* Again, they function as easily available projection objects (myths of black sexuality, animality, etc.) Or they become acceptable in two ways: either they keep to their ghettos and don't trouble us with their otherness, or they behave as we do and become replicas of the good bourgeois, their Otherness reduced to the one unfortunate difference of color. We are more likely to invite a Pakistani to dinner if he dresses in a business suit.

6. *Alternative ideologies or political systems.* The exemplary case is of course Marxism, the strategy that of parody. Still almost totally repressed within our pre-university education system (despite the key importance of Marx—whatever way you look at it—in the development of twentieth-century thought), Marxism exists generally in our culture only in the form of bourgeois myth that renders it indistinguishable from Stalinism.

7. *Deviations from ideological sexual norms—notably bisexuality and homosexuality.* One of the clearest instances of the operation of the repression/projection mechanism, homophobia (the irrational hatred and fear of homosexuals) is only explicable as the product of the unsuccessful repression of bisexual tendencies: what is hated in others is what is rejected (but nonetheless continues to exist) within the self.

8. *Children.* When we have worked our way through all the other liberation movements, we may discover that children are the most oppressed section of the population (unfortunately, we cannot expect to liberate our children until we have successfully liberated ourselves). Most clearly of all, the otherness of children (see Freudian theories of infantile sexuality) is that which is repressed within ourselves, its expression therefore hated in others. What the previous generation repressed in us, we, in turn, repress in our children, seeking to mold them into replicas of ourselves, perpetuators of a discredited tradition.

All this may seem to have taken us rather far from our immediate subject. In fact, I have been laying the foundations, stone by stone, for a theory of the American horror film which (without being exhaustive) should provide us with a means of approaching the films seriously and responsibly. One could, I think, approach any of the genres from the same starting point; it is the horror film that responds in the most clear-cut and direct way, because central to it is the actual dramatization of the dual concept of the repressed/the Other, in the figure of the Monster. One might say that the true subject of the horror genre is the struggle for recognition of all that our civilization represses or oppresses, its re-emergence dramatized, as in our nightmares, as an object of horror, a matter for terror, and the happy ending (when it exists) typically signifying the restoration of repression. I think my analysis of what is repressed, combined with my account of the Other as it functions within our culture, will be found to offer a comprehensive survey of horror film monsters from German Expressionism on. It is possible to produce "monstrous" embodiments of virtually every item in the above list. Let me preface this by saying that the general sexual content of the horror film has long been recognized, and the list of monsters representing a generalized concept of Otherness offered by the first item on my list cannot be represented by specific films.

Female sexuality. Earlier examples are the panther woman of *Island of Lost Souls* and the heroine of *Cat People* (the association of women with cats runs right through and beyond the Hollywood cinema, cutting across periods and genres from *Bringing Up Baby* to *Alien*); but the definitive feminist horror film is clearly De Palma's *Sisters* (co-scripted by the director and Louisa Rose), among the most complete and rigorous analyses of the oppression of women under patriarchal culture in the whole of patriarchal cinema.

The proletariat. I would claim here Whale's *Frankenstein*, partly on the strength of its pervasive class references but more on the strength of Karloff's costume: Frankenstein could have dressed his creature in top hat, white tie and tails, but in fact chose laborer's clothes. Less disputable, in recent years we have *The Texas Chainsaw Massacre*, with its monstrous family of retired, but still practicing, slaughterhouse workers; the underprivileged devil-worshipers of *Race with the Devil*; and the revolutionary army of *Assault on Precinct 13*.

Other cultures. In the 30s the monster was almost invariably foreign; the rebellious animal-humans of *Island of Lost Souls* (though created by the white man's science) on one level clearly signify a savage, unsuccessfully colonized culture. Recently, one horror film, *The Manitou*, identified the monster with the American Indian (*Prophecy* plays tantalizingly with this possibility, also linking it to urban blacks, before opting for the altogether safer and less interesting explanation of industrial pollution).

Ethnic groups. The Possession of Joel Delaney links diabolic possession with Puerto Ricans; blacks (and a leader clad as an Indian) are prominent in *Assault on Precinct 13*'s monstrous army.

Alternative ideologies. The 50s science fiction cycle of invasion movies are generally regarded as being concerned with the Communist threat.

Homosexuality and bisexuality. Both Murnau's *Nosferatu* and Whale's *Franken-stein* can be claimed as implicitly (on certain levels) identifying their monsters with repressed homosexuality. Recent, less arguable instances are Dr. Frank 'n' Furter of *The Rocky Horror Picture Show* (he, not his creation, is clearly the film's real monster) and, more impressively, the bisexual god of Larry Cohen's *Demon*.

Children. Since *Rosemary's Baby* children have figured prominently in horror films as the monster or its medium: *The Exorcist, The Omen,* etc. Cohen's two *It's Alive* films again offer perhaps the most interesting and impressive examples. There is also the Michael of *Halloween's* remarkable opening.

This offers us no more than a beginning from which one might proceed to interpret specific horror films in detail as well as to explore further the genre's social significance and the insights it offers into our culture. I shall add here simply that these notions of repression and the Other afford us not merely a means of access but a rudimentary categorization of horror films in social/political terms, distinguishing the progressive from the reactionary, the criterion being the way in which the monster is presented and defined.

RETURN OF THE REPRESSED

I want first to offer a series of general propositions about the American horror film and then to define the particular nature of its evolution in the 60s and 70s.

1. Popularity and Disreputability The horror film has consistently been one of the most popular and, at the same time, the most disreputable of Hollywood genres. The popularity itself has a peculiar characteristic that sets it apart from other genres: it is restricted to aficionados and complemented by total rejection, people tending to go to horror films either obsessively or not at all. They are dismissed with contempt by the majority of reviewer-critics, or simply ignored. (The situation has changed somewhat since *Psycho*, which conferred on the horror film something of the dignity that *Stagecoach* conferred on the western, but the disdain still largely continues. I have read no serious or illuminating accounts of, for example, *Raw Meat, It's Alive,* or *The Hills Have Eyes.*) The popularity, however, also continues. Most horror films make money; the ones that don't are those with overt intellectual pretensions, obviously "difficult" works like *God Told Me To* (aka *Demon*) and *Exorcist II.* Another psychologically interesting aspect of this popularity is that many people who go regularly to horror films profess to ridicule them and go in order to laugh, which is not true, generally speaking, of the western or the gangster movie.

2. Dreams and Nightmares The analogy frequently invoked between films and dreams is usually concerned with the experience of the audience. The spectator sits in darkness, and the sort of involvement the entertainment film invites necessitates a certain switching off of consciousness, a losing of oneself in fantasy experience. But the analogy is also useful from the point of view of the filmmakers. Dreams—the embodiment of repressed desires, tensions, fears that our conscious mind rejects—become possible when the censor that guards our subconscious relaxes in sleep, though even then the desires can only emerge in disguise, as fantasies that are innocent or apparently meaningless.

One of the functions of the concept of entertainment—by definition, that which we don't take seriously, or think about much ("It's only entertainment")—is to act as a kind of partial sleep of consciousness. For the filmmakers as well as for the audience, full awareness stops at the level of plot, action, and character, in which the most dangerous and subversive implications can disguise themselves and escape detection. This is why seemingly innocuous genre movies can be far more radical and fundamentally undermining than works of conscious social criticism, which must always concern themselves with the possibility of reforming aspects of a social system whose basic rightness must not be challenged. The old tendency to dismiss the Hollywood cinema as escapist always defined escape merely negatively as escape *from*, but escape logically must also be escape *to*. Dreams are also escapes, from the unresolved tensions of our lives into fantasies. Yet the fantasies are not meaningless; they can represent attempts to resolve those tensions in more radical ways than our consciousness can countenance.

Popular films, then, respond to interpretation as at once the personal dreams of their makers and the collective dreams of their audiences, the fusion made possible by the shared structures of a common ideology. It becomes easy, if this is granted, to offer a simple definition of horror films: they are our collective nightmares. The conditions under which a dream becomes a nightmare are that the repressed wish is, from the point of view of consciousness, so terrible that it must be repudiated as loathsome, and that it is so strong and powerful as to constitute a serious threat. The disreputability noted above—the general agreement that horror films are not to be taken seriously—works clearly *for* the genre viewed from this position. The censor (in both the common and the Freudian sense) is lulled into sleep and relaxes vigilance.

3. The Surrealists   It is worth noting here that one group of intellectuals did take American horror movies very seriously indeed: the writers, painters, and filmmakers of the Surrealist movement. Luis Buñuel numbers *The Beast with Five Fingers* among his favorite films and paid homage to it in *The Exterminating Angel;* Georges Franju, an heir of the Surrealists, numbers *The Fly* among his: The association is highly significant, given the commitment of the Surrealists to Freud, the unconscious, dreams, and the overthrow of repression.

4. Basic Formula   At this stage it is necessary to offer a simple and obvious basic formula for the horror film: normality is threatened by the Monster. I use "normality" here in a strictly nonevaluative sense to mean simply "conformity to the dominant social norms": one must firmly resist the common tendency to treat the word as if it were more or less synonymous with "health."

The very simplicity of this formula has a number of advantages:

It covers the entire range of horror films, being applicable whether the Monster is a vampire, a giant gorilla, an extraterrestrial invader, an amorphous gooey mass, or a child possessed by the Devil, and this makes it possible to connect the most seemingly heterogeneous movies.

It suggests the possibility of extension to other genres: substitute for "Monster" the term "Indians," for example, and one has a formula for a large number of classical westerns; substitute "transgressive woman" and the formula encompasses numerous melodramas (Vidor's *Beyond the Forest* is an especially fine example, as it links woman and Indian as "monsters").

Although so simple, the formula provides three variables: normality, the Monster, and, crucially, the relationship between the two. The definition of normality in horror films is in general boringly constant: the heterosexual monogamous couple, the family, and the social institutions (police, church, armed forces) that support and defend them. The Monster is, of course, much more protean, changing from period to period as society's basic fears clothe themselves in fashionable or immediately accessible garments—rather as dreams use material from recent memory to express conflicts or desires that may go back to early childhood.

It is the third variable, the relationship between normality and the Monster, that constitutes the essential subject of the horror film. It, too, changes and develops, the development taking the form of a long process of clarification or revelation. The relationship has one privileged form: the figure of the doppelgänger, alter ego, or double, a figure that has recurred constantly in Western culture, especially during the past hundred years. The *locus classicus* is Stevenson's Dr. Jekyll and Mr. Hyde, where normality and Monster are two aspects of the same person. The figure pervades two major sources of the American horror film—German Expressionist cinema (the two Marias of *Metropolis*, the presentation of protagonist and vampire as mirror reflections in *Nosferatu*, the very title of F. W. Murnau's lost Jekyll-and-Hyde film *Der Januskopf*), and the tales of Poe. Variants can be traced in such oppositions as Ahab/the white whale in *Moby Dick* and Ethan/Scar in *The Searchers*. The westerns of Anthony Mann are rich in doubles, often contained within families or family patterns; *Man of the West*, a film that relates very suggestively to the horror genre, represents the fullest elaboration.

I shall limit myself for the moment to one example from the horror film, choosing it partly because it is so central, partly because the motif is there partially disguised, and partly because it points forward to Larry Cohen and *It's Alive*: the relationship of Monster to creator in the *Frankenstein* films. Their identity is made explicit in *Son of Frankenstein*, the most intelligent of the Universal series, near the start of which the title figure (Basil Rathbone) complains bitterly that everyone believes "Frankenstein" to be the name of the monster. (We discover subsequently that the town has also come to be called Frankenstein, the symbiosis of Monster and creator spreading over the entire environment.) But we should be alerted to the relationship's true significance from the moment in the James Whale original where Frankenstein's decision to create his monster is juxtaposed very precisely with his decision to become engaged. The doppelgänger motif reveals the Monster as normality's shadow.

5. Ambivalence   The principle of ambivalence is most eloquently elaborated in A. P. Rossiter's *Angel with Horns*, among the most brilliant of all books on Shakespeare. Rossiter first expounds it with reference to Richard III. Richard, the "angel with horns," both horrifies us with his evil and delights us with his intellect, his art, his audacity; while our moral sense is appalled by his outrages, another part of us gleefully identifies with him. The application of this to the horror film is clear. Few horror films have totally unsympathetic Monsters (*The Thing* is a significant exception); in many (notably the *Frankenstein* films) the Monster is clearly the emotional center, and much more human than the cardboard representatives of normality. The Frankenstein monster suffers, weeps, responds to music, longs to relate to people; Henry and Elizabeth merely declaim histrionically. Even in *Son of Frankenstein*—the film in which the restructured monster is explicitly designated as evil and superhuman—the monster's emotional commitment to Ygor and grief over his death carries far greater weight than any of the other relationships in the film.

But the principle goes far beyond the Monster's being sympathetic. Ambivalence extends to our attitude to normality. Central to the effect and fascination of horror films is their fulfillment of our nightmare wish to smash the norms that oppress us and which our moral conditioning teaches us to revere.[1] The overwhelming commercial success of *The Omen* cannot possibly be explained in terms of simple, unequivocal *horror* at the devil's progress.

6. Freudian Theses   Finally, I restate the two elementary and closely interconnected Freudian theses that structure this article: that in a society built on monogamy and family there will be an enormous surplus of repressed sexual energy, and that what is repressed must always strive to return.

---

1. A game popular in British fairgrounds actually entitled "Breaking up the Happy Home" is of great interest in this connection: there are no prizes, the participants' gratification deriving purely from the smashing of china and domestic artifacts with the balls for which they pay.

✳ ✳ ✳

Before considering how the horror film has developed in the past decade, I want to test the validity of the above ideas by applying them to a classical horror film. I have chosen Robert Florey's *Murders in the Rue Morgue* (1932) because it is a highly distinguished example, and generally neglected; because its images suggest Surrealism as much as Expressionism; and because it occupies a particularly interesting place in the genre's evolution, linking two of the most famous, though most disparate, horror films ever made. On the one hand it looks back very clearly to *The Cabinet of Dr. Caligari* through the Expressionist sets and lighting, with Karl Freund as cinematographer; the fairground that provides the starting point for the action; the figure of the diabolical doctor, who shows off his exhibit and later sends it to kidnap the heroine; and the flight over the rooftops. On the other hand it looks forward, equally clearly, to *King Kong*: instead of *Caligari's* sleepwalker, a gorilla, which falls in love with the heroine, abducts her at night and is shot down from a roof. It is as important to notice the basic motifs that recur obstinately throughout the evolution of the horror film in Western culture as it is to be aware of the detailed particularities of individual films. *Murders in the Rue Morgue* responds well to the application of my formula.

1. Normality   The film is quite obsessive about its heterosexual couples. At the opening, we have two couples responding to the various spectacles of the fairground, and a scene in the middle shows numerous carefree couples disporting themselves picturesquely amid nature. Crucial to the film, however, is Pierre's love speech to Camille on her balcony, with its exaggerated emphasis on purity: she is both a "flower" and a "star"; she is told not to be curious about what goes on in the houses of the city around them ("Better not to know"); she is also prevented from obtaining knowledge of the nature of Pierre's activities in the morgue (a "horrid old place"). Even the usual gay stereotype, Pierre's plump and effeminate friend, fits very well into the pattern. He is provided with a girlfriend, to recuperate him into the heterosexual coupling of normality. His relationship with Pierre (they share an apartment, he wears an apron, cooks the dinner, fusses) is a parody of bourgeois marriage, the incongruity underlining the relationship's repressive sexlessness. And he underlines the attempts at separating "pure" normality from the pervasive contamination of outside forces by complaining that Pierre "brings the morgue into their home."

2. The Monster   *Murders in the Rue Morgue* has a divided Monster, a phenomenon not uncommon in the horror film. (In *The Cabinet of Dr. Caligari* the Monster is both Caligari and Cesar; in *Island of Lost Souls* both Dr. Moreau and his creatures.) Here the division is tripartite: Dr. Mirakle (Bela Lugosi), his servant-assistant, and

Erik, "the beast with a human soul." The servant's role is small, but important because of his appearance: half human, half animal, he bridges the gap between Mirakle and Erik. Scientist and ape are linked, however, in another way: Mirakle himself lusts after Camille, and Erik (the animal extension of himself) represents the instrument for the satisfaction of that lust. Together they combine the two great, apparently contradictory, dreads of American culture as expressed in its cinema: intellectuality and eroticism.

3. Relationship   The film's superficial project is to insist that purity-normality can be separated from contaminating eroticism-degradation; its deeper project is to demonstrate the impossibility of such a separation. In the opening sequence, the couples view a series of fairground acts as spectacles (the separation of stage from audience seeming to guarantee safety): an erotic dance by "Arabian" girls, a Wild Red Indian show, and finally Erik the ape. The association of the three is suggestive of the link between the horror film and the western—the linking of Horror, Indians, and released libido. In each case the separation of show and audience is shown to be precarious: Pierre's sidekick asks his girl if she "could learn to do that dance" for him; two spectators adopt the name "apache" to apply to the savages of Paris; the audience enters the third booth between the legs of an enormous painted ape, where its phallus would be. Dr. Mirakle's introduction uses evolutionary theory to deny separation: Erik is "the darkness at the dawn of Man." His subsequent experiments are carried out to prove that Erik's blood can be "mixed with the blood of Man"—and as the experiments all involve women, the sexual connotations are plain.

Though not obvious, the "double" motif subtly structures the film. It comes nearest to explicitness in the effeminate friend's remark that Pierre is becoming fanatical, "like that Dr. Mirakle." But Pierre and Mirakle are paralleled repeatedly, both in the construction of the scenario and through the *mise-en-scène*. At the end of the balcony love scene Florey cuts from the lovers' kiss to Mirakle and Erik watching from their carriage. Later, the juxtaposition is reversed, the camera panning from Mirakle and Erik lurking in the shadows to Pierre and Camille embracing on the balcony; it is as if the Monster were waiting to be released by the kiss. Mirakle sends Camille a bonnet; she assumes it is from Pierre. After Pierre leaves her at night, there is a knock at her door. She thinks Pierre has come back and opens; it is Mirakle. Bearing in mind that Mirakle and Erik are not really distinct from one another, one must see Pierre and this composite Monster paralleled throughout as rival mates for Camille, like Jonathan and Nosferatu, or like David Ladd and the underworld man of *Raw Meat* (*Death Line*). (The motif's recurrence across periods and different continents testifies to its importance.) At the climax, Pierre and Erik confront each other like mirror images on the rooftop, and Erik is shot down by Pierre: the hero's drive is to destroy the doppelgänger who embodies his repressed self.

Murders in the Rue Morgue is fascinating for its unresolved self-contradiction. In the fairground, Mirakle is denounced as a heretic in the name of the Judaeo-Christian tradition of God's creation of man; the whole notion of purity/normality clearly associates with this—explicitly, in the very prominent, carefully lit crucifix above Camille's bed. Yet Mirakle's Darwinian theories are also obviously meant to be correct. Erik and humanity are *not* separable; the ape exists in all of us; the "morgue" cannot be excluded from the "home."

✳ ✳ ✳

Five recurrent motifs have dominated the horror film since the 60s. The list of examples offered in each case begins with what I take to be the decisive source film of each trend—not necessarily the first film, but the one that, because of its distinction or popularity, can be thought of as responsible for the ensuing cycle. I have included a few British films that seem to me American-derived (*Raw Meat*, arguably the finest British horror film, was directed by an American, Gary Sherman); they lie outside the main British tradition represented by Hammer Productions, a tradition very intelligently treated in David Pirie's book *A Heritage of Horror*. The lists are not, of course, meant to be exhaustive.

1. The Monster as human psychotic or schizophrenic: *Psycho, Homicidal, Repulsion, Sisters, Schizo.*

2. The revenge of Nature: *The Birds, Frogs, Night of the Lepus, Day of the Animals, Squirm.*

3. Satanism, diabolic possession, the Antichrist: *Rosemary's Baby, The Exorcist, The Omen, The Possession of Joel Delaney, The Car, God Told Me To* (*Demon*), and *Race with the Devil*, which along with *High Plains Drifter* interestingly connects this motif with the western.

4. The Terrible Child (often closely connected to the above). To the first three films in the third category add: *Night of the Living Dead, Hands of the Ripper, It's Alive, Cathy's Curse*, and also, although the "children" are older, *Carrie* and *The Fury.*

5. Cannibalism: *Night of the Living Dead, Raw Meat, Frightmare, The Texas Chainsaw Massacre, The Hills Have Eyes.*

These apparently heterogeneous motifs are drawn together more closely by a single unifying master figure: the Family. The connection is most tenuous and intermittent in what has proved, on the whole, the least interesting and productive of these concurrent cycles, the revenge of Nature films; but even there, in the more distinguished examples (outstandingly, of course, *The Birds*, but also in *Squirm*), the attacks are linked to, or seem triggered by, familial or sexual tensions. Elsewhere, the connection of the Family to Horror has become overwhelmingly consistent: the psychotic/schizophrenic, the Antichrist and the child-monster are all shown as products of the family, whether the family itself is regarded as guilty (the "psychotic" films) or innocent (*The Omen*).

The cannibalism motif functions in two ways. Occasionally members of a family devour each other (*Night of the Living Dead*, and *Psycho*'s Mrs. Bates is a metaphorical cannibal who swallows up her son). More frequently, cannibalism is the family's means of sustaining or nourishing itself (*The Texas Chainsaw Massacre*, *The Hills Have Eyes*). Pete Walker's revoltingly gruesome and ugly British Horror film *Frightmare* deserves a note here, its central figure being a sweet and gentle old mother who has the one unfortunate flaw of being unable to survive without eating human flesh, a craving guiltily indulged by her devoted husband.

If we see the evolution of the horror film in terms of an inexorable return of the repressed, we will not be surprised by this final emergence of the genre's real significance. This is coupled with a sense that it becomes in the 70s the most important of all American genres and perhaps the most progressive, even in its overt nihilism—in a period of extreme cultural crisis and disintegration, which alone offers the possibility of radical change and rebuilding. To do justice to the lengthy process of that emergence would involve a dual investigation into the evolution of the horror film and into the changing treatment of the family in the Hollywood cinema, an investigation too complex for the framework of this chapter. I shall content myself here with a few further propositions.

1. The family (or marital) comedy in which the 30s and 40s are so rich turns sour (*Father of the Bride*, *The Long Long Trailer*) in the 50s and then peters out; the family horror film starts (not, of course, without precedents) with *Psycho* in 1960, and gains impetus with *Rosemary's Baby* and *Night of the Living Dead* toward the end of the decade.

2. As the horror film enters into its apocalyptic phase, so does the western. *The Wild Bunch* appeared in 1969, the year after *Rosemary's Baby*. And *High Plains Drifter* (1973) fused their basic elements in a western in which the Hero from the Wilderness turns out to be the Devil (or his emissary) and burns the town (American civilization) to the ground after revealing it as fundamentally corrupt and renaming it Hell.

3. The family comedies that seemed so innocent and celebratory in the 30s and 40s appear much less so from the vantage point of the 70s. In my book *Personal Views* I pointed to the remarkable anticipation in *Meet Me in St. Louis* of the Terrible Child of the 70s horror film, especially in the two scenes (Halloween and the destruction of the snow people) in which Margaret O'Brien symbolically kills parent figures. What is symbolic in 1944 becomes literal in *Night of the Living Dead*, where a little girl kills and devours her parents—just as the implications of another anticipatory family film of the early 40s, *Shadow of a Doubt*, become literally enacted in *It's Alive* (the monster as product of the family).

4. The process whereby horror becomes associated with its true milieu, the family, is reflected in its steady geographical progress toward America.

In the 30s, horror is always foreign. The films are set in Paris (*Murders in the Rue Morgue*), middle Europe (*Frankenstein, Dracula*), or on uncharted islands (*Island of Lost Souls, King Kong*); it is always external to Americans, who may be attacked by it physically but remain (superficially, that is) uncontaminated by it morally. The designation of horror as foreign stands even when the normal characters are Europeans. In *Murders in the Rue Morgue*, for example, the young couples, though nominally French, are to all intents and purposes nice clean-living Americans (with American accents); the foreignness of the horror characters is strongly underlined, both by Lugosi's accent and by the fact that nobody knows where he comes from. The foreignness of horror in the 30s can be interpreted in two ways: simply, as a means of disavowal (horror exists, but is un-American), and, more interestingly and unconsciously, as a means of locating horror as a "country of the mind," as a psychological state—the films set on uncharted (and usually nameless) islands lend themselves particularly to interpretation of this kind.

The Val Lewton films of the 40s are in some ways outside the mainstream development of the horror film. They seem to have had little direct influence on its evolution (certain occasional haunted house movies like *The Uninvited* and *The Haunting* may owe something to them), though they strikingly anticipate, by at least two decades, some of the features of the modern horror film. *Cat People* is centered on the repression of female sexuality, in a period where the Monster is almost invariably male and phallic. (Other rare exceptions are the panther-woman of *Island of Lost Souls* and, presumably, *Dracula's Daughter*, which I have not seen.) *The Seventh Victim* has strong undertones of sibling envy and sexual jealousy (the structure and editing of the last scene suggesting that Jacqueline's suicide is willed by her "nice" husband and sister rather than by the "evil" devil-worshipers) as well as containing striking anticipations of *Psycho* and *Rosemary's Baby*; it is also set firmly in America, with no attempt to disown evil as foreign.

Above all, *I Walked with a Zombie* explicitly locates horror at the heart of the family, identifying it with sexual repressiveness in the cause of preserving family unity. *The Seventh Victim* apart, horror is still associated with foreignness; Irena in *Cat People* is from Serbia, *Zombie* is set in the West Indies, *The Leopard Man* takes place in Mexico, etc. Yet the best of the series are concerned with the undermining of such distinctions, with the idea that no one escapes contamination. Accordingly, the concept of the Monster becomes diffused through the film (closely linked to the celebrated Lewton emphasis on atmosphere, rather than overt shock) and no longer identified with a single figure.

I Walked with a Zombie, one of the finest of all American horror films, carries this furthest. It is built on an elaborate set of apparently clear-cut structural oppositions: Canada–West Indies, white-black, light-darkness, life-death, science–black magic, Christianity-Voodoo, conscious-unconscious, etc.—and it proceeds systematically to blur all of them. Jessica is both living and dead; Mrs. Rand mixes medicine, Christianity, and voodoo; the figurehead is both St. Sebastian and a black slave; the black-white opposition is poetically undercut in a complex patterning of dresses and voodoo patches; the motivation of *all* the characters is called into question; the messenger-zombie Carrefour can't be kept out of the white domain.

The 50s science fiction cycles project horror onto either extraterrestrial invaders or mutations from the insect world, but they are usually set in America; even when they are not (*The Thing*), the human characters are American. The films, apparently simple, prove on inspection often very difficult to read. The basic narrative patterns of the horror film repeat themselves obstinately and continue to carry their traditional meanings, but they are encrusted with layers of more transient, topical material. *Them!*, for example, seems to offer three layers of meaning. Explicitly, it sets out to cope with the fear of nuclear energy and atomic experiment: the giant ants are mutants produced by the radioactive aftermath of a bomb explosion; they are eventually destroyed under the guidance of a humane and benevolent science embodied in the comfortingly paternal figure of Edmund Gwenn. The fear of Communist infiltration also seems present, in the emphasis on the ants as a subversive subterranean army and on their elaborate communications system. Yet the film continues to respond convincingly to the application of my basic formula and its Freudian implications. The ants rise up from underground (the unconscious); they kill by holding their victims and injecting into them huge (excessive) quantities of formic acid (the release of repressed phallic energy); and both the opening and the final climax of the film are centered on the destruction, (actual and potential, respectively) of family groups.

* * *

Since *Psycho*, the Hollywood cinema has implicitly recognized Horror as both American and familial—an alternative definition of those "good old values" that the Reagan administration and the 80s Hollywood cinema are trying to convince us are still capable of reaffirmation. One other crucial difference between the classical horror film and the characteristic works of the 70s needs to be noted. The typical ending of the former has the monster destroyed, the young lovers (sometimes the established family) united and safe; the typical ending of the latter insists that the monster cannot be destroyed, that the repressed can never be annihilated. The ending of *It's Alive* can be taken as representative: "Another one's been born in Seattle." In a sense, of course, the monster was always indestructible: Dracula and the Frankenstein monster could always be resurrected for sequels. But only in the 70s was this acknowledged *within the film*: it has become a cliché.

Before examining the most distinguished work of the 70s in the horror genre, I want to consider briefly two key works that offer particularly illuminating contrasts and parallels—*The Omen* and *The Texas Chainsaw Massacre*.

One can partly define the nature of each by means of a chart of oppositions:

The Omen	*The Texas Chainsaw Massacre*
big budget	low budget
glossy production values	raw, unpolished
stars	unknown actors
bourgeois entertainment	non-bourgeois "exploitation"
Good Taste	Bad Taste
"good" family	"bad" family
the Monster imported from Europe	the Monster indigenously American
child destroys parents	parent figures destroy "children"
traditional values reaffirmed	traditional values negated

I don't wish to make any claims for *The Omen* as a work of art: the most one could say is that it achieves a sufficient level of impersonal professional efficiency to ensure that the "kicks" inherent in its scenario are not dulled. (I would add here that my description above of *Massacre* as "raw, unpolished" refers to the overall effect of the film, as it seems to be generally experienced. Its *mise-en-scène* is, without question, everywhere more intelligent, more inventive, more cinematically educated and sophisticated, than that of *The Omen*. Hooper's cinematic intelligence, indeed, becomes more apparent on every viewing, as one gets over the initial traumatizing impact and learns to respect the pervasive felicities of camera placement and movement.)

In obvious ways *The Omen* is old-fashioned, traditional, reactionary: the goodness of the family unit isn't questioned; horror is disowned by having the devil-child, a product of the Old World, unwittingly *adopted* into the American family; the devil-child and his independent female guardian (loosely interpretable in mythic terms as representing child liberation and women's liberation) are regarded as purely evil (oh, for a cinematic Blake to reverse all the terms).

Yet the film remains of great interest. It is about the end of the world, but the world the film envisages ending is very particularly defined within it: the bourgeois capitalist patriarchal Establishment. Here normality—the state, the church, the family—is not merely threatened by the monster, but totally annihilated. The principle of ambivalence must once again be invoked: with a film so shrewdly calculated for box office response, it is legitimate to ask what general satisfaction it offers its audience.

Superficially, it provides the satisfaction of finding traditional values reaffirmed (even if "our" world is ending, it was still the good, right, true one); more deeply, and far more powerfully, under cover of this, it furnishes the satisfaction of the ruthless logic with which the premise is carried through—the supreme satisfaction (masquerading as the final horror) being the revelation, as the camera cranes down in the last shot, that the Devil has been adopted by the President and First Lady of the United States. The translation of the film into Blakean terms is not in fact that difficult: the devil-child is its implicit hero, whose systematic destruction of the bourgeois Establishment the audience follows with a secret relish. *The Omen* would make no sense in a society that was not prepared to enjoy and surreptitiously condone the working out of its own destruction.

As Andrew Britton pointed out to me, *The Omen* and *The Texas Chainsaw Massacre* (together with numerous other recent horror films) have one premise disturbingly in common: annihilation is inevitable, humanity is now completely powerless, no one can do anything to arrest the process. Ideology, that is, can encompass despair, but not the imagining of constructive radical alternatives. *The Omen* invokes ancient prophecy and shows it inexorably fulfilling itself despite all efforts at intervention; we infer near the opening of *Massacre* that the Age of Aquarius whose advent was so recently celebrated in *Hair* has already passed, giving way to the Age of Saturn and universal malevolence. Uncontrol is emphasized throughout the film: not only have the five young victims no control over their destiny, but their slaughterers (variously psychotic and degenerate) keep losing control of themselves and each other.

This is partly, in conjunction with the film's relentless and unremitting intensity, what gives *Massacre* (beyond any other film in my experience) the authentic quality of nightmare. I have had since childhood a recurring nightmare whose pattern seems to be shared by a very large number of people within our culture: I am running away from some vaguely terrible oppressors who are going to do dreadful things to me; I run to a house or a car, etc., for help; I discover its occupants to be precisely the people I am fleeing. This pattern is repeated twice in *Massacre*, where Sally "escapes" from Leatherface first to his own home, then to the service station run by his father.

The application of my formula to *Massacre* produces interesting results. The pattern is still there, as is the significant relationship between the terms, but the definitions of normality and monster have become partly reversed. Here normality is clearly represented by the quasiliberated, permissive young (who still form two couples and a brother-sister family unit, hence reproducing patterns of the past); the monster is the family, one of the great composite monsters of the American cinema, incorporating four characters and three generations, and imagined with an intensity and audacity that far transcend the connotations of the term "exploitation movie." It has a number of important aspects:

1. The image of the Terrible House stems from a long tradition in American and Western capitalist culture (for a fuller treatment of this, see Andrew Britton's mag-

Leatherface, the tormentor . . .

. . . and Sally, the tormented

isterial account of *Mandingo* in *Movie 22*). Traditionally, it represents an extension or objectification of the personalities of the inhabitants. *Massacre* offers two complementary terrible houses: the once imposing, now totally decayed house of Franklyn's and Sally's parents (where we keep *expecting* something appalling to happen), and the more modest, outwardly spruce, inwardly macabre villa of the monstrous family wherein every item of décor is an expression of the characters' degeneracy. The borderline between home and slaughterhouse (between leisure and work) has disappeared—the slaughterhouse has invaded the home, and humanity has begun literally to "prey upon itself, like monsters of the deep." Finally, the terrible house (whether in Poe's *Fall of the House of Usher*, in *Psycho*, in *Mandingo*, or here) signifies the dead weight of the past crushing the life of the younger generation, the future—an idea beautifully realized in the shot that starts on the ominous gray, decayed Franklyn house and tilts down to show Kirk and Pam, dwarfed in long shot, playing and laughing as they run to the swimming hole, and to their doom.

2. The contrast between the two houses underlines the distinction the film makes between the affluent young and the psychotic family, representatives of an exploited and degraded proletariat. Sally's father used to send his cattle to the slaughterhouse of which the family is a product.

3. The all-male family (the grandmother exists only as a decomposing corpse) also derives from a long American tradition, with notable antecedents in Ford's westerns (the Clantons of *My Darling Clementine*, the Cleggses of *Wagonmaster*) and in *Man of the West*. The absence of Woman (conceived of as a civilizing, humanizing influence) deprives the family of its social sense and social meaning while leaving its strength of primitive loyalties largely untouched. In *Massacre*, Woman becomes the ultimate object of the characters' animus (and, I think, the film's, since the sadistic torments visited on Sally go far beyond what is necessary to the narrative).

4. The release of sexuality in the horror film is always presented as perverted, monstrous, and excessive (whether it takes the form of vampires, giant ants, or Mrs. Bates), both the perversion and the excess being the logical outcome of repression. Nowhere is this carried further than in *Massacre*. Here sexuality is totally perverted from its functions, into sadism, violence, and cannibalism. It is striking that no suggestion exists anywhere that Sally is the object of an overtly sexual threat: she is to be tormented, killed, dismembered, eaten, but not raped. Ultimately, the most terrifying thing about the film is its total negativity; the repressed energies—represented most unforgettably by Leatherface and his continuously whirring phallic chainsaw—are presented as irredeemably debased and distorted. It is no accident that the four most intense horror films of the 70s at exploitation level (*Night of the Living Dead*, *Raw Meat*, and *The Hills Have Eyes* being the other three) are all centered on cannibalism, and on the specific notion of present and future (the younger generation) being devoured by the past. Cannibalism represents the ultimate in possessiveness, hence the logical end of

human relations under capitalism. The implication is that "liberation" and permissiveness," as defined within our culture, are at once inadequate and too late—too feeble, too unaware, and too undirected to withstand the legacy of long repression.

5. This implication connects closely with the recurrence of the "double" motif in *Massacre*. The young people are, on the whole, uncharacterized and undifferentiated (the film's energies, as usual in the horror film, are the property of its monsters, the characteristic here surviving the reversal of definitions), but in their midst is Franklyn, who is as grotesque, and almost as psychotic, as his nemesis Leatherface. (The film's refusal to sentimentalize the fact that he is crippled may remind one of the blind beggars of Buñuel.) Franklyn associates himself with the slaughterers by imitating the actions of Leatherface's brother the hitchhiker: he wonders whether he, too, could slice open his own hand, and toys with the idea of actually doing so. (Kirk remarks, "You're as crazy as he is.") Insofar as the other young people are characterized, it is in terms of a pervasive petty malice. Just before Kirk enters the house to meet his death, he teases Pam by dropping into her hand a human tooth he has found on the doorstep; later, Jerry torments Franklyn to the verge of hysteria by playing on his fears that the hitchhiker will pursue and kill him. Franklyn resents being neglected by the others, Sally resents being burdened with him on her vacation. The monstrous cruelties of the slaughterhouse family have their more pallid reflection within normality. (The reflection pattern here is more fully worked out in *The Hills Have Eyes*, with its stranded normal family besieged by its dark mirror image, the terrible shadow-family from the hills, who want to kill the men, rape the women, and eat the baby.)

6. Despite the family's monstrousness, a degree of ambivalence is still present in the response they evoke. This is partly rooted in our sense of them as a *family*. They are held together, and torn apart, by bonds and tensions with which we are all familiar—with which, indeed, we are likely to have grown up. We cannot cleanly dissociate ourselves from them. A sense also grows that they are victims, too—of the slaughter-house environment, of capitalism—*our* victims, in fact.[2] Finally, they manifest a degraded but impressive creativity. The news reporter at the start describes the tableau of decomposing corpses in the graveyard (presumably the work of the hitchhiker, and perhaps a homage to his grandparents: a female corpse is posed in the lap of a male corpse in a hideous parody of domesticity) as "a grisly work of art." The phrase, apt for the film itself, also describes the art works among

2. Anne McCoy, my manuscript editor, provides an interesting comment: "The murders are performed by a family who have been taught to kill. The grandfather (who could dispatch more 'beeves' in five minutes than anyone) is the patriarch of the business. Modern technology has made his method, i.e., hitting cattle over the head with hammers, obsolete. But the training for slaughter is still there and now displaced on to a new 'business' (the barbecue). Could this be a grotesque comment on Vietnam (returning vets, trained to kill, are filled with guilt, are displaced, sometimes act violently), as well as on the bad fruits of 'progress'?"

which the family live, some of which achieve a kind of hideous aesthetic beauty: the light bulb held up by a human hand, the sofa constructed out of human and animal bones, surmounted by ornamental skulls, the hanging lamp over the dining table that appears to be a shrunken human head. The film's monsters do not lack that characteristically human quality, an aesthetic sense, however perverted its form; they also waste nothing, a lesson we are all taught as children.

7. Central to the film—and centered on its monstrous family—is the sense of grotesque comedy, which in no way diminishes but rather intensifies its nightmare horror: Leatherface chasing Sally with the chain-saw, unable to stop and turn, skidding, wheeling, like an animated character in a cartoon; the father's response to Leatherface's devastations, which by that time include four murders and the prolonged terrorization of the heroine ("Look what your brother did to that door"); Leatherface dressed up in jacket and tie and fresh black wig for formal dinner with Grandpa; the macabre farce of Grandpa's repeated failures to kill Sally with the hammer. The film's sense of fundamental horror is closely allied to a sense of the fundamentally absurd. The family, after all, only carries to its logical conclusion the basic, though unstated, tenet of capitalism, that people have the right to live off other people. In twentieth-century art, the sense of the absurd is always closely linked to total despair (Beckett and Ionesco, for instance). The fusion of nightmare and absurdity is carried even further in *Death Trap* (aka *Eaten Alive*), a film that confirms that the creative impulse in Hooper's work is centered on his monsters (here, the grotesque and pathetic Neville Brand) and is essentially nihilistic.

The Texas Chainsaw Massacre, unlike *The Omen*, achieves the force of authentic art.[3] It is profoundly disturbing and intensely personal, yet at the same time far more than personal, as the general response it has evoked demonstrates. As a collective nightmare it brings to a focus a spirit of negativity, an undifferentiated lust for destruction, that seems to lie not far below the surface of the modern collective consciousness. Watching it recently with a large, half-stoned youth audience who cheered and applauded every one of Leatherface's outrages against their representatives on the screen was a terrifying experience. It must not be seen as an isolated phenomenon: it expresses, with unique force and intensity, at least one important aspect of what the horror film has come to signify—the sense of a civilization condemning itself, through its popular culture, to ultimate disintegration, and ambivalently (with the simultaneous horror/wish-fulfillment of nightmare) celebrating the fact. We must not, of course, see that as the last word.[4]

3. For a far less sympathetic reading of the film, see Andrew Britton's essay "The Devil, Probably: The Symbolism of Evil" in *The American Nightmare* (edited by Lippe and Wood and available from the Canadian Film Institute, Ottawa).

4. Since this was written, D. N. Rodowick's excellent analysis of *The Hills Have Eyes* has appeared in Barry K. Grant's anthology on the horror film, *Planks of Reason* (Metuchen, N.J., and London: Scarecrow Press, 1984).

6.

Normality and Monsters

THE FILMS OF LARRY COHEN AND GEORGE ROMERO

Only the major artist—or the incorrigibly obsessive one, which sometimes amounts to the same thing—is capable of standing against the flow of his period (with the concomitant dangers of isolation, of becoming fixed in an embattled position): a truism greatly compounded by the commercial nature of cinema and the problems of financing and distribution. The minor talent thrives only when the climate is congenial, when the tradition within which it operates is nourished into vigorous growth from sources within the culture. Such, precisely, is the case with the 70s horror film: within the period, within the genre, a remarkable number of talents were able to produce work of vitality, force and complexity. None has convincingly survived the retrenchments of the 80s. The 70s crisis in ideological confidence temporarily released our culture's monsters from the shackles of repression. The interesting horror films of the period, without a single exception, are characterized by the recognition not only that the monster is the product of normality, but that it is no longer possible to view normality itself as other than monstrous. I examine here the work of the two directors who produced the most consistent and impressive bodies of work, then consider briefly a number of miscellaneous horror films from the same period. What is perhaps the most brilliant of all 70s horror films—De Palma's *Sisters*—must wait till the next chapter.

LARRY COHEN: WORLD OF GODS AND MONSTERS

An attempt to define Cohen's work can profitably begin by comparing it with De Palma's; their careers to date offer remarkable parallels that serve to illuminate the differences. In their early works both directors use blacks as a threat to white supremacy, a variant on the return of the repressed theme: De Palma in the extraordinary "Be Black, Baby" section of *Hi, Mom!* (and, although not presented as a threat, Philip in *Sisters* is relevant here); Cohen in *Black Caesar, Hell Up in Harlem*, and, very impressively, in *Bone*. Both directors attempted overtly experimental works early in their careers, disrupting the conventions of realist narrative (*Greetings, Hi Mom!; Bone*). Both have returned repeatedly to the horror film (*Sisters, Carrie, The Fury, It's Alive, God Told Me To, It Lives Again*). Both have abandoned their early experimentalism, temporarily at least, to express an obviously genuine (not merely commercial) allegiance to the Hollywood tradition. Thus De Palma remade *Phantom of the Opera* as *Phantom of the Paradise, Psycho* as *Sisters, Vertigo* as *Obsession*, in each case producing a valid variation rather than imitation. In the case of Cohen, the allegiance is expressed less specifically (though *Black Caesar* very consciously transposes the structure of the 30s gangster film, drawing particularly on *Little Caesar* and *Scarface*) but seems even stronger.

One form it takes is Cohen's extensive use of Hollywood old-timers: Sylvia Sidney and Sam Levene in *God Told Me To* and most of the cast of *The Private Files of J. Edgar Hoover* (Broderick Crawford, Dan Dailey, Celeste Holm, June Havoc, Jose Ferrer). The choice of Miklos Rozsa to score *Hoover* is also relevant here, Cohen using his "stirring" final music with splendid irony.

The most obvious link is the common debt to Alfred Hitchcock, who, with *Shadow of a Doubt, Psycho, The Birds*, and *Marnie*, might reasonably be called the father of the modern horror film. Here one should include Tobe Hooper as well: the buildup to the first killing in *The Texas Chainsaw Massacre* is worthy, shot by shot, of the Master in the sophistication of its suspense devices, its play with suggestion, expectation, relaxation, and the subtle discrepancies between the characters' awareness and the audience's. The influence is most obvious in De Palma because deliberately flaunted, an aspect of the signified, but it is clear enough in Cohen, in the overt homage of the staircase assault in *God Told Me To* and more pervasively in the suspense techniques, including subjective camera, of *It's Alive*. Most specifically, both directors used Bernard Herrmann, who composed the scores for *Sisters, Obsession*, and *It's Alive*, and to whom *God Told Me To* is dedicated; he also received a posthumous credit for the score of *It Lives Again*.

De Palma's work has achieved intermittent commercial success and widespread (though still insufficient) critical attention; Cohen's has achieved neither. *It's Alive* did well enough at the box office, but *Bone, God Told Me To* and *Hoover*—all very difficult box office propositions requiring careful and intelligent handling—were thrown away. It would be an understatement to say that Cohen's work is not highly regarded by the bourgeois press: in general, it is ignored; when noticed, vilified. A *Film Comment* article summarily dismissed *It's Alive* as a "*Rosemary's Baby/Exorcist* rip-off" (it seems to me more intelligent than either, and owes them about as much as *Rio Bravo* owes *High Noon*, the relationship being more of contradiction than influence). No one has bothered to examine Cohen's work closely enough to recognize its difficulty—difficulty which, although the films are frequently incoherent, can never be reduced to a simple matter of confusion. Cohen has not achieved the brilliance or the coherence of *Sisters*, but his work in the 70s strikes me as more consistent, and more consistently satisfying, than De Palma's in the same period.

The word "brilliance" is capable of carrying a hint of pejorative overtones. *Carrie* and *The Fury* are also brilliant (indeed, more insistently so than *Sisters*), and aroused a fear (subsequently neither confirmed nor totally assuaged) that the showman in De Palma was going to take over completely, that the interest of his films, the complexity and urgency of signification, was becoming submerged beneath the desire to dazzle with an ever more flamboyant rhetoric and effects out of all proportion to meaning. Cohen, on the other hand, never attracts attention to himself; his work relates back beyond the director-as-superstar era to the classical Hollywood tradition of directorial self-effacement. I would find it difficult to describe a Cohen visual style that would clearly distinguish his work from the mainstream of contemporary cinema; like a Hawks or a McCarey, he has been content to work within the anonymity of generally accepted stylistic-technical procedures.

There is a problem here, of course: since the days of Hawks and McCarey those procedures have changed drastically, and one can argue that the tradition of filmmaking at the level of basic professionalism has become increasingly debased. The reasons for the sketchiness and sense of haste of Cohen's films are probably complex, such characteristics not to be accounted for simply in economic terms of low budgets and short shooting schedules, relevant as such conditions clearly are. The realization of the films, or more precisely, their unrealized quality, sometimes testifies to bad habits acquired from television and never quite cast off (useful, no doubt, in the saving of time and money). The conventional, at times perfunctory, ping-pong cross-cutting of dialogue scenes—Hitchcock's phrase "photographs of people talking" comes to mind—suggests a filmmaker whose ambitions don't entirely transcend expectations of casual viewing and immediate disposability (the almost total lack of critical recognition—of any interested and considered inquiry into what the films are doing—together with the absence of any sustained commercial success, is not exactly conducive to higher ambitions). It may be, however, that these are the conditions in which Cohen operates most spontaneously and effectively—the urgency and intensity of the films may be partly dependent on the speed with which they are tossed off (I once heard Cohen speculate about the film he would make with the budget De Palma had for *The Fury*. "Or rather," he added, "the three or four films"). The frequent impression of something hastily slapped together combines with Cohen's tendency to go for "impact" (the fondness for the wide-angle lens, choppy editing) to evoke—when the films are noticed at all—the term "schlock," one of those expressive but extremely ill-defined terms of abuse coined by the bourgeois press to indicate a *type* of film it considers beneath its level of "educated" taste. Thus the conceptual level of Cohen's work—the level on which it is most impressive and challenging—is ignored, the term "schlock" actually denying its existence.

Yet this is already to concede too much and to simplify a complex issue. Since a film consists only of sounds and images, some such formula as "bad films with good ideas" simply will not do: there is no conceptual level that is not at least partly realized through the organization of sounds and images. Rough and hasty as they may often appear, Cohen's films abound in ideas that are up there on the screen, dramatized in action and dialogue, in a *mise-en-scène* whose lack of refinement is the corollary of its energy and inventiveness. One can point, particularly, to the self-evident excellence with actors: outstanding performances are as much the rule in Cohen's work as they are the exception in Romero's. The urgency and intensity I noted as prime characteristics are projected through the performances of, for example, John Ryan and Sharon Farrell in *It's Alive*, Kathleen Lloyd and Frederic Forrest in the sequel, and Michael Moriarty in *Q*. Beyond that, the roughness and the emphasis on impact tend to conceal effects that are both complex and subtle. A close examination of the opening sequences of *It's Alive* will convincingly suggest the richness of Cohen's work at its best, as well as its centrality to the American tradition; it will also lead us directly into major components of the Cohen thematic.

The exposition divides into four segments (according to location): the home (Lenore is awakened by labor pangs, preparations for the hospital); the car (the drive to the hospital, leaving Chris at Charlie's house *en route*); the hospital (reception desk, corridors, Lenore's room); the hospital (waiting room with Frank and the other expectant fathers).

The first segment is built on a disturbing tension between presentation and enacted content. The introductory pan across the dark overhang of a roof, dissolving to a darkened bedroom, accompanied by ominous music, immediately evokes menace and foreboding; what we are shown is a seemingly happy, united, loving family, eager for the birth of the new child. Various stylistic features intensify the uneasiness: the edgy, elliptical editing, the low-angle hand-held tracking shot that rapidly follows the couple down a darkened hallway. But it swiftly becomes clear that this is not a matter of imposing an arbitrary ominousness on perfectly innocent subject matter, a mere business of signaling "This is a horror movie, something terrible is going to happen": a number of details relate the edginess to the familial relationship.

Lenore's attitude throughout is apologetic. We see that she is in considerable pain, but we also see her minimizing this for Frank. Even when she subsequently admits that "this one feels different," her concern seems more for the anxiety she may cause her husband than for her own physical pain. Frank's method of awakening his son—by applying the family cat to his neck—is at least curious: apparently humorous and affectionate, it also suggests aggression. The disturbing effect of the moment receives its confirmation when, in her hospital bed, Lenore expresses her anxiety lest Frank feel "tied down" again, as he did when they had Chris; we also learn that the couple (on the surface so enthusiastic about the new arrival) considered abortion. Eleven years have passed since the birth of their first child. Chris' room is decorated with wallpaper redolent of the hippy period, the time, presumably, of Frank and Lenore's early married life and the birth of Chris: the dominant motif is the word LOVE and its symbol. The detail of décor serves a dual function—the ironic contrast between flower child freedom and suburban domesticity; the need to display, to 'advertise', love, that actually calls its reality into question. Frank is in Public Relations, Lenore is the perfect bourgeois wife/mother. Frank stands in the doorway of the newly decorated nursery, surveying it with the air of a proprietor. The camera zooms out to reveal that it is all blue. The moment is answered in the second segment, when Lenore (explaining to her son that he can't accompany her to the hospital) tells Chris that they'll phone him and tell him whether he has "a baby *sister* or a baby brother," the unexpected order subtly pointed up in Sharon Farrell's delivery of the line. The suggestion is that the ideal American couple—successful businessman, devoted housewife/mother, seemingly delighted with their ideal arrangement—are in fact profoundly incompatible: what but a "monster" could such a union ultimately produce?

Clearly, the "wandering versus settling antinomy" that Peter Wollen found central to the work of Ford is central to much more: it is one of the structuring tensions within American ideology. It produces the ideal male as the wanderer/adventurer, the ideal female as housewife/mother, taught to build precisely that 'home' (literal and metaphorical) within which the man will feel trapped. In the car, a chance remark of Chris sparks off his father's imitation of Walter Brennan in *Red River*, an expression of nostalgia for the cattle drives and open prairies of the American past. Whatever the moment's origin (one's impression is of a John Ryan improvisation), its inclusion in the film represents a brilliant extension of meaning into reaches of genre and ideology: the affluent, outwardly complacent but inwardly tense and dissatisfied, nuclear family of the 70s related suddenly to the western, the pioneers, and the history/mythology of a heroic past of which they are the present product. During the same segment the freedom/entrapment opposition gets further ramification through the introduction of Charlie, the friend of the family with whom Chris is to stay. Chris is to feel sorry for Charlie because his marriage has broken up and he only sees his kids on weekends: the detail suggests an environment in which the unbroken family is no longer necessarily the norm, with the added irony that poor Charlie here and on subsequent appearances, seems consistently and spontaneously cheerful, in contrast to the strained cheerfulness of Frank and Lenore. The contrast confirms the impression of a marriage held together more by determination and willpower than by genuine desire, the strength of the film lying in the couple's representativeness (we are never encouraged to view them as monstrous *individuals*, the tension being firmly presented as arising from social structures and institutions, from ideological assumptions rather than from specific incompatibilities of character).

Nostalgia for a simpler, more primitive, less constricting past is also suggested in the third segment by Frank's exchange with the Gaelic speaking nurse about "the wee cuddies and the wee cubs." Again, one has the impression of a detail that developed spontaneously during shooting. Cohen's readiness to use such moments is an aspect of the surface aliveness of his films; it also adds to their wealth of connotation, in this case associating babies with the young of animals, taking up the animal imagery introduced with the cat (first segment) and developed in the reference to the puppy Chris has been promised as his compensation for the appearance of a sibling (second segment) that will culminate in the birth of the monstrous baby (explicitly referred to as an "animal").

The second part of the third segment (in Lenore's room, before she is taken to the delivery room) makes the familial tension explicit in ways already suggested (Lenore's anxiety lest Frank feel "tied down" again as he did with Chris, the hint that they had considered abortion). The explicitness arises naturally out of the dramatic situation (Lenore frightened by the pain she is experiencing and by her sense that "this one is *different*," her pent-up anxieties suddenly released), and its effect is to reinforce our sense of prior suppression—that in this seemingly warm, close, openly affectionate family, difficult issues are not discussed, anxieties never voiced except *in extremis*.

The most obvious function of the fourth segment (the waiting room) is to suggest (in anticipation) possible explanations for the monstrous baby: pollution and the indiscriminate use of chemicals (a new roach-killer has produced a new, more impregnably immune breed of roaches). Another possible explanation will be offered later: the irresponsible development of inadequately tested medication, birth-control pills, etc. But the "explanations" never get beyond suggestion: none is ever identified as the cause. The effect is not at all to limit the meaning of the baby, but rather to extend it: if it is the product of the contemporary nuclear family, it is also the product of a whole civilization characterized by various forms of greed and irresponsibility, a civilization for which Frank (as public relations man) is apologist and advertiser.

The density of "thinking" (whether conscious or unconscious, for clearly the unconscious thinks)—the network of interrelated connotations—that characterizes this opening is not sustained throughout the film. Passages in the middle seem comparatively thin and stretched, though any shortcomings are redeemed by the film's magnificent last twenty minutes, which project an anguish (apparently unnoticed by most critics) associated more with an Ingmar Bergman movie than with a "schlock" horror film. (Much work needs to be done on the ways in which packaging predetermines response: reviewers generally seem to see what they have been led to expect to see, whether or not it corresponds to what is actually before their eyes.) A further explanation exists beyond low budgets and temperamental urgency for Cohen's failure, to date, to produce a wholly satisfying, a wholly convincing movie: that offered in chapter 4 to explain the characteristic incoherence of the most interesting 70s films, and of particular relevance to the horror genre at this stage of its evolution. The "thinking" of the films can lead logically only in one direction, toward a radical and revolutionary position in relation to the dominant ideological norms and the institutions that embody them, and such a position is incompatible with any definable position within mainstream cinema (or even on its exploitation fringes); it is also incompatible with any degree of comfort or security within the dominant culture. The areas of disturbance exposed in the first minutes of *It's Alive*—disturbance about heterosexual relations, male/female gender roles, the family, the contemporary development of capitalism, its abuse of technology, its indifference to the pollution of the environment, its crass materialism, callousness, and greed—encompass the entire structure of our civilization, from the corporation to the individual, and the film sees that structure as producing nothing but a monstrosity.

✳ ✳ ✳

Just as the thematic structure of the horror film cannot be restricted purely to that genre (in general, genres can be clearly distinguished only in terms of their more superficial, iconographic elements), so the thematic structure of Cohen's work crosses generic boundaries, encompassing besides the horror film the "blaxploitation" movie (*Black Caesar*), the political biography (*The Private Files of J. Edgar Hoover*), and the crazy comedy (*Full Moon High*). I shall therefore not restrict the following analysis to Cohen's horror films.

Three closely interconnected thematic figures recur throughout Cohen's works and are particularly relevant to a definition of its disturbance.

1. *Undercutting the Protagonist as Hero.* Insofar as we identify ('sympathize' might be a better word here) with Cohen's male protagonists, it is in order to discover with them how wrong they have been. Frank in *It's Alive* is probably the closest to a traditional identification figure in Cohen's work, and what we share with him is the agonizing movement from repudiation of his child to acceptance of it, though too late to save its life. The films never offer us a 'correct' position dramatized within the action in relation to its conflicts. The most intellectually ambitious of Cohen's works—*Bone, God Told Me To, Hoover*—carry this furthest. The resolution of each film leaves a sense of dissatisfaction, uncertainty, loss. There is never a suggestion that things can be put right and solutions found *within the system*; the conflicts are presented as inherent in that system—fundamental and unresolvable.

2. *The Double.* What I have suggested is the privileged form of the "return of the repressed" is central to the structure of Cohen's work. One can offer a basic formula, though the films cannot be reduced to mere reiterations of it: the protagonist learns to recognize (or at the very least is haunted by a suspicion of) his identity with the figure he is committed to destroying. Again, *It's Alive* provides a particularly clear instance. The exclamatory title, of course, echoes through the horror film, but its strongest association, and presumably its source in the sound film, is James Whale's *Frankenstein.* The association is confirmed by the protagonist's name, Frank, and its significance is made explicit in his dialogue with medical authorities around the film's midpoint. Frank reminisces that when he was a child he thought "Frankenstein" was the name of the monster, not of its creator, and adds "Somehow the identities get all mixed up, don't they?"—a line that might stand as epigraph for all Cohen's films to date. Which is more monstrous, the murderous child or the father who created it and now, like Frankenstein, wants to destroy it? And are parent and offspring clearly distinguishable?–is the child not recognizable as the embodiment of the father's repressed rage and frustration, his constrained energies? Similarly, *God Told Me To* moves toward the protagonist's recognition that the beautiful, destructive "god," who (through his possessed agents) is terrorizing the city, is his brother and that he himself possesses the same powers, though repressed by his Catholic upbringing. And there is the protagonist of *Black Caesar,* who blacks with boot polish the face of the policeman who once humiliated him, before killing him, or Hoover, forever haunted by Dillinger (for whose death he was responsible, but whom he wanted to kill in person), preserving his deathmask and collecting his relics.

3. *Parents and Children.* This most problematic aspect of Cohen's work may also be the chief source of its energy. *It's Alive* clearly depicts its monstrous baby as the logical product of the tensions within the modern nuclear family, its crisis of gender roles. But what are we to make of the fact that the monster's dominant motivation is to *find* its family and to be accepted into it? On the one hand, the implication seems to be that the family must recognize and accept what they have produced, that they must account for themselves and for their own monstrousness; on the other, the film seems posited on a nostalgia for traditional family values. The tension seems at the heart of the confusion in Cohen's work. Certainly, one of the threads connecting some extremely disparate movies is the monstrous child's striving for recognition by its parents, and the impossibility of such recognition within existing familial codes and structures. Thus we have the son in *Bone* (alleged by his parents to be a Vietnam prisoner of war and actually in a Spanish jail for dope smuggling, a fate from which the parents have done nothing to extricate him) going into peels of uncontrollable laughter as, thousands of miles away, his mother beats his father to death with her handbag; thus we have "Black Caesar" motivated by an obsessive desire for parental recognition while further alienating both father and

Father and Sons: John Ryan (*right*) in *It's Alive*

mother by his every action; thus we have Hoover's relationship with his mother, and the painful scene in which the protagonist of *God Told Me To* tries to gain recognition from *his*, and is hysterically repudiated. Despite the frequent dominance of the father/son relationship, the core of the problem seems to lie in Cohen's (and our culture's) confused and ambivalent attitude to motherhood.

I want to close this section by considering what seem to me Cohen's most impressive films to date (one a horror film, the other not), which stand in one sense at opposite ends of the spectrum as, respectively, his least and most realized works: *God Told Me To* and *The Private Files of J. Edgar Hoover*.

God Told Me To remains at once one of Cohen's most fascinating works and incoherent to the point of unreadability. Again, part of the problem may be practical: the film's ambitions palpably demanded a far higher budget and longer shooting schedule, a fact more obvious here than in any other of his works. Yet it is at the conceptual level that the film's fascination and incoherence both lie. Indeed, it is organized (if that is the word) around the conflict between Cohen's potential radicalism and his fundamental inability to trust it or commit himself to it: at least that is the only way I can make sense of any kind out of its dissonances and contradictions, the sense being a matter not of rendering the film coherent but of accounting for its incoherence. As it has had little exposure (either under its original title or its alternative title, *Demon*), I offer a brief plot summary.

A police detective (Tony Lo Bianco), reared a strict Catholic but with both a wife (Sandy Dennis) and a lover (Deborah Raffin), investigates a series of apparently random and motiveless killings by various assassins, tracing them to the inspiration of a young god, born of a human virgin impregnated by light from a spacecraft. He also discovers, however, that he is himself another such god, though in him the supernatural force has been repressed by his orthodox Catholic upbringing. He kills (or seems to kill) his unrepressed 'brother', and ends convicted of murder, repeating as an explanation of his motive the phrase used earlier by each of the assassins: "God Told Me To."

The god is conceived as both beautiful and vicious. Like the snake of D. H. Lawrence's famous poem, he is associated with danger, energy, and fire—with forces that society cannot encompass and therefore decrees must be destroyed. His disruption of the social order is arbitrary, involving a series of meaningless sniper-killings, the devastating of the St. Patrick's Day Parade, and the annihilation of a family by its father; yet the imagery associated with him (the dance of light and flame) gives him stronger positive connotations than any other manifestation of the return of the repressed in Cohen's work, or indeed in any other contemporary horror film.

Crucial to the film is the god's dissolution of sexual differentiation: apparently male, he has a vagina, and invites the protagonist to father their child. The new world he envisages is, by implication, a world in which the division of sexual roles will cease to exist. What is proposed is no less than the overthrow of the entire structure of patriarchal ideology. The two god-inspired assassins whom the film presents in any detail are strongly characterized in terms of sexual ambiguity: the first (played by the actor who originated the role of the homosexual in *A Chorus Line*) is clearly meant to be taken as gay; the other (the young father who has murdered his wife and children) is also given culturally recognizable signifiers of gayness. Against all this is set the tangle and misery of the protagonist's sexual life in Judeo-Christian culture, characterized by possessiveness, secrecy, deception, and denial. Significantly, what first arouses him to open violence is the young father's sense of release and happiness after he has destroyed his family.

Like Cohen's other films, *God Told Me To* proposes no solution. If its god was ever pure, his purity has been corrupted through incarnation in human flesh and the agents he is forced to use (the disciples are businessmen and bureaucrats, the possessed executants are merely destructive). Yet, unlike the use of Catholicism in *The Exorcist*, the restoration of repression at the end of the film is not allowed to carry any positive force, uplift, or satisfaction—only a wry irony. It is not even certain that the god is dead: the narrative says he is; the images, editing and implications question it. We last see him (after he appears to have been buried in the collapse of a derelict building) rising up in flames, his native element. Nothing clearly connects the protagonist to the god's destruction, so we must assume that his conviction for murder rests on his own confession; we may infer that he has confessed in order to reassure himself that his antagonist-brother-double is really dead. In fact, the ending is left sufficiently open for one to wonder whether, had the film achieved any commercial success, Cohen would have written and directed a sequel to it rather than to *It's Alive*. Certainly, the issues it opens up are both immense and profound, and absolutely central to our culture and its future development. Perhaps, instead of regretting the film's confusion, we should celebrate its existence, the fact that Cohen had the audacity and partial freedom to imagine it at all.

The Private Files of J. Edgar Hoover is perhaps the most intelligent film about American politics ever to come out of Hollywood. I cannot speak for its historical accuracy or for the justice of its speculative audacities: that Clyde Tolson was Deep Throat; that Hoover may have been implicated in the assassination of Bobby Kennedy—a possibility, the film, keeping just the safe side of libel, allows us to infer rather than states. But the film would be no less intelligent were its entire structure fictional. It is a question, not of whether what the spectator sees on the screen is "objective truth," but of the relationship between the spectator and narrative.

The revealing comparison is with *All the President's Men*. The overall effect of Alan Pakula's film is complicated by the pervasive urban paranoia of *film noir*, a dominant element that makes the film's relationship to Pakula's *The Parallax View* less clearly one of simple contrast than the director seems to have intended. Nevertheless, it offers its audiences satisfactions that Cohen's film rigorously eschews, notably in its suspense-thriller format and its hero identification figures. *Hoover* offers no equivalent for Robert Redford and Dustin Hoffman; no heroes appear on whom we can rely to have everything put right at the end. No "correct" position is dramatized in the film with which the spectator might identify, by which he might be reassured. As there is no hero to uncover, be threatened by, and finally rectify the corruption, there can be no suspense, only analysis. Beside the obvious thriller brilliance of *All the President's Men*, the sobriety and detachment of *Hoover* might be mistaken for flatness. In fact, the narrative's ellipses and juxtapositions demand a continual activity on the part of the spectator, very different from, and incompatible with, the excitements of "What happens next?"

In the famous *Cahiers du Cinéma* analysis of *Young Mr. Lincoln*,[1] the editors claimed that the film eventually produces Lincoln as a "monster," both castrated and castrating. What is arguably implicit (or repressed) in John Ford's film is the explicit subject of Cohen's; applied to his Hoover, the *Cahiers* description is exact, word for word. Two points are made about the purity which Hoover attempts to bring to his work: that it is at all stages compromised by the corruptions of the system, and that it is itself artificial, an act of will growing out of a denial of the body. The film translates into overtly political terms the dialectic of its predecessors: nei-

1. The article first appeared in English in *Screen* (Autumn 1972); it is reprinted in Bill Nichols, ed., *Movies and Methods*, pp. 493–529 (Berkeley: University of California Press, 1976).

ther the purity nor the corruption is sanctioned; they are presented as two aspects of the same sickness. As in *It's Alive*, the monster is the logical product of the capitalist system.

Here, the "double" motif is made verbally explicit in the scene with Florence Hollister (Celeste Holm). Hoover has been responsible for the death of John Dillinger (whom he wanted to kill in person), and has since obsessively preserved his death mask and collected relics. Mrs. Hollister tells Hoover that he would secretly like to *be* Dillinger, and the context links this to Hoover's sexual repression. Having destroyed Dillinger, Hoover has internalized his violence, converting it into a repressive, castrating morality.

Essential to the repression theme is the film's treatment of Hoover's alleged homosexuality and his relationship with Clyde Tolson The presentation of Hoover-as-monster rests on the notion that his repression is total, that he is incapable of acknowledging a sexual response to anyone, male or female. The desolate little scene where he sits, in semidarkness and longshot, listening to a tape of erotic loveplay of a politician he has bugged, suggests less a vicarious satisfaction than his sense of exclusion from an aspect of life as meaningless to him as a foreign language. Elsewhere, he can innocently reminisce about the time when Bobby Kennedy, as a child, sat on his lap and asked if he was "packing a gun"; for the audience, the line evokes Mae West, yet it is clear that for Hoover the obvious implication (that the boy's proximity had given him an erection) simply does not exist.

The Tolson-Hoover relationship is treated with great delicacy and precision; out of it develops the film's culminating irony. Hoover wants publicly to repudiate the press's "slanders"; Tolson quietly advises him just to leave things alone. Tolson, in other words, is perfectly aware of what Hoover can never face: the real nature of their relationship. For a time it looks as if the film is going to produce Rip Torn as the politically aware (and heterosexual) hero who sets things right; but it is Tolson who acquires the private files, in his determination to vindicate his friend, after which the film is content enigmatically to inform us that Watergate happened a year later and Hoover couldn't have done a better job.

The film's point is that Watergate was made possible, not by the altruistic endeavors of a couple of heroic seekers after truth, but by the unfulfilled personal commitment of one man to another. Hoover's one pure achievement, that is, grows inadvertently and apolitically, after his death, out of a relationship he could never even recognize for what it was. If the film celebrates anyone it is Tolson, but he is scarcely presented as any kind of answer. *All the President's Men* communicates (at least on the surface level) that the System may be liable to corruption but will always right itself; *Hoover* views such a belief with extreme skepticism. It is scarcely surprising that, in Cohen's own words, "We soon found ourselves besieged on all sides with no political group to spring to our defense."

TESTING THE LIMITS

As a transition from Cohen to Romero I want briefly to consider three films—more than coincidentally, perhaps, they appeared within a year of each other, at that moment of ideological hesitation when the 70s became the 80s—that dramatize the essential dilemma of the horror genre. That dilemma, always present embryonically, only became manifest in the 70s, as the implications of the monster/normality dialectic became more and more explicit and inescapable. It can be expressed quite simply in a series of interrelated questions: Can the genre survive the recognition that the monster is its real hero? If the "return of the repressed" is conceived in positive terms, what happens to "horror"? And is such a positive conception logically possible? These questions are not trivial, and have ramifications far beyond the confines of a movie genre: the future of our civilization may depend upon the answer to the third.

The three films are Cohen's *It's Alive II* (*It Lives Again*), Romero's *Martin* and John Badham's *Dracula*. It is significant that all three are at once extremely interesting and extremely unsatisfactory, the interest lying in the ultimate failure as much as in the partial success. Each approaches the dilemma quite differently and attempts a quite different resolution, but they have certain basic characteristics in common. In all three, the audience is encouraged to hope for the monster's survival and possible triumph; in all three, normality is subjected to astringent criticism, seen as characterized by repression, tension, and (especially in *Martin*) misery; in all three, this critique is centered on male/female relations and gender roles; in all three, the climactic horror is the destruction of the monster, presented as more appalling than anything the monster has done.

The problem with *Martin* is that it evades the dilemma rather than resolving it: Its eponymous hero isn't really a monster, but a social misfit who has been led to *believe* he is a monster. One senses throughout the film a hesitation on Romero's part as to whether he wanted to make a horror film at all. His essential theme—a downtrodden boy struggling to achieve a sense of identity and self-worth within a totally debased, repressive and drably materialistic social milieu—lends itself most obviously to the form of realist drama. The question is, I think, one of genuine hesitation rather than commercial compromise, Romero's interest in the horror genre and his desire to extend its boundaries not being in doubt. The hesitation confuses the depiction of Martin himself and his relationship to Tata Cuda, the repressive father figure: Does his obsession with drinking blood represent the return of repressed energies, or is it merely a fantasy that has been imposed on him? The later stages of the narrative actually suggest that, by learning to have sexual intercourse instead of sucking blood, Martin can be "saved" for normality: we are not that far from the *reductio ad absurdum* enacted long before in *House of Dracula*, where the Wolf Man's lycanthropy is cured by psychoanalysis and the love of a good woman

Reinterpreting the Vampire

(*above*)
Frank Langella in *Dracula*

(*left*)
John Amplas in *Martin*

(a more generous comparison would be with Chabrol's *Le Boucher*). While normality has been demolished in the film with a ruthlessness rare in American commercial cinema, the energies that might overthrow or transcend it receive only the vaguest and most ambiguous embodiment: Martin's fantasies are mere fantasies, carrying no positive connotations.

Where *Martin* reduces vampire mythology to a cloak, makeup and imitation fangs ("You see?—there is no magic"), Badham's *Dracula* reverts to what is, as far as the cinema is concerned, its effective source in Bram Stoker's novel, and attempts to transform its sense while retaining its potency. Badham's movie has been gravely underestimated, by critics and public alike: in many ways it is quite remarkable, and as an interpretation of the novel extremely audacious. *Sight and Sound*, in one of its inimitable capsule reviews, went so far as to call it a straightforward adaptation than did not try to interpret, a startling critical aberration: For a start, this appears to be the first Dracula movie with a happy ending (of sorts), and the first in which it is van Helsing, not Dracula, who is transfixed through the heart with a stake (minor details which presumably escaped the *Sight and Sound* reviewer). Its key line is perhaps van Helsing's earlier "If we are defeated, then there is no God"; they are defeated.

The film is very much preoccupied, in fact, with the overthrow of patriarchy, in the form of the Father, van Helsing, of whom God the Father is but an extension. The ending is not merely the triumph of Dracula (who, progressively undaunted by garlic and crucifixes in the course of the film, finally flies off, burned, battered, but still alive and strong, into the sunlight) but of Oedipus, who, having carried off the woman, kills the father and flies away. The film makes clear that Lucy is still his, even though she cannot join him until the hypothetical sequel (which, in view of the poor box office response, will now never get made). Indeed, the editing suggests quite strongly that it is Lucy who gives Dracula the strength to escape. It would be nice simply to welcome the film on those terms and leave it at that. Unfortunately, the matter is not so clear-cut, and the film seems to me, though very interesting and often moving, severely flawed, compromised and problematic. Its chief effect, perhaps, is to remind us that we live in an age, not of liberation, but of pseudo-liberation.

As in the original novel and its most distinguished cinematic adaptation, Murnau's *Nosferatu*, the film's problems are centered on the woman, Lucy (the superb Kate Nelligan), and on the difficulties of building a positive interpretation on foundations that obstinately retain many of their original connotations of evil. The result is a film both confused and confusing. In response to our popular contemporary notions of feminism, Lucy's strength and activeness are strikingly emphasized and contrasted with Mina's weakness, childishness and passivity. Dracula insists that Lucy come to him of her free choice: the film makes clear that he deliberately abstains from exerting any supernatural or hypnotic power over her, as he did over Mina. The film thus ties itself in knots in first presenting Lucy as a liberated woman and then asserting that a liberated woman would freely choose to surrender herself to (of all people) Dracula. Badham wants to present the Dracula/Lucy relationship in terms of romantic passion, a passion seen as transcending everyday existence; yet he cannot free the material of the paraphernalia of Dracula mythology, and with it the notion of vampirism as evil. With its romantic love scenes, on the one hand, and the imagery that associates both Dracula and Lucy with spiders, on the other, the film never resolves this contradiction.

Although it pays a lot of attention to the picturesque details of Victoriana, Badham's movie seems far more Romantic than Victorian in feeling, and owes a lot to a tradition that has always had links with Dracula mythology: the tradition of *l'amour fou* and Surrealism. It is a tradition explicitly dedicated to liberation, but the liberation it offers; lacking any theories of feminism or bisexuality, proves usually to be very strongly male-centered, with an insistent emphasis on various forms of machismo. From *Wuthering Heights* through *L'Age d'or* to Badham's *Dracula*, *l'amour fou* is characteristically built on male charisma to which the woman surrenders. The film's emphasis on heterosexual romantic passion actually diminishes the potential for liberation implicit in the Dracula myth: the connotations of bisexuality implicit in the novel and developed in Murnau's version are virtually eliminated (Dracula vampirizes Renfield purely to use him as a slave, not for pleasure, and he does so in the form of a bat; Jonathan's visit to Transylvania is foregone, so there is no possibility of any equivalent of the castle scenes in Murnau); and the connotations of promiscuity are very much played down, with Dracula vampirizing other women almost contemptuously, his motivation centered on his passion for Lucy. Under cover of liberation, then, heterosexual monogamy is actually reinstated.

More sinister (though closely related) is the film's latent Fascism. Dracula and Lucy are to be a new King and Queen; the "ordinary" people of the film—Jonathan and Mina, for example—are swept aside with a kind of brutal contempt. Between them, Dracula and Lucy will create a new race of superhumans who will dominate the earth. Dracula's survival at the end—with Lucy's complicity—is a personalized "triumph of the will," the triumph of the superman over mere humans.

What Badham's film finally proves—and it is a useful thing to have demonstrated—is that it is time for our culture to abandon Dracula and pass beyond him, relinquishing him to social history. The limits of profitable reinterpretation have been reached (as Frank Langella's Dracula remarks, "I come from an old family—to live in a new house is impossible for me"). The Count has served his purpose by insisting that the repressed cannot be kept down, that it must always surface and strive to be recognized. But we cannot purge him of his association with evil—the evil that Victorian society projected onto sexuality and by which our contemporary notions of sexuality are still contaminated. If the return of the repressed is to be welcomed, then we must learn to represent it in forms other than that of an "undead" vampire-aristocrat.

It is characteristic of Cohen's work in general that *It's Alive II* should be at once the most careless and the most interesting of the three films. *Martin* and *Dracula* are, in their very different ways, closely worked; *It's Alive II* looks hastily thrown together, another of Cohen's rough drafts. The honesty, at once intuitive and intransigent, with which the concept is developed to the point where its inherent contradictions are exposed is also characteristic. The film develops explicitly what was already implicit in *It's Alive*: that the monstrous babies, though extremely dangerous, may represent a new stage in evolution, may actually be superior to normal human beings. It then tries to operate according to a 'double suspense' mechanics: the babies threaten the sympathetic characters who, not without doubts and qualifications, are trying to protect them; the babies are threatened by the unsympathetic authority figures who, without considering the issues involved, want to destroy them. On the simplest level, the problem with the film (accounting no doubt for its commercial failure) is that the more sympathetic the babies become, the less frightening they are. At the same time they remain monstrous, grotesquely ugly (and we are allowed to see far more of them than in the original) and fundamentally inhuman; the visual conception totally lacks the fire-and-light connotations of the god of *God Told Me To*, along with the suggestions of a revolutionary sexuality. The babies' superiority is also problematic, remaining a given rather than a concept that is explored and defined. They are telepathic, and develop very fast; they may have great intellectual potential. But these are fairly commonplace characteristics of monsters in the horror/science fiction genres (from "The Thing" to the "Midwich Cuckoos"): the notion that the babies may represent a valid human (or superhuman) future never becomes very compelling. The film is finally confused by Cohen's recurrent preoccupation with biological parentage: the babies' demand to be accepted into an impossible nuclear family, the inherent tensions and inequities of which the film has already thoroughly exposed, seems an intrinsically unprofitable line of narrative development. Yet if the film lacks the surface viability of *Martin* and *Dracula*, it reveals even more nakedly the intractability of the traditional monster/normality conflict for radical development beyond a certain point. For such a development to become possible, the conflict itself needs to be redefined, the monstrousness returned to the normality where it belongs. Such a strategy is apparent in the "living dead" films of Romero.

GEORGE ROMERO: *Apocalypse Now*

Night of the Living Dead (1968) and *Dawn of the Dead* (1979) represent the first two parts of a trilogy which Romero plans to complete later with *Day of the Dead*.[2] They are

2. See chapter 14.

among the most powerful, fascinating and complex of modern horror films, bearing a very interesting relationship both to the genre and to each other. What I want to examine here is their *divergence*: together, they demand a partial redefinition of the principles according to which the genre usually operates, and they are more distinct from each other—in character, tone and meaning—than has generally been noted (*Dawn of the Dead* is much more than the elaborate remake it has been taken for).

The differences—both from other horror films and between the two films—are centered on the zombies and their function in relation to the other characters. The zombies of *Night* answer partly to the definition of monster as the return of the repressed, but only partly: they lack one of the crucial defining characteristics, energy, and carry no positive connotations whatever. In *Dawn*, even this partial correspondence has almost entirely disappeared. On the other hand, the zombies of both films are not burdened with those actively negative connotations ("evil incarnate," etc.) that define the reactionary horror film. The earlier films to which the living dead movies most significantly relate are both somewhat to one side of the main development of the horror film: *The Birds* (*Night* more than *Dawn*) and *Invasion of the Body Snatchers* (*Dawn* more than *Night*). The strategy that connects all four films (and at the same time distinguishes them from the most fully representative specimens of the genre) is that of depriving their monsters of positive or progressive potential in order to restore it to the human characters. From this viewpoint, *Dawn of the Dead* emerges as the most interesting of the four films (which is not to say that it is better—more complex, more suggestive, more intelligent—than *The Birds*).

Much has been made of the way in which *Night of the Living Dead* systematically undercuts generic conventions and the expectations they arouse: the woman who appears to be established as the heroine becomes virtually catatonic early in the film and remains so to the end; no love relationship develops between her and the hero. The young couple, whose survival as future nuclear family is generically guaranteed, is burned alive and eaten around the film's midpoint. The film's actual nuclear family is wiped out; the child (a figure hitherto sacrosanct—even in *The Birds*, which appeared the same year as *Rosemary's Baby*, children sustain no more than superficial injuries) not only dies but comes back as a zombie, devours her father, and hacks her mother to death. In a final devastating stroke, the hero of the film and sole survivor of the zombies (among the major characters) is callously shot down by the sheriff's posse, thrown on a bonfire, and burned.

But the film's transgressions are not just against generic conventions: those conventions constitute an embodiment, in a skeletal and schematic form, of the dominant norms of our culture. The zombies of *Night* have their meaning defined fairly consistently in relation to the Family and the Couple. The film's debt to *The Birds* goes beyond the obvious resemblances of situation and imagery (the besieged group in the boarded house, the zombies' hands breaking through the barricades like the birds' beaks). The zombies' attacks, like those of the birds, have their origins in (are the physical projection of) psychic tensions that are the product of patriarchal male/female or familial relationships. This is established clearly in the opening scene. Brother and sister visit a remote country graveyard (over which flies the Stars and Stripes: the metaphor of America-as-graveyard is central to Romero's work, the term "living dead" describing the society of *Martin* as aptly as it does the zombies). Their father is buried there, and the visit, a meaningless annual ritual performed to please their mother, is intensely resented—actively by the man, passively by the sullen woman. They take their familial resentments out on each other, as the film indicates they have always done; the man frightens his sister by pretending to be a monster, as he used to do when they were children; the first zombie then lurches forward from among the graves, attacks them both, and kills the man. At the film's climax, when the zombies at last burst into the farmhouse, it is the brother who leads the attack on his sister, some obscure vestige of family feeling driving him forward to devour her.

In between, we have the film's analysis of its typical American nuclear family. The father rages and blusters impotently, constantly reasserting a discredited authority (the film continually counterpoints the disintegration of the social microcosm, the patriarchal family, with the cultural disintegration of the nation, the collapse of confidence in authority on both the personal and political level). The mother, contemptuous of her husband yet trapped in the dominant societal patterns, does nothing but sulk and bitch. Their destruction at the hands of their zombie daughter represents the film's judgment on them and the norm they embody.

The film has often been praised for never making an issue of its black hero's color (it is nowhere alluded to, even implicitly). Yet it is not true that his color is arbitrary and without meaning: Romero uses it to signify his difference from the other characters, to set him apart from their norms. He alone has no ties—he remains unconnected to any of the others, and we learn nothing of his family or background. From this arises the significance of the two events at the end of the film: he survives the zombies, and he is shot down by the posse. It is the function of the posse to restore the social order that has been destroyed; the zombies represent the suppressed tensions and conflicts—the legacy of the past, of the patriarchal structuring of relationships, "dead" yet automatically continuing—which that order creates and on which it precariously rests.

Almost exactly halfway between the two living dead films, and closely related to both, is *The Crazies*, an ambitious and neglected work that demands parenthetical attention here for its confirmation of Romero's thematic concerns and the particular emphasis it gives them: The pre-credits sequence is virtually a gloss on the opening of *Night of the Living Dead*, with brother and sister as young children and the acting out of tensions dramatized within the family. Again, brother teases sister by pretending to be a monster coming to kill her; abruptly, their "game" is disturbed by the father, the first "crazy" of the title, who has already murdered their mother and is now savagely destroying the house. The subsidiary family of the main body of the film (here father and daughter), instead of killing and devouring each other, act out the mutual incestuous desire on whose repression families are built. In general; however, the film moves out from *Night*'s concentration on the family unit into a more generalized treatment of social disintegration (a progression *Dawn* will complete).

The premise of the film is similar to that of Hawks' *Monkey Business* (that the same premise can provide the basis for a crazy comedy and a horror movie is itself suggestive of the dangers of a rigid definition of genres, which are often structured on the same sets of ideological tensions): a virus in a town's water supply turns people crazy, their craziness taking the form of the release of their precariously suppressed violence, its end result either death or incurable insanity. The continuity suggested by the opening between normality and craziness is sustained throughout the film; indeed, one of its most fascinating aspects is the way the boundary between the two is continually blurred. In the first part of the film after the declaration of martial law and the attempt to round up and isolate all the town's inhabitants, the local priest finds his authority swept aside and the sanctuary of his church brutally repudiated. He becomes increasingly distraught, and publicly immolates himself. We never know whether he is a victim of the virus (acting, in his case, on a desire for martyrdom). Once such a doubt is implanted, uncertainty arises over what provokes the uncontrolled and violent behavior of virtually everyone in the film. The hysteria of the quarantined can be attributed equally to the spread of contagion among them or to their brutal and ignominious herding together in claustrophobically close quarters by the military; the various individual characters who overstep the bounds of recognizably normal behavior may simply be reacting to conditions of extreme stress. The crazies, in other words, represent merely an extension of normality, not its opposite. The spontaneous violence of the mad appears scarcely more grotesque than the organized violence of the authorities.

The end of *Night of the Living Dead* implies that the zombies have been contained and are in the process of being annihilated; by the end of *Dawn of the Dead* they have apparently overrun everything, and nothing remains but to flee. Yet *Dawn* (paradoxically, taking the cue from its title) comes across as by far the more optimistic of the two films. This is due partly to format (bright colors, as opposed to *Night*'s grainy and drab black and white), partly to setting (the garish and brilliantly lit shopping mall, contrasted with the shadowy, old-fashioned farmhouse), partly to tone (in *Night*, the zombies are never funny, the film's black humor being mainly restricted to the casual brutalism of the sheriff's posse). But these are only the outward signs of a difference which is basically conceptual. Both films are built upon all-against-all triangular structures, strikingly similar yet crucially different:

NIGHT
Besieged

Zombies   Posse

DAWN
Besieged

Zombies   Gang

(*The Crazies* essentially repeats the pattern of *Night*, with crazies instead of zombies and the military substituting for the posse.)

The functions of the sheriff's posse in *Night* and the motorcycle gang in *Dawn* are in some ways very similar. They constitute a threat both to the zombies and to the besieged (even if in *Night* inadvertently, by mistaking the hero for a zombie); more important, both dramatize, albeit in significantly different ways, the possibility of the development of Fascism out of breakdown and chaos. The difference is obvious: the purpose of the posse is to destroy the zombies and to restore the threatened social order; the purpose of the gang is simply to exploit and profit from that order's disintegration. The posse ends triumphant, the gang is wiped out.

The premise of *Dawn* in fact is that the social order (regarded as in all Romero's films as obsolete and discredited) *can't* be restored; its restoration at the end of *Night* simply clinches the earlier film's total negativity. The notion of social apocalypse is succinctly established in *Dawn*'s TV studio prologue: television, the only surviving medium of national communication whereby social order might be maintained, is on the verge of closing down; as a technician tells Fran, "Our responsibility is at an end." The characters of *Night* were still locked in their responsibility to the value structure of the past; the characters of *Dawn* are at the outset absolved from that responsibility—they are potentially free people, with new responsibilities of choice and self-determination. Since the zombies' significance in both films depends entirely on their relationship to the main characters, it follows that their function here is somewhat different. They are no longer associated with specific characters or character tensions, and the family as a social unit no longer exists (it is only reconstituted in parody, when the injured Roger becomes the-baby-in-the-pram, wheeled around the supermarket by his "parents" as he shoots down zombies with childish glee). The zombies instead are a given from the outset; they represent, on the metaphorical level, the whole dead weight of patriarchal consumer capitalism, from whose habits of behavior and desire not even Hare Krishnas and nuns, mindlessly joining the conditioned gravitation to the shopping mall, are exempt.

As in *The Crazies*, the seemingly clear-cut distinctions between the three groups are progressively undermined (aside from the obvious visual differentiation between zombies and humans). The motorcycle gang's mindless delight in violence and slaughter is anticipated in the development of Roger; all three groups are con-

Lover as Zombie: David Emge in *Dawn of the Dead*

taminated and motivated by consumer greed, which the zombies simply carry to its logical conclusion by consuming *people*. All three groups, in other words, share a common conditioning: all are predators. The substance of the film concerns the four characters' varying degrees of recognition of, and varying reactions to, this fact. Two become zombies, two (provisionally) escape.

In place of *Night*'s dissection of the family, *Dawn* explores (and explodes) the two dominant couple relationships of our culture and its cinema: the heterosexual couple (moving inevitably toward marriage and its traditional male/female roles) and the male "buddy" relationship with its evasive denial of sexuality (the pattern is anticipated in the central triangle relationship of the three principles of *The Crazies*). Through the realization of the ultimate consumer society dream (the ready availability of every luxury, emblem, and status symbol of capitalist life, without the penalty of payment) the anomalies and imbalances of human relationships under capitalism are exposed. With the defining motive—the drive to acquire and possess money, the identification of money with power—removed, the whole structure of traditional relationships, based on patterns of dominance and dependence, begins to crumble.

The heterosexual couple (an embryonic family, as Fran is pregnant) begins as a trendy variation on the norm: they are not legally married, and the woman is allowed a semblance of independence through her career; but as soon as the two are together the conventional assumptions operate. It is the man who flies the helicopter and carries the gun—the film's major emblems of sexual/patriarchal authority. At various points in the narrative Fran nostalgically re-enacts the role of female stereotype, making up her face as a doll-like image for the male gaze, skating alone on the huge ice rink—woman as spectacle, without an audience. But in the course of the film she progressively assumes a genuine autonomy, asserting herself against the men, insisting on possession of a gun, demanding to learn to pilot the machine. The pivotal scene is the parody of a romantic dinner with flowers and candlelight— the white couple in evening dress cooked for and waited on by the black—with the scene building to the man's offer and the woman's refusal of the rings that signify traditional union.

The closest link between *Night* and *Dawn* is the carry-over of the black protagonist, his color used again to indicate his separation from the norms of white-dominated society and his partial exemption from its constraints. Through the developing mutual attachment between him and Roger, the film takes up and comments on the buddy relationship of countless recent Hollywood movies and its implicit sexual undercurrents and ambiguities. Neither man shows any sexual interest in the woman, yet both are blocked by their conditioning from admitting to any in each other. Hence the channeling of Roger's energies into violence and aggression, his uncontrolled zest in slaughter presented as a display for his friend. The true nature of the relationship can be tacitly acknowledged only after Roger's death, in the symbolic orgasm of the spurting of a champagne bottle over his grave.

Both the film's central relationships are broken by the death of one of the partners. The two who die are those who cannot escape the constraints of their conditioning, the survivors those who show themselves capable of autonomy and self-awareness. The film eschews any hint of a traditional happy ending, there being no suggestion of any romantic attachment developing between the survivors. Instead of the restoration of conventional relationship patterns, we have the woman piloting the helicopter as the man relinquishes his rifle to the zombies. They have not come very far, and the film's conclusion rewards them with no more than a provisional and temporary respite: enough gasoline for four hours, and no certainty of destination. Yet the effect of the ending is curiously exhilarating. Hitherto, the modern horror film has invariably moved toward either the restoration of the traditional order or the expression of despair (in *Night*, both). *Dawn* is perhaps the first horror film to suggest—albeit very tentatively—the possibility of moving beyond apocalypse. It brings its two surviving protagonists to the point where the work of creating the norms for a new social order, a new structure of relationships, can begin—a context in which the presence of a third survivor, Fran's unborn child, points the way to potential change. Romero has set himself a formidable challenge, and it will be interesting to see how the third part of the trilogy confronts it.

NEGLECTED NIGHTMARES

Romero's work represents the most progressive potentialities of the horror film, the possibility of breaking the impasse of the monster/normality relationship developed out of the Gothic tradition. But the final emphasis here must be on the genre rather than on the work of an individual director, for it is the vitality of the genre itself—fed, in the 70s, by the whole pervasive sense of ideological crisis and imminent collapse—that is so remarkable in this period. I want to end, then, by examining a handful of neglected (in some cases virtually unknown) films by directors either not particularly associated with the horror film (Stephanie Rothman), or whose careers have proved subsequently disappointing (Wes Craven, Bob Clark).

If I begin with Craven's *Last House on the Left* it is partly because it has achieved at least a certain underground notoriety; it surfaced briefly in the pages of *Film Comment* (July-August 1978) as one of Roger Ebert's *Guilty Pleasures*. I had better say that the Guilty Pleasures feature seems to me an entirely deplorable institution. If one feels guilt at pleasure, isn't one bound to renounce either one or the other? Preferably, in most cases, the guilt, which is merely the product of that bourgeois elitism that continues to vitiate so much criticism. The attitude fostered is essentially evasive (including *self*-evasive) and anti-critical: "Isn't this muck—to which of course I'm really so superior—*delicious?*"

Ebert's *Guilty Pleasures* (which may be *Last House*'s only recognition so far by a professedly serious critic) is brief enough to quote in full:

> The original *Keep repeating—It's Only a Movie!!!* movie. The plot may sound strangely familiar. Two young virgins go for a walk in the woods. One is set upon by vagabonds who rape and kill her. The other escapes. The vagabonds take their young victim's clothes and set on through the wood, coming at last, without realizing it, to the house of the victim's parents. The father finds his daughter's bloodstained garments, realizes that he houses the murderers, and kills them by electrifying the screen door and taunting them to run at it, whereupon they slip on the shaving cream he's spread on the floor, fall into the screen, and are electrocuted.

> Change a few trifling details (like shaving cream) and you've got Bergman's *Virgin Spring*. The movie's an almost scene-by-scene ripoff of Bergman's plot. It's also a neglected American horror exploitation masterpiece on a par with *Night of the Living Dead*. As a plastic Hollywood movie, the remake would almost certainly have failed. But its very artlessness, its blunt force, makes it work.

Pleasure or not, Ebert has plenty here to feel guilty about:

1. The virginity of one of the girls (Phyllis) is very much in question. The relationship between them is built on the experienced/innocent opposition (as in Bergman's original, the plot of which, by the way, was also a "scene-by-scene rip-off" of a medieval ballad), though the innocence of Mary (the nice bourgeois family's daughter) is also questioned: she is a flower child with an ambiguous attraction to violence.

2. The girls meet the "vagabonds" in the latter's apartment in the city: they are on their way to a concert by a rock group noted for its onstage violence, and pause to try to buy some dope from the youngest of the gang, who is lounging about on the front steps.

3. Ebert is decently reticent about the "vagabonds" (their background, relationships, sex, and even their number). His association of them with "the wood" deprives them of the very specific social context that Craven in fact gave them. There are four: as escaped killer, his sadistic friend Weasel, their girl Sadie, and the killer's illegitimate teenage son Junior.

4. I am not clear which girl Ebert thinks "escapes." Phyllis gets away briefly but is soon recaptured, tormented, repeatedly stabbed, and (in the original, though Craven himself wonders if a print survives anywhere with this included) virtually disemboweled. The abridged version leaves no doubt that she is dead. Mary staggers into the water to cleanse herself after she is raped, and is repeatedly shot; her parents later find her on the bank, and she dies in their arms.

5. The "vagabonds" do not take Mary's clothes. Her body, which they presume dead, is drifting out in the middle of a large pond. The mother (as in Bergman), searching the men's luggage after overhearing some semi-incriminating dialogue and one of the gang calling out in his sleep, finds the peace pendant her husband gave Mary at the start of the film, and blood on the *men's* clothes.

6. No one in the film dies from electrocution. The father spreads shaving cream outside the upstairs bedroom door to slow his victims down, and electrifies the screen door to prevent their escaping by it. The gang are disposed of as follows: the nice bourgeois mother seduces Weasel out in the dark by the pond where Mary was raped, fellates him, and bites off his cock as he comes; the killer contemptuously persuades his son Junior to blow out his own brains; the mother cuts Sadie's throat outside in an ornamental pond while her husband dispatches Junior's father with a chain saw—presumably decapitating him, and thereby completing the parallel between the simultaneous actions (though this is about the only thing that Craven doesn't show).

That Ebert's plot synopsis sets a new record in critical inaccuracy (combined with characteristic critic-as-superstar complacency) says less about him personally than about a general ambiance that encourages opinion-mongering, gossip, Guilty Pleasures, and similar smart-assery—and, as an inevitable corollary, actively discourages criticism and scholarship. What does it matter whether he gets the plot right or not? Hell, it's only a movie, and an exploitation movie at that, albeit an "American horror exploitation masterpiece on a par with *Night of the Living Dead*," which Ebert mercilessly slammed when it came out. (Is this supposed to be his public retraction?)

What I mean by bourgeois elitism could as well be illustrated from the writings of John Simon or Pauline Kael. What the critic demands, as at least a precondition to according a film serious attention, is not so much evidence of a genuine creative impulse (which can be individual or collective, and can manifest itself through *any* format) as a set of external signifiers that advertise the film as a Work of Art. No one feels guilty about seriously discussing *The Virgin Spring*, though the nature of Bergman's creative involvement there seems rather more suspect than is the case with *Last House*. What is at stake, then, is not merely the evaluation of one movie but quite fundamental critical (hence cultural, social, political) principles—issues that involve the relationship between critic and reader as well as that between film and spectator.

The relationship of *Last House* to *The Virgin Spring* is not, in fact, close enough to repay any detailed scrutiny, though one might remark that, if the term "rip-off" is appropriate here, it is equally appropriate to the whole of Shakespeare, the debt being one of plot outline and no more. The major narrative alterations—the transformation of Ingeri into Phyllis and of the child goat-herd into the teenage Junior, the killing of *both* girls, the addition of Sadie, the mother's active participation in the revenge, the destruction of Junior by his own father—are all thoroughly motivated and in themselves indicate the creative intelligence at work.

The most important narrative change is that of overall direction and final outcome. Bergman's virgin is on her way to church, and the film leads to the somewhat willed catharsis of her father's promise to build a new church, and the "answer" of a spurious and perfunctory miracle. Craven's virgin is on her way to a rock concert by a group that kills chickens on stage and, as the recurrent pop song on the soundtrack informs us, "the road leads to nowhere." The last image is of the parents, collapsed together in empty victory, drenched in blood.

But the crucial difference is in the film-spectator relationship, especially with reference to the presentation of violence. Joseph Losey saw Bergman's film as "Brechtian," but I think its character is determined more by personal temperament than aesthetic theory: the ability to describe coldly and accurately, without empathy—or, perhaps more precisely, with an empathy that has been repressed and disowned. If there is something distasteful in the film's detailing of rape and carnage, it is because Bergman seems to deny his involvement without annihilating it, and to communicate that position to the spectator.

The Virgin Spring is Art; *Last House* is Exploitation. One must return to that dichotomy because the difference between the two films in terms of the relationship set up between audience and action is inevitably bound up with it. I use the terms Art and Exploitation here not evaluatively, but to indicate two sets of signifiers—operating both within the films as "style" and outside them as publicity, distribution, etc.—that define the audience-film relationship in general terms. As media for communication, both Art and Exploitation have their limitations, defined in both cases, though in very different ways, by their inscriptions within the class system. Both permit the spectator a form of insulation from the work and its implications—Art by defining seriousness in aesthetic terms implying class superiority (only the person of education and refinement can appreciate Art, i.e., respond to that particular set of signifiers), Exploitation by denying seriousness altogether. It is the work of the best movies in either medium to transcend or transgress these limitations, to break through the spectator's insulation.

In organizing a horror film retrospective for the 1979 Toronto film festival, Richard Lippe and I also set out to transgress. We wanted (through the accompanying booklet and the directors' seminars, which only a very small proportion of our audience attended) to cut through the barriers bourgeois society erects as protection against the genre's implications—defenses that take many forms: laughter, contemptuous dismissal, the term "schlock," the phenomenon of the late-night horror show, the treatment of the horror film as Camp. In a way, *Last House* succeeded where we failed. A number of our customers—even in the context of a horror retrospective, even confronted by a somewhat bowdlerized print—gathered in the foyer after the screening to complain to the theater management that the film had been shown at all. Clearly, the film offers a very disturbing experience, its distinction lying in both the degree and nature of the disturbance. It is essential to this that its creation was a disturbing experience for Craven himself, a gentle, troubled, quiet-spoken ex-professor of English literature. The exploitation format and the request from the producer to "do a really violent film for $50,000" seem to have led him to discover things in himself he scarcely knew were there, which is also the effect it has on audiences. As Craven said:

> I found that I had never written anything like this, and I'd been writing for ten to twelve years already. I'd always written artistic, poetic things. Suddenly, I was working in an area I had never really confronted before. It was almost like doing a pornographic film if you'd been a fundamentalist. And I found that I was writing about things that I had very strong feelings about. I was drawing on things from very early in my own childhood, things that I was feeling about the war, and they were pouring into this very simple B-movie plot.

That extraordinary linking of "things from very early in my childhood" to "things that I was feeling about the war" is the kind of central perception about a film that criticism strives for and often misses. The connection between Vietnam and the fundamental structures of patriarchal culture is one I shall return to in discussing *The Night Walk*.

The reason people find the violence in *Last House* so disturbing is not simply that there is so much of it, nor even that it is so relentlessly close and immediate in presentation. (Many, myself included, have come to praise films for being "Brechtian," but it should also be acknowledged that distanciation is not the only valid aesthetic method.) I want to draw here on ideas derived from an admirable book, *Violence in the Arts* by John Fraser. The book is one of the rare treatments of this subject that manages to be intelligent and responsible without ever lapsing into puritanism, hypocrisy, or complacency. Its weakness is, I think, a failure to argue clearly as to whether violence is innate in "the human condition," a product of specific social structures, or a combination of the two—to speculate, that is, on the degree to which violence would disappear within a truly liberated society.

Violence, whether actual or implicit, is so powerfully and obstinately inherent in human relationships as we know them (structured as they are on dominance and inequality) that the right to a pure denunciation of it must be a hard-won and precarious achievement. It is difficult to point to such an achievement in the cinema: perhaps Mizoguchi (the brandings and cutting of the tendon in *Sansho the Bailiff*), perhaps Fritz Lang (the scalding of Gloria Grahame in *The Big Heat*—but even there, what feelings are aroused by her eventual retaliation?) As for myself, I am a committed pacifist who has experienced very strong desires to smash people's faces in, and who can remember incidents when I joined in the persecution of those in an inferior position and took pleasure from it; I have also, not infrequently, been a victim, and my greatest dread is of total helplessness at the mercy of tormentors. It is these three positions—the position of victim, the position of violator, the position of righteous avenger—and the interconnections among them that *Last House on the Left* dramatizes. Its distinction lies in the complex pattern of empathies that it creates.

To empathize exclusively with the victims is to see the violators as strictly Other, nonhuman, to erect a clear-cut boundary between one's own humanity and the inhumanness of someone "out there"; it is the grave error Michael Cimino makes in the Vietnam sequences of that nonetheless great movie *The Deer Hunter*. On the other hand, to empathize exclusively with the violators is to adopt the position of the sadist, seeing the victims as mere objects; it is a position to which Tobe Hooper's *The Texas Chainsaw Massacre* comes perilously close, in its failure to endow its victims with any vivid, personalized aliveness. *Last House* involves the spectator, simultaneously and inescapably, in the experience of both violator and victim.

How does one recognize the aliveness of characters in a movie? What I am pointing to is not merely a matter of subjective impression; nor is it a matter of those "rounded," "complex" characters beloved of critics whose aesthetic criteria are derived from the psychological novel. What is crucial is the suggestion of common intimate experience shared between character and spectator, particularly the suggestion of vulnerability. It is there in the nervous, darting glances of the Viet Cong tormentor in *The Deer Hunter*—though not sufficiently to offset the film's horrified repudiation of him. It exists much more strongly in *The Texas Chainsaw Massacre*, especially in the little scene (echoed in *Eaten Alive* with Neville Brand) where Leatherface is seen alone and appears at a loss what to do next, but also in his curiously endearing dressing up for the family dinner, complete with curly wig. In Hooper's films, however, such moments are reserved for the monstrous figures. The young people are scarcely more than objects, capable of nothing beyond a completely generalized and stereotypical display of pain and terror.

In *Last House*, all the major characters are allowed these moments of particularized vulnerability (except perhaps the father, the center of Bergman's film, relatively peripheral in Craven's). As the two girls rest in the woods on their way to the concert, Mary talks shyly and hesitantly to Phyllis about her sense of awakening womanhood, her developing breasts, her awareness of her own sexuality. The moment involves the spectator in an intimate relationship with her that makes objectification impossible. Yet her counterpart Sadie is equally alive, always groping toward an awareness that is beyond her grasp: she is acquainted with Frood, and knows that a telegraph pole is "not just a telegraph pole but a giant phaylus"; she has also been brushed by feminism, to the extent that she can sum up one of the men who pushes her around as a "male chauvinist dog."

The men, corrupt and brutalized, never cease to be recognizably human. Weasel's horrendous castration nightmare, wherein the father, a dentist, prepares to knock out his front teeth with hammer and chisel, attests to a continuing capacity for Oedipal guilt. As for Junior, we have his embarrassed, puzzled, troubled reaction to the extraordinary moment where Mary, in a desperate attempt to seduce him into a relationship with her and break through the gang's objectification of her, confers upon him the name Willow and proceeds to offer to steal him a fix from her father's house. One incident in Craven's original version clearly dramatized the breakdown of objectification; it must have been the most disturbing moment in this most disturbing of films, bringing home the common humanity of violators and victim. It may have been cut from all prints, but we have Craven's account of it.

The killing of Phyllis is very sexual in feeling, and ended with her being stabbed not only by the men but by the woman repeatedly. Then she fell to the ground and Sadie bent down and pulled out a loop of her intestines. They looked at it and that's where it all stopped. That's when they realized what they had done, and they looked at each other and walked away. They were disgusted at what they had done. It was as if they had been playing with a doll, or a prisoner they thought was a doll, and it had broken and come apart and they did not know how to put it back together again. Again, there were parallels with what I was seeing in our culture, where we were breaking things that we did not know how to put back together.

The film offers no easily identifiable parallels to Vietnam (in the somewhat opportunistic, though eminently well-intentioned, manner of *Little Big Man*). Instead, it analyzes the nature and conditions of violence and sees them as inherent in the American situation. Craven sees to it that the audience cannot escape the implications. We are spared nothing in the protracted tormenting of the two girls—our having to share the length of their ordeal is part of the point—and we cannot possibly enjoy it. They are *us*. Yet we also cannot disengage ourselves from their tormentors: *They* are *us*, too. We can share the emotional and moral outrage of the parents, yet they take hideous revenge on characters we have entered into an intimate relationship with, and we are kept very much aware that it is the revenge of the haves on the have nots—that the gang's monstrousness is the product of the inequalities and power structures of a class system into which all the characters are bound. No act of violence in the film is condoned, yet we are led to understand every act as the realization of potentials that exist within us all, that are intrinsic to our social and personal relationships.

The domination of the family by the father, the domination of the nation by the bourgeois class and its norms, and the domination of other nations and other ideologies (more precisely, attempts at domination that inevitably fail and turn to mutual destruction)—the structures interlock, are basically a single structure. My Lai was not an unfortunate occurrence *out there*; it was created within the American home. No film is more expressive than *Last House* of a(n) (inter)national social sickness; and no film is richer in Oedipal references—an extension, in its widest implications, of the minutiae of human relations under patriarchal capitalist culture. Craven is fully aware of this macrocosm-microcosm relationship: I leave the last word to him, adding merely that these concerns are taken up (with great intelligence, a higher budget, more polish, but less disturbing intensity) in *The Hills Have Eyes*, a work that, while it has not to my knowledge received serious critical treatment, is scarcely unknown.

> The family is the best microcosm to work with. If you go much beyond that you're getting away from a lot of the roots of our own primeval feelings. Let's face it, most of the basic stories and the basic feelings involve very few people: Mommy, Daddy, me, siblings, and the people in the other room. I like to stay within that circle. It's very much where most of our strong emotions or gut feelings come from. It's from those very early experiences and how they are worked out. I grew up in a white working-class family that was very religious, and there was an enormous amount of secrecy in the general commerce of our getting along with each other. Certain things were not mentioned. A lot of things were not spoken of or talked about. If there was an argument it was immediately denied. If there was a feeling it was repressed. As I got older I began to see that as a nation we were doing the same thing.

* * *

Throughout the series of directors' seminars that formed part of the horror film retrospective one question recurred: What was the filmmaker's attitude to the possibility of social change, and did s/he feel a responsibility in that direction? The responses of the five directors we interviewed seem closely relevant to their work—indeed, almost deducible from it, though such correspondences are not as common as one might logically expect.

For Brian De Palma, the cultural situation is beyond any hope, social change is impossible, and all one has left is to enjoy the fascinating spectacle of corruption and disintegration as best one can. Generally, he wanted to discuss his films as formal exercises (invoking Hitchcock as precedent), disclaiming much interest in what they were about. David Cronenberg's attitude was, roughly, that as we all die in the end anyway, what does it matter? He resisted any social analysis of his films in favor of a metaphysical reading (they are about "mortality"). George Romero gave what was at once the most equivocal, guarded, and complex answer. He by no means rejected notions of social engagement, but didn't think of his work primarily in such terms; the desire to change society might be present but was not a primary, conscious motivation. Only Stephanie Rothman and Wes Craven gave unequivocal affirmative answers on the subject of the artist's responsibility; both wished to make films that engaged directly and progressively with social issues.

I certainly don't wish to attribute any absolute authority to an artist's view of her/his own work. But my growing distrust of De Palma's work, my hatred of Cronenberg's,[2] and my increasing interest in and respect for that of the other three directors received support from their statements. Equally, of course, one must resist any simplistic equation between conscious social engagement and artistic merit: it is the work that confers significance on the artist's statement, not vice versa.

* * *

The interest of Stephanie Rothman's films has been noted in a number of places—for example, in the work of feminist critics and in a *Film Comment* article by Terry Curtis Fox (November-December 1976). Only one of her films, *The Velvet Vampire*, belongs within the horror genre, though we also screened *Terminal Island* for its treatment of violence as a response to oppression.

Rothman's work embodies a vitality and inventiveness that suggest a potential

2. The hatred does not extend to *The Dead Zone*, arguably the finest of all screen adaptations of Stephen King to date and a revelation of Cronenberg's potential when released from his constricting personal obsessions.

far beyond the films' actual achievement. I have not seen a Rothman film for which I would stick out my neck, as I would for Larry Cohen's *Demon*, De Palma's *Sisters*, Romero's *Dawn of the Dead*, or *Last House on the Left*. But perhaps the absence from her work to date of the fully convincing, fully realized film should not be seen in personal terms or even in terms of the specific production setups (with obvious deficiencies of budget, casting and shooting schedules) of each film.

Rothman's films—and particularly *The Velvet Vampire*—raise the question of whether a feminist intervention in heavily male-dominated and traditionally sexist genres can be more than disruptive, can produce more than sketchy, fragmented and self-contradictory texts. De Palma's *Sisters* (co-written by Louisa Rose) suggests that a coherent feminist horror movie is possible, though only in negative terms: the systematic analysis of the oppression of women and of the annihilation of any movement of revolt. It is Rothman's desire to offer more positive statements that makes her films at once so sympathetic and so problematic. *Group Marriage*, for example, is one of the only American films actually to propose alternatives to the battered ideological tradition of monogamous relationships, but it evades most of the problems it raises under the alibi of being a light comedy.

The inclusion of *Terminal Island* in the retrospective foregrounded, among other things, the perennial quandary of genre movies with ulterior motives. For me, the film, though invigorating and effective (unlike Terry Curtis Fox, I don't sense any inhibitions whatever in Rothman's treatment of violence), is too clear-cut, too pared down to the bare lines of a thesis; a message movie is a message movie, even if one likes the message. Yet, to judge from the reactions of our audience, most people respond only to the generic signifier and miss the message altogether. Despite all the work on genre and entertainment that has been done in film education, reactions to films remain largely determined by the spectator's cultural position. To recognize a film as Exploitation, etc., is instantly to know how to respond to it, and all local particularities and inflections become obliterated.

As a "fable for our time," *Terminal Island* works beautifully. To save the taxpayers' money, convicts who would otherwise be subject to the death penalty or life imprisonment are released to fend for themselves on a small island off the coast of California. The action begins and ends with the arrival of the boat that periodically deposits new islanders. A woman who arrives at the start finds a state not without parallels in the real world: on the one hand, a primitive quasi-Fascist dictatorship based on force and terrorization, in which women are prostitutes ignominiously servicing the men; on the other, a band of guerrillas, disruptive and violent but ultimately impotent and disorganized. The women escape to the guerrillas, help overthrow the dictatorship, and exert their new power to create a free democracy based on true equality (including, of course, full sexual equality). When the boat arrives at the end, it brings a new murderess and a pardon for the doctor convicted of euthanasia. The doctor decides not to leave—not, as in the traditional genre movie, because he has fallen in love, but because he recognizes the superiority of the new order to the "civilized" world that awaits him. The new woman is welcomed into the order by her sisters.

The film works partly because the action movie format permits the simplification of the issues and problems arising from the contemporary crisis in male and female roles. But the film's limitations are not, I think, solely explicable in terms of generic determinants. Rothman's work suggests that she is more a liberal feminist than a radical feminist; the key issue of bisexuality is repeatedly evaded, or refused recognition as an issue. *Terminal Island* seems to be stating that men and women should collaborate and accept each other on equal terms. Fine, of course, as far as it goes, but it leaves undisturbed the fact that the terms "men" and "women" are, beyond the simple biological facts, themselves culturally defined.

The group in *Group Marriage* explicitly rejects bisexuality; on the periphery of the group hovers a gay couple conceived in terms of the most blatant sexual stereotyping. The film does not treat them unkindly; they are permitted to join the group wedding ceremony at the film's climax, but as a couple who tag along, not as full members. Rothman's feminism never wants to acknowledge that the male and female roles of our culture are built upon the repression of bisexuality and the resultant separation and reinforcing of masculinity and femininity. She wants men and women to be men and women as our culture defines and conditions them.

Bisexuality is allowed far greater freedom in *The Velvet Vampire*, but is treated very equivocally. Both the release and the equivocation are characteristic of the horror genre. I find the film very difficult to come to terms with: it is imaginative and audacious, gaining a strong impetus from Rothman's interest in Surrealism (in her seminar she expressed a debt to and great admiration for Jean Cocteau and Georges Franju), but riven by contradictory impulses and confusions.

The feminist inflection actually intensifies the genre's unresolvable quandary. *The Velvet Vampire* never progresses beyond confusion, but its internal contradictions are very interesting. They are centered, of course, in the vampire Diane herself. The plot concerns her shifting relationship with a normal young couple (quasi-liberated, i.e., bourgeois-trendy) whom she picks up at an art exhibition and invites to her desert retreat, where she seduces them both (thereby anticipating *The Rocky Horror Show* by several years). Logically, she should represent a deeper level of sexual liberation than the young couple have hitherto experienced, and this meaning does seem to be intermittently present. This reading is undermined, however, by the fact that Diane is most obviously associated with decadence and perversity. Rothman, in other words, equivocates with her very much as Bernardo Bertolucci equivocates with the Dominique Sanda character of *The Conformist.*

The issue is obfuscated further by the fact that Diane is obsessively tied to a husband (apparently one of those "real men" who, once bedded, is never forgotten) to whom she is faithful in her fashion; the husband is long dead, so necrophilia enters in as well. By the end of the film the character, in terms of the values she is meant to embody, seems quite unreadable. Rothman produces a splendid climax, with Diane destroyed in the Los Angeles sunshine by an impromptu lynch mob of young people mindlessly waving at her crosses snatched from a souvenir stall: repression restored by the permissive young having a ball. But the kind of liberation Diane embodies, if indeed she can be said to embody any at all (if she doesn't, then what is the film about?), is by this time so unclear that the spectator scarcely knows how to react.

* * *

The great period of the American horror film was the period of Watergate and Vietnam: the genre required a moment of ideological crisis for its full significance to emerge, the immediate cultural breakdown calling into question far more than a temporary political situation. It is scarcely a coincidence that both Wes Craven and George Romero see certain of their films—*The Hills Have Eyes* and *The Crazies* respectively—as deliberate, if oblique, commentaries on Vietnam and its impact on the structures of American society. The reference of Bob Clark's *The Night Walk* (also known, in the manner of commercially dubious propositions, by the aliases *Death Dream* and *Dead of Night*) is more direct. The film, made in 1972, seems to have been almost entirely buried; it is certainly worth digging up again. It shares with Bob Clark's subsequent films (*Black Christmas, Murder by Decree*) a certain laboriousness at the level of *mise en scène*, an overanxiety that points be clearly made. But the concept is remarkable and rigorously worked out; the film accumulates tremendous force by the time its climactic sequences are reached.

Its premise is that a young man, killed in Vietnam, is willed home by his mother (Lynn Carlin). He returns as a zombie, able to sustain himself only on human blood and driven by a desire for revenge on the society that sent him to war. The film's resonances develop out of the three-way connection set up among the raw materials of the horror film, the family, and Vietnam. Its anticipations are very striking; not just the basic concept (the monster as product of the family) but whole sequences evoke *It's Alive* and Romero's *Martin*. The coincidental proximity of these three distinguished films, without any direct connecting links or influence, greatly strengthens the argument that to study the evolution of a genre is to study the evolution of a national (un)consciousness.

Few horror films have been so explicit about the monstrousness of patriarchal family structures. Within the home, the mother rules—the reward for her exclusion from the world of money, power and politics. She devotes her frustrated energies entirely to the perpetuation of patriarchy, in the shape of her obsessively adored son, relegating her daughter to unconsidered subordination and an impotent and furtive complicity with the ineffectual father (John Marley). The family is seen as a structure of relationships based on hate masquerading as love; everything is to be sacrificed for the son, the future patriarch, the most "loved," hence the most resented, of the family group. Of Andy the son the film offers (by presentation and implication) a double image: nice, unremarkable boy and devouring ghoul—a figure quite inadequate to sustain the ideological burden he is meant to carry. The film never falls into the simplistic trap of innocent-boy-corrupted-by-horrors-of-war. It was not Vietnam alone that produced Andy's monstrousness.

The dinner scene near the beginning of the film, before Andy's return, establishes the theme succinctly. The roast is brought in, and the mother insists that the father carve it; she loves to watch the head of the family carve. Andy has already learned to carve beautifully, as befits a future head of a future family. It is the symbol of his position and the duties that go with it, duties which clearly extend to "serving his country," killing and being killed. Imperialism begins at home. So the father carves, very awkwardly and badly, as his wife watches admiringly.

The film builds logically from that moment to a climax of sustained hysteria, the mother frantically driving her vampire son to the grave he has prepared for himself before he can wreak further destruction on the community and the family. The film's ultimate insight is remarkable: that, under patriarchy, the patriarch suffers as much as anyone, and from the very assumptions that enthrone him as an ideologically privileged figure. The film is also a useful reminder that a radical statement about Vietnam must be a statement about much more.

7.

Brian De Palma

THE POLITICS OF CASTRATION

CASTRATION

Brian De Palma's interesting, problematic, frequently frustrating movies are quite obsessive about castration, either literal (*Sisters, Dressed to Kill*) or metaphorical (all the rest).[1] This "Obsession"—the significant title of one of his films—seems a legitimate way into a discussion of his work, its relation to the films of Hitchcock, and its place within 70s Hollywood cinema. In the interests of clarity, I shall preface this discussion with an examination of Freudian castration theory and the use that has been made of it in recent film criticism.

Freud's own accounts of castration anxiety attribute it to two major sources: The development of the Oedipus complex where the boy fears castration as his logical punishment for desiring the mother and wishing the father dead; the discovery of sexual difference, when he finds that little girls don't have penises, and becomes afraid that he may lose his. Conversely, there arises here the concept of female castration: the girl, finding that little boys do have penises, fears that she has already lost hers.

It has been thoroughly documented that in Freud's time castration anxiety (whatever one may think of the theoretical basis baldly outlined above) was also rooted in practical familial realities: little boys were actually threatened with castration as punishment for masturbation, if not directly ("If you do that I'll cut it off"), then indirectly ("If you do that it will drop off"). That monstrous, much-trans-

---

1. Since this chapter was written, *Body Double* (though it is far from being among De Palma's best films) has amply confirmed its argument.

lated, widely distributed "children's book" *Struwwelpeter*—surely among the most disgusting works of literature ever produced, especially given its intentions and presumed readership—testifies eloquently to the reality and pervasiveness of the threat. Similarly, it seems logical to assume that the traumatic shock of the discovery of sexual difference was greatly exacerbated, if not actually produced, by the secrecy with which sexuality was surrounded, the parental insistence on the shamefulness and "dirtiness" of the "private parts," which must always be concealed. Little information exists as to just how thorough and how widespread through the various social strata change has been. The practice of sex education within the institutionalized educational system and through popular manuals, counseling services, etc., although obviously compromised and co-opted by the bourgeois capitalist establishment (a true sex education would promote revolution), has presumably made some inroads, so that infantile masturbation is more tolerated, and both infantile and parental nudity are more widely accepted, less accompanied by damaging inhibitions. One needs to know what effect this has had on castration anxiety (some, surely, though a study of our current cinema would swiftly suggest that we shouldn't overrate it). Meanwhile, many film theorists appear to continue to accept castration theory as it came from the mouth of Freud, as if no changes had occurred whatever.

For this, Freud himself is partly to blame. It is one of the paradoxes of his work that, while he strove all his life toward the formulation of a psychoanalytical theory of human history, he had so little awareness of the cultural/historical specificity of his own work. Hence his habitual lapses into an essentialism in which valid and radical discoveries derived from investigations into the neuroses of upper middle-class turn-of-the-century Vienna are assumed to offer permanent and universal insights into the entire human race. For example, his discovery of the Oedipus complex and its multifarious ramifications has clearly proved invaluable as a means toward understanding the construction of the socialized individual within our culture. Yet only recently—such is Freud's authoritativeness—have we come to realize that the complex is far more likely to be something imposed on children by their parents within the structures of the bourgeois nuclear family, than something that develops inevitably and "naturally" in every child ever born. A constant problem with Freud is that the very cogency of his arguments, combined with this pervasive essentialist fallacy, tends to impose those arguments as representing conditions that are unchangeable. So with castration theory, which is obviously closely bound up with the immense symbolic significance accumulated by "the phallus" in patriarchal society. I am not asserting that, in an achieved socialist-feminist culture, castration anxiety would disappear altogether (it refers, after all, to a part of the anatomy which men are likely to continue to value), but it would clearly be very different in nature and scope, restricted to a perfectly legitimate sensitivity to the possibility of physical mutilation.

For it is when one considers the symbolic extensions of castration anxiety that the problems really thicken. The mystique of the phallus appears to rest upon no more impressive a foundation than the fact that, in childhood (before girls develop breasts, when boys and girls alike may have long or short hair, etc.), it is the one sign that clearly differentiates the sexes. Hence, for patriarchy, it can be invested with the utmost mythic/symbolic importance. There is even, for example, the myth that power, strength, and charisma are somehow attributes of the phallus (a myth most strikingly developed in the work of D. H. Lawrence, whose genius invested it, for a time, with a spurious plausibility). Given the false premise the symbolic extensions are perfectly logical, taking in every form of male power and, especially, those forms that have as their function the domination of women. I list here but a few.

1. Positions of Authority   Under this rubric fall the Father and his Law (both terms to be understood literally and symbolically): the father of the family, the President or King as "father" of the nation, the Pope as "Father of the Church," together with father figures from ministers of state through judges to policemen (not forgetting university professors). Sometimes, of course, women fill these roles, but, in the overwhelming majority of what is only a tiny minority of cases, only if they are able to convince men that they pose no threat, that they will slot safely in to the patriarchal institutions.

2. Money   In capitalist society possession of money is the most obvious manifestation of power; translated beyond the individual into class terms, it is also, of course, the most real one. Hence possession of money equals possession of the phallus, a point magnificently confirmed by such impressive but variously doomed transgressive heroines of the 40s and 50s as Mildred Pierce, Ruby Gentry and Mamie Stover, usurpers of the phallus.

3. The Voice   The voice of authority in the home has traditionally been that of the father; for all the myths about American matriarchy: "Stop it, or I'll tell your father." Outside the home, all the institutionalized voices of our culture—government, the church, the law, education, the media—have been dominated and controlled by men (occasionally, again, by nonfeminist women, but they are merely individuals rather than representatives of collective authority).

4. The Look   In relation to the visual arts, "the look" is logically the most theorized extension of the phallus: see, most obviously, John Berger's *Ways of Seeing* and Laura Mulvey's seminal article *Visual Pleasure and Narrative Cinema*. The simplest way of examining the male domination of women through the organization of "the look" is the study of advertisements. Two favorite patterns recur insistently, and they roughly correspond to Mulvey's presentation of Hawks and von Sternberg, respectively. In the case of advertisements featuring both a male and a female, the female looks out at us—or at nothing; the male looks at *her*, his look becoming the mediation of our own. With advertisements (usually for cosmetics) featuring a female alone, displayed for the camera—for our gaze, our appropriation—without the need of mediation, the male viewer symbolically possesses her through "the look"; the female viewer is encouraged to "be" her, the passive looked-at. It must be added that as soon as we move from advertising to cinema, that is, to narrative, with all its potential tensions, complexities and contradictions, the situation immediately becomes less simple. Mulvey's article, like so many seminal works, has proved quite inadequate and oversimplified in its actual reading of films: von Steinberg's work, for example, cannot be seen merely as reproduction/reinforcement of the objectification of women; it also operates consistently as a critique of it. This does not invalidate Mulvey's premises, which have proved invaluable as a starting point for exploration.

The symbolic phallus has as its logical corollary the notion of symbolic castration: the male fears the loss of power as castration, the powerless woman is already castrated. For a particularly vivid cinematic image of the castrated woman, one might evoke Liv Ullmann in *Persona*, cowering back against the wall of her hospital bedroom away from the television newscast of the burning monk in Vietnam, appalled not only at horror itself, but at the utter powerlessness of women in a world whose horrors are constructed and perpetrated by men. If one accepts the Freudian premise, then the no-win, Catch-22 situation of women in our culture becomes clear: men hate and fear them because as castrated they perpetually reactivate childhood fears of literal castration, and because they may at any point reject their status as castrated and attempt to appropriate the symbolic phallus. They can be accepted, grudgingly, only if they willingly accept a subordinate position and show themselves to be happy in their own castration. Conversely, any attempt to possess the phallus is simultaneously perceived as a threat to castrate the male: see the extraordinary introduction of Charlton Heston in *Ruby Gentry*, where Jennifer Jones captures him in the beam of her powerful flashlight, blinding him with its brilliance, violently inverting the looker/looked-at relationship.

The problem (for political purposes, i.e., from the viewpoint of producing fundamental transformation) lies in the relationship between the literal and symbolic levels. One can scarcely doubt that a relationship exists. It is vouched for in popular idiom. Consider, for example, the link between phallus and "look" epitomized in that favorite threat of castration-as-punishment-for-masturbation "Do that and you'll go blind," or the common usage of the term "castrating bitch," signifying the woman's rebellion (which, of course, can take very "unpleasant" forms) against her assigned passivity and subordination. The psychoanalytical argument (supported by our culture's pervasive acceptance of the phallus as the major symbol of power) is partly that symbolic castration inevitably reactivates the primal terrors of childhood. Yet it seems essential that the link be broken. If the struggle for women's liberation is to be won, men must learn to relinquish the domination that is central to socially constructed masculinity, and to relinquish it not in the name of liberal condescension and fair play but as an act that liberates them, too: in psychoanalytical terminology, they must learn to accept castration. Yet it is obviously impossible for anyone, male or female, short of a criminal psychopath, to think the term castration positively. The problem cannot be reduced to one of mere terminology: while the link between the literal and symbolic phallus remains, the term will retain its symbolic relevance. One's hope must be that as more enlightened attitudes to sex education, nudity, infantile masturbation, and parent/child relations develop, as literal castration fears diminish, the link will gradually weaken to the point where separation becomes possible, and men can view their relinquishment of domination as a relinquishment of a set of social conditions that oppresses *everybody*. Meanwhile, it is the dramatization of these quandaries—though frequently incoherent and confused—that gives De Palma's work its resonance.

DE PALMA AND HITCHCOCK

The common adverse account of De Palma starts from (and in effect ends at) the charge that he can do nothing but produce imitations. *Phantom of the Paradise* is a remake of *Phantom of the Opera*, *Scarface* a remake of the Hawks classic. Above all, of course, De Palma imitates—or, more brutally, plagiarizes—Hitchcock. I want here to define more precisely the relationship between the two bodies of work.

It has become a critical commonplace that we live in an age of remakes, and in general this can be taken as one sign among many of the bankruptcy of contemporary Hollywood cinema (another closely connected sign is the spinning off of sequels). As the bankruptcy is artistic but not by any means commercial (sequels, especially, are "what the public wants"), one can certainly see this as reflecting the bankruptcy of contemporary American culture, or capitalism in general. First, then, I want firmly to distinguish De Palma's Hitchcock-inspired films from this widespread tendency: their characteristics are quite distinct. A way of putting this distinctness positively is to say that the relationship of De Palma to Hitchcock is centered on a complex dialectic of affinity and difference, whereas the overwhelming majority of contemporary remakes and sequels are constructed on the simple premise that a formula that worked before will work again.

A brief consideration of De Palma's two non-Hitchcock remakes will define this distinction further. *Phantom of the Paradise* belongs, in fact, with the "Hitchcock" films (significantly, it contains an overt Hitchcock reference, what still remains the wittiest parody of the *Psycho* shower murder) and is related closely to the De Palma thematic. With Hawks, on the contrary, De Palma has shown no affinity whatever:

Scarface, for all its distinction, has far more in common than the "Hitchcock" films with the general conglomeration of contemporary remakes. Its weakest aspects are those derived without significant transformation (remade rather than made over) from the original: witness the uninteresting and perfunctory treatment of the incest theme. Everything that really works in the film is new: the explicit and devastating critique of contemporary American capitalism; the extraordinary climactic restaurant scene in which, first, Scarface is denounced by his wife, who walks out on him, and subsequently, Scarface denounces the entire restaurant clientele and walks out on *them*, retreating into final and irremediable isolation from his society, the audacious "excessive" images (ridiculous, of course, in the eyes of journalist critics who place their notion of the plausible above any attempt to read the film's symbolic progress) of the protagonist desperately burying his face in a mound of cocaine, emblem at once of his wealth and bankruptcy.

It is interesting that, in an age of generally inert remakes and imitations, there is still such insistence on the Romantic concept of originality. In terms of the Hollywood cinema and its critical reception, the term has become thoroughly debased. A film is perceived as original either if the reviewer is ignorant of its sources or if it imitates a (generally European) model of critically ratified "genius": when De Palma works his variations of *Psycho*, this is imitation or plagiarism, whereas when Bob Fosse or Woody Allen imitates Fellini or Bergman this is somehow, mysteriously, evidence of his originality. Debased or not, the cult of originality is of comparatively recent date. Renaissance painting is rich in acknowledged masterpieces which draw from pre-existing models not only their subject (let us say, the Madonna and Child) but their iconography, their composition, their relation of foreground and background, and their deployment of colors. In such a context, originality (and one really needs to substitute another word like authenticity) can be judged only by the use to which the formulas have been put, evaluation becoming a matter of discriminating between the inert and the creative. De Palma's variations on Hitchcock—confused, unsatisfactory, maddening perhaps—are never inert.

What, then, does De Palma borrow from Hitchcock? Most obviously, certain plot structures: *Sisters* and *Dressed to Kill* both derive from *Psycho*, *Obsession* from *Vertigo*, *Blow Out* (much less closely) from *Rear Window* (as well as from Antonioni's *Blow Up*, as De Palma's title candidly confesses). *Rear Window* also provides the basis for specific sequences in *Sisters* and *Dressed to Kill*, an influence already anticipated in a hilarious scene in the early *Hi, Mom*. Beyond these, *Carrie* owes something to *Marnie* (the mother/daughter relationship), and Richard Lippe has brilliantly suggested a much less obvious, perhaps unconscious relationship between *North by Northwest* and *The Fury*: both are journey movies built on "double chase" structures (the male protagonist both pursued and pursuer); both plots are activated by an American government secret organization headed by a manipulative father figure (Leo G. Carroll, John Cassavetes); both journeys move progressively from city to country, and culminate in a private and sinister house which the hero must infiltrate; the climax of both shows the hero trying to save a person he loves from falling from a great height. I shall show that, while some of the films follow the original plot structure closely, each of them significantly transforms its meaning.

It is the existence of much deeper affinities that validates De Palma's borrowings of Hitchcock plot structures; what is at issue is not the cynical appropriation of commercially successful formulas but a symbiotic relationship whose basis is a shared complex of psychological/thematic drives. These are so closely interconnected in the work of both filmmakers that it is difficult to separate them out, but in the interests of clarity we may attempt a list of the major components, restricting the Hitchcock examples to the films De Palma has demonstrably used, a small group of late works.

1.Voyeurism   This is already strikingly in evidence in *Hi, Mom!*, a film made before any clear connections between De Palma and Hitchcock had been established. It is only retrospectively that one connects with *Rear Window* the sequence in which Robert De Niro, attempting to make a pornographic film, sets up his camera to film his own seduction of Jennifer Salt in the opposite apartment block. As with Hitchcock, the attitude to voyeurism is complex, the desire to watch from a position of secrecy and immunity being both indulged and chastised. Both directors extend this principle to cinematic practice itself, with the spectator as the ultimate voyeur. *Rear Window* has been widely interpreted as an allegory about cinema; De Palma makes the connection between voyeurism and the visual media explicit, in, for example, the *Hi, Mom!* sequence just cited and in the magnificent opening of *Sisters*, and, further extended to include listening, it forms the very basis of *Blow Out.*

2. Romantic Obsession   In Hitchcock, this is always qualified by irony and skepticism: in *Vertigo*, James Stewart's obsession with Kim Novak is defined in terms of an impossible and ultimately regressive wish fulfillment fantasy; in *Marnie*, Sean Connery's obsession with Tippi Hedren is bound up with his perception of her as dangerous and neurotic, so that one of several factors qualifying the sense of a happy ending is the unanswered question of what happens when she is "cured." With De Palma, there is less direct ironic commentary on the male characters' romantic obsession, but it is invariably presented as hopeless, incapable of fulfillment: in *Phantom of the Paradise* the male protagonist (William Finley), never physically attractive, becomes so hideously disfigured that he cannot even show himself; in *Obsession*, the object of the hero's desire turns out to be his own daughter. *Sisters* most rigorously subjects romantic obsession to criticism, the fixation of Dr. Breton (William Finley again) on Dominique/Danielle being perceived as the desire of the male to construct and possess (and thereby symbolically castrate) the female, depriving her of all autonomy.

3. Male Sexual Anxiety The association of romantic passion with the male power drive has as its corollary the fear of losing that power, the fear of impotence or castration. The subjugation of female desire to male desire, the containment of the female within patriarchal normality, is typically dramatized in Hitchcock's films as the male's assertion, as his means of assuaging castration fears, that he and he alone possesses the phallus. Hitchcock's films—they amount to one of the most eccentric bodies of work within the Hollywood cinema, though our sense of the eccentricity has been partly dulled by familiarity and popular acceptance—are only precariously contained within the patterns of classical narrative. They move obediently toward the formulaic reestablishment of the patriarchal order (the death of Judy, the marriage of Roger Thornhill and Eve Kendall, the elimination of Norman Bates, the cure of Marnie), yet the reestablishment is invariably undercut (by irony, by a sense of desolation arising out of irremediable loss, by a sense of the emptiness, the emotional bankruptcy, of the order itself). No Hitchcock film lacks a sense of disturbance; the degree of that disturbance, varying enormously from film to film, corresponds closely to the degree to which male sexual anxiety is granted reassurance—the difference between, for example, *North by Northwest* and *Vertigo*. I should make clear that I do not wish to claim that De Palma's films are more radical than Hitchcock's (when one moves away from messages and concentrates on ideological tensions, the notion of what constitutes a radical film becomes obviously problematic). But in certain specific, hence limited, ways, they go further: the alleged structuring principle of classical narrative, the restoration of the patriarchal order, collapses altogether. The most extreme instance is the end of *The Fury*, a resolution unthinkable in Hitchcock: the "good father" (Kirk Douglas) voluntarily falls to his death after failing to save his son Robin (Andrew Stevens); as Robin dies he transmits his powers to the already psychically endowed daughter/sister figure (Amy Irving); she uses her accumulated telekinetic potency to explode (literally) the evil father figure (John Cassavetes). The "Oedipal trajectory" of classical narrative (see Raymond Bellour's celebrated reading of *North by Northwest*), in which the symbolic father is reinstated and the woman is restored to her "correct" (i.e., castrated) position, is here spectacularly negated.

4. Female Sexuality/Energy/Autonomy The necessary corollary of the male's fear of losing the phallus is the fear that the female may appropriate it. The transgressive female is a recurrent figure throughout Hitchcock's work; invariably (unlike the majority of her male counterparts) her guilt is real and her own, not a matter of an "exchange"; invariably she is punished by death if her transgression is irrecuperable (Judy in *Vertigo* is an accessory to murder), by emotional and physical chastisement if her sin is less extreme (like Tippi Hedren in *The Birds* and *Marnie*). Superficially, the films lie open to feminist attack in quite obvious ways; on a deeper level they strongly repudiate it. The woman's punishment is never endorsed, the spectator is never permitted to feel satisfaction in it; what the films finally enact (and in enacting expose) is the intolerable strain that is the cost of the imposition of male dominance.

De Palma, again, carries this even further. The continuity is clear enough: the murder of Angie Dickinson in *Dressed to Kill* closely parallels the murder of Janet Leigh in *Psycho* (registered in both cases as the most grotesquely excessive punishment in either director's work); the anguish and attempted suicide of Sandra (Genevieve Bujold) in *Obsession* parallels, though much less closely, the death of Judy in *Vertigo*. But De Palma's identification with the female position is in general much more unambiguous than Hitchcock's, and, correspondingly, the male position is much more unambiguously undermined. Female activity and autonomy are not inevitably punished (see the end of *The Fury*); when punished, the activity is also clearly endorsed, so that the monstrousness of the punishment is foregrounded. The key film here is *Sisters*, which I discuss in detail later. For the moment, I shall consider *Obsession* and its relation to *Vertigo* (of all Hitchcock's films, the one in which the mechanisms and motivations of the male power drive are subjected to the most ruthless and uncompromising critique).

The crucial difference between the two films lies in the nature of the heroine's involvement in the convoluted criminal plot. In *Vertigo*, Judy's role is purely instrumental ("You were the victim, I was the tool," as her letter to Scottie declares); her motivation is money and the man's favors. In *Obsession*, although Sandra is involved in the machinations of an evil man, her motivation is autonomous: she is avenging herself and, more important, her mother. The opening of the film sets up the couple as, in the words of Bob (John Lithgow), "this world's last romantics"; to the ideal romantic couple is added the ideal family. Yet, as father dances with daughter, mother rather pointedly withdraws. Central to the film's development is the daughter's growing identification with the mother who, within the structures of the nuclear family, was initially her rival. One of the film's key moments is when Sandra, many years later and about to become her father's bride, reads her dead mother's diary, and the romantic love that is the basis of the entire action is abruptly revealed as a male-imposed illusion: the mother, on her side of the ideal union, felt unhappy and neglected. The film dramatizes, and systematically undermines, two manifestations of the male power drive, the assertion of the phallus: the imposition of romantic love and the potency signified by money. Hence the emotional force of the extraordinary final moments. Courtland (Cliff Robertson) rushes toward the woman who is the seeming reincarnation of his romantic ideal (explicitly, the Beatrice to his Dante, with whom he was going to begin the "vita nuova") armed with two objects—the suitcase of money that proves the greatness of his love for her, and the gun with which he means to kill her for betraying that love. As the suitcase bursts open and the banknotes are dispersed, she reveals in a word that she is his daughter. The ensuing reunion—ecstatic on her side, profoundly troubled on his—

Genevieve Bujold in *Obsession*

is modeled on the famous climactic moment of *Vertigo*, the moment (circling lovers, circling camera) of simultaneous fulfillment and disillusionment. Here, however, what is expressed are the triumph of the woman and the defeat of the man (though a defeat he comes, in the final seconds, graciously to accept): the celebration of her identification with the mother, ironically fused with the destruction of romantic illusion.

5. Gender Ambiguity The problematic of castration (both male and female, literal and symbolic) inevitably merges with, and becomes confused with, other questions of sexuality: the social construction of gender roles and the repression of bisexuality, of the masculinity of women and the femininity of men. *Psycho* (significantly, with *Rear Window*, the Hitchcock film that most haunts De Palma's work) produces at its center, and as its problem, the figure of Norman Bates, the feminized male who becomes transformed into the masculinized female, the avenging mother: a figure of extraordinary resonance in relation to all the relationships (both sexual and familial) in the film. In close parallel *Dressed to Kill* produces as its center Dr. Elliott (Michael Caine), a feminized male so horrified by his own masculinity that he feels compelled to murder any woman who arouses it. The whole film moves toward the explicit statement of castration—Nancy Allen's detailed description, in the restaurant, of the operation that would have converted Dr. Elliott into a woman. For the contemporary viewer and reader, the ending of the film irresistibly evokes Balzac's *Sarrasine*, as read by Roland Barthes in *S/Z*: the revelation of castration makes it impossible for the heterosexual couple to make love. The question has been raised, in relation to *S/Z*, as to whether *Sarrasine* is really about castration or rather about bisexuality; precisely the same question could be asked of *Dressed To Kill*, which provides no coherent answer.

The other literary reference the film evokes for me, equally irresistibly, is Eliot's famous cryptic note to part 3 of *The Wasteland*: "All the men are one man, all the women are one woman, and the sexes meet in Tiresias." (De Palma has assured me that the use of the name Elliott for *his* Tiresias is purely coincidental; he also admits to familiarity with Eliot's poem. What exactly is coincidence?) As fascinating in its suggestiveness as it is infuriating in its incoherence, *Dressed to Kill* plays intricately throughout on doubles and on ambiguities of sexual identity. The first female transgressor (Angie Dickinson) finds her reflection, even as she dies, in the second (Nancy Allen), as they stretch out hands to each other across the entrance to the elevator; both are reflected in Bobby, Elliott's female persona, as, in women's clothes, she wields the castrating razor. Bobby, in turn, finds her double in the masculine police woman assigned to protect Liz (Nancy Allen) but mistaken by her for the killer. An extraordinary sequence using cross-cutting and split screen juxtaposes Liz with Dr. Elliott and both with an actual transsexual being interviewed on television: the man who wants to lose the phallus (literally) mirror-imaged by the woman who wants to acquire it (symbolically, in the form of money—she speculates on the stock exchange, and is involved in business calculations throughout the sequence). Less obvious, but most intriguing of all, Peter (Keith Gordon) becomes, as feminized and asexual male, the echo of the would-be-castrated Dr. Elliott. The original intention was that the role be played by a child; when this proved impractical De Palma made the character a young man without apparently altering his function in the film. The connotations of asexuality may therefore be accidental (but what exactly is accident?). It seems extremely important that the film should produce as its male hero a gentle and feminine character who is excluded (why is never gone into) from becoming the female hero's lover. The film, in other words, while built on the horrors arising from sexual difference, can see, (like *Sisters* before it), no resolution of that difference except through castration. (Consider how different the final effect would have been if Peter had been characterized as gay.) This may be why De Palma's habitual identification with women is accompanied, paradoxically, by an apparent animus against them, the contradiction often expressing itself in the treatment of a single character: Kate (Angie Dickinson) in *Dressed to Kill* is the most obvious example, but there is also Grace (Jennifer Salt) in *Sisters*, the major flaw of which is De Palma's inability to take her seriously. The artistic personality the films define is that of a fundamentally feminine man who, because he *is* a man within a patriarchal culture, can view his femininity only in terms of castration.

✳ ✳ ✳

I shall conclude by examining in more detail De Palma's two finest, most fully realized works to date, *Sisters* and *Blow Out*. By way of transition, it is illuminating to
formulate more systematically the structural parallels between *Psycho*, *Sisters* and
Dressed to Kill, and the play of difference those parallels make possible.

Psycho	*Sisters*	*Dressed to Kill*
Bedroom	Locker room	Shower/bedroom
Office (money)	TV show (prizes)	Kate/Peter
		*Kate/Dr. Elliot
Theft	Danielle propositions	Kate picks up man
	Philip	
Car journey	Ferry to Staten Island	Taxi to man's apartment
Norman/Mother	Danielle/Dominique	
dialogue	dialogue	
Norman/Marion		
Murder of Marion	Murder of Philip	Murder of Kate
	xIntroduction of Grace	xIntroduction of Liz
Cleaning/swamp	Cleaning/couch	
	Grace/police	Liz/police
xIntroduction of Lila		
Introduction of Arbogast	Introduction of Larch	Peter as investigator
Arbogast to motel	Larch to apartment	Peter filming
Murder of Arbogast	Larch almost caught	Subway scene
Visit to sheriff	Visit to McClennan	
(Revelation: Mrs. Bates	(Revelation: Dominique	
dead)	dead)	
	Siamese twin tape	Transsexual on TV
Mrs. Bates to cellar		Elliott to psychiatrist
Lila into Bates house	Grace into clinic	Liz into Elliott's house
Lila finds Mrs. Bates	Grace "becomes"	Liz/Bobby confrontation
	Dominique	
Psychiatrist's explanation		Psychiatrist's explanation
Norman in cell	Grace in child's	Liz's nightmare
	bedroom	

In each film a crucial point of transference occurs, a transition from one character to another as the center of interest; in each case the transition and its significance are in key respects quite different:

Psycho	*Sisters*	*Dressed*
Marion—Norman	Philip—Grace	Kate—Liz
Female—Male	Male—Female	Female—Female
Neurosis—Psychosis	Possession of "the look"	Progression in female sexuality, assertion, activeness

The above chart, while largely self-explanatory, requires a few elucidatory comments. First, it will be clear that the parallels range from the close and obvious to the relatively esoteric. Second, they do not always obey a parallel chronology: those that occur "out of synch," as it were, are linked by typographical signs. Third, many of the parallels, whether close or not, in synch or out, serve to highlight the differences between the films and in some cases give those differences richer significance (perhaps, instead of talking about plagiarism critics might begin talking about intertextuality). I shall discuss a few of the more important differences here.

Psycho, from being initially deplored or regarded as a joke, has become something of a critical fetish object, to the extent that one feels a certain trepidation in suggesting that it has any flaws whatever. After a number of viewings of which I long ago lost count, the first half of the film remains as engrossing, and seemingly inexhaustible, as ever; the film picks up again with Lila's exploration of the Bates house. The half hour in between becomes more tedious with every viewing: shot like a TV movie ("photographs of people talking"), it consists largely of Hitchcock laboriously maneuvering his characters into position for the next incursion into the Bates domain. De Palma in both films solves at a blow the structural problem that defeated Hitchcock and his writer Joseph Stephano in adapting Robert Bloch's novel: the investigator in the film's second half witnesses the murder that closes its opening movement, and the narrative hiatus is abruptly bridged.

This strategy has a further extension. The reader may have noticed that my chart of narrative transitions appears to cheat: the second character in each of the De Palma films is not the one who corresponds to Norman Bates (the logical parallel would replace Grace and Liz with, respectively, Danielle/Dominique and Dr. Elliott/Bobby). However De Palma achieves a marked shift of emphasis: where Hitchcock kept Sam and Lila quite nondescript and undercharacterized, mere projections of the curious spectator into the film, De Palma centers our attention on the investigator, who happens to be in both instances a woman. One might loosely claim Lila Crane as a transgressor: she assumes an active role and an active "look." But women have explored sinister houses virtually since cinema began. Grace and Liz are transgressors in far more specific ways; they are also more drastically punished. The shift, one might argue, is motivated by De Palma's characteristic disturbance about women (identification with/animus against).

Accordingly, the *meaning* of the transition changes significantly, the centering of the conflict on female transgression becoming increasingly explicit and emphatic. All three films move toward the revelation that the woman, usurper of "the look," must finally confront. Lila faces, in the form of the dead/alive Mrs. Bates, the ultimate horror of the Oedipal tensions produced by the nuclear family; Grace is forced to witness and participate in the castration of woman under patriarchy; Liz, the appropriator of the symbolic phallus, confronts her inverted mirror image and the horror of a sexual difference that can neither be accepted nor transcended.

Sisters

I have argued elsewhere that horror films can be profitably explored from the starting point of applying a simple all-purpose formula, Normality is threatened by the Monster, and that the formula offers three variables with which to work on the analysis of individual films: the definition of normality, the definition of the monster, and, crucially, the definition of the relationship between the two. As a general rule, the less easy the application, the more complex and interesting the film, though no horror film is entirely simple (i.e., with the monster as purely external threat). Take *War of the Worlds* (Haskin/Pal, 1953) as an example of the horror film at its simplest as far as meaning is concerned. On the surface, Normality = humans, the Monster = Martians; this covers (not very concealingly) a second level where Normality = the free world and the Monster = Communism (the news bulletins in the film name every major country but Russia as the victim of Martian invasion, an absence that leaves the audience to make a simple deduction). Yet even here the threat only *appears* purely external. The topical fear of Communist invasion in its turn covers a more fundamental fear, the true subject of horror films—the fear of the release of repressed sexuality. The Martian machines are blatantly phallic, with their snakelike probing and penetrating devices, it is the monogamous heterosexual couple (Classical Hollywood's habitual basic definition of normality) who are centrally threatened, and the film ends with God and Nature combining, at the very moment when the whole world (i.e., normality) is in imminent danger of destruction, to reunite the couple, annihilate the invaders, and restore repression. The film is also crudely sexist. Lip service is paid to female equality, the heroine being supplied with an M.A. in technological science, but once that's been established, her only function is to scream every time a Martian phallus pokes in through her window. *War of the Worlds*, then, to which the formula applies very simply, is like thousands of other films reducible to the simplest and crudest patriarchal ideology.

The great horror movies demand a far more complex application of the formula. For example, *I Walked with a Zombie* is structured on a complicated set of oppositions (crudely reducible to normality/monster) which the film systematically undermines until everything is in doubt; in *Psycho* normality and the monster no longer function even superficially as separable opposites but exist on a continuum which the progress of the film traces. *Psycho* is clearly a seminal work, definitively establishing (if hardly inventing) two concepts crucial to the genre's subsequent development: the monster as human psychotic/schizophrenic and the revelation of horror as existing at the heart of the family. The continuum is represented not only by the transition from Marion Crane to Norman Bates, but by the succession of references to parent/child relationships that starts with Marion's mother's picture on the wall overseeing the respectable steak dinner and culminates in Mrs. Bates. Since *Psycho*, and particularly in the 70s, the definition of normality has become increasingly uncertain, questionable, open to attack; accordingly, the monster becomes increasingly complex.

The force and complexity of *Sisters*, De Palma's finest achievement prior to *Blow Out* and one of the great American films of the 70s, can be demonstrated through the ways in which it responds to the formula. Traditional normality no longer exists in the film as actuality but only as ideology—as what society tries, at once unsuccessfully and destructively, to impose. Specifically, it is what Grace Collier's mother wants to do to Grace (Jennifer Salt) and what Emile Breton (William Finley) wants to do to Danielle/Dominique (Margot Kidder). Grace's mother speaks condescendingly of her daughter's journalist career as her "little job," regards it as a phase she is going through, looks forward to her marrying, and proposes an appropriate suitor; Emile's obsessive project has been to create Danielle as a sweet, submissive girl at the increasing expense of Dominique (eventually provoking Dominique's death). Normality, therefore, is still marriage, the family and patriarchy—all that the monster of the horror movie has always implicitly threatened. But whereas in the traditional horror film there had to be an appearance of upholding normality, however sympathetic and fascinating the monster, in *Sisters* normality is not even superficially endorsed. If the monster is defined as that which threatens normality, it follows that the monster of *Sisters* is Grace as well as Danielle/Dominique—a point the film acknowledges in the climactic hallucination/flashback sequence wherein Grace becomes Dominique, joined to Danielle as her Siamese twin, the film's privileged moment on which its entire structure hinges. Simply, one can define the monster of *Sisters* as women's liberation; adding only that the film follows the time-honored horror film tradition of making the monster emerge as the most sympathetic character and its emotional center.

Sisters analyzes the ways in which women are oppressed within patriarchal society on two levels, the professional (Grace) and the psychosexual (Danielle/Dominique). Grace's progress in the film can be read as a depiction of how women are denied a voice. At times this can be taken literally: the police inspector denies Grace the right to ask questions or to make verbal interventions; in the asylum she is prevented from using the phone, her attempts to assert her sanity (and even her own name) are overruled, and she is silenced by being put to sleep. More widely, her professional potency is frustrated at every step: the police refuse to believe her story; her editor habitually gives her ludicrous assignments such as the convict who has carved a model of his prison out of soap; her mother tries to make her normal. Even when she gets permission to pursue her investigations, it must be under the guidance of a male private detective (Charles Durning), who rejects her spontaneous ideas in favor of the methods he has been taught in training school. Finally, rendered powerless by a drug, she is given her words by Emile Breton: all she will be able to repeat when she wakes up is "There was no body because there was no murder." At the end of the film she is reduced to the role of child, tended by her mother, surrounded by toys, and denying the truth of which she once alone had possession.

Also—and this is where the Hitchcock/De Palma fascination with voyeurism becomes incorporated significantly into the film's thematic structure—Grace transgresses by her desire to usurp the male prerogative of "the look." The opening of *Sisters* succinctly establishes the gaze as another means of male dominance: Danielle is blind; not only does Philip watch her begin to undress, but we, the cinema audience (thus defined by identification as male), also watch. This is of course immediately and brilliantly undercut: we discover that, having allowed ourselves to be drawn into the voyeuristic act, we have identified ourselves less with Philip than with the lewd and philistine panel (with male *and* female members) of a particularly mindless TV show. But, having established looking as a theme at the outset, De Palma can take it up again later when Grace aspires to the look of dominance, the look that will give her knowledge. It is for this that she is most emphatically punished: the hallucination sequence is introduced by Emile's telling her that, as she wanted to see, she will now be forced to witness everything, and is punctuated by huge close-ups of her terrified eye. What Grace sees is the ultimate subjugation (castration) of woman by man.

When Danielle/Dominique murders Philip, her attack is on the two organs by which male supremacy is most obviously enforced, the phallus and the voice; the logic of the film perhaps would also demand that she blind him. Through the presentation of Danielle/Dominique the theme of women's oppression is given another dimension on an altogether more radical level. Crucial to it is the opposition the film makes between "freaks" and mad people. Freaks are a product of nature; the insane are a product of society (normality). The two mad people we see are simply carrying to excess two of society's most emphasized virtues, tidiness and cleanliness, the man obsessively trimming hedges with his shears in the night, the woman with her cleaning cloth terrified of the germs that can be transmitted through the telephone wires; both pervert the "virtue" into aggression. (One might note here that the detective's van assumes two disguises in the course of the film: first that of a house-cleaning firm, later that of Ajax Exterminators.)

Freaks, on the other hand, are natural: it is normality that names, degrades, rejects or seeks to remold them (see Danielle's horror, in the hallucination sequence, not of being a freak but of being *named* as one). The morality of using real freaks (the photographs of genuine Siamese twins in the videotape Grace is shown, the various freaks discernible in the hallucination sequence) may be touched on here, with the essential point made by comparing De Palma's use of them with Michael Winner's in the worst—most offensive and repressive—horror film of the 70s, *The Sentinel.* Winner, with his usual taste and humanity, uses real freaks, unforgivably, for their (socially defined) ugliness, to represent demons surging up out of hell. De Palma uses them, in a film that consistently and subversively undercuts *all* assumptions of the normal, to symbolize everything that normality cannot cope with or encompass. To object, in this context, to the association of women's liberation with freaks would be simply to endorse normality's definition. Freaks only become freaks when normality names them; to her mother, as to the police inspector, Grace is clearly a freak—hence the mother's appearance with a camera in the hallucination sequence where Grace becomes Dominique. Danielle/Dominique function both literally and symbolically: literally, as freaks whom normality has no place for, must cure, hence destroy; symbolically, as a composite image of all that must be repressed under patriarchy (Dominique) in order to create the nice, wholesome, submissive female (Danielle). Dominique's rebellion against patriarchal normality took the extreme but eloquent form of killing Danielle's unborn baby with garden shears; after which Emile killed her by separating her from her twin. What is repressed is not of course annihilated: Dominique continues to live on in Danielle. Further, the point is made (and underlined by repetition in the speech of the priest in the videotape that recurs during the hallucination sequence) that Danielle's sweetness depends on the existence of Dominique, on to whom all her "evil" qualities can be projected. Equally, Dominique is Danielle's potency: the scar of separation, revealed by the slow zoom-in to her body as she and Philip make love, is also the "wound" of castration. Having deprived Danielle of her power (creating her as the male ideal of the sweet girl), Emile can realize a union with her only when she (or the repressed Dominique), in turn, has castrated *him*, signified by his pressing their clasped hands into the blood of his wound.

The intelligence and radicalism of the film are manifested in its refusal to produce a scapegoat, in the form of an individual male character who can be blamed. Philip is an entirely sympathetic figure, Emile ultimately a pathetic one (he loves Danielle in precisely the way ideology conditions men to love women). He is also one of De Palma's hopeless romantic lovers, played by William Finley who was to fill the same role a year later in *Phantom of the Paradise.*

Philip, moreover, provides a further extension of the oppression theme by being black. The film at no point presents his color as an issue, but shows it as an issue for white-dominated normality (his prize for his TV appearance is dinner for two in

"The African Room"; the police sergeant's comment is that "those people are always stabbing each other"). The amiable private investigator asserts his authority over Grace because he is placed in that position. The final image of him (last shot of the film) up a telegraph pole by a tiny railway depot somewhere in remote Quebec watching the sofa containing Philip's body, with nobody left alive to collect it, is at once funny and poignant. The assertion of male dominance in the film is shown everywhere as destructive, nowhere as successful: it is variously misguided, disastrous, and futile.

One must not, however, look to *Sisters* for any optimistic portrayal of liberation. If the horror film of the 70s has lost all faith in normality, it simultaneously sees all that it repressed (the monster) as, through repression, perverted beyond redemption. In its apocalyptic phase, the horror film, even when it is not concerned literally with the end of the world (*The Omen*), brings its own world to cataclysm, refusing any hope of positive resolution (see, to name three distinguished and varied examples, *Carrie*, *God Told Me To*, and *The Texas Chainsaw Massacre*). The most disquieting aspect of *Sisters* is that the two components of its composite monster, Grace and Danielle/Dominique, are in constant and unresolved antagonism. They operate on quite distinct levels of consciousness: Danielle tells Philip near the beginning of the film that she is not interested in women's liberation; Grace clearly is, but only on the professional level. Even when forced together (as Siamese twins) they are constantly straining apart. The deeper justification for the use of split screen (which also works brilliantly on the suspense level) is that it simultaneously juxtaposes and separates the two women, presenting them as parallel yet antagonistic.

The question as to whether *Sisters* is really about the oppression of women or is "just" a horror movie is one that I decline to discuss. It is, however, illuminating to place it beside a Hollywood film whose concern with women's liberation is conscious and overt, *Alice Doesn't Live Here Anymore*. *Alice* (a charming, indeed disarming, film) is a perfect example of what Roland Barthes calls "inoculation": ideology inoculates itself with a small dose of criticism in order to distract attention from its fundamental evils. The opening of the film (after the childhood prologue) depicts an impossible marital situation, wherein the woman is ignored, taken for granted or maltreated, her role as wife and mother being assumed to be all she needs. The end of the film unites her with a man who will treat her well, permit discussion, and perhaps allow her to pursue her own career on the side: the patriarchal order is restored, suitably modified. *Sisters* is beyond such inoculation.

Blow Out

Both *Rear Window* and *Blow Out* have as their underlying premise male castration anxiety and the search for reassurance or compensation. This is obvious in Hitchcock's film, which takes as its starting point Jefferies' broken leg and the transference of phallic power to "the look": one of Hitchcock's funniest and most serious gags is the systematic growth of the look-as-phallus-substitute—eyes, binoculars, a huge telescope. In *Blow Out* Jack Terry (John Travolta) bears no physical mark of castration; yet he shows no sexual interest in women (although he feigns it when it suits his purposes), and all his energies are displaced on to his work as sound man. The sequence that follows the credits—Jack on the bridge in the woods recording his sound effects—visually establishes his microphone as phallic symbol. Where Jefferies finds compensatory power in looking, Jack finds it in listening; in both cases, the man's sense of his own manhood, conceived essentially in terms of dominance, comes to depend upon his proving the truth of what he believes he has seen or heard; both films move toward his confrontation with his alter ego, the spied-upon, in each case a murderer.

Weaving through *Blow Out* like a guiding thread is the suggestion that Jack's "disinterested" search for truth is not in fact disinterested at all: its true motivation is the assertion of his own ego. The film is also quite clear that this assertion is realized at the expense of women. The connection with *Rear Window* has been often noticed; as far as I know, no one has commented on *Blow Out*'s relationship to another great Classical Hollywood movie, Fritz Lang's *The Big Heat*. There Debbie (Gloria Grahame), a gangster's kept woman, becomes attracted to the hero, Bannion (Glenn Ford), and specifically to his "disinterested" nobility; she dies helping him successfully extirpate the city's corruption. Bannion's motivation is presented as mixed: his integrity is indirectly responsible for the death of his wife, from which point he is motivated as much by the desire for personal revenge as by a desire to clean up the city. His responsibility for Debbie's death is kept carefully ambiguous. He leaves her a gun, ostensibly for her own protection, perhaps (unconsciously?) so that she will do what he, with his nobility and integrity, cannot: murder Martha Duncan. One might say that the subtext of *The Big Heat* (the hero's use of a woman to whom he feels morally superior to serve his own ends, and his responsibility for her death) becomes the overt, dominant text of *Blow Out*. One can trace its development throughout the film.

1. During the scene on the bridge, Jack records—at first inadvertently—the conversation of a young couple. The man is leading the woman on, plainly bent on seducing her against her better judgment. Jack's knowing smile aligns him at the outset with the manipulative male, at which moment the girl becomes aware of his presence, and his voyeuristic complicity is made explicit ("What is he, a peeping tom or something?").

2. The establishment of Jack's relationship with Sally (Nancy Allen) in the hospital is already characterized by deception, albeit of an innocent if patronizing sort: knowing that she is about to succumb to sedation, he tells her he will fetch her clothes so that she can leave.

3. When he discovers what he has recorded (the sound of a gunshot, establishing the "blow out" as nonaccidental), he attempts to enlist Sally's aid. When she resists, he immediately abandons rational argument and resorts to emotional blackmail ("I saved your life, the least you can do is have a drink with me"). The entire sequence is very interesting in its relation to audience expectations. He has brought her to a motel bedroom and has stayed there himself; the conventions of Hollywood narrative demand that he show at least some sexual interest, but he shows none, spending the night obsessively replaying his tape. In the context of De Palma's relationship to Hitchcock, the parallel here would seem to be with *Vertigo* (the man rescues the woman from drowning and puts her to bed), a parallel that underlines Jack's sexual indifference.

4. When they meet for a drink, Jack deliberately manipulates Sally into missing the train that would take her to a safe seclusion. His method is to feign interest in her professional accomplishments as makeup artist. When she realizes that she is being both exploited and patronized ("You're not interested in this at all. . . . You just kept me talking so that I'd miss my train"), he switches abruptly to the use of his own attractiveness and supposed *personal* interest in her ("No, that's not true, Sally, I just didn't want you to go"). In fact, Sally's job and Jack's job offer suggestive parallels: she falsifies people's appearances by applying makeup, he falsifies bits of film by applying sound effects.

5. Jack finds that all his tapes have been erased. The film's midpoint/turning point is thus a form of symbolic castration whose importance De Palma marks by two of his most "excessive" rhetorical gestures, a seemingly interminable, dizzying circular pan and a vertiginous overhead shot. After that Jack's more or less subtle manipulation of Sally escalates into overt bullying.

6. In the scene where Jack makes Sally miss her train, he subsequently confesses his responsibility for the death of Freddie Corvo, the direct consequence of Jack's wiring him (again, in the apparent interests of truth, and in the real interests of Jack's own ego). In the final scenes, he wires Sally when he sends her to her fatal meeting with Burke, the bogus Frank Donohue, without any sense of repeating his own earlier actions. He is too preoccupied with his own self-vindication ("I'm going to cover all the bases. Nobody's going to fuck me this time"), and his concern is for the safety, not of Sally, but of Manny Karp's film.

If the subject of *Sisters* is the oppression (castration) of women under patriarchy, *Blow Out* can be read as its corollary: an uncompromising critique of the machinations of the male ego to assert its possession of the phallus. It is crucial that Jack Terry (one of Travolta's most disciplined performances) remain a sympathetic character throughout: the male spectator is permitted no comforting or distancing superiority ("Of course, I wouldn't behave like that"). The critique, however, goes far beyond the development of linear narrative I have so far described. Supporting and extending it is a systematic symbolic structure built upon the figure of the dou-

Male Manipulation in *Blow Out*

Dennis Franz and Nancy Allen

John Travolta and Nancy Allen

ble. Jack, as sympathetic character, as the film's main identification figure, finds significant reflection in three other male characters, none of whom is sympathetic in the least and one of whom is explicitly psychopathic. I deal with them in ascending order of importance.

Frank Donohue. The connection between Jack and Donohue (the investigative reporter for "City News" and illustrious television personality) is the only one not underlined by either narrative echoes or the reiterative use of specific cinematic codes, perhaps because it is the simplest and most obvious. Donohue's verbal manipulation of Jack closely reflects Jack's of Sally. He is another, cruder example of ego-serving masquerading as the search for truth. As he persuades Jack to "go public" on his news show, the "disinterested" desire to reveal truth quickly slips into "It's a great story." When Jack initially resists—as Sally initially resisted—Donohue moves immediately into a direct appeal to Jack's need for personal recognition: "Frank Donohue believes it. And he's got eight million people every night that watch him. . . . All those sons of bitches are going to believe Jack Terry's story, I promise you that." Jack capitulates.

Manny Karp. By withholding crucial information from her, Karp has manipulated Sally into playing her role in the blow out plot, closely anticipating Jack's use of her (subtler, but scarcely less reprehensible) in the plot *he* is trying to construct. Karp's motivation, pure material greed, is altogether cruder than Jack's, yet the stripping away of the camouflage of disinterestedness merely reveals the drive of personal egoism the more clearly (Karp's phallus is money). Hence the overhead shot when Jack discovers that his tapes have been erased is precisely answered by the overhead shot when Sally knocks Karp out and steals his film, source of all his expectations.

Burke. The film's key scene—its "primal scene," one is tempted to say—juxtaposes (when "what actually happened" is revealed) Burke, Karp and Jack Terry: Burke causes the death of "the father" (Governor George McRyan, probable future President of the United States), Karp films it, Jack records it: all three are voyeurs at a scene where "the father" is caught with a woman *in flagrante delicto*. Burke and Jack are subtly paralleled throughout the film. Both begin by doing a professional job, both continue with that job for their personal satisfaction after their employers have disowned it. Jack's personal satisfaction involves the manipulation of women, Burke's *is* the murder of women; both drives come together in the death of Sally, caused by Jack, executed by Burke. Both secretly listen in to and record other people's conversations (Jack and the young couple at the bridge, Burke's tapping of Jack's phone). Jack's responsibility for the death of Freddie Corvo is directly linked to Burke's murder of the prostitute at the station: each is a death-by-hanging, in a public washroom. Both men, and their responsibility for people's deaths, are associated by wire: Jack "wires" Freddie Corvo and "wires" Sally; Burke uses wire as his murder weapon. Finally, Jack's hysterical execution of Burke at the film's climax closely imitates Burke's mutilation of his victims by multiple stab wounds in the belly. The effect is similar to that of Ethan Edwards' scalping of Scar in *The Searchers*: the hero inadvertently acknowledges his affinity with the villain by duplicating his actions.

* * *

Blow Out strikingly combines the overtly political concerns of *Hi, Mom!* with the sexual politics of De Palma's Hitchcock variations. The attitude to the American political system is characteristically pessimistic: the electorate can only choose between corrupt liberalism and corrupt conservatism, the corruption presented as all-pervading and irremediable. One would scarcely wish to argue with such a view. The problem is, of course, the one I have already indicated in relation to progressive Hollywood cinema generally, but in De Palma's work (and this is both its major distinction and its major limitation) it reaches its most extreme expression: the blockage of thought arising from the taboo on imagining alternatives to a system that can be exposed as monstrous, oppressive, and unworkable but which must nevertheless not be *constructively* challenged. Cynicism and nihilism: the terms can no more be evaded in relation to De Palma than in relation to Altman. Obviously, De Palma's work suffers—as any body of work must—from an inability to believe, not necessarily in systems and norms that actually exist, but in any imaginable alternative to them. Yet it seems to me that his work is less vulnerable to attack along these lines than Altman's. At least he never hides behind the superior snigger, never treats his characters or his audience with contempt, and in his best films his thematic concerns achieve remarkably complete realization. Undoubtedly compromised from a purely feminist or purely radical viewpoint, his films offer themselves readily—one might say generously—to appropriation by the Left.

Blow Out explicitly invites us to look for connections between its two political levels, the national and the sexual: the television newscaster, reporting on the discovery of the body of Burke's first female victim, asks what connection can be made between the "upcoming Liberty Day celebrations" and the pattern of the wounds in the shape of the Liberty Bell. In fact, the motivation for the murders combines the political and the sexual: Burke was initially employed by the right wing to discredit the liberal McRyan; the murder of Sally, politically expedient, is to be disguised to look like one of a series of sex crimes; and in effect that is precisely what the killings are (Burke clearly enjoys his work). Politics is presented as rivalry between males, even the most liberal of whom is not above exploiting women: when he dies, McRyan (presented as a Kennedy-type—the implicit reference to Chappaquiddick has been much noticed) is cheating on his wife and using a prostitute. Above all, the film's unifying theme of male ego-boosting masquerading as disinterestedness extends to the political level, is seen, in fact, as the defining characteristic of American party politics.

The climactic sequence of *Blow Out*, where everything comes together, seems to me among the most remarkable achievements of modern Hollywood cinema: the excess, the flamboyance, the cinematic rhetoric, are here entirely earned by the context. As Sally dies, the Liberty Bell rings out: the irony (as crude and obvious as you please) is, in its savage bitterness, the culmination of the whole film. The celebration of a liberty created by males, for males, at the expense of women, within a culture the film has characterized as at every level corrupt and manipulative, coincides with the death of its latest victim. After which, Jack, distraught, his responsibility for what has happened forced home, cradles Sally's body against a background of orgasmically exploding fireworks: an object lesson in the cost of phallic assertion. What is there left for him to do—given the impossibility, within De Palma's work and the Hollywood cinema, of envisaging and dramatizing political alternatives, whether sexual or national—but to give Sally's death scream to the producer of a schlock horror movie? The final moments reveal the action's hideous cynicism as the male protagonist's desperate self-laceration. For me, no film evokes more overwhelmingly the desolation of our culture.

8.

Papering the Cracks
FANTASY AND IDEOLOGY
IN THE REAGAN ERA

THE LUCAS-SPIELBERG SYNDROME

The crisis in ideological confidence of the 70s visible on all levels of American culture and variously enacted in Hollywood's "incoherent texts," has not been resolved: within the system of patriarchal capitalism no resolution of the fundamental conflicts is possible. Instead, it has been *forgotten*, though its specter, masquerading as idealized nostalgia for lost radicalism, still intermittently haunts the cinema (*The Big Fix, The Big Chill, Return of the Secaucus Seven*). Remembering can be pleasant when it is accompanied by the sense that there is really nothing you can do any more ("Times have changed"). Vietnam ends, Watergate comes to seem an unfortunate aberration (with a film like *All The President's Men* actually feeling able, though ambiguously, to celebrate the democratic system that can expose and rectify such anomalies); the Carter administration, promising the sense of a decent and reassuring liberalism, makes possible a huge ideological sigh of relief in preparation for an era of recuperation and reaction. *Rocky* and *Star Wars*—the two seminal works of what Andrew Britton (in an article in *Movie* 31/32 to which the present chapter is heavily indebted) has termed "Reaganite entertainment"—appear a few years before Reagan's election, and are instant, overwhelming commercial successes. Their respective progenies are still very much with us.

Reassurance is the keynote, and one immediately reflects that this is the era of sequels and repetition. The success of *Raiders of the Lost Ark, E. T.*, and the *Star Wars* movies is dependent not only on the fact that so many people go to see them, but also that so many see them again and again. The phenomenon develops a certain irony in conjunction with Barthes' remarks on "rereading," in *S/Z*: "Rereading [is] an operation contrary to the commercial and ideological habits of our society, which would have us 'throw away' the story once it has been consumed ('devoured'), so that we can then move on to another story, buy another book, and which is tolerated only in certain marginal categories of readers (children, old people, and professors)."

Clearly, different kinds of rereading occur, (children and professors do not reread in quite the same way or for the same purpose): it is possible to "read" a film like *Letter from an Unknown Woman* or *Late Spring* twenty times and still discover new meanings, new complexities, ambiguities, possibilities of interpretation. It seems unlikely, however, that this is what takes people back, again and again, to *Star Wars*.

Young children require not-quite-endless repetition—the same game played over and over. When at last they begin to weary of exact repetition they demand slight variation: the game still easily recognizable, but not entirely predictable. It can be argued that this pattern forms the basis for much of our adult pleasure in traditional art. Stephen Neale, in one of the very few useful works on the subject (*Genre*, British Film Institute, 1980), discusses the Hollywood genres in such terms. The distinction between the great genre movies and the utterly uncreative hack work (between, say, *Rio Bravo* and *The Man Who Shot Liberty Valance* on the one hand, and the Roy Rogers or Hopalong Cassidy series on the other) lies very largely in the relationship between the familiar and the surprising—in the length of the leap the spectator is asked to make from generic expectations to specific transformations, the transformations being as much ideological as conventional. The repetition-and-sequel pattern of the 80s is obviously of a very different order: despite the expensiveness of the films and their status as "cultural event," it is closer to Roy Rogers than to Ford and Hawks. The satisfactions of *Star Wars* are repeated until a sequel is required: same formula, with variations. But instead of a leap, only an infant footstep is necessary, and never one that might demand an adjustment on the level of ideology.

Hence the ironic appositeness of Barthes' perception that rereading is tolerated in children. The category of children's films has of course always existed. The 80s variant is the curious and disturbing phenomenon of children's films conceived and marketed largely for adults—films that construct the adult spectator as a child, or, more precisely, as a childish adult, an adult who would like to be a child. The child loses him/herself in fantasy, accepting the illusion; the childish adult both does and does not, simultaneously. The characteristic response to *E. T.* (heard, with variations, over and over again) was "Wasn't it *wonderful?*" followed instantly by a nervously apologetic "But of course it's pure fantasy." In this way, the particular satisfactions the films offer—the lost breast repeatedly rediscovered—can be at once indulged and laughed off. That the apology (after all, the merest statement of the obvious) has to be made at all testifies to the completeness of the surrender on another level to the indulgence.

It remains to define just what those satisfactions are, the kinds of reassurance demanded and so profitably supplied. It will be scarcely surprising that they—as it were, incidentally and obliquely—diminish, defuse, and render safe all the major radical movements that gained so much impetus, became so threatening, in the 70s: radical feminism, black militancy, gay liberation, the assault on patriarchy. Before cataloguing them, however, it is as well to foreground certain problems that arise in discussing (and attacking) the films. It is, in fact, peculiarly difficult to discuss them seriously. The films themselves set up a deliberate resistance: they are so insistently not serious, so knowing about their own escapist fantasy/pure entertainment nature, and they consistently invite the audience's complicity in this. To raise serious objections to them is to run the risk of looking a fool (they're "just entertainment," after all) or, worse, a spoilsport (they're "such fun"). Pleasure is indeed an important issue. I had better confess at once that I enjoy the *Star Wars* films well enough: I get moderately excited, laugh a bit, even brush back a tear at the happy endings, all right on cue: they work, they are extremely efficient. But just what do we mean when we say "they work"? They work because their workings correspond to the workings of our own social construction. I claim no exemption from this: I enjoy being reconstructed as a child, surrendering to the reactivation of a set of values and structures my adult self has long since repudiated, I am not immune to the blandishments of reassurance. Pleasure itself, in fact, is patently ideological. We may be born with the desire for pleasure, but the actual gratifications of the desire are of necessity culturally determined, a product of our social conditioning. Pleasure, then, can never be taken for granted while we wish to remain adult; it isn't sacrosanct, purely natural and spontaneous, beyond analysis which spoils it (on many levels, it is imperative that our pleasure be spoiled). The pleasure offered by the *Star Wars* films corresponds very closely to our basic conditioning; it is extremely reactionary, as all mindless and automatic pleasure tends to be. The finer pleasures are those we have to work for.

I do not want to argue that the films are intrinsically and uniquely harmful: they are no more so than the vast majority of artifacts currently being produced by capitalist enterprise for popular consumption within a patriarchal culture. In many ways they resemble the old serials (Buck Rogers, Superman, Batman, etc.) that used to accompany feature films in weekly installments as program fillers, or get shown at children's matinees. What I find worrying about the Spielberg-Lucas syndrome is the enormous importance our society has conferred upon the films, an importance not at all incompatible with their not being taken seriously ("But of course, it's pure fantasy"): indeed, the apparent contradiction is crucial to the phenomenon. The old serials were not taken seriously on any level (except perhaps by real children, and then only young ones); their role in popular culture was minor and marginal; they posed no threat to the co-existence of challenging, disturbing or genuinely distinguished Hollywood movies, which they often accompanied in their lowly capacity. Today it is becoming difficult for films that are not like *Star Wars* (at least in the general sense of dispensing reassurance, but increasingly in more specific and literal ways, too) to get made, and when they do get made, the public and often the critics reject them: witness the box office failure of *Heaven's Gate*, *Blade Runner*, and *King of Comedy*.

These, then, are what seem to me the major areas in which the films provide reassurance. I have centered the argument in the *Star Wars* films (*E. T.* is dealt with separately afterward), but it will be obvious that most of my points apply, to varying degrees, over a much wider field of contemporary Hollywood cinema.

1. Childishness I cannot abandon this theme without somewhat fuller development. It is important to stress that I am not positing some diabolical Hollywood-capitalist-Reaganite conspiracy to impose mindlessness and mystification on a potentially revolutionary populace, nor does there seem much point in blaming the filmmakers for what they are doing (the critics are another matter). The success of the films is only comprehensible when one assumes a widespread *desire* for regression to infantilism, a populace who wants to be constructed as mock children. Crucial here, no doubt, is the urge to evade responsibility—responsibility for actions, decisions, thought, responsibility for changing things: children do not have to be responsible, there are older people to look after them. That is one reason why these films must be intellectually undemanding. It is not exactly that one doesn't have to think to enjoy *Star Wars*, but rather that thought is strictly limited to the most superficial narrative channels: "What will happen? How will they get out of *this*?" The films ore obviously very skillful in their handling of narrative, their resourceful, ceaseless interweaving of actions and enigmas, their knowing deployment of the most familiar narrative patterns: don't worry, Uncle George (or Uncle Steven) will take you by the hand and lead you through Wonderland. Some dangers will appear on the way, but never fear, he'll also see you safely home; home being essentially those "good old values" that Sylvester Stallone told us *Rocky* was designed to reinstate: racism, sexism, "democratic" capitalism; the capitalist myths of freedom of choice and equality of opportunity, the individual hero whose achievements somehow "make everything all right," even for the millions who never make it to individual heroism (but every man can be a hero—even, such is the grudging generosity of contemporary liberalism, every woman).

2. Special Effects These represent the essence of Wonderland Today (Alice never needed reassurance about technology) and the one really significant way in which the films differ from the old serials. Again, one must assume a kind of automatic doublethink in audience response: we both know and don't know that we are watching special effects, technological fakery. Only thus can we respond simultaneously to the two levels of "magic": the diegetic wonders within the narrative and the extra-diegetic magic of Hollywood (the best magic that money can buy), the technology on screen, the technology off. Spectacle—the sense of reckless, prodigal extravagance, no expense spared—is essential: the unemployment lines in the world outside may get longer and longer, we may even have to go out and join them, but if capitalism can still throw out entertainments like *Star Wars* (the films' very uselessness an aspect of the prodigality), the system must be basically OK, right? Hence, as capitalism approaches its ultimate breakdown, through that series of escalating economic crises prophesied by Marx well over a century ago, its entertainments must become more dazzling, more extravagant, more luxuriously unnecessary.

3. Imagination/Originality A further seeming paradox (actually only the extension of the "But of course it's pure fantasy" syndrome) is that the audiences who wish to be constructed as children also wish to regard themselves as extremely sophisticated and "modern." The actual level of this sophistication can be gauged from the phenomenon (not unfamiliar to teachers of first-year film studies in universities) that the same young people who sit rapt through *Star Wars* find it necessary to laugh condescendingly at, say, a von Sternberg/Dietrich movie or a Ford western in order to establish their superiority to such passé simple-mindedness. "Of course it's pure fantasy—but what imagination!"—the flattering sense of one's own sophistication depends upon the ability to juggle such attitudes, an ability the films constantly nurture. If we are to continue using the term "imagination" to apply to a William Blake, we have no business using it of a George Lucas. Imagination and what is popularly referred to as pure fantasy (actually there is no such thing) are fundamentally incompatible. Imagination is a force that strives to grasp and transform the world, not restore "the good old values." What we can justly credit Lucas with (I use the name, be it understood, to stand for his whole production team) is facility of invention, especially on the level of special effects and makeup and the creation of a range of cute or sinister or grotesque fauna (human and non-human).

The "originality" of the films goes very precisely with their "imagination": window dressing to conceal—but not entirely—the extreme familiarity of plot, characterization, situation, and character relations. Again, doublethink operates: even while we relish the originality, we must also retain the sense of the familiar, the comforting nostalgia for the childish, repetitive pleasures of comic strip and serial (if we can't find the lost breast we can at least suck our thumbs). Here doublethink becomes almost a synonym for sophistication. The fanciful trimmings of the *Star Wars* saga enable us to indulge in satisfactions that would have us writhing in embarrassment if they were presented naked. The films have in fact largely replaced Hollywood genres that are no longer viable without careful "it's pure fantasy" disguise, but for whose basic impulses there survives a need created and sustained by the dominant ideology of imperialist capitalism. Consider their relation to the 40s war movie, of which Hawks' *Air Force* might stand as both representative and superior example: the group (bomber crew, infantry platoon, etc.) constructed as a microcosm of multiracial democracy. The war movie gave us various ethnic types (Jew, Polack, etc.) under the leadership of a WASP American; the Lucas films substitute fantasy figures (robots, Chewbacca) fulfilling precisely the same roles, surreptitiously permitting the same indulgence in WASP superiority. *Air Force* culminates in an all-out assault on the Japanese fleet, blasted out of the sea by "our boys": a faceless, inhuman enemy getting its just deserts. Today, the Japanese can no longer be called Japs ("One fried Jap going down"—*Air Force*'s most notorious line), and are no longer available for fulfilling that function (we are too "sophisticated"). However, dress the enemy in odd costumes (they remain faceless and inhuman, perhaps even totally metallic) and we can still cheer our boys when they blast them out of the sky as in the climax of *Star Wars*, etc.: the same indoctrinated values of patriotism, racism and militarism are being indulged and celebrated.

Consider also the exotic adventure movie: our white heroes, plus comic relief, encounter a potentially hostile tribe; but the natives turn out to be harmless, childlike, innocent—they have never seen a white man before, and they promptly worship our heroes as gods. You can't do that any more: such movies (mostly despised "B" movies anyway) don't get shown now, and if we saw one on late-night television we would have to laugh at it. But dress the natives as koala bears, displace the god identity on to a robot so that the natives appear even stupider, and you can still get away with it: the natives can still be childlike, lovable, and ready to help the heroes out of a fix; the nature of the laughter changes from repudiation to complicity.

4. Nuclear Anxiety This is central to Andrew Britton's thesis, and for an adequately detailed treatment I refer readers to the article cited above. The fear of nuclear war—at least, of indescribable suffering, at most, of the end of the world, with the end of civilization somewhere between—is certainly one of the main sources of our desire to be constructed as children, to be reassured, to evade responsibility and thought. The characteristic and widespread sense of helplessness—that it's all out of our hands, beyond all hope of effective intervention, perhaps already predetermined—for which there is unfortunately a certain degree of rational justification, is continually fostered both by the media and by the cynicism of politicians: whether we can actually do anything (and to escape despair and insanity we must surely cling to any rational belief that we can), it is clearly in the interests of our political/economic system for us to believe we can't. In terms of cinema, one side of this fear is the contemporary horror film, centered on the unkillable and ultimately inexplicable monster, the mysterious and terrible destructive force we can neither destroy, nor communicate with, nor understand. The Michael of *Halloween* and the Jason of the later *Friday the 13th* films are the obvious prototypes, but the indestructible psychopath of Michael Miller's *Silent Rage* is especially interesting because he is actually signified as the product of scientific experimentation with nuclear energy. The other side is the series of fantasy films centered on the struggle for possession of an ultimate weapon or power: the Ark of the Covenant of *Raiders of the Lost Ark*, the Genesis project of *Star Trek II*, "the Force" of *Star Wars*. The relationship of the two cycles (which developed simultaneously and are both extremely popular with, and aimed at, young audiences) might seem at first sight to be one of diametrical opposition (hopelessness vs. reassurance), yet their respective overall messages—"There's nothing you can do, anyway" and "Don't worry"—can be read as complements rather than opposites: both are deterrents to action. The pervasive, if surreptitious, implication of the fantasy films is that nuclear power is positive and justified as long as it is in the right, i.e., American, hands. *Raiders* is particularly blatant on the subject, offering a direct invitation to deliberate ignorance: you'll be all right, and all your enemies will be destroyed, as long as you "don't look"; nuclear power is synonymous with the power of God, who is, by definition, on our side. The film is also particularly blatant in its racism: non-Americans are in general either evil or stupid. The disguise of comic strip is somewhat more transparent than the disguise of pure fantasy. Nonetheless, it can scarcely escape notice that the arch-villain Khan of *Star Trek II* is heavily signified as foreign (and played by a foreign actor, Ricardo Montalban), as against the American-led crew of the spaceship (with its appropriate collection of fantasy-ethnic subordinates). The younger generation of *Star Wars* heroes is also conspicuously American.

The question has been raised as to whether the *Star Wars* films really fit this pattern: if they contain a fantasy embodiment of nuclear power it is surely not the Force but the Death Star, which the Force, primarily signified in terms of moral rectitude and discipline rather than physical or technological power, is used to destroy. Can't they then be read as *anti*-nuclear films? Perhaps an ambiguity can be conceded (I concede it without much conviction). But moral rectitude has always been an attribute of Americans in the Hollywood war movie; the Death Star was created by the Force (its "dark side," associated with the evil-non-Americans); and the use of the Force by Luke Skywalker in *Star Wars* is undeniably martial, violent, and destructive (though *Return of the Jedi* raises some belated qualms about this). Given the context—both generic and social-political—it seems to me that the same essential message, perhaps more covert and opaque, can be read from the *Star Wars* trilogy as from *Raiders* and *Star Trek II*.

5. Fear of Fascism I refer here not to the possibility of a Fascist threat from outside but from *inside*: the fear, scarcely unfounded, that continually troubles the American (un-)consciousness that democratic capitalism may not be cleanly separable from Fascism and may carry within itself the potential to become Fascist, totalitarian, a police state. The theme has been handled with varying degrees of intelligence and complexity in a number of overtly political films—supremely, *Meet John Doe*, but also a range of films from *All the King's Men* through *Advise and Consent* and *The Parallax View* to *The Dead Zone*, the theme particularly taking the form of the demagogue-who-may-become-dictator by fooling enough of the people enough of the time. The fear haunts the work of Hitchcock: the U-Boat commander of *Lifeboat* is of course German and explicitly Fascist, but he is not clearly distin-guishable in his ruthlessness, his assumption of superiority and his insidious charm from the American murderers of *Shadow of a Doubt* and *Rope*. More generally, how does one distinguish between the American individualist hero and the Fascist hero? Are the archetypes of westerner and gangster opposites or complements? The quandary becomes ever more pressing in the Reagan era, with the resurgence of an increasingly militant, vociferous and powerful Right, the Fascist potential forcing itself to recognition. It would be neither fair nor accurate to describe *Rocky* and *Raiders of the Lost Ark* as Fascist films; yet they are precisely the kinds of entertain-ment that a potentially Fascist culture would be expected to produce and enjoy (what exactly are we applauding as we cheer on the exploits of Indiana Jones?).

The most positively interesting aspect of the *Star Wars* films (their other inter-ests being largely of the type we call symptomatic) seems to me their dramatization of this dilemma. There is the ambiguity of the Force itself, with its powerful, and powerfully seductive, dark side to which the all-American hero may succumb: the Force, Obi One informs Luke, "has a strong influence on the weak-minded," as had Nazism. There is also the question (introduced early in *Star Wars*, developed as the dominant enigma in *The Empire Strikes Back*, and only resolved in the latter part of *Return of the Jedi*) of Luke's parentage: is the father of our hero *really* the prototyp-ical Fascist beast Darth Vader? By the end of the third film the dilemma has devel-oped quasi-philosophical dimensions: as Darth Vader represents rule-by-force, if Luke resorts to force (*the* Force) to defeat him, doesn't he become Darth Vader? The film can extricate itself from this knot only by the extreme device of having Darth Vader abruptly redeem himself and destroy the unredeemable Emperor.

The trilogy's simple but absolutely systematic code of accents extends this theme in the wider terms of the American heritage. All the older generation Jedi knights, both good and evil, and their immediate underlings, e.g. Peter Cushing, have British accents, in marked contrast to the American accents of the young heroes. The contradictions in the origins of America are relevant here: a nation founded in the name of freedom by people fleeing oppression, the founding itself an act of oppression (the subjugation of the Indians), the result an extremely oppressive civ-ilization based on the persecution of minorities (e.g., the Salem witch-hunts). Britain itself has of course markedly contradictory connotations—a democracy as well as an imperialist power ("the Empire"), which America inherited. It is there-fore fitting that both Obi One and Darth Vader should be clearly signified as British, and that doubt should exist as to which of them is Luke Skywalker's father, whether literal or moral/political. Hence the films' unease and inability satisfactorily to deal with the problem of lineage: what will the rebels against the Empire create if not another empire? The unease is epitomized in the final sequence of *Star Wars*, with its visual reference (so often pointed out by critics) to *Triumph of the Will*. A film buff's joke? Perhaps. But Freud showed a long time ago that we are often most serious when we joke. From the triumph of the Force to the Triumph of the Will is but a step.

Parenthetically, it is worth drawing brief attention here to John Milius' *Conan the Barbarian*, perhaps the only one of these 80s fantasy films to dispense with a liberal cloak, parading its Fascism shamelessly in instantly recognizable popular signifiers: it opens with a quotation from Nietzsche, has the spirit of its dead heroine leap to the rescue at the climax as a Wagnerian Valkyrie, and in between unabashedly celebrates the Aryan male physique with a singlemindedness that would have delighted Leni Riefenstahl. Its token gay is dispatched with a kick in the groin, and its arch-villain is black. There is an attempt, it is true, to project Fascism on to *him* (so that he can be allotted the most gruesome of the film's many grisly deaths), but it is difficult to imagine a more transparent act of displacement.

6. Restoration of the Father   One might reasonably argue that this constitutes—and logically enough—the dominant project, ad infinitum and post nauseam, of the contemporary Hollywood cinema, a veritable thematic metasystem embracing all the available genres and all the current cycles, from realist drama to pure fantasy, taking in en route comedy and *film noir* and even in devious ways infiltrating the horror film. The Father must here be understood in all senses, symbolic, literal; potential: patriarchal authority (the Law), which assigns all other elements to their correct, subordinate, allotted roles; the actual heads of families, fathers of recalcitrant children, husbands of recalcitrant wives, who must either learn the virtue and justice of submission or pack their bags; the young heterosexual male, father of the future, whose eventual union with the "good woman" has always formed the archetypal happy ending of the American film, guarantee of the perpetuation of the nuclear family and social stability.

The restoration of the Father has many ramifications, one of the most important of which is of course the corresponding restoration of women, after a decade of feminism and "liberation." The 80s have seen the development (or, in many cases, the resurrection) of a number of strategies for coping with this project. There is the plot about the liberated woman who proves she's as good as the man but then discovers that this doesn't make her happy and that what she really wanted all the time was to serve him. Thus Debra Winger in *Urban Cowboy* proves that she can ride the mechanical bull as well as John Travolta but withdraws from competition in order to spend the future washing his socks. Or Sandra Locke in *Bronco Billy* demonstrates that she can shoot as well as Clint Eastwood but ends up spread out

Mark Hamill as Luke
Skywalker in *Return
of the Jedi*

on a wheel as his target/object-for-the-gaze. (The grasp of feminist principle
implicit in this—that what women want is to be able to do the same things men do
because they envy them so much—is obviously somewhat limited.) The corollary
of this is the plot that suggests that men, if need arises, can fill the woman's role just
as well if not better (*Kramer vs. Kramer, Author! Author!, Mr. Mom*). It's the father,
anyway, who has all the real responsibility, women being by nature irresponsible, as
in the despicable *Middle Age Crazy*, which asks us to shed tears over the burden of
"being the daddy," the cross that our patriarchs must bear.

   If the woman can't accept her subordination, she must be expelled from the narrative altogether, like Mary Tyler Moore in *Ordinary People* or Tuesday Weld and
Dyan Cannon in *Author! Author!*, leaving the father to develop his beautiful relationship with his offspring untrammeled by female complications. *Ordinary People*
makes particularly clear the brutality to the woman of the Oedipal trajectory our
culture continues to construct: from the moment in the narrative when our young
hero takes the decisive step of identification with the father/acquisition of this own

woman, the mother becomes superfluous to Oedipal/patriarchal concerns, a mere burdensome redundancy. The father, on the other hand, must be loved, accepted and respected, even if he is initially inadequate (*Kramer vs. Kramer*) or generally deficient, unpleasant or monstrous (*Tribute*, *The Great Santini*). Even a non-family movie like *Body Heat* can be read as another variant on the same pattern. Its purpose in reviving the *film noir* woman of the 40s so long after (one had innocently supposed) her cultural significance had become obsolete seems to be to suggest that, if women are so perverse as to want power and autonomy, men are better off without them: at the end of the film, William Hurt is emotionally "with" his male buddies even though ruined and in prison, while Kathleen Turner is totally isolated and miserable even though rich and free on a Mexican beach. Clearly, what she really needed was the love of a good man, and as she willfully rejected it she must suffer the consequences. Seen like this, *Body Heat* is merely the *Ordinary People* of *film noir*.

Back in the world of pure fantasy (but we have scarcely left it), we find precisely the same patterns, the same ideological project, reiterated. Women are allowed minor feats of heroism and aggression (in deference to the theory that what they want is to be able to behave like men): thus Karen Allen can punch Harrison Ford in the face near the beginning of *Raiders*, and Princess Leia has intermittent outbursts of activity, usually in the earlier parts of the movies. Subsequently, the Woman's main function is to be rescued by the men, involving her reduction to helplessness and dependency. Although Princess Leia is ultimately revealed to be Luke Skywalker's sister, there is never any suggestion that *she* might inherit the Force, or have the privilege of being trained and instructed by Obi One and Yoda. In fact, the strategy of making her Luke's sister seems largely a matter of narrative convenience: it renders romance with Luke automatically unthinkable and sets her free, without impediments, for union with Han Solo. Nowhere do the films invite us to take any interest in *her* parentage. They play continually on the necessity for Luke to confirm his allegiance to the "good father" (Obi One) and repudiate the "bad father" (Darth Vader), even if the latter proves to be his *real* father. With this set up and developed in the first two films, *Return of the Jedi* manages to cap it triumphantly with the redemption of Darth Vader. The trilogy can then culminate in a veritable Fourth of July of Fathericity: a grandiose fireworks display to celebrate Luke's coming through, as he stands backed by the ghostly figures of Obi One, Darth and Yoda, all smiling benevolently. The mother, here, is so superfluous that she doesn't figure in the narrative at all—except, perhaps, at some strange, deeply sinister, unconscious level, disguised as the unredeemably evil Emperor who, as so many people have remarked, seems modeled on the witch in *Snow White* (the heroine's stepmother). Her male disguise makes it permissible to subject her to the most violent expulsion from the narrative yet. Read like this, *Return of the Jedi* becomes the *Ordinary People* of outer space, with Darth Vader as Donald Sutherland and Obi One and Yoda in tandem as the psychiatrist.

If the *Star Wars* films—like the overwhelming majority of 80s Hollywood movies—put women back where they belong (subordinate or nowhere), they do the same, in a casual, incidental way, for blacks and gays. The token black (Billy Dee Williams) is given a certain token autonomy and self-assertiveness, but he has a mere supporting role, in all senses of the term, on the right side, and raises no question of threat or revolution. Gays are handled more surreptitiously. Just as the 40s war movie generously included various ethnics in its platoon/bomber crew, so its 80s equivalent has its subordinate, subservient (and comic and timid) gay character, in the entirely unchallenging form of an asexual robot: CP-30, with his affected British accent, effeminate mannerisms, and harmlessly pedophile relationship with R2D2 (after all, what can robots do?). On the other hand, there is the *Star Wars* rendering of a gay bar, the clientele exclusively male, and all grotesque freaks.

Thus the project of the *Star Wars* films and related works is to put everyone back in his/her place, reconstruct us as dependent children, and reassure us that it will all come right in the end: trust Father.[1]

SPIELBERG AND *E. T.*

While it is in many respects permissible to speak of a Lucas-Spielberg syndrome—films catering to the desire for regression to infantilism, the doublethink phenomenon of pure fantasy—Spielberg and, especially, *E. T.* also demand some separate consideration. The *Star Wars* films are knowing concoctions, the level of personal involvement (that facility of invention that I have granted them) superficial. *Raiders of the Lost Ark* belongs with them, but with *Close Encounters of the Third Kind* and *E. T.* there is a certain sense of pressure, of personal necessity. Semiologists would call this the inscription of the author in the film; the popular response is to applaud Spielberg's "sincerity." However one takes it—as evidence of a genuine creative drive, or as simply one further level of signification—I am not arguing that it necessarily

1. It is striking that, since this chapter was written, the essential ugliness of the 80s science fiction/comic strip project—hitherto concealed beneath the sweetness-and-light of patriarchal morality—has risen to the surface: witness the obsessive violence of *Indiana Jones and the Temple of Doom* and the pervasively sick imagery of *Gremlins* (which Spielberg "presented"). *Dune* is the culmination of the exposure of rottenness. It is the most obscenely homophobic film I have ever seen, managing to associate with homosexuality in a single scene physical grossness, moral depravity, violence and disease. It shows no real interest in its bland young lovers or its last-minute divine revelation, all its energies being devoted to the expression of physical and sexual disgust. Much of the imagery strongly recalls David Lynch's earlier *Eraserhead*, but the film seems only partly explicable in auteurist terms; the *choice* of Lynch as writer-director would also need to be explained, and the film must be seen in the wider context as a product of the 80s Hollywood machine.

makes the films better than the *Star Wars* movies. Sincerity is a difficult concept (Spielberg's, in conjunction with the films' extraordinary efficiency, makes him a lot of money) and in itself carries no connotations of value; popularly, it tends to get confused with "giving us a nice feeling," but logically there is no more reason to credit Spielberg with it than, say, Mickey Spillane, whose novels also carry a charge of personal investment, If the Spielberg films are in some ways more interesting than the *Star Wars* trilogy, it is because the personal investment has as its corollary, or perhaps its source, a certain disturbance; the sincerity seems in large part the need to cover over that disturbance, a *personal* need for reassurance (which the *Star Wars* films peddle as a commodity), the desire to "believe." Another way of saying this is to suggest that the patriarchal/Oedipal trajectory is never quite as simple, direct or untroubled, and takes more curious and deviant routes, in the Spielberg movies. That the films fail to be more interesting than they are testifies to the success of the fantasy: the disturbance is covered over very effectively, almost obliterated. Illuminating comparisons might be made with two of *E. T.*'s thematic antecedents: Lewton's *Curse of the Cat People* and Cohen's *It's Alive* movies.

One needs to distinguish carefully between the childlike and the childish (just as one needs to distinguish the true innocence of childhood from the sentimental, sanitized, desexualized version of bourgeois ideology). Peter Coveney's admirable *The Image of Childhood* undertakes just such a distinction, examining the differences between the Romantic concept of the child (Blake, Wordsworth) as symbol of new growth and regeneration (of ourselves, of civilization) and the regressive Victorian sentimentalization of children as identification figures for "childish adults," the use of the infantile as escape from an adult world perceived as irredeemably corrupt, or at least bewilderingly problematic.[2] Both models persist, intermittently, in our culture: within the modern cinema, one might take as an exemplary reference point the Madlyn of *Céline and Julie Go Boating* and the multiple suggestions of growth and renewal she develops in relation to the four women of the film. Spielberg in *E. T.* seems to hesitate between the two concepts (Elliott's freshness and energy are seen in relation to a generally oppressive civilization, though he is never Blake's "fiend hid in a cloud") before finally committing himself to the childish. If Spielberg is the ideal director for the 80s, it is because his "sincerity" (the one quality that the *Star Wars* films are vaguely felt to lack) expresses itself as an emotional investment in precisely that form of regression that appears to be so generally desired.

The attitude to the patriarchal family implicit in Spielberg's films is somewhat curious. In *Jaws* the family is tense and precarious; in *Close Encounters* it disintegrates; in *E. T.* it has already broken up before the film begins. The first part of

2. It is peculiarly appropriate that a new version of *Peter Pan* should be among Spielberg's current projects.

E. T. quite vividly depicts the oppressiveness of life in the nuclear family: incessant bickering, mean-mindedness, one-upmanship. This state of affairs is the result of the father's defection, perhaps: the boys have no one to imitate, as Roy Scheider's son in *Jaws* had. But he has defected only recently, and the *Close Encounters* family is scarcely any better. Yet Spielberg seems quite incapable of thinking beyond this: all he can do is reassert the "essential" goodness of family life in the face of all the evidence he himself provides. Hence the end of *E. T.* surreptitiously reconstructs the image of the nuclear family. Spielberg is sufficiently sophisticated to realize that he can't bring Dad home from Mexico for a last-minute repentance and reunion (it would be too corny, not realistic, in a film that for all its status as pure fantasy has a great stake in the accumulated connotations of "real life"). But he produces a paternal scientist in Dad's place (an even better father who can explicitly identify himself with Elliott—"When I was ten I was just like you," or words to that effect). A climactic image groups him with mother and daughter in an archetypal family composition, like a posed photograph. For Spielberg it doesn't really matter that the scientist has no intimate relationship with the mother, as his imagination is essentially presexual: it is enough that he stands in for Elliott's missing father.

It follows that the position of women in Spielberg's work is fairly ignominious. Largely denied any sexual presence, they function exclusively as wives and mothers (especially mothers), with no suggestion that they might reasonably want anything beyond that. The two women in *Close Encounters* typify the extremely limited possibilities. On the one hand there is the wife of Richard Dreyfuss (Teri Garr), whom the film severely criticizes for not standing staunchly by her husband even when his behavior suggests that he is clearly certifiable: she has to be dismissed from the narrative to leave him free to depart in the spaceship. On the other hand there is the mother (Melinda Dillon) whose sole objective is to regain her child (a male child, inevitably). No suggestion is made that *she* might go off in the spaceship, or even that she might want to. The end of *E. T.* offers the precise complement to this: the extraterrestrial transmits his wisdom and powers to the male child, Elliott, by applying a finger to his forehead, then instructs the little girl to "be good": like Princess Leia, she will never inherit the Force.

As for men, Spielberg shows an intermittent desire to salute Mr. Middle America, which is not entirely incompatible with his basic project, given the way in which serious (read subversive) thought is repressed by the media: at the end of *Jaws*, Roy Scheider destroys the shark after both the proletarian and the intellectual have failed. By inclination, however, he gravitates toward the infantile, presexual male, a progression obviously completed by Elliott. (No one, of course, is really presexual; yet the myth of the pre-sexuality of children remains dominant, and it is logical that the desire for regression to infantilism should incorporate this myth.) Roy Neary in *Close Encounters* is an interesting transitional figure. As he falls under the influence of the extraterrestrial forces his behavior becomes increasingly infantile (given the dirt he deposits all over the house, one might see him as regressing to the pre-toilet training period). Divested of the encumbrances of wife and family, he proceeds to erect a huge phallus in the living room; but, before he can achieve the actual revelation of its meaning, he must learn to slice off its top. As with the mother and the scientist of *E. T.* the film contradicts generic expectations by conspicuously not developing a sexual relationship, although Neary's alliance with Melinda Dillon makes this more than feasible—generically speaking, almost obligatory. Instead, the symbolic castration makes possible the desexualized sublimation of the ending: Neary led into the spaceship by frail, little, asexual, childlike figures, to fly off with a display of bright lights the Smiths of *Meet Me in St. Louis* never dreamed of. The logical next step (leaving aside the equally regressive comic strip inanities of *Raiders of the Lost Ark*) is to a literal, but still necessarily male, child as hero.

Spielberg's identification with Elliott (that there is virtually no distance whatever between character and director is clearly the source of the film's seductive, suspect charm) makes possible the precise nature of the fantasy *E. T.* offers: not so much a child's fantasy as an adult's fantasy about childhood. It is also essentially a male fantasy: apart from Pauline Kael (whose feminist consciousness is so undeveloped one could barely describe it as embryonic), I know of no women who respond to the film the way so many men do (though not without embarrassment), as, in Kael's term, a "bliss-out." The film caters to the wish—practically universal, within our culture—that what W. B. Yeats so evocatively called "the ignominy of boyhood" might have been a little less ignominious. It is the fulfillment of this wish that most male adults find so irresistible. It is however, always worth examining what precisely it is that we have failed to resist. The film does for the problems of childhood exactly what Spielberg's contribution to *Twilight Zone* did for the problem of old age: it raises them in order to dissolve them in fantasy, so that we are lulled into feeling they never really existed. Meanwhile boyhood (not to mention girlhood) remains, within the patriarchal nuclear family, as ignominious as ever.

Such a view of family life, male/female relations, and compensatory fantasy is obviously quite curious and idiosyncratic, always verging on the exposure of contradictions that only the intensity of the commitment to fantasy conceals. The essential flimsiness and vulnerability of the fantasy are suggested by the instability of E. T. himself as a realized presence in the film. Were it not for Spielberg's sincerity (a sincerity unaccompanied by anything one might reasonably term intelligence, and in fact incompatible with it)—his evident investment in the fantasy— one might describe the use of E. T. as shamelessly opportunistic. From scene to scene, almost moment to moment, he represents whatever is convenient to Spielberg, and to Elliott: helpless/potent, mental defective/intellectual giant, child figure/father figure.

The film's central theme is clearly the acceptance of Otherness (that specter that

Cary Guffey with Melinda Dillon in *Close Encounters of the Third Kind*

Henry Thomas in *E. T.*

haunts, and must continue to haunt, patriarchal bourgeois society)—by Elliott, initially, then by his siblings, eventually by his mother, by the benevolent scientist, by the schoolboys. On the surface level—"E. T." as an e. t.—this seems quite negligible, a nonissue. This is not to assert that there are no such things as extraterrestrials, but simply that, as yet, they haven't constituted a serious social problem. They have a habit of turning up at convenient moments in modern history: in the 50s, with the cold war and the fear of Communist infiltration, everyone saw hostile flying saucers, and Hollywood duly produced movies about them; at a period when (in the aftermath of Vietnam and Watergate, and with a new Vietnam in Central America hovering over American heads) we need reassurance, Hollywood produces *nice* extraterrestrials. (The 50s produced some benevolent ones, too—*It Came from Outer Space*, for example—but they proved less profitable; contrariwise, the hostile, totally intractable kind are still with us—witness Carpenter's *The Thing*, released almost simultaneously with *E. T.*—but the model is definitely not popular.)

Unfortunately, on a less literal level, as a more general representation of Otherness, E. T. almost totally lacks resonance ("zero charisma," one might say). All the Others of white patriarchal bourgeois culture—workers, women, gays, blacks—are in various ways threatening, and their very existence represents a demand that society transform itself. E. T. isn't threatening at all: in fact, he's just about as cute as a little rubber Martian could be. This, it seems to me, is what makes the film (for all its charm, for all the sincerity) in the last resort irredeemably smug: a nation that was founded on the denial of Otherness now—after radical feminism, after gay liberation, after black militancy—complacently produces a film in which Otherness is something we can all love and cuddle and cry over, without unduly disturbing the nuclear family and the American Way of Life. E. T. is one of us; he just looks a bit funny.

※ ※ ※

Poltergeist requires a brief postscript here. It is tempting to dismiss it simply as Tobe Hooper's worst film, but it clearly belongs to the Spielberg *oeuvre* rather than to Hooper's. Its interest and the particular brand of reassurances it offers both lie in its relation to the 70s family horror film—in the way in which Spielberg enlists the genre's potential radicalism and perverts it into 80s conservatism. One can discern two parallel and closely related projects: First, the attempt (already familiar from *Jaws*) to separate the American family from "bad" capitalism, to pretend the two are without connection: there are a few greedy people, putting profit before human concerns, who bring on catastrophes, whether by keeping open dangerous beaches or not removing the bodies before converting cemeteries into housing developments. The project has a long history in the American cinema (its inherent tensions and contradictions wonderfully organized by Capra, for example, in *It's a Wonder-*

ful Life). With Spielberg it becomes reduced merely to a blatant example of what Barthes calls "inoculation," where ideology acknowledges a minor, local, reformable evil in order to divert attention from the fundamental ones. Second, the attempt to absolve the American family from all responsibility for the horror. In short, a cleansing job: in the 70s, the monster was located within the family, perceived as its logical product. *Poltergeist* appears at first to be toying with this concept, before declaring the family innocent and locating the monstrous elsewhere: it is defined in terms of either meaningless superstition (corpses resent having swimming pools built over them) or some vague metaphysical concept of eternal evil ("the Beast"—superstition on a more grandiose scale), the two connected by the implication that the latter is evoked by, or is working through, the former. In any case, as in *E. T.*, the suburban bourgeois nuclear family remains the best of all possible worlds, if only because any other is beyond Spielberg's imagination. One might suggest that the overall development of the Hollywood cinema from the late 60s to the 80s is summed up in the movement from Romero's use of the Star Spangled Banner (the flag) at the beginning of *Night of the Living Dead* to Spielberg's use of it (the music) at the beginning of *Poltergeist.*

Blade Runner

Blade Runner was released in the United States simultaneously with *E. T.* and for one week was its serious challenger at the box office; then receipts for *Blade Runner* dropped disastrously while those for *E. T.* soared. The North American critical establishment was generally ecstatic about *E. T.* and cool or ambivalent about *Blade Runner. E. T.* was nominated for a great many Academy Awards and won a few; *Blade Runner* was nominated for a few and won none. I take these facts as representing a choice made in conjunction by critics and public, ratified by the Motion Picture Academy—a choice whose significance extends far beyond a mere preference for one film over another, expressing a preference for the reassuring over the disturbing, the reactionary over the progressive, the safe over the challenging, the childish over the adult, spectator passivity over spectator activity.

Admirers of the original novel (Philip Dick's *Do Androids Dream of Electric Sheep?*) tend to regard the film with some hostility. But *Blade Runner* is not really an adaptation: rather, the film is built upon certain ideas and motifs selected from the novel. Its aim, argument and tone are so different that it is best to regard it as an autonomous work. Gone or played down are most of the novel's major structuring premises: the nuclear war that has rendered the earth unsafe for the support of life and health; the use of animals as rare, expensive, coveted status symbols; the pseudoreligion of "Mercerism." One might define the fundamental difference thus: the concerns of the novel are predominantly metaphysical, those of the film pre-

Jobeth Williams in *Poltergeist*

dominantly social. Some of the features discussed here derive (in most cases rather loosely) from the book; others do not. They are so well integrated that it seems unnecessary to spell out the distinction in each individual case.

Fantasy, by and large, can be used in two ways—as a means of escaping from contemporary reality, or as a means of illuminating it. Against the Spielbergian complacency of *E. T.* can be set *Blade Runner*'s vision of capitalism, which is projected into the future, yet intended to be clearly recognizable. It is important that the novel's explanation of the state of the world (the nuclear war) is withheld from the film: the effect is to lay the blame on capitalism directly. The society we see is our own writ large, its present excesses carried to their logical extremes: power and money controlled by even fewer, in even larger monopolies; worse poverty, squalor, degradation; racial oppression; a polluted planet, from which those who can emigrate to other worlds. The film opposes to Marx's view of inevitable collapse a chilling vision of capitalism hanging on, by the maintenance of power and oppression, in the midst of an essentially disintegrated civilization.

The depiction of the role played in this maintenance by the media is a masterly example of the kind of clarification—a complex idea compressed into a single image—advocated by Brecht: the mystified poor are mostly Asians; the ideal image they are given, therefore, dominating the city in neon lights, is that of a beautiful, richly dressed, exquisitely made-up female oriental, connected in the film (directly or indirectly) with emigration, Coca-Cola and pill-popping, various forms of consumption, pacification and flight.

The central interest of the film lies in the relationship between the hero, Deckard, and the "replicants"; the hero, one might add, is interesting *only* in relation to the replicants. The relationship is strange, elusive, multi-leveled, inadequately worked out (the failure of the film is as striking as its evident successes): the meeting of Raymond Chandler and William Blake is not exactly unproblematic. The private eye/*film noir* aspect of the movie is strongly underlined by Deckard's voice-over narration, demanded by the studio after the film's completion because someone felt that audiences would have difficulty in following the narrative (justifiably, alas: our own conditioning by the contemporary media is centered on, and continually reinforces, the assumption that we are either unable or unwilling to do any work). But that aspect is clearly there already in the film, which draws not only on the Chandler ethos but also on the rethinking of it in 70s cinema (Altman's *The Long Goodbye*, more impressively Penn's *Night Moves*): the moral position of Chandler's knight walking the "mean streets" can no longer be regarded as uncompromised. Deckard's position as hero is compromised, above all, by the way the film draws upon another figure of *film noir* (and much before it), the figure of the double—which brings us to the replicants.

If *Blade Runner*'s attitude to American capitalism is at the opposite pole to Spielberg's, the logical corollary is that the film's representation of the Other is at the opposite pole to that of *E. T.*, though without falling into the alternative trap embodied by Carpenter's "Thing." The replicants (I am thinking especially of Roy and Pris) are dangerous but fascinating, frightening but beautiful, other but not totally and intractably alien; they gradually emerge as the film's true emotional center, and certainly represent its finest achievement. Their impressiveness depends partly on their striking visual presence, but more on the multiple connotations they accrue as the film proceeds, through processes of suggestion, association, and reference.

The central, defining one is that established by the near-quotation from Blake with which Roy Batty introduces himself (it has no equivalent in the novel):

Fiery the angels fell; deep thunder rolled
Around their shores, burning with the fires
of Orc   (*America: A Prophecy*, lines 115–16)

Blake's poem is a celebration of the American Revolution, a narrative about the founding of modern America, interpreted on a spiritual/symbolic plane. Orc leads the revolt against oppression; he is one of Blake's devil-angels, descendant of Milton's Lucifer as reinterpreted by Blake ("Milton was of the devil's party without knowing it"), the spirit of freedom, "Lover of wild rebellion and transgression of

God's law," consistently associated with fire ("the fiery joy"). Roy, however, misquotes: Blake's original reads "Fiery the angels *rose*," the rising of the angels signifying the beginning of the revolt which is to found the free democratic state that, two hundred years ago, could be viewed idealistically as a step in humanity's progress toward the New Jerusalem. The change from "rose" to "fell" must be read, then, in terms of the end of the American democratic principle of freedom, its ultimate failure: the shot that introduces Roy, the rebel angel, links him in a single camera movement to the imagery of urban squalor and disintegration through which he is moving. Clearly, in the context of 80s Hollywood, such an implication could be suggested only in secret, concealed in a particularly esoteric reference. Subsequently, Roy's identification with the Blake revolutionary hero is rendered visually: stripped to the waist for the final combat with Deckard, he could have stepped straight out of one of Blake's visionary paintings.

The other connotations are less insistent, more a matter of suggestion, but (grouping themselves around the allusion to Blake) they add up to a remarkably complex and comprehensive definition of the Other. First, the replicants are identified as an oppressed and exploited proletariat: produced to serve their capitalist masters, they are discarded when their usefulness is over and "retired" (i.e., destroyed) when they rebel against such usage. Roy tells Deckard: "Quite an experience to live in fear. That's what it is to be a slave." They are also associated with racial minorities: when Deckard's boss refers to them by the slang term "skin-jobs," Deckard immediately connects this to the term "niggers." Retaining a certain sexual mystery, they carry suggestions of sexual ambiguity: Rachael's response to one of Deckard's questions in the interrogation scene is "Are you trying to find out if I'm a replicant or if I'm a lesbian?"; the climactic Roy/Deckard battle accumulates marked homoerotic overtones (made explicit in Roy's challenge "You'd better get it up"), culminating in his decision to save Deckard's life. The replicants have no families: they have not been through the bourgeois patriarchal process known euphemistically as socialization. They appear to be of two kinds—those who are not supposed to know they are replicants (Rachael) and have accordingly been supplied with "memory banks," false family photographs, etc., and who are therefore more amenable to socialization, and those who know they are other (Roy/Pris) and live by that knowledge. Roy and Pris are also associated with childhood, not only by the fact that they are literally only four years old, but by their juxtaposition with the toys in J. F. Sebastian's apartment, an environment in which they are so at home that Pris can be assimilated into it, becoming one of Sebastian's creations when she hides from Deckard. Pris, made up as a living doll, irresistibly evokes punk and the youth rebellion associated with it. As in Blake, the revolution is ultimately against the Father, the symbolic figure of authority, oppression and denial ("Thou shalt not"); it is therefore appropriate that the film should move toward Roy's murder of Tyrell, his creator, owner, and potential destroyer.

Blake's Rebel Angel:
Rutger Hauer in
Blade Runner

The parallels that seek to establish Roy as Deckard's double are fairly systematic but not entirely convincing, the problem lying partly in the incompatibility of the film's literary sources (Philip Marlowe can scarcely look into the mirror and see Orc as his reflection). Rachael's question (never answered) "Did you ever take that test yourself?" suggests that Deckard could be a replicant; Deckard's own line, "Replicants weren't supposed to have feelings, neither were blade runners," develops the parallel. The crosscutting in the battle with Roy repeatedly emphasizes the idea of the mirror image with the injured hands, the cries of pain. The relationship is above all suggested in Roy's contemptuously ironic "Aren't you 'the good man'?": hero and villain change places, all moral certainties based upon the status quo collapse.

The more often I see *Blade Runner* the more I am impressed by its achievement and the more convinced of its failure. The problem may be that the central thrust of the film, the source of its energy, is too revolutionary to be permissible: it *has* to be compromised. The unsatisfactoriness comes to a head in the ludicrous, bathetic ending, apparently tacked on in desperation at the last minute. But how should the film end? In the absence of any clear information, two possibilities come to mind, the choice depending, one might say, on whether Philip Marlowe or Orc is to have the last word. The first scenario involves the *film noir* ending in which Rachael is retired by Deckard's superior who is then killed in turn by Deckard (himself mortally wounded, perhaps) in a final gun battle. In the second, Deckard joins the replicant revolution. The former is probably too bleak for 80s Hollywood, the latter too explicitly subversive for any Hollywood. Either would, however, make some sense and would be the outcome of a logical progression within the film, whereas the ending we have makes no sense at all: Deckard and Rachael fly off to live happily ever after (where?—the film has clearly established that there is nowhere on earth to go). The problem partly lies in the added voice-over commentary, the only evidence we are given that Rachael has been constructed without a "determination date": were she about to die, the notion of a last desperate fling in the wilderness would make slightly more sense, and we would not be left with the awkward question of how they are going to survive.

The film's problems, however, are not confined to its last couple of minutes: just as its strengths are centered in the replicants, so too are its weaknesses. If Roy is the incarnation of the Blakean revolutionary hero, he also, especially in association with Pris, carries other connotations that are much more dubious, those of an Aryan master race. This is very strongly suggested by the characters' physical attributes (blondness, beauty, immense strength), but it is also, more worryingly, signified in their ruthlessness: the offscreen murder of J. F. Sebastian (not in the novel) seems completely arbitrary and unmotivated, put in simply to discredit the replicants so that they cannot be mistaken for the film's true heroes. The problem is rooted in the entire tradition of the Gothic, of horror literature and horror film: the problem of the positive monster, who, insofar as he becomes positive, ceases to be monstrous, hence no longer frightening. It is the problem that Cohen confronted in the *It's Alive* movies (and failed to resolve in the second) and that Badham confronted in *Dracula* (a film that, like *Blade Runner*, develops disturbing Fascist overtones in its movement toward the monster's rehabilitation).

The central problem, however, is Rachael and her progressive humanization. The notion of what is human is obviously very heavily weighted ideologically; here, it amounts to no more than becoming the traditional "good object," the passive woman who willingly submits to the dominant male. What are we to make of the moment when, to save Deckard's life, Rachael shoots a fellow replicant? Not, clearly, what other aspects of this confused movie might powerfully suggest: the tragic betrayal of her class and race.

The film is in fact defeated by the overwhelming legacy of classical narrative. It succumbs to one of its most firmly traditional and ideologically reactionary formulas: the elimination of the bad couple (Roy, Pris) in order to construct the good couple (Deckard, Rachael). The only important difference is that in classical narrative the good couple would then settle down ("I'll take you home now"), whereas here they merely fly away to nowhere. Long ago, *Stagecoach* had its couple drive off, "saved from the blessings of civilization," to start a farm over the border; *The Chase* was perhaps the first Hollywood film to acknowledge, ahead of its time, that there was no longer any home to go to. Seventeen years later, *Blade Runner* can manage no more than an empty repetition of this—with the added cynicism of presenting it as if it were a happy ending.

Blade Runner belongs with the incoherent texts of the 70s: it is either ten years behind its time or hopefully a few years ahead of it. If the human race survives, we may certainly hope to enter, soon, another era of militancy, protest, rage, disturbance, and radical questioning, in which context *Blade Runner* will appear quite at home.

Postscript 2003: Since this book was written, Ridley Scott's original cut of *Blade Runner* has become available. There are three major differences, all improvements: the absurd "happy ending" has gone; the voiceover narration has been omitted; the suggestion that Deckard may himself be a replicant has been considerably strengthened. The film's major problems, however, remain.

9.

Horror in the 80s

The transition from the incoherent texts of the 70s to the all-too-coherent ones of Lucas and Spielberg is paralleled by the progress—more accurately, regression—of the horror film. Of the filmmakers whose work I examined in chapters 5 and 6, only Larry Cohen could be said to have remained obstinately true to himself, and that at the cost of virtual obliteration: at time of writing he has no fewer than four completed films unreleased. *Q* scarcely marks an advance on his earlier work, or adds significantly to its thematic complex, but it is characteristically odd, subversive, inventive, and marvelously acted, if once again confused and unsatisfying. One may also reasonably hold out hope for Tobe Hooper (despite his nominal involvement in *Poltergeist*). *The Fun House*, while burdened, especially in its second half, with the ritualistic formula of the "teenie-kill pic," achieves a genuine if intermittent distinction. Of the others, Bob Clark, with the upward mobility of someone ready to take on anything, has moved from *The Night Walk* to *Porky's* and its sequel (on which he produced the memorable comment that it contains less social comment than its predecessor). Wes Craven's career has achieved a certain consistency, in that each of his films since *Last House on the Left* has been worse than the one before. *Deadly Blessing*, with potentially rich material, is so incoherent as to be virtually unreadable; *Swamp Thing* is merely childish. The intensity and disturbance that gave *Last House* its peculiar and appalling distinction have not been in any way resolved—they have simply evaporated.

Saddest of all is the case of Romero, because after *Dawn of the Dead* it seemed legitimate to expect of him the most. *Knight Riders* has a certain symptomatic interest in relation to the persistent quandary of the American radical who wants to make some kind of positive statement yet is barred from embracing any coherent political alternative: essentially, the film is another *Alice's Restaurant*, ten years too late, and lacking Penn's sensitivity and complexity. It is the archetypal liberal American movie, with something nice to say about every minority group, some pious

Vestiges of a Tradition: Wayne Doba and Kevin Conway in *The Fun House*

platitudes about the corrupting power of commercialism, and a lament for the failure of a counterculture that couldn't possibly succeed. Nothing, however, had prepared one for *Creep Show*, either here or in any of the early work. It combines the worst of Romero with the worst of Stephen King, without bearing any interesting relation to the work of either. It is, in fact, almost indistinguishable from the British Amicus productions of the 70s: a series of empty anecdotes in which nasty people do nasty things to other nasty people, the nastiness being the entire point and purpose. One continues to hope, of course, that Romero will recover, and his current projects (at time of writing) encourage such a hope: *Day of the Dead* (the completion of the trilogy) and a film version of *Pet Sematary*, one of King's most haunting and disturbing works.

There is indeed little to salvage from the period: a few minor works such as *Alligator* and *Blood Beach* which represent the vestigial traces of the 70s tradition. Certainly, they no longer represent a mainstream. At the end of the 70s, the prevailing current began to flow in quite another direction, the decisive film being *Halloween*, with its great commercial success.

THE REACTIONARY WING

I suggested earlier that the theory of repression offers us a means toward a political categorization of horror movies. Such a categorization, however, can never be rigid or clear-cut. While I have stressed the genre's progressive or radical elements, its potential for the subversion of bourgeois patriarchal norms, it is obvious that this potential is never free from ambiguity. The genre carries within itself the capability of reactionary inflection, and perhaps no horror film is entirely immune from its operations. It need not surprise us that a powerful reactionary tradition exists—so powerful it may under certain social conditions become the dominant one. Its characteristics are, in extreme cases, very strongly marked.

Before noting them, however, it is important to make one major distinction between the reactionary horror film and the apocalyptic horror film. The latter obviously expresses despair and negativity, yet its very negation can be claimed as progressive: the apocalypse, even when presented in metaphysical terms (the end of the world), is generally reinterpretable in social/political ones (the end of the highly specific world of patriarchal capitalism). The majority of the most distinguished American horror films, especially in the 70s, are concerned with this particular apocalypse. They are progressive in so far as their negativity is not recuperable into the dominant ideology, but constitutes, on the contrary, the recognition of that ideology's disintegration and its untenability, as all it has repressed explodes and blows it apart. *The Texas Chainsaw Massacre*, *Sisters*, *Demon* are all apocalyptic in this sense; so are Romero's two "living dead" movies.

Outlined here are some of the characteristics that have contributed to the genre's reactionary wing:

1. The designation of the monster as simply evil. Insofar as horror films are typical manifestations of our culture, the dominant designation of the monster must necessarily be evil: what is repressed (in the individual, in the culture) must always return as a threat, perceived by the consciousness as ugly, terrible, obscene. Horror films, it might be said, are progressive precisely to the degree that they refuse to be satisfied with this simple designation—to the degree that, whether explicitly or implicitly, consciously or unconsciously, they modify, question, challenge, and seek to invert it. All monsters are by definition destructive, but their destructiveness is capable of being variously explained, excused and justified. To identify what is repressed with evil incarnate (a metaphysical, rather than a social, definition) is automatically to suggest that the only recourse is to strive to *keep* it repressed. Films in which the monster is identified as the devil clearly occupy a privileged place in this group, though even the devil can be presented with varying degrees of deliberate or inadvertent sympathy and fascination—*The Omen* should not simply be bracketed with *The Sentinel* for consignment to merited oblivion.

2. The presence of Christianity (insofar as it is given weight or presented posi-

tively) is in general a portent of reaction. (This is a comment less on Christianity itself than on what it signifies within the Hollywood cinema and the dominant ideology.) *The Exorcist* is an instructive instance—its validity is in direct proportion to its failure convincingly to impose its theology.

3. The presentation of the monster as totally nonhuman. The progressiveness of the horror film depends partly on the monster's capacity to arouse sympathy; one can feel little for a mass of viscous black slime. The political (McCarthyite) level of 50s science fiction films—the myth of Communism as total dehumanization—accounts for the prevalence of this kind of monster in that period.

4. The confusion, in terms of what the film wishes to regard as monstrous, of *repressed* sexuality with sexuality itself. The distinction is not always clear-cut; perhaps it never can be, in a culture whose attitudes to sexuality remain largely negative and where a fear of sex is implanted from infancy. One can, however, isolate a few extreme examples where the sense of horror is motivated by sexual disgust.

A very common generic pattern plays on the ambiguity of the monster as the return of the repressed and the monster as punishment for sexual promiscuity (or, in the more extreme puritanical cases, for any sexual expression whatever: two teenagers kiss; enter, immediately, the Blob). The *Jaws* films—their sources in both 50s McCarthyite science fiction and all those beach party-monster movies that disappeared with the B feature—are obvious recent examples, Spielberg's film being somewhat more complex and less blatant than its sequels, though the difference is chiefly one of ideological sophistication.

John Carpenter's films reveal in many ways an engaging artistic personality: they communicate, at the very least, a delight in skill and craftsmanship, a pleasure in play with the medium, that is one of the essential expressions of true creativity. Yet the film-buff innocence that accounts for much of the charm of *Dark Star* can go on to combine (in *Assault on Precinct 13*) *Rio Bravo* and *Night of the Living Dead* without any apparent awareness of the ideological consequences of converting Hawks' Fascists (or Romero's ghouls, for that matter) into an army of revolutionaries. The film buff is very prominent again in *Halloween*, covering the film's confusions and its lack of real thinking with a formal/stylistic inventiveness that is initially irresistible. If nothing in the film is new, everything testifies to Carpenter's powers of assimilation, as opposed to mere imitation: as a resourceful amalgam of *Psycho, The Texas Chainsaw Massacre, The Exorcist* and *Black Christmas, Halloween* is cunning in the extreme.

The confusions, however, inform its very foundation, in the conception of the monster. The opening is quite stunning both in its virtuosity and its resonances. The long killer's point-of-view tracking shot with which the film begins establishes the basis for the first murder as sexual repression: the girl is killed because she arouses in the voyeur-murderer feelings he has simultaneously to deny and enact in the form of violent assault. The second shot reveals the murderer as the victim's bewildered six-year-old brother. Crammed into these first two shots (in which *Psycho* unites with the Halloween sequence of *Meet Me in St. Louis*) are the ingredients for the definitive family horror film: the child-monster, product of the nuclear family and the small-town environment; the sexual repression of children; the incest taboo that denies sexual feeling precisely where the proximities of family life most encourage it. Not only are those implications not realized in the succeeding film, their trace is obscured and all but obliterated. The killer is identified with "the Bogeyman," the embodiment of an eternal and unchanging evil which, by definition, can't be understood; and with the Devil ("those eyes . . . the Devil's eyes"), by none other than his own psychoanalyst (Donald Pleasence)—surely the most extreme instance of Hollywood's perversion of psychoanalysis into an instrument of repression.

The film proceeds to lay itself wide open to the reading Jonathan Rosenbaum offered in *Take One*: the killer's victims are all sexually promiscuous, the one survivor a virgin; the monster becomes, in the tradition of all those beach party-monster movies of the late 50s and early 60s, simply the instrument of puritan vengeance and repression rather than the embodiment of what puritanism repressed.

Halloween is more interesting than that, if only because more confused. The basic premise of the action is that Laurie is the killer's real quarry throughout (the other girls merely distractions *en route*), because she is for him the reincarnation of the sister he murdered as a child (he first sees her in relation to a little boy who resembles him as he was then, and becomes fixated on her from that moment). This compulsion to reenact the childhood crime keeps Michael tied at least to the possibility of psychoanalytical explanation, thereby suggesting that Donald Pleasence may be wrong. If we accept that, then one tantalizing unresolved detail becomes crucial: the question of how Michael learned to drive a car. Only two possible explanations present themselves: either he *is* the devil, possessed of supernatural powers; or he has not spent the last nine years (as Pleasence would have us believe) sitting staring blackly at a wall meditating further horrors. (It is to Carpenter's credit that the issue is raised in the dialogue, not glossed over as an unfortunate plot necessity we aren't supposed to notice, but he appears to use it merely as another tease, a bit of meaningless mystification.) The possibility this opens up is that of reading the whole film against the Pleasence character: Michael's evil is what his analyst has been projecting on to him for the past nine years. Unfortunately, this remains merely a possibility in the material that Carpenter chose not to take up; it does not constitute a legitimate (let alone a coherent) reading of the actual film.

RETURNING THE LOOK

Confronted over the past few years with the proliferation of increasingly violent and gruesome low-budget horror movies centered on psychopathic killers, one may take away the impression of one undifferentiated stream of massacre, mutilation and terrorization, a single interminable chronicle of blood-letting called something like "When a Stranger Calls after Night School on Halloween or Friday the Thirteenth, Don't Answer the Phone and Don't Go Into the House because He Knows You're Alone and is Dressed to Kill." In fact, however one may shrink from systematic exposure to the films or deplore the social phenomena and ideological mutations they reflect, distinctions can be made in terms both of function and quality. Their popularity, especially—indeed, almost exclusively—with youth audiences, suggests that, even if they were uniformly execrable, they shouldn't be ignored; an attempt both to understand the phenomena and to discriminate among the films seems valid and timely.

The films fall into two partially distinguishable categories, answering to two partially distinguishable cultural needs: the violence against women movie (of which *Dressed to Kill* is the most controversial, as well as the most ambitiously "classy," example), and what has been succinctly dubbed the "teenie-kill pic" (of which the purest—if that is the word—examples are the four *Friday the 13th* movies). The distinction is never clear-cut: the two cycles have common sources in The *Texas Chainsaw Massacre* and *Halloween* (which in turn have a common source in *Psycho*); the last survivor of the teenie-kill movies, endurer of the ultimate ordeals, terrors and agonies, is invariably female; the victims in the violence against women films are predominantly young. But the motivation for the slaughter on both the dramatic and ideological levels is somewhat different: in general, the teenagers are punished for promiscuity, while the women are punished for being women.

Both types represent a sinister and disturbing inversion of the significance of the traditional horror film. There, the monster was in general a creature from the id, not merely a product of repression but a protest against it, whereas in the current cycles the monster, while still produced by repression, has essentially become a superego figure, avenging itself on liberated female sexuality or the sexual freedom of the young. What *hasn't* changed, making the social implications even more sinister, is the genre's basic commercial premise—that the customers continue to pay, as they always did, to enjoy the eruptions and depredations of the monster. Where the traditional horror film invited, however ambiguously, an identification with the return of the repressed, the contemporary horror film invites an identification (either sadistic or masochistic or both simultaneously) with punishment.

On the whole, the teenie-kill pic seems the more consistently popular, which can be interpreted as a logical consequence of a "permissive" (as opposed to a liberated) society. The chief (indeed almost the only) characteristic of the films' teenagers (who are obviously meant to be attractive to the youth audience as identification figures) is a mindless hedonism made explicit by a character in *Friday the 13th, Part 3*, who remarks without contradiction that the only things worth living for are screwing and smoking dope. The films both endorse this and relentlessly punish it;

they never suggest that other options might be available (what, after all, might happen if young people began to *think*?). What is most stressed, and nowhere *explicitly* condemned, is promiscuity—the behavior that consumer capitalism in its present phase simultaneously "permits" and morally disapproves of. The satisfaction that youth audiences get from these films is presumably twofold: they identify both with the promiscuity and with the grisly and excessive punishment. The original *Friday the 13th* dramatizes this very clearly: most of the murders are closely associated with the young people having sex together (a principle that reaches ludicrous systematization in the sequels, where one can safely predict that any character who shows sexual interest in another will be dead within minutes); the psychopathic killer turns out to be a woman whose son Jason drowned because the camp counselors who should have been supervising him were engaged in intercourse. In the sequels, Jason himself returns as a vaguely defined mutant monster, virtually indistinguishable from the Michael of the *Halloween* films, which introduces another indispensable component of the cycle, the monster's unkillability: the sexual guilt which the characters are by definition incapable of analyzing, confronting or understanding can never be exorcized.

The violence against women movies have generally been explained as a hysterical response to 60s and 70s feminism: the male spectator enjoys a sadistic revenge on women who have begun to refuse to slot neatly and obligingly into his patriarchally predetermined view of the way things should naturally be. This is convincing as long as one sees it as accounting for the intensity, repetitiveness and ritualistic insistence of these films, and not for the basic phenomenon itself: from *Caligari* to *Psycho*, women have always been the main focus of threat and assault in the horror film. A number of variously plausible explanations may account for this: First, that, as women are regarded as weak and helpless, it is simply more frightening if the monster attacks *them*; the male spectator can presumably identify with the hero who finally kills the monster, the film thereby indulging his vanity as male protector of the helpless female. That he may also, on another level, identify with the monster in no way contradicts this: it merely suggests its inadequacy as total explanation. Second, that, as men in patriarchal society have set women up on compensatory pedestals, thereby constructing them as oppressive and restrictive figures, they have a strong desire to knock them down again. As in every genre, the archetypal male-constructed opposition of wife/whore operates here: in the traditional horror film the women who get killed are usually whore figures, punished for bringing out the beast in men; the heroine who gets terrorized and/or abducted, but is eventually rescued, is the present or future wife. The ideological tensions involved here are still central to our culture. Third, that the films obliquely express what Hitchcock's films, for example, have consistently dramatized—the anxiety of the heterosexual male confronted by the possibility of an autonomous female sexuality he can't control and organize. But the key point, for present purposes, is that in the traditional horror film the threatened heroine was invariably associated with the values of monogamous marriage and the nuclear family (actual or potential): the eruption of the Frankenstein monster during the preparations for his creator's wedding in the 1931 James Whale movie is the *locus classicus*. What the monster really threatened was a repressive, ideologically constructed bourgeois normality. Today, the women who are terrorized and slaughtered tend to be those who *resist* definition within the virgin/wife/mother framework.

The dominant project of both these overlapping, interlocking cycles is, then, depressingly reactionary. However, as both can be shown to have their source in contemporary ideological tension, confusion and contradiction, both carry within them the potential for subverting that project. There is, for example, no inherent reason why a filmmaker of some intelligence and awareness should not make a teenie-kill movie that, while following the general patterns of the genre, analyzed sexual guilt and proposed opposition to it: it would chiefly require characters who were not totally mindless, for whom both filmmaker and spectator could feel some respect. The recent *Hell Night* perhaps shows vestiges of such an ambition (it at least produces an active and resourceful heroine—Linda Blair—capable of doing more than screaming and falling over), but in general the apparently total complicity of the youth audience in these fantasies of their own destruction has licensed a corresponding mindlessness in the filmmakers.

Feminists (of both sexes) have, on the other hand, been quite vociferous on the subject of violence against women, and this can be credited with provoking various degrees of disturbance in recent specimens of the genre, ranging from vague uneasiness to an intelligent rethinking of the conventions. In *Dressed to Kill* the violence to women is consistently countered by a critique of male dominance and an exposure of male sexual insecurities. *He Knows You're Alone*, while finally very confused, makes a highly sophisticated attempt through a conscious, intermittently self-reflexive play with narrative to analyze violence against women in terms of male possessiveness and the fear of female autonomy. It is certainly worth discriminating between it and *Don't Go into the House*, which may be taken as representing the cycle at its most debased: a film in which the most disgusting violence (flaying alive with a blowtorch) is significantly juxtaposed with some more than usually strident dialogue about "faggots" in a way that may be taken as indicating, however inadvertently, some of the sexual tensions that motivate the cycle as a whole.

Ken Wiederhorn's *Eyes of a Stranger* strikes me as the most coherent attempt to rework the conventions of the cycle so far, resulting in a film that, while it doesn't escape contamination (the generic patterns are to some degree intractable), comes closest to embodying a systematic critique of the dominant project. Disgracefully mishandled and thrown away by its distributors, it seems to have come and gone virtually unnoticed on both sides of the Atlantic, apart from some predictable abuse from journalist-critics incapable of distinguishing between different uses of the

The Terrorization of Women

(right)
Friday the 13th,
Part 2

(below)
Halloween

same generic material. The film follows the basic rules of the cycle very faithfully, so the necessary plot synopsis can be brief: a psychopath is terrorizing women (obscene phone call, followed by rape and murder); a TV news reporter (Lauren Tewes) comes correctly to suspect a man in the apartment opposite her own; she endangers her own life by searching his apartment for evidence while he is out; he discovers who is harassing him and, in the climactic scene, invades her apartment in return, assaulting her younger sister (Jennifer Jason Leigh), who is blind, mute, and deaf from shock at being raped and beaten when she was a child. I shall restrict analysis to three aspects, representing the major components of the genre.

1. The Psychopath, "The Look"   Much has been made of the strikingly insistent use (in both teenie-kill and violence against women movies) of first-person camera to signify the approach of the killer, seen by many critics as an invitation to sadistic indulgence on the part of the spectator. A simple alternative explanation for the device, which in fact works with rather than against this, is the need to preserve the secret of the killer's identity for a final "surprise" The latter motivation might be seen merely as supplying a plausible alibi for the former: the sense of indeterminate, unidentified, possibly supernatural or superhuman menace feeds the spectator's fantasy of power, facilitating a direct spectator/camera identification by keeping the intermediary character, while signified as present, as vaguely defined as possible. In *Eyes of a Stronger* the psychopath's identity is revealed quite early in the film: a rather ordinary-looking, confused, ungainly, unattractive man who strongly evokes memories of Raymond Burr in *Rear Window*. The (for the genre, surprisingly infrequent) point-of-view shots of strippers, naked women, etc., are always attached to an *identified* figure: if the male spectator identifies with the point-of-view, he is consistently shown precisely whom he is identifying with. Hence, although the film is posited on the terrorization of women (and, during its first half, certainly gets too much mileage out of that for its own good), this is never presented with simple relish, and the sadism can never be simply enjoyed (it is difficult to imagine audiences cheering the murders—a not uncommon phenomenon within this cycle— deprived as they are of all possible perverse glamour).

2. The Other Male Characters   The two "attractive" young men (potential hero figures, though one is murdered very early in the film) are both associated with the killer on their first appearances, a device also employed, though less strikingly, in *He Knows You're Alone*. The first (when the film's first victim is already threatened— we know, but she doesn't, that the murderer is in her apartment) frightens her by appearing in her doorway wearing a grotesque mask that resembles the killer's face under its concealing stocking; the second (Lauren Tewes' lover, the film's apparent male lead) leaps on her violently in bed in a parody of sexual assault. Male aggression is thus generalized, presented as a phenomenon of our culture (the lover, significantly, is trying throughout the film to circumscribe Tewes within his values and his apartment).

Consistently, the men in the film are either unhelpful, uncomprehending, or active impediments. The police refuse to investigate the first victim's reports of harassment in time to save her because Tewes' fully justified warning newscast has provoked an epidemic of obscene calls that turn out to be jokes (compare the lover's pretended assault). The lover refuses to accept Tewes' evidence (circumstantial, but strong, and strongly supported by that intuition men like to see as the prerogative of the female so that they can condescend to it) until it's too late, because of his commitment as a lawyer to one of the dominant institutions of patriarchy. Tewes' attempts to express her concern on television are met by her fellow newscaster with bland indifference; the film is very shrewd in pinpointing the tendency of television to cancel out and reassure, Tewes' warning to women being immediately followed by the determinedly comic antics of the male weather-reporter.

3. The Women   The film is consistently woman-centered. Our identification figures are exclusively female, and the temptation to produce a male hero who springs to the rescue at the last moment is resolutely resisted, the women handling everything themselves. Tewes and Leigh are both presented—in their different ways, and within the limitations of the generic conventions—as strong, resourceful, and intelligent. Here, too, comparison with *Rear Window* is interesting. When Grace Kelly, in Hitchcock's film, invades the murderer's apartment, it is in order to demonstrate her courage to a man; Tewes' motivation in the corresponding scene of *Eyes of a Stranger* is a genuine and committed social concern. Although this is shown to have roots in personal psychology (her feeling for her younger sister, and largely irrational guilt about what happened to her), the film strongly suggests that this has become generalized into a concern about the victimization of women in contemporary society. Crucial to the film is its reversal of the patterns of male domination: the turning point is the moment when Tewes phones the killer, to persuade him to turn himself in, but also to let him know what it feels like to be on the receiving end of an anonymous phone call.

The conclusion of the film is particularly satisfying by virtue of its play on "the look" and the way in which it answers the beginning. The opening images show a man photographing marine life along the Florida coastline, who suddenly finds himself photographing a woman's body: the look, innocent enough on the personal level, is symbolically established as male, the looked-at female and passive. The psychosomatically blind sister's recovery of her sight during the murderer's assault—dramatically predictable and, if you like, corny (I find it, like many "obvious" moments in the cinema, very moving)—takes on corresponding significance in relation to this and to the film's play on looking throughout (from its title onwards). Tracy's regaining of her sight and her voice can be read in terms of "pop" psychology, that is, the reliving of a traumatic experience; the film also makes clear that she sees at the moment when she finally realizes she has to fight for her life. The regaining of sight represents the renunciation of the passivity into which she has withdrawn: immediately, the power of the look is transferred to the power of the gun with which she shoots the murderer, the reappropriation of the phallus. In accordance with current convention he isn't really dead, and Tewes, returning just in time, has to shoot him again; unlike Michael and Jason, however, he is by no means signified as indestructible. The contemporary horror film has, typically, two possible endings (frequently combined): the heroine/last survivor alive but apparently reduced to insanity; the suggestion that the monster is still alive. (Like so much else in these twin cycles, the endings were initiated by *The Texas Chainsaw Massacre* and *Halloween* respectively.) *Eyes of a Stranger* ends with the murderer, definitely dead, slumped ignominiously in the bathtub, his eyes closed, his glasses still perched incongruously on his nose—an unflattering reflection for any male in the audience who has relished the sadistic assaults.

10.

Images and Women

HOLLYWOOD FEMINISM: THE 70S

In order to be admitted to the Hollywood cinema at all, feminism had to undergo various drastic changes, the fundamental one, from which all the rest follow, being the repression of politics. In Hollywood films—even the most determinedly progressive—there is no "women's movement"; there are only individual women who feel personally constrained.

Hollywood's intermittent concern with social problems has, in fact, almost never produced radically subversive movies (and if so, then incidentally and inadvertently). A social problem, explicitly stated, must always be one that can be resolved within the existing system, i.e., patriarchal capitalism; the *real* problems, which can't, can only be dramatized obliquely, and very likely unconsciously, within the entertainment movie. Just as *Cruising* can tell us far more about the relationship between patriarchy and homophobia than *Making Love*, so *Looking for Mr. Goodbar* can tell us far more about the oppression of women and the tensions inherent in contemporary heterosexual relations than *An Unmarried Woman.*

The two films generally singled out to represent Hollywood feminism are Paul Mazursky's *An Unmarried Woman* and Martin Scorsese's *Alice Doesn't Live Here Anymore.* It seems superfluous at this point to rehearse yet again their limitations. What seems not to have been noticed is that they share a common structure, in which those limitations are embodied. The significance of this—given that there are no tangible connections between the two films, in the form of common writers, producers, directors, stars, studios—should be obvious: the structure defines the limits of the ideologically acceptable, the limits that render feminism safe. It is with structure rather than texture that I shall be concerned here, so I shall preface the account by saying that Scorsese's film seems to me not just the more immediately engaging (by virtue of that surface aliveness that is due, especially, to Scorsese's work with actors) but the richer and more complex work, despite the fact that

Ellen Burstyn in *Alice Doesn't Live Here Anymore*

With Diane Ladd

With Alfred Lutter

superficially it appears the more compromised, the heroine's capitulation being more complete. Partly, this is bound up with its working-class milieu: it is simply too easy to make a film about the liberation of an upper-class career woman with a lucrative position in the fashionable art world. Scorsese's film cannot resolve its problems satisfactorily, but at least it doesn't so glibly evade them.

The common structure can be broken down into its main components (for the sake of brevity, I shall indicate variations on the pattern by the directors' initials):

1. At the outset, the heroine is married (in M. apparently happily, in S. unhappily).

2. She has a child, signified as on the verge of or just into adolescence (M.: a daughter; S.: a son). Despite the gender difference, the resemblance is remarkable, the dominant characteristic being precocity. In both films the child is young enough to be still dependent; mature enough to be a semi-confidant, engaging with the mother in arguments and intimate exchanges; independent enough to demand his/her own rights. Hence, the child functions in both films as a problem, and simultaneously provides reassurance that the marriage breakdown isn't *irremediably* damaging.

3. The marriage ends (M.: the husband leaves the heroine for another woman; S.: the husband is killed in an accident), and the woman has to make a new life for herself and the child.

4. The heroine is already (M.) or becomes (S.) involved in a group of women who provide emotional support (M.: Erica's friends; S.: the other waitresses). The development of Alice's mutually supportive relationship with Flo is among the most positive and touching things in Scorsese's film.

5. The heroine has an unsuccessful and transitory relationship with an unsatisfactory lover (M.: because he is promiscuous and rejects commitment; S.: because he is psychotic and already married). Harvey Keitel, in a generally atypical film, is in the direct line of descent of Scorsese's male protagonists, complete with Scorpio pendant.

6. The heroine meanwhile pursues, or attempts to pursue, a career that satisfies her need for self-respect (M.: successfully, as a receptionist in an art gallery; S.: unsuccessfully, as a singer).

7. In the course of her work, she meets a non-oppressive male to whom she can relate on equal terms and with whom she develops a satisfying, if troubled, relationship.

This last development—felt in both cases as the film's necessary culmination—is obviously crucial. It occurs roughly two-thirds of the way through, and represents the end of the heroine's trajectory; both men (M.: Alan Bates; S.: Kris Kristofferson), despite the fact that one is an artist and the other a rancher, are strikingly similar in type: burly, bearded, emphatically masculine, physically strong, and emotionally stable: reassuring, not only for the woman in the film, but for women in the audience and—perhaps most important of all—for *men* in the audience. The films share a certain deviousness. On the explicit level, both preserve a determined ambiguity, refusing to guarantee the permanence of the happy ending. Yet the final effect is of a huge communal sigh of relief: the women don't *have* to be independent after all; there are strong, protective males to look after them. Their demand for independence is accordingly reduced to a token gesture, becoming little more than an irrational "feminine" whim. The "nonoppressiveness" and the "equality," though heavily signaled, are also extremely problematic, existing purely on the personal level in terms of sympathetic individual men and never clearly examined in terms of social positions. *Alice Doesn't Live Here Anymore*, with its richer generic background, develops a particular irony here, although it is never brought to a sharp focus: the Western traditionally offered women two options, the rancher's wife or the saloon entertainer; they remain, in a consciously feminist film of 1974, precisely the options open to Alice.

In a brilliant article in the 1983 *Socialist Register* ("Masculine Dominance and the State"), Varda Burstyn distinguishes between women's *liberation* and women's *equality*:

The notion of equality for women rather than the notion of women's liberation denies a transformative dynamic to women's struggles . . . . It implicitly but firmly sets the lifeways and goals of masculine existence as the standards to which women should aspire and against which official estimates of their "progress" will be made. It poses the problem as one of the women's "catching up to men," rather than as a problem for women and men to solve together by changing the conditions and relations of their shared lives—from their intimate to their large-scale social interaction.

What *Alice Doesn't Live Here Anymore* and *An Unmarried Woman* offer is, at best, equality, not liberation, and even the equality is precarious and compromised.

HOLLYWOOD ANTIFEMINISM: THE 80S

The precariousness of what was achieved in the 70s can be gauged from the ease with which it has been overthrown in the 80s. The pervasiveness of antifeminism in current Hollywood cinema (it is seldom of course explicitly presented as such, and often embodied merely in the reinstatement of traditional role models, as if nothing had happened) has been noted elsewhere in this book. Here I want to focus simply on two pairs of parallel examples, one from the beginning of the period and one representing the subsequent, more brazen development of the implications. The examples are offered as representative: if they stand out, it is only by virtue of their clarity.

Urban Cowboy and *Bronco Billy* were released almost simultaneously in 1980. The dramatic tension in both is centered on the efforts of an active, even aggressive woman to assert herself within a strongly male-dominated environment, in activities associated with masculinity: Debra Winger proves that she can ride the mechanical bull at least as well as John Travolta; Sondra Locke proves herself at least as good a sharp-shooter as Clint Eastwood. The narrative then moves to the point, where the woman comes to understand that she isn't happy with this "equality": Debra Winger realizes that what she's really wanted all along is to wash her husband's socks; Sondra Locke ends up spreadeagled on a revolving wheel, as Bronco Billy's target in his traveling Wild West show. Both films, though contemporary in setting, explicitly locate themselves in the tradition of the Western, and use this as a means of putting assertive women back where they belong—respectively, as wife and object-of-the-gaze; both narratives teach the woman to be fully complicit in her own oppression. One must also note the uncomprehending vacuity of the underlying premise: the principles of feminism reduced to the demand to participate in the violent rites of masculinity.

Two of the ugliest moments in recent Hollywood films occur in *An Officer and a Gentlemen* and in *Terms of Endearment*. In the first, Debra Winger turns on her friend and denounces her for having pretended to be pregnant in order to trap a man into marriage ("God help you"). In the second, Debra Winger turns on a group of her New York acquaintances and denounces them for their divorces, abortions, etc. Both narratives are careful to justify the outburst dramatically: in the former, the feigned pregnancy has precipitated the lover's suicide; in the latter, the New York friends are presented, stereotypically, as superficial, trendy and blasé. Yet again, the alibi of realism masks ideology: the insidious purpose of each film is to suggest that the only alternative for a woman to being a "good" wife/mother is to be duplicitous or fashionably desensitized.

The two moments have a good deal in common. Each occurs at roughly the same point in the narrative (about two-thirds through the film, around the point where the development of the relationship with the acceptable male occurred in the 70s movies), and marks a decisive step in its progression. Each uses a woman to denounce other women, the woman in both cases having come fully to accept her correct traditional role, even though both she and the film know that role to be fairly ignominious (affirmation in the 80s is never free of cynicism). In *An Officer and a Gentleman* this movement is used to support the film's glorification of militarism, the ultimate embodiment of masculinity. Just what it supports in *Terms of Endearment* is less easy to define, though central to it is a mystique of motherhood—hence the emphasis on abortion—that has given the film an unfortunate credibility for many women (in combination with its maddening "great acting," which amounts to no more than a relentless parade of knowing mannerisms). There is also, of course, the presence in both films of Debra Winger. One might say that Winger, having learned to oppress herself in *Urban Cowboy*, has gone on to dedicate her career to the oppression of other women. But that is perhaps putting it too personally. What is at issue is not Winger's acting ability or even her presence as a personality (both could be inflected in various ways), but the star image that has been constructed around her: Winger-as-star has become the indispensable 80s woman, a major focus for the return to the good old values of patriarchal capitalism and the restoration of women to their rightful place.

It is a profoundly depressing and alienating experience to sit in a packed auditorium watching these films with an audience who actually cheer their grossest moments. Doubtless, at the end of the world, bourgeois society will sit dying among the ruins still congratulating itself on the rightness of its good old values: a spectacle literally enacted in Lynne Littman's *Testament*.

DIRECTING WOMEN

The first great wave of feminism, around the turn of the century, coincided roughly with the invention of cinema; the second, through the 60s and 70s, produced an impressive body of critical/theoretial work and some distinguished avant-garde, "alternative" filmmaking. Neither, so far, has managed radically to affect the structures of mainstream film production (either the economic and power structures of an overwhelmingly patriarchal industry or the aesthetic and thematic structures of the films it turns out). It would be wrong, however, to assume that feminism has had no effect on Hollywood whatever. On the level of content it has provoked, negatively, a massive retaliation (ranging from the shameless grossness of the mad slasher movie to the far more insidious reinstatement of compliant women to their safe, traditional roles enacted in films like *An Officer and a Gentleman* and *Terms of Endearment*) that testifies at least to the magnitude of the threat; less negatively, if not entirely positively, feminism has aroused a pervasive sense of disturbance and unease. On the professional level, the grudging recognition that women can do the work of men (a superficial but not unimportant response to feminism) has made it somewhat less difficult, if by no means easy, for women to work as directors. During the past ten years or so we have seen more or less distinguished films by Elaine May (*The Heartbreak Kid*), Claudia Weill (*Girl Friends*), Joan Micklin Silver (*Chilly Scenes of Winter*), Jane Wagner (*Moment by Moment*), Lee Grant (*Tell Me a Riddle*), Amy Heckerling (*Fast Times at Ridgemont High*), Lynne Littman (*Testament*) and Barbra Streisand (*Yentl*), together with entirely negligible ones by Joan Rivers (*Rabbit Test*), Joan Darling (*First Love*), Nancy Walker (*Can't Stop the Music*), Barbara Peeters (*Humanoids from the Deep*) and Martha Coolidge (*Joy of Sex*). I have not seen Anne Bancroft's *Fatso*. In terms of numbers, the tally is unprecedented in any previous period, though of course still enormously outweighed by the films made by men.

The continuing inequality between the sexes can be measured not only in numbers but in terms of the conditions under which women are permitted to make films (and that word "permitted," deliberately chosen, speaks volumes). Ten of the fourteen in the above list have made, at time of writing, only one commercial theatrical movie, though Heckerling is currently working on a second;[1] six of the fourteen established themselves as performers first (a route proportionately uncommon for men); none has so far managed to establish a stable, continuous career (May, with three films, has not directed since 1974; Silver, also with three, not since 1979; Weill, with two, not since 1980). One may ask why no woman (Streisand the partial exception) has ever made a really big-grossing box office hit. Treating the possible sexist response with the contempt it deserves, one may suggest that one reason is that no woman (Streisand again excepted) has been entrusted with the kind of material from which box office hits ore made: the projects that women directors have been able to set up are, typically, modest, low-budget affairs on unassuming subjects, usually without major stars. During the Classical Hollywood period, Dorothy Arzner (20s to 40s), working intermittently with major female stars (Hepburn, Crawford), was able to build an impressively solid body of films, but always on projects regarded by the studios as minor and feminine, which came to the same thing. Ida Lupino (again an established star before becoming a director) made half-a-dozen films in the 50s, all B movies on restricted budgets. Stephanie Rothman, courageously plunging into the exploitation field of beach parties, horror, violence and sex, practiced some remarkable, though not widely celebrated, strategies of subversion in the 60s and early 70s, and has been unable to set up a film since, though still eager and certainly able.

So much for statistics. The problems they indicate go far beyond what might seem the simple, obvious explanation that men continue to resent women in positions of power—which is not to deny that that explanation carries a lot of weight. The male aversion seems to be primarily a practical one: less objection exists to women's power behind the scenes, as screenwriters or producers; the aversion is to women's power made visible and concrete. An obvious parallel: there are very few female orchestral conductors, and no very famous ones. A woman can be a pianist or violinist of international status (and presumably Cécile Ousset and Kyung-Wha Chung, when they play concertos, determine the tempi and overall conception), but she cannot stand up in front of an orchestra composed mainly of males and be seen to direct and dominate them. I have heard wonderful broadcast concerts by

---

1. *Johnny Dangerously* has appeared just in time for a footnote which, alas, it barely deserves: Heckerling has allowed herself to be absorbed (temporarily, one hopes) into a comic mode that derives from TV (*Saturday Night Live* is the most obvious influence) in which a woman's discourse is quite obliterated, and the film proves no more than that women can make movies that are just as bad as most of those made by men.

the Milwaukee Symphony under Margaret Hawkins, but Ms. Hawkins, as far as I know, never leaves Milwaukee for the international tours taken for granted by her male, and often inferior, jet-setting counterparts.

The deeper problem can be suggested through a series of questions: What films might women of integrity *want* to make? If no woman has made an overwhelming box office smash, may this be because no woman in her senses would *want* to make *Raiders of the Lost Ark, An Officer and a Gentleman,* or *Return of the Jedi?* Entrusted with such projects, what could a woman director decently do but struggle to subvert them? Their commercial success is intimately bound up with their flattering of patriarchy. What possibilities exist for a female (not necessarily feminist) discourse to be articulated within a patriarchal industry through narrative conventions and genres developed by and for a male-dominated culture? The closure of classical narrative (of which the Hollywood happy ending is a typical form) enacts the restoration of patriarchal order; the transgressing woman is either forgiven and subordinated to that order, or punished, usually by death. The seminal writings of Claire Johnston and Pam Cook on Dorothy Arzner suggest that Arzner's intervention in patriarchal projects could do little to alter the course of such narrative conventions; what it *could* do was to create disturbances and imbalances, rendering the happy ending problematic or unsatisfying. In effect, the films are being praised for their incoherence, their unresolved contradictions, their tendency to leave audiences dissatisfied—scarcely a recommendation within a commercially motivated industry (try going to a producer with "I've got this great idea for a really incoherent movie").

I shall consider here some of the genuinely distinguished achievements of women directors in the past decade (especially Grant, Weill, Silver, and Heckerling). First, however, it seems fitting to focus briefly on *Yentl,* because it provides apparent answers to some of the problems. It is a big-budget production obviously intended to have wide popular appeal, directed, co-produced, and co-written by a woman as her own cherished project, on an explicitly feminist theme (a woman's rebellion against patriarchal constraints), quite free of any of the obvious symptoms of incoherence (awkwardness, tentativeness, strain, imbalance, working against the grain). Yet—while a generally agreeable entertainment with a few wonderful moments—*Yentl* is really the answer to nothing. It is scarcely a breakthrough for women directors, as its existence is entirely dependent on Streisand's status as Superstar. Its precise nature seems determined by her desire to give her audiences what they expect of her: there was a neat, sharp little ninety-minute movie there somewhere, but it has become almost submerged in lush production values (*Sound of Music* meets *Fiddler on the Roof)* and an inordinate number of songs as undistinguished as they are superfluous. Apart perhaps from some interesting if equivocal play with gender roles and sexual ambiguity, the film offers no challenge to anyone: its feminist theme is placed in the context of a culture so remote from our own that we can view it with a complacent sense of "how things used to be," a sense confirmed by the ending, where Yentl emigrates to America and emancipation. As for the film's coherence, it is precisely that of classical narrative, left completely undisturbed: the exceptional individual (Young Mr. Lincoln, Shane, Yentl) leaves a society too narrow to contain her/him, but only after ensuring the continuance of the patriarchal order through the reconstitution of the family or the couple. The general sense the film communicates of unearned self-congratulation calls to mind the slogan on the notorious advertisement for Virginia Slims: "You've come a long way, baby." For truly progressive work by women in mainstream cinema we must look elsewhere.

FOUR FILMS

It will be clear from the works I discuss (Claudia Weill's *Girl Friends*, Lee Grant's *Tell Me a Riddle*, Joan Micklin Silver's *Chilly Scenes of Winter*, and Amy Heckerling's *Fast Times at Ridgemont High*) that I am using the term "mainstream" somewhat loosely. Of the four, the first two were produced independently on the margins of the industry, and would never have been made but for the pertinacity of the filmmakers; only the last belongs squarely within the contemporary development of Hollywood genres and cycles. I use the term solely to distinguish fictional feature films intended to reach general audiences from experimental or avant-garde work produced without expectation of widespread distribution and standing resolutely apart from anything that could reasonably be called "entertainment." Many feminist critics have argued persuasively that the language (what one might call the organization of the look, both within the film and of the spectator) of mainstream cinema was developed by patriarchy for patriarchy and must be rigorously rejected; certain feminist filmmakers have put that argument into practice (the Laura Mulvey/Peter Wollen *Riddles of the Sphinx* is among the most impressive examples). Yet it seems to me desirable that all avenues be kept open, that the widest range of strategies and practices be attempted; it remains unproven that the patriarchal language of mainstream narrative film cannot be transformed and redeemed, that a woman's discourse cannot speak through it. The four films on which I here offer brief notes (each deserves detailed attention) provide some evidence to the contrary.

It is significant that only the two independent movies embody overtly feminist projects, and even they never manage to acknowledge the existence of a political women's movement: the obligatory conditions for a woman working for a major studio would appear to be discretion, subterfuge, deviousness, and compromise. *Girl Friends* is the only American commercial movie I can think of that explicitly calls marriage as an institution into question, as opposed to admitting that there are unsuccessful marriages, though a number of mainstream Hollywood movies (von Sternberg's *Blonde Venus*, Sirk's *There's Always Tomorrow*, Cukor's *Rich and*

Famous—which owes a lot to *Girl Friends*) can be read as suggesting this implicitly, under cover of being "just entertainment." *Tell Me a Riddle* is the only commercial American movie I can think of that explicitly parallels feminism and socialist revolution (though somewhat tactfully). Why should major studios, which are patriarchal capitalist structures from top to bottom, be expected to finance films that call into question their very premises? It is surprising enough that they agreed to distribute them. A culture committed to freedom of speech but built on money and private enterprise has a very simple means of repressing the former by using the latter, with no inconvenient or disturbing sense of hypocrisy. *Girl Friends* presents marriage as patriarchy's means of containing and separating women: the friendship of the title is effectively destroyed by the marriage of one of the women, whose priorities then *necessarily* become her house, her husband, her child. The view of marriage in *Tell Me a Riddle*, though less negative, is not entirely dissimilar. Here, the husband feels threatened, not by a female friendship, but by the woman's intellectual interests and revolutionary sympathies—in both cases, but in different ways, by the possibility of her autonomy. What is unique, and deeply moving, about Grant's film is its generosity in allowing the husband to recognize, though much too late, the destruction his attitude has caused: the scene of marital reconciliation is among the great moments in modern American cinema, not least because it triumphantly breaks another taboo by permitting old people erotic contact.

The independence of these two films is as much a matter of narrative/thematic content as of production setup. Neither fits comfortably into traditional generic expectations. *Girl Friends*, predominantly comic in tone but taking up the themes (marriage vs. career, etc.) of the "woman's melodrama," ends on a note of regret at the formation of the heterosexual couple rather than the traditional glow of relief and satisfaction; *Tell Me a Riddle* continues beyond the reconciliation scene to the old woman's death, the husband's remorse at lost opportunities, the younger woman's confirmed independence. The latter film, especially, is an extremely unorthodox project even aside from its feminist thrust: one of a very small handful of commercial films from *any* country on the highly uncommercial subject of old age.[2]

The achievement of *Chilly Scenes of Winter* and *Fast Times at Ridgemont High*, by contrast, can really only be appreciated in relation to the generic expectations and formulae they at once part fulfill, part undermine. *Chilly Scenes* is one of the very few woman-directed films centered on a male consciousness (men have never hesitated to make films centered on women, whereas women are always assigned or permitted feminine projects): an interesting strategy for the indirect expression of a woman's discourse.

2. For a detailed analysis of *Tell Me a Riddle*, see the article by Florence Jacobowitz and Lori Spring in *CineAction*, no. 1.

Marriage vs. Women's Solidarity: Anita Skinner, Bob Balaban, and Melanie Mayron in *Girl Friends*

Undermining the Comic Stereotype: Gloria Grahame and John Heard in *Chilly Scenes of Winter*

The relationship of the film to Ann Beattie's novel is complex, balancing fidelity with subtle transformation. Silver, who wrote the screenplay as well as directing the film, retains Beattie's premise, plot, and characters (realized with wonderful delicacy and precision by the actors), adding inventions of her own (some of the flashbacks, Charles' construction of the model of Laura's house, his visit with Sam to the actual house, hence the entire scene with Laura and her husband) that are perfectly compatible with the original but give Beattie's somewhat tenuous narrative, with its frequent recourse to internal monologues, a more concrete dramatization. Much of the dialogue is taken from the book, the film preserving the quality of its oblique, offbeat humor. However, the spirit of the book is subtly transformed. The transformation is due partly to the fact that the film owes as much to Hollywood—to a specific Hollywood tradition—as to its literary source. Its essence can be made clear by comparing Beatties's and Silver's endings. To put it succinctly, where Beattie gives us an unhappy happy ending, Silver substitutes a happy unhappy ending. (I am discounting here the ending that was tacked on to the film for its initial release, when its title was also changed to *Head Over Heels*.) At the end of the novel, the lovers get back together, yet it is clear that Laura has merely given up the struggle and is now wearily acquiescing to the insistence of Charles' romantic (and thoroughly possessive) passion for her: nothing has changed, neither has learned anything. The book's highly idiosyncratic and engaging humor becomes complicit in its defeatism: as people are incapable of growth or change, there is really nothing to do but laugh sadly and ironically at their predicament. Silver's film ends with the lovers separated and with Charles at last finding himself able to accept the separation: each has learned to recognize, slowly and painfully, the oppressiveness of romantic possession/dependence. It is perhaps the first Hollywood film where the happy ending consists, not in the lovers' union, but in their relinquishing its possibility.

The genre to which *Chilly Scenes* relates is not exactly topical: essentially, it belongs to the type of light comedy that flourished in the 30s and now seems virtually a lost art. The closeness of the fit can be suggested by the simple expedient of recasting it. The male protagonist trying to regain the woman he loves would have been Cary Grant, with Irene Dunne opposite him once again; the alternative but impossible lovers—"dumb blonde" secretary, dull businessman—would have been Lucille Ball and (of course!) Ralph Bellamy, with Billie Burke as the hero's comic-eccentric, scatterbrained mother. Once one has grasped the pattern, Silver's subtle inflections of it become quite fascinating. Crucial to the operation is her refusal to take romantic love for granted as an unquestionable value, or to assume the happy ending as the hero's inalienable right. Our classical prototype would have been what Stanley Cavell calls a "comedy of remarriage": the final reunion of the estranged couple would have been guaranteed from the outset by the fact that they were husband and wife. But in *Chilly Scenes* the male protagonist is the other man, the *husband* the dull businessman, and the woman ultimately rejects them both. Silver's handling of the comic female stereotypes (secretary, mother) is also idiosyncratic: if still comic, they are also disturbingly vulnerable, so that our laughter is made uneasy.

If I devote more space to *Fast Times at Ridgemont High*, it is not because I consider it a better film, but because it was made right in the mainstream of contemporary Hollywood production and because it belongs to a cycle one would never have expected a woman of intelligence and integrity to be able, or indeed want, to infiltrate. If *Eyes of a Stranger* proves that the terms of even the most apparently intractable generic formulae can be partially subverted (on the condition of meeting the demand that they also be partially fulfilled), the same can be argued far Amy Heckerling's disarming and exhilarating movie.

The terms of the 80s high school cycle (the obvious touchstones are *American Graffiti* and *Porky's*, respectively its pre-80s initiation and its most fully representative 80s manifestation) can be set forth quite succinctly:

1. **Sex** Even though school is the setting, the films at no point show the slightest interest in education (unless negatively, as a nuisance). The need to graduate may occasionally be an issue, but chiefly because it interferes with the real one. The cynicism (typical in general of our civilization, but especially a feature of the 80s) is total, and totally taken for granted; to the extent that reviewers never comment on it, one assumes they share it. There is never any hint of serious or reasoned rebellion against the educational system: education is a nuisance and a farce, yet somehow mysteriously necessary: one must study in order to graduate, and one must graduate in order to take one's place within the adult society one despises. The only film I have seen (marginal to the cycle, as its leading characters are preadolescent) that allows its characters to express overt antagonism to the educational system is Ronald Maxwell's *Kidco*: the objection is that school fails to teach children how to make money. Generally, the assumption is that teenagers could not possibly be interested in anything except sex, and it would be rather absurd to expect it (serious students are by definition "nerds"—though nerds need not be serious students). The films are at once a significant product and reinforcement of the commodification of sex in contemporary capitalist culture, most of the consumer products of which must be advertised and sold on their sexual appeal, blatant or subtle.

2. **The Suppression of Parents** Given that the teenagers of the films still live at home, the almost total absence of parents is rather remarkable. Peewee's mother (in *Porky's*) appears in one brief scene; Stacey's mother (in *Fast Times*) appears in one shot; fathers are either absent altogether or, in the case of the violent macho father of *Porky's*, so obviously monstrous as to be easily repudiated. Like education, parents are a mysteriously necessary evil, to be avoided whenever possible. Of course, what the films dare not suggest (they would instantly lose all their appeal) is that these

teenagers will grow up—inevitably, given their total lack of political awareness—to be replicas of their parents. Like education, parents interfere actually or potentially with the pursuit of sex: the less they are present in the films, the better. They are, in fact, reduced to the ignominious role of supplying occasional suspense (can the son/daughter get away in time for the next sexual encounter?).

3. Multicharacter Movies   The aim is to reach and satisfy as wide a youth audience as possible; there must, therefore, be a range of identification figures, and no minority group (with one significant exception) must be entirely neglected (though arranged within a careful hierarchy).

4. Hunter/Hunted   Two male figures recur, with variations, often in close juxtaposition—the one (there are likely to be several) who "knows all about it" and the one who doesn't. A central plot thread concerns the male virgin who has to "get laid." With both figures, the innocent and the experienced, the basic pattern is the same: male as hunter, female as hunted, male as looker, female as looked-at. The initiation of the male virgin is clearly crucial: the emphasis is less on his desire to achieve a pleasure already experienced by his fellows than on his need to prove himself, to become a "real man": Getting laid is the guarantee of masculinity/heterosexuality, the denial of a possibility that the films cannot even mention.

5. The Repression of Homosexuality   There are no gay teenagers in America: such, at least, is the films' implicit message.[3] No surprise, of course. What is marginally more surprising is that the films never acknowledge the possibility of teenage homosexual *behavior*, despite the fact that this is widely recognized as a normal phase in the progress toward true normality ("normally abnormal" might put the attitude more precisely). The phenomenon is common enough to demand explanation, various of which have been given: adolescent boys need sexual outlets, and girls are not always (or are not perceived to be) readily available, so they take "second best"; adolescents need to experiment in order to reject the inferior form of sexuality for the superior; the onset of adult sexuality can be experienced as frightening, and many boys are intimidated by the implicit demands on their potency. All these explanations are variously homophobic in asserting the superiority of heterosexuality over homosexuality. The most logical explanation—which is not homophobic—is consistently repressed: that the phenomenon represents the final struggle of our innate bisexuality to find recognition, before it capitulates to the

3. Since this was written the curious and confused *Revenge of the Nerds* has supplied a gay college student. The film carefully compounds his otherness by making him black as well as gay and, in one disarming but not exactly uncompromised moment, equips him with a "limp-wristed javelin" with which to win a sporting event.

demands of normality, the nuclear family and the patriarchal order. The films' often quite hysterical and obsessive emphasis on "getting laid" can be seen as an unconscious acknowledgment of the reality of the threat: though the adult world is treated with contempt, no *serious* challenge to normality can be countenanced.

By this point it will be clear that the syndrome I have described is shared by another, exactly contemporary and equally popular, cycle discussed in the previous chapter: the teenie-kill pic. The parallel development is intriguing, especially as the overall import of the two cycles is (superficially at least) quite opposite: in the high school movies promiscuity is generally indulged, in the teenie-kill pics it is ruthlessly punished. The opposition may be less total than it first appears (see, for example, the obsessive emphasis on castration in *Porky's*). The cycles seem premised on a common assumption: that, despite all the lip service to female equality, it is still the male who decides what movie young heterosexual couples will go to. Audiences for both cycles have been (in my experience) predominantly male, with all-male groups quite common. Any satisfaction the films offer the female spectator seems at once marginal and perverse: she is invited to contemplate, as something at once funny and desperately important, male initiation rites; or she is invited to contemplate reiterated punishment for sexual pleasure, with a special emphasis on female pleasure. One can see well enough why young males conditioned by the ideological assumptions of our culture in its current phase should want to drag their compliant girlfriends along to participate in what are essentially male rituals of desire and guilt, part of the films' function being the reinforcement of that compliance.

The relation of *Fast Times at Ridgemont High* to this syndrome is extremely complex. Clearly, there are certain bottom-line generic conditions that must be satisfied for such a film to get made at all (just as *Eyes of a Stranger* could not exist if it did not contain sequences in which women are terrorized and brutally murdered): here, heterosexism and the commodification of sex. In fact, the film's treatment of adolescent sexuality is consistently enlightened and intelligent, but it is compelled to subscribe to the myth that sex is all teenagers ever think about, with all its consequent ramifications. "Packaging"—a term that encompasses all the purely commercial interests involved from conception to publicity—is crucial here: it is interesting that the last line of dialogue ("Awesome—totally awesome"), which in the film has nothing whatever to do with sexual activity, was lifted out of context and used as an advertising slogan.

Where *Fast Times* succeeds, against all reasonable expectations, is in constructing a position for the female spectator that is neither masochistic nor merely compliant. One may begin at the end where Heckerling, in a single simple gesture, quietly rectifies the sexism of *American Graffiti*. Lucas ended his film with captions succinctly synopsizing the destinies of his four *male* characters; the implication was that the females were either of no consequence or so dependent on the men as to *have* no destinies of their own. Heckerling repeats the device, but allows the women

Amy Heckerling directing Judge Reinhold

Male Confrontation: Robert Romanus and Brian Backer

full equality. Nor is this a mere afterthought; rather, it concludes the logic of the entire film. Heckerling's six main characters include four males and two females. Yet, if there is a character who takes precedence over the others, it is clearly Stacey (Jennifer Jason Leigh). Where the cycle as a whole is obsessed with male sexual desire and anxieties (the girls in *Porky's* have no problems, and exist purely in relation to the boys, whose "needs" they either satisfy or frustrate), *Fast Times* allows its young women both desire and disturbance: see, for example, the delightful scene in which Linda (Phoebe Cates), with the aid of a carrot, instructs an anxious Stacey in the techniques of the "blow job." And, as the women cease to be objects of the male gaze, their autonomous desire is used to express, not merely an appreciation of male beauty ("Did you see his cute little butt?"), but a critique of male presumption. When Stacey responds to her date's "You look beautiful" with an enthusiastic "So do *you*," the film immediately registers his discomfiture, and the reaction prepares us for his behavior in the ensuing scene of intercourse: he shows no concern for Stacey's sexual pleasure and no awareness of her pain (she was a virgin). During it, Heckerling cuts in a shot from Stacey's point-of-view: a graffito, "Surf Nazis," scrawled on the wall above her.

Similar strategies characterize the treatment of Stacey's brief relationship with Mike (Robert Romanus), the school lady-killer. It is she who takes the initiative, and the film suggests that this is what undermines him: he is accustomed to being the hunter. His sexual insecurity surfaces in the changing-cabin by Stacey's family's pool when Stacey asks, "You want to take off your clothes, Mike?' and his automatic response ("You first") is answered by her "Both of us at the same time"; he then "comes too soon." Subsequently (*before* he learns that she is pregnant), he is too embarrassed to confront her, evading her friendly overtures: the film is clear that what is being "put down" is not sexual failure in itself, but the male vanity that makes so much of it.

The principle of rectifying the cycle's sexist imbalance is not restricted to the development of the narrative; it determines the details of shooting and editing. This is established right at the outset, during the brilliantly precise and economical credits sequence: the second shot—Mike eyeing a girl—is answered instantly by the third, in which two girls eye Brad (Judge Reinhold). A little later, a traveling shot along a row of asses in tight jeans bent over pinball machines looks like a typical sexist cliché until one realizes that the asses are not identifiable as female. Two sequences are built upon the visual objectification of women; both are defined as male fantasies and are clearly placed by the context within which they occur. In one, Spicoli (Sean Penn) fantasizes his victory as surfing champion, a beautiful bikini-clad girl on each arm (the film elsewhere gives him no contact with real females whatever, defining his existence in terms of permanently doped amiability). The other is treated even more pointedly. Brad (Stacey's brother), arriving home in the Captain Hook uniform of the fish restaurant where he works, finds Linda beside the pool and is embarrassed at being seen in a costume; he watches her from the washroom, fantasizes that she is offering herself to him, and begins to masturbate; entering the washroom without knocking, she catches him in the act.

The film takes up many of the cycle's recurrent schemata but always uses them creatively. The economy of the various plot expositions depends upon the instant recognizability of the characters, but in every case the stereotype is resourcefully extended, varied or subverted. Especially interesting is the treatment of the male virgin, Mark (Brian Backer): the whole progression of his relationship with Stacey is built, not upon his desire to "get laid"—to become a "real man"—but on his continuing sexual reticence and diffidence, maintained beyond the ending of the film, where we are informed that he and Stacey are having a passionate love affair but still haven't "gone all the way." On the other hand the film, while firmly implying that the best relationships are based upon mutual respect and concern, is strikingly non-judgmental in its treatment of promiscuity and experimentation. It is also firmly "pro-choice": abortion is certainly not presented as a pleasant experience, but neither is it treated as in the least shocking. The abortion episode is also used to establish what is otherwise conspicuously absent from the cycle, the positive potential of certain family ties, in Brad's gentle, understanding, and nonpaternalist acceptance of his sister.

The film's unobtrusive critique of male positions exists within the context of Heckerling's generosity to all her characters, male and female alike. The film manages the extremely difficult feat of constructing a tenable position for the female spectator without threatening the male: this defines, one might say, both its success and its limitations. It is clearly impossible, in the current phase of social evolution, for a film that rigorously and radically explores the oppression of women to be non-threatening. *Fast Times* must be seen as a reflection of current attitudes rather than a radical challenge to them; what it proves—a very rare phenomenon in contemporary Hollywood cinema—is that it is still possible to reflect (hence reinforce) the progressive tendencies in one's culture, not merely the reactionary ones. Flawlessly played by a uniformly wonderful cast (Heckerling is obviously marvelous with actors), it restores a certain credibility to the concept of "entertainment." Of the four films discussed *Fast Times* is predictably enough the only one that has had an appreciable box office success. It pays a price for this, of course. The other three women whose films I have considered are paying a different price: none is currently working on a theatrical feature film.

11.

From Buddies to Lovers

O ur civilization's great next step forward—if it is permitted one—will be the recognition and acceptance of constitutional bisexuality: an advance comparable to, and in certain respects more important than, the general acceptance of birth control. It had better be said at once that the reader who cannot entertain this proposition, at least as a working hypothesis, is going to have great difficulty with much of the remainder of this book.

Skeptics, however, might consider the logic of evolution, both in the biological/Darwinian sense and in the sense of social evolution. Homosexual choice begins with the primates. Rats, for example, indulge in homosexual activity only if deprived of access to the opposite sex; apes, on the other hand, can freely enjoy sexual activity with either sex. The implications of this are far-reaching. Before animals began to walk on their hind legs, the pleasure of sex was strictly contingent upon the need for procreation, for the continuance of the species. With creatures who walked upright (exposing and making openly accessible those parts of the body that the socialized human being is taught—and forced by law—to hide), the sexual instinct began to evolve into an end in itself, a means of pleasure and communication to which procreation became incidental. From the moment that principle is accepted, there is no logical reason why such a means of pleasure and communication should be restricted to members of the opposite sexes. Within social evolution, the acceptance of birth control implies precisely the same logic: a general recognition that the primary significance of sexuality lies in pleasure/communication, that procreation is a mere by-product that one can choose or not; therefore, that no logical reason remains why sexuality should be restricted to heterosexuality.

The logic that holds up heterosexuality as the norm is merely the perverted logic of patriarchy, that massive force that continues to impede the rightful progress of civilization and evolution. Patriarchy depends upon the separation of the sexes, hence upon the continued repression of bisexuality in order that masculinity and femininity may continue to be constructed. And the logical end result of the construction of masculinity (in terms of domination, aggression and competition) is nuclear war. The more immediate result—in the sense of being already a reality, not just a threat—is the extreme difficulty, for men whose femininity has been systematically repressed, of identifying with a female position, of bridging a gulf between the sexes that is itself ascribable to social construction rather than to nature. The phenomenon, discernible all around us and analyzable at virtually every point in contemporary mainstream cinema, is both the overall catastrophe of our civilization and the cause of innumerable personal tragedies.

This chapter will examine certain traces of repressed bisexuality that lurked (always ambiguously) in 70s Hollywood cinema, and will go on to consider the 80s films on explicitly gay themes that may seem, at first glance, to have brought those traces to the surface, but which may actually be the means of their obliteration. As a prelude, however, I want to digress briefly outside the proposed limits of this book, to consider, as exemplary of the tensions I have just defined, the work of Jean-Luc Godard. The justification for such a digression is simple: Godard, clearly one of the most important and most progressive filmmakers in the history of cinema, his work dedicated to a radicalism that, while varying in its specific allegiances, has remained uncompromisingly antagonistic to the norms of establishment society, achieving formal and political audacities and subversions that no one working in the Hollywood cinema has ever dared dream of, remains nonetheless trapped in the very same prison of masculinity that limits the work of a Scorsese or a Cimino, and that totally invalidates most of the remainder of contemporary Hollywood cinema. I want, in other words, to suggest that to be aesthetically and politically revolutionary carries no guarantee of exemption from the most obstinate, fundamental ideological constraints.

Godard's early work, from *Breathless* to *Pierrot le Fou*, covering his first ten features, provides an interesting extension of Laura Mulvey's famous thesis about the Hollywood action narrative, that the male protagonist (active, bearer of the look) carries forward the action while the woman (passive, the looked-at) repeatedly interrupts it, holds it up. The films centered on men (*Breathless*, *Pierrot*) are action films in which Godard clearly identifies with his male heroes (the women remain enigmas, potentially or actually treacherous, in the manner of *film noir*); those centered on women (*Vivre So Vie*, *Une Femme Mariée*) are sociological studies, in which the object of study is not so much prostitution, alienation, etc. as the woman herself.

Masculin, Féminin, which immediately followed *Pierrot*, is clearly a key work in Godard's development. The male protagonist is split into two. Paul is a gentler version of Godard's previous doomed drop-out heroes, seeking a "personal solution" in a relationship with a woman; with Robert, Godard introduces an explicit revolutionary political position into his work for the first time. It is Robert who tells Paul that a personal solution can't work. At the end of the film Paul dies (in a kind of accidental suicide) and Robert survives—to go on to become the Maoist militants of *La Chinoise* and *Vent d'Est*.

Although, characteristically, *Masculin, Féminin* raises and interconnects a wide range of concerns, its title directs our attention clearly to *sexual* politics; it also seems to promise an equal weighting between the sexes, a promise that is not fulfilled. It is perhaps Godard's most openly misogynistic film, the tentative commitment to revolutionary politics finding no counterpart on the level of heterosexual relations. The main plot line reproduces and reinforces the male myth of the sensitive, intelligent, vulnerable young man destroyed by the insensitive, egocentric, rather stupid woman (very disturbingly, this is carried over intact into *Crystal Gazing*, the film by those committed feminists Laura Mulvey and Peter Wollen that is obviously in part a remake of Godard's film). Women throughout are presented as essentially self-enclosed and unreachable. In the two extended scenes in which a male and a female character interview each other (Paul/Madeleine, Catherine/Robert), there seems to be some conscious attempt at equalizing the participants, but in both cases the balance is tipped, in obvious and subtle ways, in favor of the man. (Obvious: the male is permitted far more questions in both interviews, and far more screen time is devoted to his interrogation of the woman than to hers of him. Subtle: the women's responses are in both cases partly discredited, Madeleine's interview centering on the question of her "lying," Catherine's answers being evasive—like Eve, she eats an apple throughout.) The imbalance is confirmed by the long interview of "Miss Nineteen," the one-sidedness of which is emphasized by the man's remaining off-screen. The interview (apparently genuine, i.e., not acted) is one of the highlights of the film, a devastating exposure of the emotional and intellectual bankruptcy, the complacent unawareness, of this typical "consumer product" (as the film describes her) who is also a product of higher education. Yet important questions arise: Why this particular selection of women? Were there no intelligent, enlightened, politically aware young women available in Paris in 1966? (We are told, when she is introduced into the film, that Catherine is such, but nothing in her subsequent behavior or speeches supports the assertion.) Conversely, were there no unintelligent, self-enclosed, politically ignorant young men who might have been exposed to the merciless scrutiny of Godard's questions and camera?

The starting point for *Masculin, Féminin* was Guy de Maupassant's marvelous *La Femme de Paul* (which Ophuls had earlier wanted to use as the final story of *Le Plaisir*). What Godard does with his source is extremely illuminating. The lesbianism, both in the popular sexual sense and in the wider sense of women's bonding together to resist male definition, that is so prominent and so positively treated in Maupassant's story is all but suppressed in *Masculin, Féminin*: the traces of a lesbian involvement between Madeleine and Elizabeth are so fleeting and ambiguous that the spectator can be forgiven for missing them altogether. The film treats women's bonding wholly negatively: in so far as it exists, it is seen entirely from Paul's perspective, as a threat. It is significant that Elizabeth is virtually denied a voice: of the three female characters, she is the only one who is not interviewed. Even more significant—in view of the title's suggestion of a balance between gender-positions—is the fact that the women are only fleetingly allowed a scene alone together (Catherine and Elizabeth briefly discussing sexuality), whereas Paul and Robert have extended scenes of intimate, though never, of course, physical, contact. Indeed, it might be said that *only* the two men are permitted intimacy in the film in any real sense of the word, the male/female confrontations being posited on the assumption of insurmountable barriers and possible scenes of female/female contact without male surveillance suppressed altogether.

One can argue that in Godard's films as in dreams the seemingly inconsequential and irrelevant moments are in fact of particular significance. One such moment occurs in *Masculin, Féminin*. Paul, during the visit to the cinema, goes to the washroom and finds two men embracing in the cubicle; he then scrawls on the door "à bas la République des lâches" ("Down with the cowards of the Republic"). The moment (which appears to have nothing whatever to do with anything else in the film—one can certainly read it as an unconscious displacement of the lesbianism of *La Femme de Paul*) is ambiguous: the men may be cowards because they don't come out and fight for their rights or make love in public, or simply because they are homosexuals (the heterosexual myth that a "real man" is defined by the ability and desire to possess women, on which Maupassant's story can be read as an ironic commentary). The former meaning is merely uncharitable and irresponsible, taking no account of the social pressures that make the act of embracing in a public washroom in fact moderately heroic (this is, after all, 1966, when gay liberation and gay consciousness were scarcely in their infancy). I'm afraid, in the context of the whole film and of Godard's work generally, one is forced to prefer the latter reading, far more reactionary and reprehensible. A fairly strict correlation always exists between a heterosexual male's attitude to women and his attitude to gays ("the two others," in Andrew Britton's useful phrase), to the extent that the one can usually be deduced from the other. The repudiation of male as well as female homosexuality parallels the perception of women as, incorrigibly and unreachably, "other," and underpins the impossibility of transsexual identification.

It is depressing to find, fifteen years later, precisely the same formation recurring in *Sauve Qui Peut*: after all, radical feminism and gay liberation had both vociferously intervened. Feminism has obviously left its mark on Godard, strongly affecting the surface of his films from *Numéro Deux* onwards; unfortunately, it seems to have left their basic assumptions about the unbridgeability of sexual difference untouched. In *Sauve Qui Peut* there is an obvious, agonized effort to adopt a female viewpoint: the greater part of the film's running time is devoted to the parallel struggles for survival of Nathalie Baye and Isabelle Huppert (the inveterate sexism of our culture and its embedding in language are epitomized in the Anglo-American title, "Every *Man* for *Himself*"). The fleeting contact between them in a car, though brief and without sequel, is clearly the most positive moment in the film. Yet, for all the effort to the contrary, the true emotional center of the film remains the male protagonist, his death (though "accidental," as in *Masculin, Féminin*) implicitly blamed on recalcitrant women—the wife and daughter who, like Jean Seberg at the end of *Breathless*, turn and walk away. The film's interesting paradox is that this is the case despite the fact that, on the explicit level, the female protagonists are presented far more sympathetically than the man. His name happens to be Paul Godard. Godard has been eager to tell us in interviews that Paul was his father's name (a fact of seemingly total irrelevance): one is surely at liberty to relate this Paul to the Paul of *Masculin, Féminin* and, through him, to the Paul of *La Femme de Paul*.

The unconscious formation seems confirmed, again, by the film's repudiation of male homosexuality (here far more violent, obtrusive and unambiguous—the corollary, no doubt, of the film's superficial commitment to feminism and the female viewpoint). In the first few minutes Godard introduces an adult bellboy who is determined to seduce "Paul Godard," who is presented by Godard the filmmaker as a comic grotesque, and who is then vehemently rebuffed by Godard the character.

The above account is obviously very partial; it must not be understood as a dismissal of Godard, whose work remains among the most important produced during the past twenty-five years of cinema. What I have tried to fix here is the sense of a continuing *block*, for Godard apparently insurmountable, that has prevented his films from ever achieving the uncompromised progressiveness at which they clearly aim, and which can be argued to be responsible for the persistent sense of desperation and frustration that characterizes them. The obstinacy of that block in the work of a filmmaker who has consistently wished to be, and in many respects has been, in the forefront of cinematic and societal progress testifies to its formidable general presence in our culture, and to the sustained effort on the part of men and women alike that will be necessary to remove it. No unambiguously radical or progressive treatment of these issues within mainstream commercial cinema can be expected. The traces, however, remain worth investigating.

BUDDIES

Within their social context, the 70s "buddy" movies seem to me more interesting than is generally recognized. They have frequently been explained, or explained away, as a reaction to the women's movement. This is doubtless an important factor in their constitution, but it is not the only one nor necessarily the prime determinant. Certainly the treatment of women in the films is extremely demeaning, both in their relegation to marginality and in the nature of the roles they are allocated. However, an interesting corollary accompanies this: if women can be dispensed with so easily, a great deal else goes with them, including the central supports of and justification for the dominant ideology: marriage, family, home.

It seems to me that the basic motivating premise of the 70s buddy movie is not the presence of the male relationship but the absence of home. The cycle (it has, of course, many precursors, going back to *Huckleberry Finn* and beyond) was effectively launched in 1969 by the appearance of three films that, between them, account for all the factors on whose permutations the subsequent films were built— *Butch Cassidy and the Sundance Kid, Easy Rider, Midnight Cowboy.* The later films, of which *Thunderbolt and Lightfoot, Scarecrow,* and *California Split* are the most distinguished and idiosyncratic, are all variations on the principles established in 1969:

1.The Journey   Although the main body of *Midnight Cowboy* takes place in one city, the film opens with the male protagonist entering it and ends with him leaving it; similarly, the Las Vegas of *California Split* is a place the men come to and leave. In both cases the cities are stages in a journey. All the other films mentioned are structured upon journeys. The essential point is that either the journey has no goal or its ostensible goal proves illusory: "Florida" in *Midnight Cowboy* is obviously not intended to represent a possibility of resolution or fulfillment; Francis' journey in *Scarecrow* is to an illusion he has constructed, to which the reality bears no resemblance.

2. The Marginalization of Women   Of the six films, only *Butch Cassidy* has what appears to be a traditional female lead (Katherine Ross), and she is eliminated from the narrative some time before the film's climax. Otherwise, women are merely present for casual encounters *en route*, "chicks" for the boys to pick up and put down. In *Scarecrow*, the pathetic, oppressed and vindictive woman Francis has abandoned (with child) years previously, and now intends to return to, confirms rather than contradicts the sudden unavailability of the woman-as-wife to provide a happy end.

3.The Absence of Home   At the end of *California Split* George Segal (ditching his compulsive gambler buddy Elliott Gould) abruptly announces that he is going "home" but the film has made it clear that he no longer has any home to go to. In the films, home doesn't exist, the journey is always to nowhere. "Home," here, is of course to be understood not merely as a physical location but as both a state of mind and an ideological construct, above all as ideological *security.* Ultimately, home is America ("God bless America, my home, sweet home," as the characters whose ethnic home America has effectively destroyed sing at the end of *The Deer Hunter*). The essential spirit of the buddy movie was marvelously epitomized in the advertising campaign for *Easy Rider*, which told us that the film was about two men who went searching for America and "couldn't find it anywhere": the films are the direct product of the crisis in ideological confidence generated by Vietnam and subsequently intensified by Watergate.

4. The Male Love Story   For the moment, let us leave the word "love" in all its ambiguity (Howard Hawks, who resolutely denied the existence of any gay subtext in his films, described two of them as "a love story between two men"), and simply say that in all these films the emotional center, the emotional charge, is in the male/male relationship, which is patently what the films are *about*. Obvious, of course: yet the fact stands in direct opposition to the usual account of the Classical Hollywood text in terms of the happy ending in heterosexual union, promising the continuance of the nuclear family.

5. The Presence of an Explicitly Homosexual Character   In the three 1969 movies, this occurs only in *Midnight Cowboy* (but there, twice). Yet it rapidly became a standard component of the cycle: the clownish gay of *Mean Streets* (a film in some respects central, in others peripheral), the transvestite of *California Split*, the brutal and frustrated prison inmate of *Scarecrow*. The overt homosexual (invariably either clown or villain) has the function of a disclaimer—our boys are not like *that*. The presence of women in the films seems often to have the same function: they merely guarantee the heroes' heterosexuality.

6. Death   In *Butch Cassidy* and *Easy Rider* both men die; in *Midnight Cowboy* one does. The pattern remains fairly consistent throughout the cycle, with variations: in *Scarecrow*, Francis becomes catatonic and may never recover; in *California Split*, Elliott Gould is trapped in the world of casinos, from which his partner can extricate himself. The male relationship must never be consummated (indeed, must not be *able* to be consummated), and death is the most effective impediment.

If the films are to be regarded as surreptitious gay texts, then the strongest support for this comes, not from anything shown to be happening between the men, but, paradoxically, from the insistence of the disclaimers: by finding it necessary to deny the homosexual nature of the central relationship so strenuously, the films actually succeed in drawing attention to its possibility. Read like this, the films are guilty of the duplicitous teasing of which they have often been accused, continually suggesting a homosexual relationship while emphatically disowning it. But this leaves many questions unanswered: Why did so many films of this kind get made in the 70s? Why did so many filmmakers apparently want to make them? If the answer to that is "because they made money," then why were they so commercially successful? And why, in the 80s, have they virtually disappeared?

The formulation "surreptitious gay texts" is in fact too simple: it carries the suggestion that the central characters in the films are really homosexual, but the film can't admit this. Such a suggestion, in its turn, rests on that strict division of heterosexual and homosexual which is one of the regulations on which patriarchy depends: if it is forced to admit that there are recalcitrant people who don't or won't conform to its norms, and if it recognizes that (perhaps) it should extend to them the magnanimity of toleration, then at least it can continue to set them aside, to separate them out.

I have suggested that what is fundamental to these films, as to so much of 70s Hollywood cinema, is the disintegration of the concept of home. That concept could also be named (one thinks here of course of the horror film) "normality": the heterosexual romance, monogamy, the family, the perpetuation of the status quo, the Law of the Father. In discussing the horror film, I outlined the Freudian and post-Freudian account of the construction of that normality, its terrible cost, and its dependence upon the repression of an innate, free sexuality. What happens, then, when that normality collapses? What happens, specifically, within a cinema made by men and primarily *for* men? It produces male protagonists, identification figures for the male audience, the efficient socialization of whose sexuality can no longer be a given. The characters themselves are, of course, without exception social outcasts, voluntary dropouts; frequently criminals, they have placed themselves outside the pressures of patriarchy, which are all that stand in the way of the recognition and acceptance of constitutional bisexuality. They are also the protagonists of films made within an overwhelmingly patriarchal industry: hence they must finally be definitively separated, preferably by death. The films belong not only to social history but to social progress. Their popularity testifies, no doubt, to the contemporary "heterosexual" male audience's need to denigrate and marginalize women, but also, positively, to its unconscious but immensely powerful need to validate love relationships between men. However one may regret the strategies of disownment, the films would admittedly be unthinkable without them: the heterosexual male spectator's satisfaction would quickly be replaced by panic, and the films' commercial viability would instantly disintegrate.

If I focus now on *Thunderbolt and Lightfoot*,[1] it is not merely because it was

1. Since I completed this essay, a friend has directed my attention to an article on the film in *Jump Cut*, November/December 1974, by Peter Biskind ("Tightass and Cocksucker: Sexual Politics in *Thunderbolt and Lightfoot*"). Biskind's account of the film is far more hostile than my own: he seems unduly disturbed by what he sees as "its frank and undisguised contempt for heterosexuality," without at any point acknowledging the "frank and undisguised" contempt for homosexuality that pervades our entire culture. Nevertheless, there are considerable areas of overlap in our interpretations.

directed by Michael Cimino: indeed, the link with his subsequent work is somewhat tenuous, and one could certainly not deduce from it the ambitions and audacity that were to produce *The Deer Hunter* and *Heaven's Gate*. Of all the films in the cycle it comes closest to explicitness about the sexual nature of the male relationship (while still, of course, coding this rather than directly dramatizing it); it also, especially through its generic connotations, connects the male love story very directly with other aspects of the 70s action movie that reflect the collapse of confidence in home/America.

The film begins in a church and ends (almost) in a one-room schoolhouse: its action is framed between two of the major historical institutions for socialization, for the construction of normality, both marked by the presence of the American flag. Both, however, are presented explicitly as obsolete, empty shells rather than repositories of value. The church is the setting for a sermon by a phony clergyman, bank robber/con man, interrupted by a gunman's attempt to assassinate him. The schoolhouse has been removed from its original location and fossilized as historical monument; its value within the narrative resides in its use as a hiding place for the loot—behind the blackboard, a secret ironic lesson in American capitalism. Thunderbolt/Clint Eastwood, contemplating the schoolhouse near the end of the film, respectfully murmurs 'History!': the admittedly peripheral concern with the image and reality of America, with American past and American present, links the film both to the western and to Cimino's subsequent work. Church and schoolhouse (together with the middle-aged heterosexual bourgeois couples, both caricatured, associated with each) represent all that is left in the film of the concept of home. As for actual homes, none of the characters has one, or appears to regret its absence: Lightfoot, asked if he has "people," remarks 'I don't even know any more, that's weird.'

Despite its central relationship, the film from which *Thunderbolt and Lightfoot* derives most directly is none of the three source movies listed above, but *Bonnie and Clyde*. The basic narrative pattern is very close: the starting point of both films is the fortuitous encounter of two characters who, immediately attracted to each other, swiftly become a team; later, they are joined by a second, somewhat older couple with whom one of the initial couple has past links. The four become a gang, and plan and execute robberies. Ultimately, everything falls apart, and there is catastrophe and death. There are many incidental differences, but the major one is that *both* the heterosexual couples of Penn's film become male couples in Cimino's, where women play no part whatever in the central action, and from which the nostalgia for a lost home that haunts *Bonnie and Clyde* is conspicuously absent.

While women have no significant role in *Thunderbolt and Lightfoot*, the film's treatment of them is not totally ignominious or without interest. One charming little scene (perhaps unique in the 70s buddy movie, where, typically, the women appear grateful for any crumb of attention the heroes may throw their way) actually foregrounds the feminist revolt against objectification: Lightfoot/Jeff Bridges, driving his truck, attempts to pick up a woman motorcyclist who responds by smashing at the truck with a hammer. The film is quite clear that the joke is on Lightfoot, not the woman. Totally irrelevant to the narrative, the moment, with its active and sympathetically presented woman engaged in a masculine pursuit and responding with aggressive behavior, is not irrelevant to the film's pervasive if incoherent and unformulated sense of changing gender roles.

The relationship between Thunderbolt and Lightfoot is built throughout on ambiguities of sexuality and gender role. Their names carry obvious connotations of masculine and feminine, strength and grace, respectively, and these are systematically developed as the film proceeds. At times, the overt sexuality that is inevitably repressed in the *mise-en-scène* returns in the implications of the editing. The opening of the film crosscuts (before the two men have met) between Thunderbolt's sermon and Lightfoot's theft of a car from a second-hand dealer's lot. From Thunderbolt's text, " . . . and the leopard shall lie down with the kid," we cut immediately to the first shot of Lightfoot, whom Thunderbolt will refer to as "kid" throughout the movie; the text is repeated, without obvious narrative motivation, later in the film, as if to underline its implications.

Two other components of the structure of character relationships serve in different ways to validate the Thunderbolt-Lightfoot relationship as the film's emotional center. The obligatory sex scene involving women, whose usual function, as already noted, is merely to guarantee the men's heterosexuality, is used here to suggest Thunderbolt's lack of sexual interest in women and Lightfoot's casual attitude to them. (It is interesting that, if one reads the central relationship as basically sexual, it is Lightfoot, at once the more feminine and the more childlike of the two men, who is the more clearly presented as bisexual, or whose sexuality might be regarded as undefined and open; in this respect he can be considered a forerunner of the Christopher Walken character in *The Deer Hunter*.) The second male relationship, Red and Goody (George Kennedy, Geoffrey Lewis), is used throughout as a foil to the growing commitment of Thunderbolt and Lightfoot. The two couples, in fact, aside from being male, correspond closely to the good couple/bad couple opposition so common in Classical Hollywood cinema, where the narrative moves toward the elimination of the bad couple in order to construct the good. Here, the Red-Goody relationship is characterized by disorder, tension and contempt (culminating in Red's brutal dumping from a car of the wounded Goody— "You're gonna be dead soon anyway"), in contrast to the increasing mutual trust and dependence of Thunderbolt and Lightfoot. It is appropriate, then, that Kennedy's brutal masculinity should be used in one scene to highlight, favorably, Lightfoot's sexual ambiguity: Lightfoot, responding to the older man's question as to what he did with a naked woman, enrages him by kissing him on the mouth (though placing his own hand in between). Red's outrage expresses itself in an indignant "You kids don't believe in anything anymore," to which Lightfoot responds by blowing kisses at him.

The film moves toward the climactic robbery sequence throughout which Lightfoot is disguised as a woman. The narrative pretext for this is fairly flimsy, its logical necessity seeming to lie rather in the development of the relationship. Lightfoot's masquerade interestingly avoids the obvious twin temptations of female impersonation in the Hollywood cinema—on the one hand, the caricature of femininity, on the other, the playing up of masculine clumsiness and awkwardness in the interests of comedy: without being particularly graceful or ungainly, he makes an attractive and appealing young woman. Significantly, from the point where the disguise is adopted, the film keeps the two men apart for as long as possible, and the sexual overtones are restricted again to the implications of the editing. Lightfoot walking the street in drag is intercut with Thunderbolt removing his clothes in preparation for the robbery; Lightfoot's masquerade is then juxtaposed with the "erection" of Thunderbolt's enormous cannon. This culminates in the film's most outrageous moment: in a washroom Lightfoot, back to camera, bends over the watchman he has knocked out, his skirt raised to expose his ass clad only in the briefest of briefs, from which he extracts a revolver; the film immediately cuts to Thunderbolt, fixing his cannon in its fully erect position. In its recent overt treatments of male homosexuality, the Hollywood cinema has never dared give us anything comparable to that.

The ending, with the bad couple destroyed, initially celebrates the union of the heroes with the abrupt discovery of the relocated schoolhouse and the recovery of the hidden money, a celebration clinched by Thunderbolt's gift to his buddy of the possession he has always coveted, a white Cadillac. Lightfoot's declaration that they are "heroes" crystallizes much of the spirit of the 70s interlocking road-movie, buddy-movie, gangster-movie cycles: the heroes of American culture can now exist and operate only outside the confines and norms of the American establishment, the schoolhouse a historical relic of an obsolete socialization. The definition of the heroism is not merely in terms of criminality, but in terms of escaping the constraints of normality. The two men drive off together, not to but *away from* home: there is no sense of a specific destination, rather of an extended honeymoon after what amounts to a wedding celebration complete with extravagant gift. Of course, Lightfoot is already dying (a delayed reaction to his brutal beating by Red): given the cultural constraints, it is one of the most necessary deaths in the Hollywood cinema. It is important that he be the one to die, rather than the stoical, resolutely and unambiguously masculine Thunderbolt, whose sexuality is, on the level of overt signification, of gender stereotyping, never in question (after all, he is played by Clint Eastwood). It is the essentially gentle Lightfoot, with his indeterminate sexuality, his freedom from the constraints of normality's gender roles, and his air of presocialized child, who constitutes the real threat to the culture.

✳ ✳ ✳

Dog Day Afternoon provides the ideal transition from *Thunderbolt and Lightfoot* to the gay-themed movies of the 80s, combining as it does dropout bank robbers with explicitly gay characters. The film's movement is central to the American cinema since *The Chase*: a rapidly escalating progress from a precarious, already troubled order into breakdown and chaos—a progress expressed through the shift of tone from comedy to desperation and underlined by the movement from light to darkness in the film's strict time scheme. The shift is centered on the feature that gives *Dog Day Afternoon* its particularity, the protagonist's gayness: from the moment of the revelation that his second "wife" (the one he is most eager to contact and the raison d'être of the robbery) is male, the presentation changes. This is most obviously signaled through the changed attitude of the audience *within* the film, the crowd that collects to watch: having adopted Pacino as a sort of anti-authoritarian folk hero and identification figure during the first part of the film (especially as a means of expressing resentment of the police), they detach themselves from him after the appearance of his lover Leon: an audience participation "happening" becomes a spectacle, almost the "freak show" Pacino denounces. For the cinema audience there is a parallel (but not identical, and much less extreme) modulation. At screenings I have attended, members of the audience have audibly taken time to adjust, but it is to the film's credit that its gays never become a freak show for anyone outside it (the one ominous moment, Leon fainting in the arms of the police in apparent stereotypical effeminacy, is quickly explained: he has been brought straight from hospital). But it is from the time we know he is gay that we are also invited to see Sonny as neurotic (rather than just endearingly incompetent)—particularly through Leon's account of the impossibility of life with him.

The treatment of gayness in *Dog Day Afternoon* defines very precisely the ideological limits within which the contemporary American cinema operates. It is, I believe, the first American commercial movie in which the star/identification figure turns out to be gay, a revelation cunningly withheld—in the terms in which the narrative is constructed, irrespective of factual foreknowledge—until the audience has been drawn into a qualified but sympathetic complicity with him. It is also (and I am grateful for this to Lumet, Pacino, and Chris Sarandon) one of the only films with gay characters that I can watch without anger—anger from which Fassbinder, for example, is not exempt. *Fox*, whatever its quasi-Marxist intentions, seems to go out of its way to reinforce stereotyped images of gay men (petty and malicious unless just stupid like the hero) and gay relationships (destructive and exploitative) for the bourgeois audience: see most of our "liberal" journalists' enthusiastic reviews, celebrating the film's truth and honesty about "the homosexual condition."

Dog Day Afternoon reinforces the popular association of gayness with neuroticism and necessary unhappiness, but at least the film works against any assumptions in the audience of superiority or safe detachment. Indeed, one of the most inter-esting aspects of the film is its assimilation of gayness into the syndrome of exis-tential uncertainty, breakdown-of-traditional-values, dissolution-of-borderlines, so central to the contemporary American cinema. Another is its curious inverse rela-tion to the male duo/road subgenre: there, the male couple are together all the time, traveling freely across the continent in close comradeship, and the films are careful to signal their interest in women (albeit casual and, in most cases, degradingly "merely" sexual); in *Dog Day Afternoon* the couple are explicitly gay, their relation-ship is disastrous, each is trapped in a separate building, and they converse only by telephone. Keeping Sonny and Leon apart (like Thunderbolt and Lightfoot when the latter is in drag) spares the spectator the potential embarrassment of imagining anything they might do in bed together. It is also consistent with the film's general desexualization of Sonny: his other wife is a comic grotesque, fat and hysterical, and although she is the mother of his two children we are never invited to imagine any sexual attraction between them.

If gay stereotyping is intelligently avoided in the performances of Pacino and Sarandon, it forces its way, significantly, back in at a later point: the lateral track along the line of gay militants reveals all the usual stock figures that represent the popular concept of the overt homosexual. Inherent in the gay liberation movement is a significance going far beyond the rights of homosexuals: it offers the most direct and practical challenge imaginable to the central, stubborn feature of the dominant ideology, the traditional concept of marriage and family. It cannot, therefore, within the popular commercial cinema, be treated seriously, at least in its militant and organized aspects. The effects of this in *Dog Day Afternoon* go far beyond the brief unfortunate moment of the militant gay demonstration; the particular nature of the hero is also determined by the same ideological constraints. Our sympathy for him is clearly meant to *increase* because the militants opportunistically try to use him for their cause: he is essentially the little guy, minding his own business (apart from rob-bing a bank), tossed about by rival factions, who just wants to be himself—a rela-tively safe liberal concept which the establishment has never had much difficulty in assimilating. Despite armed robbery, gayness, and an occasional spontaneous protest outburst, Sonny is not an ideologically dangerous character. The film makes him comically incompetent as a robber, carefully dissociates his gayness from any organ-ized movement, and repeatedly stresses his political (or apolitical) confusion: he fought in Vietnam and isn't ashamed of it, and he used to be a Goldwater supporter.

LOVERS

At first sight, the 80s movies on gay themes (of which I shall discuss *Making Love* and *Victor, Victoria*, the two that most interestingly raise the problems of treating the subject of male homosexuality positively in mainstream cinema) might appear an unambiguous advance on the 70s buddy movie: the sexuality is openly acknowledged, male couples are shown embracing and/or in bed together, women are no longer marginalized or reduced to mere alibis. Certainly there are positive things to be said, and I shall say these first; ultimately, however, the constraints within which the films operate seem more illuminating than the superficial advances in frankness and liberalism. Apparently representing the only progressive trend in 80s Hollywood cinema, the films in fact belong very much to their period, constitute no real anomaly, paradox or problem.

Insofar as such things can be calculated, one can deduce that the direct social effect of *Making Love* has probably been (within its somewhat limited commercial success, and in relation to the somewhat limited audiences at which it seems to have been aimed) very good. It seeks discreetly to acclimatize its audience to homosexual lovemaking, presenting it no differently from the ways in which a bourgeois cinema dedicated to "good taste" and the family audience has typically presented heterosexual embraces; it suggests (within careful ideological limits, to which I shall return) that it is legitimate to choose to live as gay, with a lover of the same sex; it offers two attractive, moderately popular young stars, potential identification figures, as homosexual lovers. Unlike, for example, *Taxi zum Klo*, it is the kind of film to which your average gay bourgeois male might profitably take his parents. Further, such a film might help a number of hitherto closeted gays to "come out": its very existence as a popular entertainment, its very format of compressed soap opera, its public display for general audiences, all suggest the growing acceptance of gayness, its potential respectability. In addition, the screenwriter, Barry Sandler, himself felt able to come out during the making of the film: incredible as it seems, he appears to be still the only *openly* gay figure in the Hollywood industry (although George Cukor managed nobly to declare himself before he died). His screenplay, cunningly contrived in relation to the engagement and leading on of middle America, with a number of extremely well-observed and well-written scenes, is clearly the film's major strength, together with the performances of Michael Ontkean and Harry Hamlyn, which avoid all the obvious pitfalls of stereotyping and condescension. Conversely, the film's most apparent limitation is blazoned in the opening credits: "An Arthur Hiller Film." Like every other Arthur Hiller film its directorial ambitions nowhere transcend the constrictions of a professionally efficient made-for-TV movie, ensuring that any continuing interest it has will be purely sociological and historical.

The comic vitality of *Victor, Victoria*, on the other hand, should ensure it a life after its sociological and historical interest has lost its topicality. It is also, in many respects, a very pleasurable film for gay people to share with large general audiences. Having promised Julie Andrews and comedy in the opening credits, the film is confident enough to confront its audience with male homosexuality in its first shot: the camera moves back from a window overlooking a Paris street, moves left over a bed-side table on which is a photograph of Marlene Dietrich (Sternberg period) in male clothes, to show Toddy (Robert Preston) asleep in bed, then continues its progress to reveal that his bed companion is another man. It is important that it is set, as the first view of the stylized street set establishes, in an artificial never-never land: Paris and the 30s, but not a real place or a real time. Its play with artifice is suggested by giving its leading French character (Toddy) an American name and its leading American character (James Garner) a French one (Marchand), and by its refusal to make language and accent problematical, giving French accents only to peripheral comic characters, such as Graham Stark's skeptical waiter. We are led at once into a world whose relation to our own is far more ambiguous and fanciful than that offered by the simple contemporary representationalism of *Making Love*. From there, the film quickly gains the complicity of its audience with the introduction of Andrews and a series of brilliantly executed comic scenes built upon our identifi-cation with her and her predicament (impoverished singer in a foreign city) and culminating in the establishment of her friendship with Toddy.

The complicity is strong enough to take in its stride some directly (and, for Hol-lywood, outspokenly) didactic moments such as Andrews' assertion to Garner that the only people who consider homosexuality sinful are "respectable clergymen and terrified heterosexuals," and some magnificent moments of gay-positive comedy. Gay people are accustomed to experiences of discomfort in the cinema: all those moments when a grotesque or monstrous stereotypical gay character appears and certain—shall we say?—more uninhibited members of the audience shout out "Faggot!" at the screen (personal memories of this include Siegel's *Escape from Alca-traz* and Wiederhorn's *Meatballs II*). The experience is not unlike what Jewish peo-ple might have felt had they wandered inadvertently into screenings of the anti-Semitic films made in Germany under the Nazi regime. It is to the credit of films like *Making Love* and *Victor, Victoria* that they have made it—temporarily at least—less easy for Hollywood filmmakers to capitalize on such prejudice except on the lowest levels of mindless exploitation. Consider, as an example of the successful reconditioning of the mainstream audience, the following moment from *Victor, Victoria* (greeted, on both occasions on which I saw the film in a full house, by spontaneous applause). Victoria (Andrews), her clothes shrunk by rain, dresses in a suit left behind by Toddy's obnoxious and venal lover. The lover returns unexpect-edly, and Victoria hides in the closet. As he opens the closet to retrieve his clothes, the lover contemptuously addresses Toddy as "You pathetic old queer." In immedi-ate response, Victoria bursts from the closet, punches him in the nose, and subse-quently boots him out of the apartment. Previous movies would have got their laugh, and their applause, on the lover's remark; this film gets it on Victoria's reac-tion. There is also the later moment, also commonly applauded, when Toddy, informed by Norma (Lesley Ann Warren) that she thinks a good woman could reform him, responds that *he* thinks a good woman could reform *her*. From that, it is but a step (though still an audacious one) to the moment where King Marchand's hefty bodyguard Mr. Bernstein (Alex Karras) comes out, kissing his boss on the cheek. At its best, *Victor, Victoria* is a salutarily educational movie, undermining and transforming its audience's entrenched and continually reinforced attitudes through sympathy and laughter.

I do not wish to be ungenerous to these movies (some will say that I have already conceded too much, but I think their positive aspects have been consistently under-rated in the gay and radical press). It has become increasingly clear, however, since their release, that they are oppositional films only on the most superficial levels. On deeper levels, they retain their niche within the dominant ideology of 80s America. That familiar monster "the dominant ideology" is—even in an overwhelmingly reactionary period like our own—neither monolithic nor static. It might be likened to a protean octopus: like Proteus, it can perpetually transform its appearance while remaining the same underneath; like an octopus, it can reach out in all directions and engorge whatever it thinks it can digest (also like an octopus, it sometimes makes mistakes). Films like *Making Love* and *Victor, Victoria* testify to the continu-ance of the tradition of American liberalism; they also testify to its frailty and to its vulnerability to the pressures of compromise. Liberalism has always been a phe-nomenon the octopus digests quite easily.

The background to the 70s buddy movies was, we have seen, the collapse of the concept of home, with all its complex associations; the background to the 80s gay movies is, precisely, its restoration and reaffirmation, an operation that makes clear the extent to which the restoration of home is synonymous with the restoration of the symbolic Father. (The Father may either forbid or permit; the permitting is just as authoritarian as the forbidding.) In fact, two ideological strategies, closely inter-connected, operate within the films:

1. Separation   I argued that the ambiguity or evasiveness of the buddy movies can be read positively in the context of the collapse of confidence in normality and in relation to Freudian theories of constitutional bisexuality: the men are explicitly defined as heterosexual yet involved in what can only be called a "male love story." It is striking that, just before the sudden outcrop of explicitly gay movies, the buddy cycle virtually ends. *My Bodyguard*, with its extraordinary motorbike-riding mon-tage sequence in which the two male teenagers are seen trying out all available posi-tions, is perhaps its last fling; *An American Werewolf in London* might be seen as a corrupt mutant form, the male relationship made repulsive and impossible by the fact that one of the partners is progressively decomposing throughout the film. It is precisely sexual ambiguity that *Making Love* and *Victor, Victoria* avoid: sexual ori-entation is separated out; there are heterosexuals and homosexuals, but they are two distinct species.

Julie Andrews as a woman impersonating a man impersonating a woman

Images of masculinity: Alex Karras and James Garner

From Buddies. . . (Chris Makepeace and Adam Baldwin in *My Bodyguard*) . . . to Lovers (Harry Hamlin and Michael Ontkean in *Making Love*)

Certain explicit aspects of the two films appear to counter this assertion. Zack (Michael Ontkean) is, after all, apparently happily married until he "discovers" he is gay; Victoria (as Victor) challenges Marchand as to whether he's never had any doubts about his sexuality. But such moments are negated by the overall movement of the films. From the time when Zack defines himself as gay there is never the slightest indication that he might relate sexually to women as well as men; the implication (strengthened by a few more or less subtle hints) is that his relationship with his wife was based on friendship and mutual respect, and that, although he was able to function sexually with her, that side of the marriage was always a bit of a strain. The problem here is, of course, that this depiction is not only plausible but probable: our culture is committed to separating out, true bisexuality seemingly being very rare: the infant is "ideally" constructed as exclusively heterosexual and becomes exclusively homosexual if the programming somehow "goes wrong." The film can plead the usual alibi of realism. Yet nothing in its generally glib and superficial analysis raises the essential questions. By merely reproducing the notion that everyone is, in some inexplicable way, either exclusively one thing or the other, it reinforces and perpetuates it.

Victor, Victoria is somewhat more complex: it does contain one scene that raises the issue of innate bisexuality—significantly, a scene many have found redundant, unnecessary, or obscure. Marchand and Victoria (disguised as a man but known by Marchand to be a woman) go dancing in a gay male club. After a while, Marchand becomes so disturbed by the presence of the male couples dancing in close proximity to him that he feels compelled to leave. Instead of going back to the hotel with Victoria, however, he goes alone to a laborers' bar, where he deliberately provokes the clientele into a brawl; after violently punching each other, the men end up (as buddies) singing in each other's arms. One must, I think, read the scene as follows: Marchand's disturbance at the gay couples is more than mere homophobia; he feels his own manhood threatened, and goes off ostensibly to reaffirm it; however, what he really wants is the close physical companionship of other males, though, because of his inhibitions, he can permit himself this only under cover of an overt display of masculinity (violence, aggression).

That scene apart, however (and in its inexplicitness it scarcely goes further than the buddy movies or, for that matter, Hawks' *A Girl in Every Port*), the film is every bit as systematic as *Making Love* in sorting out its gays from its straights. What should have been its most audacious moment—Marchand telling Victor/Victoria that he wants to kiss her even if she *is* a man—is in effect its most pusillanimous: we know that he knows that she isn't. And Victoria's own heterosexuality, despite her own didactic utterances, is never called into question.

2. The Restoration of the Father This sorting out serves, in fact, a further purpose: the consigning of gays to their place within a liberal hierarchy in which the symbolic Father (the heterosexual male) remains the dominant figure. What happens in both films is in effect—an effect quite contrary to the filmmakers' very evident good intentions—the putting down of gayness. As Richard Dyer has pointed out in conversation, the implication of the ending of *Making Love* (it derives, significantly, from *Les Parapluies de Cherbourg*) is that, for all their protestations to the contrary, the two leading characters are both unhappy: if only Zack had not been gay, everything would have been perfect. The film does nothing very effective to counter this: Zack's permanent gay relationship is presented in the most perfunctory manner possible, the little we see of it suggesting that it is an imitation of heterosexual marriage, only lacking the child (significantly, a son) Zack always wanted and that his ex-wife now has with her new husband. As for Bart (Harry Hamlyn), although the opening of the film very emphatically accords him equal prominence with Claire (Kate Jackson), from the point where he rejects the possibility of a monogamous union with Zack the narrative can no longer encompass him: he disappears into a *film noir*-ish blur of sidewalks and neon lights. Earlier, the film tries very earnestly to permit him a voice—to permit, that is, a defense of independence and promiscuity; the attempt signally fails, leaving us with the heterosexual couple or its gay imitation as the only valid life-style. This reading is thoroughly confirmed by the presentation of the other promiscuous gay man Claire visits in her search for Zack: he reveals himself as insensitive, materialistic, devoid of aspirations beyond an endless procession of "tricks." The restoration of normality, the elimination from the narrative of any ideological threat to it, is underlined by the way in which both Zack and Claire are shown to have teamed up with father figures. Predictably, the film's putting in place of gay liberation is accompanied by a parallel operation in relation to feminism: Claire, who was earlier allowed to assert that she *thought* she could be independent, ends up apparently content with her role as wife and mother, with no further mention made of her work.

The same parallel operations are performed in *Victor, Victoria*: its last scene simultaneously confirms the position of gays as comic and the position of women as inevitably subordinate. Throughout the film, Victoria's essentially compliant female sexuality (for all her masquerade) has been contrasted favorably with the aggressive female sexuality of Norma, presented as grotesque and castrating. In the final scene, in direct contradiction to her earlier assertions, Victoria abandons the freedom of her male disguise in favor of her relationship with Marchand, while Toddy performs in her place in drag. The film utilizes a so-called time-honored tradition going back through Mozart and Shakespeare, but which was never free of class connotations: the comic couple used as a foil to the serious couple. Typically, in the past, the serious couple was aristocratic, the comic couple servants or commoners; now, the serious couple is straight, the comic gay. The Victoria/Marchand relationship is presented in terms of a commitment deserving sacrifices; the Toddy/Bernstein relationship is allowed no real importance whatever, and is further undermined by Toddy's casual and brutal reference to Bernstein's "making a permanent dent in the bed." (*Silkwood* performs a precisely analogous serious couple/comic couple strategy for dealing with lesbians.)

One is forced finally to reflect that, while they dramatize and promote certain liberal attitudes toward homosexuality that are without precedent in the Hollywood cinema, the ultimate and insidious ideological function of these films is to close off the implications of a threatening, antipatriarchal bisexuality that were opened surreptitiously in the 70s. Then, of course, one or both of the male protagonists had to die: patriarchy could not safely contain their relationship. Today, the explicitly gay couple can be permitted to survive and even be designated happy (though the happiness is never dramatized)—provided they accept their place.

12.

Two Films by Martin Scorsese

THE HOMOSEXUAL SUBTEXT: *Raging Bull*

Without taking bisexuality into account, I think it would be scarcely possible to arrive at an understanding of the sexual manifestations that are actually to be observed in men and women.   —Freud, *Three Essays on the Theory of Sexuality*

Although this discussion will eventually center upon Scorsese's *Raging Bull*, its concerns are far wider than a reading of a single film. I want to develop certain ideas or trains of thought, which remain as yet somewhat tentative and fragmentary, arising out of recent critical explorations into the operations of classical narrative. I will focus especially on the notion that classical narrative is centrally concerned with the organization of sexual difference within the patriarchal order, a project whose ultimate objective must be the subordination of female desire to male desire and the construction/reinforcement of a patriarchally determined normality embodied by the heterosexual couple. Clearly, *Raging Bull* should strictly be described as postclassical, but there is obviously no clean break, and I shall be as concerned to establish continuity as divergence. Scorsese's film—which I see as possessing both the distinction and the representativeness whose fusion has always been a necessary, defining characteristic of great art—relates to classical Hollywood narrative very interestingly and continues to reveal many of its structural operations: those principles of symmetry, repetition, variation, and closure ("the end answers the beginning") that, especially, Raymond Bellour has investigated systematically. One of my aims is to rescue both classical and postclassical narrative from that school of criticism (in relation to which I find Bellour's position curiously ambiguous and undefined) that would jettison it altogether in favor of avant-garde experimentation, on the grounds that narrative *can only* lead to the reconstitution of the patriarchal order, the reinforcement of patriarchal ideology.

Using Hitchcock as a reference point, but also pointing beyond him to the work of post-classical filmmakers like Scorsese, I want to start by raising three questions (or question clusters) about classical narrative and the restoration of order that I don't think have yet been definitively answered or closed off.

1. Order   If classical narrative moves toward the restoration of an order, must this be the patriarchal status quo? Is this tendency not due to constraints imposed by our culture rather than to constraints inherent within narrative itself? Does the possibility not exist of narrative moving toward the establishment of a *different* order, or, quite simply, toward irreparable and irreversible breakdown (which would leave the reader/viewer the options of despair or the task of imagining alternatives)?

2. Tone   If a given narrative does move toward the restoration of the patriarchal order, what is the work's attitude to that restoration? The order itself may, after all, have been called into question and undermined, its monstrous oppressiveness exposed. The attitude to its restoration, then, need by no means be one of simple optimism or endorsement: it could be tragic or ironic. Tone is a phenomenon with which semioticians appear to have great, if unacknowledged, problems, which they ignore rather than resolve: hence Bellour can pursue at length the "Oedipal trajectory" of *North by Northwest* without ever considering that its major father figure, the Professor (Leo G. Carroll), is presented consistently as a cynical opportunist. Hitchcock's resolutions, in fact, are frequently characterized by an idiosyncratic fusion of the ironic and the tragic. The narratives of *Shadow of a Doubt*, *Rear Window*, and *Strangers on a Train* all move toward the construction of the heterosexual couple and the restoration of patriarchal normality, but the audience is left with a feeling of tension, frustration and emptiness rather than satisfaction (let alone plenitude): the films have systematically dismantled the order that is perfunctorily (some might say cynically) restored.

3. Identification   I remain dissatisfied with the current theoretical accounts of the construction of the viewer's position by classical cinema, especially with regard to the dichotomy of male/female spectatorship. More work needs to be done on the phenomenon of transsexual identification and the complex implications of this. I don't believe that Hitchcock's films (which frequently encourage identification with the female position for viewers of either sex) construct a position for women that merely teaches them to acquiesce in punishment for transgression and to submit to the male order; nor do they construct the complementary position for men. Take, as the extreme case, *Vertigo*: from the moment when Hitchcock allows us access to the consciousness of Judy/Kim Novak, the male identification position is undermined beyond all possibility of recuperation; no spectator of either sex, surely, acquiesces in Judy's death or perceives the male protagonist's treatment of her as other than monstrous and pathological. Hitchcock's *narratives* (if one reduces the term to story line) may move toward the restoration of the patriarchal order; their *thematic* might be defined as the appalling cost, for men and women alike, of that restoration, and the exposure of heterosexual male anxieties.

This begins, I hope, to suggest ways in which the current impasse in criticism of classical narrative—the jaded sense that all narratives are really the same and that the critic's task is to demonstrate this over and over again—might be broken. I want now, however, to take a giant step further, with the help of Freud, in an attempt to open up new paths of exploration. I take as a starting point what may yet prove to be the most important of all Freud's discoveries (though it wasn't only his), the implications of which he himself was obviously reluctant to pursue—a reluctance that our culture has in general continued to share: the discovery of constitutional bisexuality. Freud found, to his own evident surprise and discomfiture, that in every case he analyzed, without exception, the analysis revealed at some level the traces of repressed homosexuality; this revelation accorded with his investigations into the sexuality of children, the theory of the infant's "polymorphous perversity," and the existence in children of all those erotic impulses that our adult world of patriarchal normality labels "perversions." It need not surprise us that Freud, himself an eminent turn-of-the-century Viennese patriarch with his own stake in that normality, was quite incapable of following through on the revolutionary implications of this discovery: he could only fall back lamely on the ideological assumption, never questioned or subjected to scrutiny, that the process of repression, the progress toward and into normality, was both desirable and inevitable, despite his very clear awareness that that very normality was characterized by misery, frustration and neurosis. For it is upon the repression of bisexuality that the organization of sexual difference, as enacted within our culture and as represented upon our cinema screens, is constructed. There is no reason to assume, as Freud appears to have assumed, that repression is somehow necessary for the development and continuance of human civilization in any form; it is necessary only for the continuance of *patriarchal* civilization, with its dependence upon a specific, rigid and repressive organization of gender roles and sexual orientation. It seems probable that the contemporary crisis in heterosexual relations can be satisfactorily resolved only by reversing the process of repression, liberating what is repressed, and restoring to humanity that portion of its rightful legacy that our culture has consistently denied it. This gives a new definition to the project known as gay liberation, which has generally been taken to mean something like "society should tolerate homosexuals." This in itself constitutes an interesting ideological strategy, redolent of the nervous compromises of liberalism: homosexuals are identified as a separate, fundamentally different group; thus homosexuality is simultaneously tolerated and disowned by being defined as "other." The gay liberation that I have in mind involves, obviously, the liberation of *heterosexuals*; *Rag-*

ing Bull—to leap ahead for a moment—can be read as an eloquent sermon on the urgency of such a project.

What is repressed is never, of course, annihilated: it will always strive to return, in disguised forms, in dreams, or as neurotic symptoms. If Freud was correct—and I see no reason to suppose otherwise—we should expect to find the traces of repressed homosexuality in every film, just as we should expect to find them in every person, usually lurking beneath the surface, occasionally rupturing it, inform-ing in various ways the human relationships depicted. It is my purpose to examine the manifestations of those traces in *Raging Bull*, a film in which they exist threat-eningly close to the surface, to the film's conscious level of articulation, accounting for its relentless and near-hysterical intensity. The title of my chapter comes from Martin Scorsese himself: he told me in a conversation that, though he was not aware of it while making the film, he now saw that *Raging Bull* has a "homosexual subtext." However, my title refers, at least by implication, far beyond the homo-sexual subtext of one film to the homosexual subtext of our culture.

Before I turn to Scorsese's film, however, let me throw in one last aside on Hitch-cock to complement, in the light of Freud, what I have said above. Everyone should be aware of the pronounced strain of homophobia that runs through Hitchcock's work, although it is homophobia of a very peculiar kind, as much fascination as repulsion. A significant number of his villains are coded, more or less explicitly, as homosexual (together, curiously, with one of his most morally admirable charac-ters, Louis Jourdan in *The Paradine* Case): the transvestite killer in *Murder*, Judith Anderson in *Rebecca*, John Dall in *Rope*, Robert Walker in *Strangers on a Train*. Fur-ther, these figures relate closely to others whose homosexual connotations (if they exist) are unclear but who are all associated with perverse sexuality: Joseph Cotten in *Shadow of a Doubt*, Anthony Perkins in *Psycho*, Barry Foster in *Frenzy*. The atti-tude to these characters is always ambivalent: if evil—all are murderous, and all but one are actual killers—they are also arguably the most attractive, certainly the most *fascinating* figures in their respective films, and the films' true sources of energy. No one, to my knowledge, appears to have connected this striking phenomenon with Hitchcock's treatment of heterosexual relations. Homophobia is, in fact, a very interesting illness. It is characterized by the sense that it doesn't need an explana-tion, that it is somehow natural to hate homosexuals, and by its total irrationality, the fact that no possible explanation for it exists outside the psychoanalytical one. It is clearly enough a particular form of heterosexual anxiety: the homophobe hates the precariously repressed homosexual side of himself. Future work on Hitchcock might profitably pursue the connection between the sexual anxiety expressed in the homophobia and the sexual anxiety expressed in the treatment of heterosexual rela-tions—the absence, in Hitchcock's films, of *any* presentation of a mutually fulfill-ing sexual relationship, the emphasis throughout his work being on the obsession with domination and power. One can certainly see the films (and herein lies their potential for revolutionary use) as foregrounding and exposing the mechanics of the heterosexual male power drive, the obsession with controlling, containing, defining or punishing female sexuality.

* * *

At first sight, *Raging Bull* seems a particularly difficult *kind* of film to which to gain critical access. The performance style favored by Scorsese and De Niro—derived from the Actors' Studio and the Method school, with its emphasis on spontaneity, improvisation and behaviorism—tends to deflect attention from structure and the kinds of meaning generated by structural interaction and instead to focus it upon acting and character study. Thus one of the common misconceptions of *New York, New York* is that it is "simply" about two individuals; and Andrew Sarris can complain of Scorsese's lack of a sense of structure (meaning, presumably, that the films do not correspond to the well-made scenario of classical Hollywood) and see *Raging Bull* as the stringing together of a number of extraordinary moments. The question has also been raised as to why Scorsese wanted to make a film about so unattractive, unpleasant and limited a character as the Jake La Motta created by himself and De Niro. The meaning the film finally seems to offer its audience—La Motta's progress toward partial understanding, acceptance or "grace"—must strike one as quite inadequate to validate the project, and actually misleading: the film remains extremely vague about the nature of the grace or how it has been achieved. Any suggestion of that kind is in fact thoroughly outweighed by the sense the film conveys of pointless and *unredeemed* pain, both the pain La Motta experiences and the pain he inflicts. But, if one rejects the film's invitation (at best half-hearted, and deriving, one may assume, more from Schrader than Scorsese) to read it in terms of a movement toward salvation, one must accept the invitation to read it centrally as a character study (though "case history" might be the more felicitous term). The film's fragmented structure can be read as determined by La Motta's own incoherence, by Scorsese's fascination with that incoherence and with the violence that is its product. That audiences are also fascinated, not merely appalled, by La Motta, testifies to the representative quality that the film's apparent concentration on a singular individual seems to deny. If we can make sense of La Motta we shall make sense of the film's structure and, simultaneously, be in a position to explain the fascination that La Motta and the film hold for our culture at its present stage of evolution.

Seeking a way into the film, we may begin with the montage sequence that intercuts La Motta's home movies with a series of his fights. The sequence is privileged in two ways: first, it is a very unusual *kind* of sequence, virtually unclassifiable within the categories of Metz's "Grande Syntagmatique" (it combines certain defin-

Raging Bull:
Jake's Marriages

Jake La Motta (Robert
De Niro) above with his first
wife (Lori Anne Flax) . . .

. . . and his second wife
(Cathy Moriarty).

ing characteristics of the bracket syntagma, the alternating syntagma and the episodic sequence); second, it is marked by the only intrusion into the film (opening credits apart) of color. The intercutting suggests an intimate relationship between two seemingly disparate aspects of La Motta's life—that the fights are somehow necessary to the construction of "domestic happiness" that is the home movies' raison d'etre. By this point (about a third of the way through) the film has definitively established black and white as its reality; conversely, then, color signifies illusion. This illusion of domestic happiness is presented clearly as Jake's construction: he "directs" the movies, he brings Vickie gifts, he drops her in the swimming pool, etc. At the same time, the fights are given an illusory quality of another order through the use of technical devices such as stills and slow motion: reality as dream.

Jake's exclusion from a lived reality is dramatized particularly in his relationship with women, characterized by an inability to respond to them as persons. It is one of the film's finest achievements, given the extent to which it is centered on Jake's consciousness, to convey to the audience (through the performance of Cathy Moriarty, but also through the very small role of Jake's first wife) a female response that is shown simultaneously to be beyond Jake's comprehension. For Jake, Vickie is from first to last an object, without independent existence. The film associates her repeatedly with swimming pools (the tenement pool where Jake first sees her, the pool of the home movies, the pool of their Miami home) and with the Lana Turner image (the most plastic and constructed of all the Hollywood star images): she is first shown posed by the pool in 1941, the release year of *Honky Tonk, Johnny Eager, Ziegfeld Girl* and *Dr. Jekyll and Mr. Hyde*—the year of Turner's rise to the position of major star and glamour symbol. The image is completed in the 1946 home movies (release year of *The Postman Always Rings Twice*) by her adoption of the famous white turban and sunsuit. Vickie is shown as at once complicit in her own objectification and yet having an existence outside it. In the course of the film Jake undergoes striking physical transformations (also made much of in the publicity surrounding De Niro) while Vicky remains unchanged, as Jake's object/construction/possession. Specifically, Jake can't relate to *mature* women or to women who demand recognition as autonomous beings (witness the casting off of the first wife). The scene in his Miami nightclub contrasts his flirtations with the teenage girls (who "prove" they're not under age by kissing him) with his animus against mature women (when he kisses the state attorney's wife he simultaneously upsets a drink all over her).

The film counterpoints two forms of violence: violence against women and violence against men, the latter subdivided between the socially licensed violence in the ring and the socially disapproved, spontaneous violence in public and private places outside the ring. While the motivations for these different manifestations of violence may seem quite distinct—Jake's pursuit of a boxing career, his jealousy concerning Vickie—I think a true understanding of the film depends on our ability to grasp the relationship between them. The film suggests that there is quite clearly a connection: on two occasions, Jake's fears of being overweight (i.e., of not being allowed to fight a man in the ring) are closely linked to another explosion of paranoid jealousy about (potential or actual violence toward) Vickie. Through a repeated motif the film also connects phallus and fist: Jake douses his cock with cold water to prevent himself reaching orgasm, and in a subsequent moment marked by a close-up plunges his fist into an ice bucket to cool it after a fight. Both forms of violence can in fact be interpreted as Jake's defenses against the return of his repressed homosexuality, and I shall presently invoke Freud himself to demonstrate this. First, however, it is important to notice that the violence, though centered on Jake, is by no means exclusive to him but is generalized as a characteristic of the society, the product of its construction of sexual difference. It will be clear, also, that by "the society" I mean something much wider than the specific Italian-American subculture within which the film is set.

As a conclusion to his analysis of the Schreber case, Freud offers a general statement about paranoia and the principal forms of paranoid delusion that seems as relevant to the Jake La Motta of *Raging Bull* as to Senatspräsident Schreber:

> We are in point of fact driven by experience to attribute to homosexual wishful phantasies an intimate (perhaps an invariable) relation to this particular form of disease. Distrusting my own experience on the subject, I have during the last few years joined with my friends C. G. Jung of Zurich and Sandor Ferenczi of Budapest in investigating upon this single point a number of cases of paranoid disorder which have come under observation. The patients whose histories provided the material for this enquiry included both men and women, and varied in race, occupation, and social standing. Yet we were astonished to find that in all of these cases a defence against a homosexual wish was clearly recognizable at the very centre of the conflict which underlay the disease, and that it was in an attempt to master an unconsciously reinforced current of homosexuality that they had all of them come to grief.   (p. 196)

(Four pages later Freud throws out in the manner of a casual aside the remark that "a similar disposition would have to be assigned to patients suffering from . . . schizophrenia," demonstrating that he had come close to a position where he was ready to posit repressed homosexuality as a major source of most serious mental illness.)

We can now consider the La Motta of *Raging Bull* in relation to the "forms of paranoia." "The familiar principal forms of paranoia can all be represented as contradictions of the single proposition: '*I* love *him*' " (p. 200). Freud lists four of these forms, of which no less than three apply strikingly to *Raging Bull*; the fourth (the second of Freud's categories) applies more tenuously but is not irrelevant.

1. "I do not *love* him—I *hate* him." According to. Freud, this usually requires the pseudo-justification of delusions of persecution, as the hatred must be felt to be morally and rationally motivated ("I hate him because he persecutes me"). But it is precisely Jake's profession that renders such a cover superfluous: as a boxer, he is licensed to express his animus against male bodies directly, and in public, before an approving audience. Two points need to be made here, that lead in somewhat opposed directions. First, Jake is presented as an exceptional case, a boxer noted not for his skill, grace, and agility, but for obsessive ferocity and excess. This of course confirms the Freudian diagnosis of La Motta as an individual "case," but it may deflect us from the more general implications of boxing as a social institution. Therefore, as a second point, we should not lose sight of wider issues, though it is beyond the scope of the present article to pursue them far: I refer to the cultural significance of boxing itself as licensed and ritualized violence in which one man attempts to smash the near-naked body of another for the satisfaction (surely fundamentally erotic) of a predominantly male mass audience. It would be interesting to discover whether there is any significant correlation between an enthusiasm for boxing and homophobia.

2. The least relevant of Freud's categories is what one might call the Don Juan syndrome where homosexuality is denied by means of obsessive pursuit of women ("I don't love men—I love women"). Losey seems to have wanted to suggest something of this in his pretentious, humorless, strikingly de-eroticized and anti-Mozartian film of *Don Giovanni*. It is not presented as a prominent symptom of the La Motta case history, though strong traces of it manifest themselves in the later part of the film, in Jake's need to be admired by women (especially attractive *young* women) in his nightclub, at the expense of Vickie and the domestic happiness constructed in the home movies. Three points: It is essential that this display take place in public: its motive is Jake's preservation of an image as a man both attractive to and attracted by women, rather than any actual erotic satisfaction. The form it finally takes is Jake's trick with the champagne glasses (a marvelously evocative image): the construction in public, before the admiring female gaze, of an imaginary phallus. (We discover subsequently that it is precisely during this action that Vickie is preparing finally to leave him.) The drive for women's admiration manifests itself only after Jake has been denied the *real* erotic satisfaction (phallus/fist) of pummeling men in the ring. The public display of "I don't love men—I hate them" gives way to the public display of "I don't love men—I love women (and they love me)."

3. Freud's final category contains his explanation of the close connection between paranoia and megalomania: the ultimate denial, "I don't love at all," in fact has its corollary "I love only myself": megalomania is "a sexual overvaluation of the ego." The relevance of this to La Motta seems obvious.

4. I have left to last what is actually the third of Freud's categories, because, in

relation to *Raging Bull*, it is the most resonant of all. This is the form of "sexual delusions of jealousy," and we should not let ourselves be diverted from its implications by Freud's association of it with alcohol, which is clearly inessential. He writes:

> It is not infrequently disappointment over a woman that drives a man to drink— but this means, as a rule, that he resorts to the public-house and to the company of men, who afford him the emotional satisfaction which he has failed to get from his wife at home. If now these men become the objects of a strong libidinal cathexis in his unconscious he will ward it off with the third kind of contradiction: "It is not *I* who love the man—*she* loves him," and he suspects the woman in relation to all the men whom he himself is tempted to love.   (p. 202)

We can examine one manifestation of this last form of paranoia in the "Pelham, 1947" section of the film, the series of scenes that culminates in the Janiro fight. The structure is as follows: a. Domestic scene (Jake's family, Joey's family), linking Jake's anxiety about his weight to his anxiety about Vickie. b. The Copacabana scene: Vickie is invited over to another table (presided over by Tommy, the "godfather" figure) and kissed by other men. This is followed by Jake's obsessive questionings and distrust. He accepts the invitation to join the other men, and the conversation shifts to Janiro's physical beauty. Jake remarks, as a joke, "I don't know whether to fuck him or fight him." c. At home, Jake awakens Vickie and resumes the interrogation about other men, finally attributing remarks about Janiro's beauty to *her*. "I don't even know what he looks like," she replies. d. The fight: Jake deliberately destroys Janiro's face, with a complicit smile at Vickie. He has effectively destroyed the threat Janiro posed, not as attractive to Vickie, but as attractive to *himself*.

This is perhaps the most obvious instance in the film of the kind of internal logic it is my purpose to trace; it is certainly not the only one. Near the beginning of the film, at the start of Jake's career, we are confronted with his apparently irrational and never adequately explained hatred of Salvy, who is both a friend of Jake's brother Joey and, because of his Mafia connections, a potential booster of Jake's professional advancement. Salvy is with Vickie when Jake sees her for the first time at the tenement pool and immediately becomes fixated on her as an object. The film dramatizes here, very precisely, the relationship between "I don't love him—I *hate* him" and "I don't love him—I love *her*"—the possibility of movement from one of the forms of paranoia to another. Subsequently, Salvy becomes recruited into the ever growing ranks of men Jake believes Vickie to have had sex with.

We must now confront one possible objection to this reading of La Motta, and of the film: apart from Janiro, with his disturbing physical beauty, and Salvy, with his florid good looks, the two men who precipitate Jake's outbursts of paranoid jealousy are the sexually unattractive old man Tommy and Jake's own brother Joey.

Here we may have the film's most remarkable insight and the one that will be hardest to accept. It is exactly at this point that the parallels between the film and Freud's analysis of the Schreber case are most fascinating. Freud maintains that Schreber's original love objects, for whom all later men were stand-ins, must have been his own father and brother. Tommy potently functions in the film as the father figure; Joey is Jake's actual brother. The film's insights, in fact, are closely in line with Freud's insistence that erotic impulses take as their first objects the members of the immediate family circle (one might note here the closeness of Italian-American family relationships, while again rejecting any invitation to restrict the film's implications to any specific milieu). What provokes the ultimate, cataclysmic explosion of Jake's paranoid fantasy is Vickie's defiant, sarcastic assertion that she sucked Joey's cock.

We can now return to the principles of classical narrative, and especially the familiar one of closure: "the end answers the beginning." Despite the frequent complaint that Scorsese lacks a sense of structure, *Raging Bull* relates to this formula very interestingly. The partial correspondence suggests, however, that the principles of symmetry and closure do not necessarily entail a restoration of the patriarchal order: rather, their function may be that of carefully marking the point the narrative has reached, by returning our memories to its starting point. One can single out the following points of reference:

1. The film (after the credits, before the final epigraph) begins and ends with Jake, fat, middle-aged, alone in his dressing room (1964) practicing his act. At the beginning of the film he is inarticulate, thoroughly incompetent, unable to master his lines, a potential laughingstock; at the end, he is able to deliver his monologue in a way that will at least not destroy his dignity.

2. Near the beginning, during the violent row between Jake and his first wife, an unseen neighbor shouts that they are "animals" (compare also the film's title and Jake's predilection for dressing in animal skins for his entries into the ring). This is followed immediately by the scene with Joey, shortly after Joey has raised the question of why Jake can't stand Salvy, in which Jake demands that his brother punch him in the face. These moments are answered by the prison sequence near the end where Jake, in the most extreme instance of self-punishment, repeatedly beats his head against the wall of his cell after asserting "I'm not an animal," and then by the scene in the garage to which he follows Joey, repeatedly embracing him and kissing him on the face. The moment can be read as an ironic inversion of the notion of the kiss as a privileged climactic moment of classical cinema, epitomizing the construction of the heterosexual couple.

3. We may also adduce here the moment at the beginning when Jake and Joey leave for the nightclub and Jake's wife screams after him "Fucking queer." The prison and garage scenes, in fact, answer *all* these moments from the beginning: if Jake behaves like an animal (violently, toward both men and women), it is because

Raging Bull: Jake La Motta (Robert De Niro) with father figure (Nicholas Colasanto)
. . . and brother (Joe Pesci)

he is blocked from loving either; his insistence that Joey punch him in the face is answered by the embrace. The self-punishment motif, in relation to Joey, is not only taken up symmetrically at the end, it is also treated very thoroughly earlier, in the climactic fight with Robinson, the point of Jake's retirement from the ring, which immediately follows his failure to apologize to Joey on the phone—the fight in which Jake allows himself to be beaten to a pulp, scarcely retaliating, with the one face-saving proviso that he was never knocked down.

This is one instance in the film where screen time takes precedence over narrative chronology: we don't know how much time has elapsed between the abortive phone call and the Robinson fight, but in Scorsese's montage the latter directly follows the former, obeying the inner logic of psychological movement. We have, finally, to confront the puzzle of the film's end, which represents a more drastic use of the same license. At the opening of the film, Jake is patently incompetent, about to humiliate himself; at the end, he has mastered himself and his material (the *On the Waterfront* speech of Brando to Steiger in the taxi) sufficiently to maintain his dignity. The problem here—a very intriguing one—is of chronology. The film ends where it begins, in Jake's dressing room. But is it the same night?—the film doesn't tell us. Why is Jake totally incompetent at the start, adequate at the end?—the film doesn't tell us. One is forced, I think, to posit two chronologies at work: the diegetic chronology (within which Jake's transformation makes no sense whatever), and the actual movement of the film, in which the final scene directly follows the garage scene and the embrace. The film specifies a six-year gap between the two; the editing has one follow on from the other, as if its logical consequence. It is as if Scorsese wished simultaneously to assert and deny that the embrace was what made it possible for Jake to go through with his act—a speech, after all, about one brother's unsatisfied emotional dependence upon another ("I could have been a contender . . . ").

The narrative of *Raging Bull*, then, has its own inner logic, its own internal correspondences and interrelationships. Far from being a rambling and structureless stringing together of moments or a mere character study, it is among the major documents of our age: a work single-mindedly concerned with chronicling the disastrous consequences, for men and women alike, of the repression of constitutional bisexuality within our culture.

FATHER'S SHOES: SCORSESE'S RADICALISM

King of Comedy puzzled many people, including many of Scorsese's admirers. Yes, the end more or less recapitulated the end of *Taxi Driver*, but otherwise, how does one relate it to the previous films? An anomaly, a dead end, a new departure? Certainly, it seemed at first glance a "minor" work, more limited in scope and ambition than any of its three narrative feature predecessors, and one of the problems of becoming a superstar director within the prevailing critical climate is that every work is expected to be "major." Yet the attribution of minor status to the film now seems based partly on false assumptions (tragedy is major, comedy is minor), but more on a misconception of what the film actually does. It was generally taken at face value as a satire on notions of celebrity and an attack on the debasement of values within the mass media, specifically television. Of course, it *is* that. I want to argue here that it is also much more: one of the greatest, and certainly one of the most radical, American films about the structures of the patriarchal family. Viewed as such, the film immediately makes sense within the inner logic of the progress of Scorsese's work, as a necessary follow-up to *New York, New York* and *Raging Bull.*

First, I should define what I mean here by radicalism. The films express no overt political commitment; one cannot take from them any coherently articulated Marxist critique of capitalism or feminist critique of patriarchy, and they give no reason to suppose that Scorsese would subscribe to either of those ideologies. One deduces from the films that his starting point is always an imaginative engagement with a subject, in the most concrete and specific sense: a character, a relationship, a situation; and, no doubt, perhaps simultaneously with the actors who will give them their dramatic embodiment. Yet every subject available must inevitably be structured by the major conflicts within the culture; what distinguishes the major artist is not an explicit ideological stance but his/her ability to pursue the implications of a given subject rigorously, honestly and without compromise, until its basis in those conflicts is revealed. Given that our culture is built upon interlocking structures of domination and oppression, such a pursuit (however innocent of any conscious ideological position) must inevitably produce radical insights—insights that can then be legitimately appropriated by overtly radical movements.

If I choose not to discuss *New York, New York* in these pages, this is purely because Richard Lippe has already done so.[1] All great works constantly change their meanings or reveal new ones, in dynamic relationship with the historical/cultural situation within which they are perceived, and doubtless in the next decade further accounts of *New York, New York* will be needed; but for the moment, Lippe's seems definitive. The film is exemplary of Scorsese's method and of his radicalism. Starting from a subject in the concrete sense (relationship between a jazz saxophone player and a pop singer after the Second World War), the film gradually reveals its true subject—the impossibility of successful heterosexual relations within the existing sexual organization, with its construction of hopelessly incompatible gender roles. Perhaps the saddest moment in an overwhelmingly sad movie is one that Lippe does not, in fact, mention (it is virtually thrown away, as if it were of no significance—a phenomenon not uncommon in Scorsese's work): the moment when the son of the impossible couple informs his father that he's glad he takes after him

1. *Movie* 31–32, pp. 95–100.

King of Comedy: Martin Scorsese directing Robert De Niro

because he wouldn't want to be like a girl, and we see the whole sorry mess beginning again. *New York, New York* brilliantly *describes*, it doesn't *explain*, beyond a
fairly rudimentary level (e.g., men can't live with women who are more successful
than they are, they are afraid of being trapped in domesticity, and so on).

The explanation is begun in *Raging Bull*, with its analysis of the construction of
masculinity upon the basis of the repression of bisexuality, a masculinity that creates the man as a martyr as well as monster. Still lacking is an explanation of the
role played in that construction by the family. Families are quite strikingly absent
from Scorsese's work. The only family in *Taxi Driver* is Iris' (strictly off-screen and
marginal); neither Jimmy Doyle nor Francine Evans appears to have any parents;
Jake LaMotta's are mentioned but never seen, and are allowed no explicit influence
on the film's events. It is as if Scorsese felt compelled to resist and repress any confrontation with the ways in which the individual is constructed within and by the
family. It is not surprising that even in *King of Comedy*—which continues and
extends the explanation of *Raging Bull*—he can approach the family only obliquely,
albeit with the most extraordinary incisiveness and intransigence.

As with *Raging Bull*, whatever the film's direct, unconscious impact, *King of
Comedy* is accessible to interpretation only by the use of psychoanalytical theory;
and the context within which I want to consider it is that of Freudian and post-

Freudian accounts of the construction of children (male and female) within the structures of the patriarchal nuclear family. Crucial to that construction is what might be called the "battle for the phallus." I discussed and I hope resolved, in the chapter on De Palma, the problems of this terminology: that the term "phallus," like the term "castration," must be understood as both literal and metaphorical, the latter usage being by far the more widespread and inclusive, but always carrying connotations of the fundamental meaning, which gives the terms their suggestive resonance. The phallus—penis, power, authority, domination, control of money, etc.— is the attribute of the Father (another literal/symbolic term); the mother is defined essentially by its absence. The little boy's difficult and painful passage through the Oedipus and castration complexes (marked by a series of renunciations—his erotic attachments to *both* parents) leads to an "inevitable" resolution, against which homosexuality or neurosis is the only available form of revolt: he accepts symbolic castration, hence his powerlessness, on the understood condition that "one day" he will acquire the mother after all, in the form of a substitute woman. The logical corollary of this is that he learns to identify with the father, whom he will one day become. It follows from this that, from the moment of this identification and the simultaneous promise of possession of his own woman, the actual mother becomes increasingly irrelevant—a useless, castrated figure of no further significance; she might as well not exist. The little girl's passage through socialization is perhaps even worse. From the outset, she must recognize that she can never "be" the father: her identification figure is, necessarily, the mother, who also represents to her her own castration. As she cannot hope to be the father, she can only hope, a least, to have him, again in the form of a substitute male, to whom she will offer her castrated person as a replica of the mother with whom she is forced to identify and whom she hates, both for the castration and the enforced identification.

Freud's limitations cannot be stressed too often (neither can his greatness). He never fully confronted the horror of this process, the horror of the patriarchal family, because he could envisage no alternative to it. Today we can. Men and women *can* achieve equality, if women, and some men, are willing to fight hard enough for it, and "the phallus" can become quite simply the penis, all its metaphorical extensions stripped away, hopefully by mutual agreement. The "division of labor" can cease to exist, nurturing can become a function of men and women equally, and our long-repressed bisexuality can be reinstated. Meanwhile, despite the sweeping social changes that have occurred within the last few decades, we remain essentially within the situation Freud described: the present social/political/so-called moral climate is characterized by a desire to set us back in it permanently. Immediately relevant here is what underlies (and is produced by) this whole process of repression and socialization—a nausea and horror, originating in early infancy, which is never lost, a potential for rebellion which we may justly call instinctive, as its roots are in the pleasure principle with which we are born and the repression of most of its major and natural constituents. All this explains a phenomenon most of us recognize, emotionally if not intellectually, despite the pressures on us to not recognize it: the child's simultaneous love and hate for its parents, inevitably carried over into adult life: the real subject of *King of Comedy.*

It is instructive at this point to introduce, for comparison, a film that I have already referred to in passing and which, as a phenomenon; has obvious symptomatic importance in the early 80s. *Ordinary People* belongs to sociology rather than aesthetics, which is to say that its interest lies, not in itself (it seems to me negligible) but in its great critical/commercial success. (But who, only a few years after its release, still talks about it? Who, two years from now, will still be talking about *Terms of Endearment?* The "masterpieces" that bourgeois journalism is able confidently to identify seldom prove to have much staying power.) *Ordinary People* is not, then, a film that demands detailed attention; indeed, it seems almost sufficient in this context merely to name it. The film belongs, unambiguously, to 80s reaction; its relevance here lies purely in its particularly precise and schematic, almost textbook, account of the Oedipal trajectory I have just described. The son progresses toward identification with the father, achieving this with the help of psychiatry (psychoanalysis institutionalized, conscripted into the service of the patriarchal order after being emptied of all its subversive content); the progress involves his acquisition of his own woman. The mother, redundant and inconvenient, can then be expelled from the narrative, leaving father and son in the plenitude of their Oedipal reconciliation. The film's popularity, within its social context, was presumably due to its total complacency and complicity. If anything disturbs its equanimity it is, quite simply, the face of Mary Tyler Moore expressing the mother's refusal to participate in or endorse a process that renders her superfluous. Otherwise, nothing in the film challenges or troubles: its quite insistent play on the emotions does not correspond to any disturbance of establishment values or dominant ideological assumptions. The ignominious position of women within the patriarchal family system is never acknowledged (if the mother can't accept it, that's *her* problem; the "nice girl" functions purely as support for the son and is given no autonomous existence whatever). The archetypal patriarchal resolution is offered without a hint of irony, criticism or complexity of attitude.

The distinction of *King of Comedy* is precisely that it subjects to rigorous, astringent, profoundly malicious analysis what *Ordinary People* reassuringly endorses and reinforces; the appearance of the film in the context of the 80s, in opposition to the whole movement of contemporary Hollywood cinema, testifies once again to Scorsese's salutary intransigence. It is the most obviously economical of his films to date (though the occasional sense of redundancy and repetition in *New York, New York* and *Raging Bull* disappears when one grasps what the films are actually doing): every scene and every aspect have their precise place in the analysis. For this reason, it is convenient to break the film down into its components.

1. As a preliminary, we may note that Scorsese has implicitly acknowledged that this is a film about the family by including his own family in it: his sister is the autograph hunter who intrudes upon Rupert Pupkin's fantasy lunch with Jerry Langford; his father is the man at the bar who objects to Rupert's changing the television channel to the show on which he will appear; his mother (heard but not seen) is Rupert's mother; Scorsese himself appears as the director of the Jerry Langford Show. Ambivalence—that simultaneous love and hate—toward the family could not be more succinctly epitomized: Scorsese expresses his affection for his family by putting them in his film, yet the subject of that film is the intrinsic monstrousness of the patriarchal family structures.

2. Rupert's real father is absent from the film and is presumably dead. Jerry Langford functions both as a substitute father (because he is an actual person) and as the symbolic Father, (because of his prestige and authority as celebrity).

3. The projects of the "son" (Rupert) and the "daughter" (Masha) fit perfectly into the Oedipal pattern: Rupert wants to become the father (on whom he admits he has patterned his act) as the next "king of comedy." Masha, on the other hand, shows no sign anywhere of wanting to achieve celebrity: her ambition is not to be the father but to have him.

4. Rupert perceives Rita as his woman, but he can claim her only when his identification with the father has been established, at least in fantasy: as soon as he can delude himself into believing that Langford has accepted him, he goes straight to Rita's bar to establish possession, despite the fact that they haven't met for so long that at first she doesn't recognize him. Scorsese achieves here with Diahanne Abbott something of what he achieved with Cathy Moriarty in *Raging Bull.* The narrative is again completely male-dominated, which is to say not so much that men have the principal roles as that its every step is determined by the processes and concerns of patriarchy. Rita, accordingly, can function in it only as a pawn in the game, a token whose acquisition marks the male's entry into the patriarchal order, rather than an autonomous human being. At the same time, Abbott is allowed (or encouraged) to bring to the role a degree of skepticism and resistance that repeatedly disturbs Rita's overall complicity in the trajectory the film analyzes. She is conspicuously absent from the ending.

5. The culmination of this aspect of the film takes place, not as the traditional happy end, but as mere wish fulfillment: the wedding ceremony that Rupert fantasizes, staged and organized by the Father on his own talk show. The wish fulfillment is completed and the absurdity reinforced by the duplication of Langford with another father, Rupert's high school principal (retired, now a Justice of the Peace), who not only performs the ceremony but clinches the fantasy with a public apology to Rupert for all the wrongs done him in his youth. The sequence enacts the impossible wish that the Father (here again both substitute and symbolic, patriarchy personified) should apologize for "the ignominy of boyhood."

6. The film opens with Rupert's imaginary identification with the father. The redundancy of the mother is signified in the most direct manner possible: she never appears in the movie, is reduced to an offscreen voice that gratingly intrudes on Rupert's "important" and totally illusory pursuits. Thus disembodied and reduced to a mere incomprehending superfluous nuisance with no further role to play in the processes of patriarchy, she can then be killed off by Rupert in his climactic comic monologue (if his mother were here tonight "I'd say, 'Mom, what are *you* doing here?, you've been dead nine years' ").

7. The visit to Langford's country home, in response to an invitation issued within one of Rupert's fantasies, and Rita's participation in it are essential to Rupert's project (and the failure of the visit is essential to the motivation of the rest of the narrative): the father must acknowledge the son, and the son's acquisition of the woman (his accession to manhood), on his own territory, in his own home.

8. The kidnapping is provoked by the blocking of the two Oedipal projects: the humiliating defeat of the visit to Langford and Masha's failure to get her love letter to him. "Brother" and "sister," hostile to one another throughout the film, can precariously join forces in the frustration of their (superficially similar, profoundly incompatible) drives to possess the father.

9. There follows immediately, however, the extraordinary "sibling rivalry" sequence, in which the brother/sister antagonism resurfaces. The two compete, hilariously and pathetically, for the father's attention as he is held at gunpoint (though even the gun is an illusion—they don't really have the phallus). The means of gaining that attention vary significantly, however, corresponding precisely to the positions of the son and daughter within patriarchy: Rupert demands Langford's interest in his tape (or rebukes him for his lack of it)—the tape is the evidence that he is the new king of comedy; Masha, on the other hand, woos Langford with the scarlet sweater she is knitting for him. They embody the drives that patriarchy constructs out of the free, indeterminate, bisexual libido with which we are born: to usurp the father's position, to become his wife. Essential to both is the refusal to recognize Langford as a human individual: he is not a person but the phallus.

10. The ruthless logic with which Scorsese pursues his premises is exemplified again in the recognition that the Oedipal projects of the children can only be realized (in a way that simultaneously frustrates them) by reducing the father to total impotence, indeed, total immobility. The importance of the moment when Rupert begins actually to tape Langford to his chair, virtually mummifying him, so that he can barely even turn his head, is signaled by the film's solitary recourse to an unusual camera angle: the overhead shot. It is the ultimate denial of Langford-as-person: he becomes an inanimate object who can then be supplanted by the son and made love to by the daughter.

11. With the father bound, Rupert can leave to become him on the show. (This is not of course strictly accurate: Langford's literal replacement as host is Tony Ran-

dall. Yet the validity of the reading is not affected by this: in the conversation in Langford's car at the beginning of the film Rupert makes it clear that his choice of Langford is dependent on the latter's gifts as a comedian, and the casting of Jerry Lewis clinches the matter. We may further note that when Rupert finally leaves Langford outside his apartment building, the self-proclaimed future king of comedy already, in anticipation, demotes his predecessor: "Jerry, you're a prince.") Meanwhile Masha (in Sandra Bernhard's astonishing incarnation) proceeds with her campaign to seduce the immobile and determinedly impassive father, first with a candlelight dinner, then with reminiscences of her real parents ("I never told my parents I loved them"—though she once carried golf clubs for her father, and Langford is a golfer), and finally with a romantic song, "Come Rain or Come Shine," first heard over the opening credits sung by Ray Charles. The moment is one of the most extraordinary in a remarkably consistent, coherent, tightly organized film in which every moment is extraordinary: although Scorsese's work has little discernibly in common with Brecht, a remarkable instance of "making the familiar strange." The song, of a type our culture has come to take for granted, suddenly reveals previously unimagined meanings in the context within which it is performed. The intensity of the Oedipal investment is there in the opening "I'm gonna love you/like nobody's loved you/come rain or come shine." In fact, Masha commences the song with its later, corresponding verse, which gives us the other side of the impossible bargain: "You're gonna love me/like nobody's loved me." The Oedipal basis of romantic love is cruelly, relentlessly exposed, the impossible demands that men and women, within our culture, make on one another related back to their roots in the overwhelming desires that patriarchy at once nurtures and frustrates.

12. Rupert arrives at the television studio, identifies himself as "the King," and Miss Long, Langford's secretary, for the first time gets his name right (he has previously been put through every variation: Pumpkin, Pipkin, Popkin). The name itself has obvious significance (the "pup" who insists on his "kin"-ship to the father). But it is only when Rupert becomes the father (the king) that his identity is at last established.

13. It is not enough that Rupert become the father: his woman must see that he has become it. Hence the necessity of transferring the spectacle of Rupert's empty, barren triumph to Rita's bar. She is even (as a woman under patriarchy, the barmaid, not the owner) impressed, though still skeptical.

14. The whole film moves—again, with that remorseless Scorsesian logic—to Rupert's monologue, which is obsessively concerned with his parents. The mother, as already noted, is brutally eliminated ("dead nine years"). As for the father, Rupert is now standing in his shoes (metaphorically), and the monologue's crowning joke is about his vomiting over them (literally): the son's simultaneous love/hatred for the father could scarcely be more succinctly or more brilliantly expressed. Yet it can

Father-fantasy (Jerry Lewis and Robert De Niro)

Robert De Niro and Sandra Bernhard

be argued that the film goes even beyond this statement of the filial ambivalence the patriarchal family engenders. The shoes that are vomited over are new shoes, the shoes Rupert is metaphorically now standing in. The hatred for the father whom he is obsessed with becoming is also, and crucially, *self*-hatred, self-contempt: the nausea the patriarchal process generates is ultimately nausea at oneself, as its latest recruit and representative.

15. Langford's presence (Lewis' splendid performance, disciplined, precise, self-effacing) is itself eloquent: a pathetic, bitter, empty, totally isolated figure, he epitomizes the bankruptcy of patriarchy at this phase of consumer capitalism, the symbolic Father essentially meaningless and obsolete, though still hysterically pursued. The chain of "great" father figures that passes through the entire development of Hollywood cinema, endowed with attributes of moral/spiritual grandeur and divine authority (of which Abraham Lincoln, in his various cinematic incarnations, can stand as exemplary) has dwindled to a lonely, barren man in an immense apartment of cold glass and glitter. (For an alternative—parallel but very different—critique of the symbolic Father, the hero, see *The Deer Hunter*, discussed in the next chapter.)

16. Within the psychoanalytical context I have defined, the satire on the media takes on a resonance it entirely lacks when seen as the film's sole and simple subject. Today, the media have become the vehicle for the perpetuation of patriarchy, a patriarchy emptied of its earlier force and potency, continuing as longed-for fantasy fulfillment (consider not only television, but the *Star Wars* phenomenon analyzed in a previous chapter). The ambivalence toward the Father inherent in the patriarchal family structure is repeated in the transference to the media: endless promise, endless frustration, since the promise can be fulfilled only in fantasy and one is always cheated. (The murder of John Lennon, which the film has been widely held to evoke, has its relevance here.)

17. The film's rigorous attitude toward its characters makes possible the precisely focused irony of the ending, so similar to that of *Taxi Driver* yet so different. The absence of Schrader from the project is doubtless significant here: there is no suggestion of a drive toward a personal transcendence or redemption (never mind the cost). The absurdity of Rupert's status as celebrity—the total emptiness of this new signifier of success, stardom, king, father—is firmly held. The emptiness of *King of Comedy* against the plenitude of *Ordinary People*: no wonder the public, the establishment press, the Motion Picture Academy, in short, America, preferred the latter. Yet it is the emptiness of Scorsese's film that exposes the illusoriness of *Ordinary People*'s plenitude, by subjecting to analysis the structures through which it is achieved and the cost of the patriarchal process to the human psyche, both male and female.

Two Films by Michael Cimino

"THINGS FALL APART . . . ": *The Deer Hunter*

he Deer Hunter raises fundamental questions about the relationship
between politics and aesthetics. It has been lavishly praised as realistic and roundly condemned as reactionary; neither response seems
to me either justified or helpful, at least without modifications so sweeping as to
transform either verdict into something quite different. The use of the term "realistic" is—here as elsewhere—merely obfuscatory: if not exactly without meaning, its
meaning is so vague and diffuse, so prone to slipping from one sense into another
(so that all precise meanings are collapsed into an amorphous mass from which you
can extract whatever sense suits your convenience) as to invalidate it for critical use.
The politically reactionary tag raises another issue, the familiar but still challenging
question of whether it is valid to reject a work of art because of its ideological position. My own answer is no, but with the immediate proviso that certain ideologies
are fundamentally inimical to art. The extraordinary poverty of the cinema of Stalinist and post-Stalinist Russia, or of Nazi Germany, testifies to this. The Fascist ideology can only produce ugly, simplistic, brutalized art: Riefenstahl's films, far from
being the exception to this thesis that liberal film historians (intimidated, no doubt,
by the films' insistence on the paraphernalia of "the cinematic") would have us
believe, represent its thorough confirmation. It is the essential characteristic of the
Fascist or Stalinist ideology totally to repress contradiction or complexity. The "democratic" bourgeois ideology is another matter altogether: in order to justify its claim
to being democratic, it has to accommodate so much, to be prepared to bend and
stretch in so many directions, that contradiction and complexity are its ineradicable
qualities. If the idea of a great Fascist work of art is a contradiction in terms, there
are innumerable great democratic bourgeois works of art, and I shall argue that *The
Deer Hunter*, for all its areas of vagueness and confusion, is patently one of them.

This is not to concede that the film is, in any simple or unambiguous way, reactionary. It is interesting that, by and large, the people ready to brand it as such in order to reject it have been defensive liberals rather than radicals: the dismissal has less to do with the "common pursuit of true judgment" than with a desire to look good. Certainly, the film offers itself (in its candor, offers itself *up*—for it is part of Cimino's greatness that he is never afraid to expose himself) for just such a ritual of liberal self-approval. From a position left of center, it must be admitted that its presentation of the Vietnam war raises severe problems, established immediately in the first Vietnam sequence. Women and children hide in a dugout shelter; a Vietnamese soldier casually lifts the trapdoor and rolls in a grenade; explosion; Mike (Robert De Niro), who has witnessed the atrocity, righteously executes the soldier with his flamethrower. Cimino's aim (brilliantly realized on the level of realistic effect) was clearly to convey the sense of horror and confusion through the abrupt and elliptical images. Yet the *sense* of confusion becomes, for the audience, a dangerous *actual* confusion as to what exactly is happening. I assumed initially that the perpetrator of the atrocity was a member of the Vietcong, and most people I have consulted made the same assumption (no one challenged it when Richard Lippe and I reviewed the film for Toronto's *Body Politic*). It is, when one thinks about it, clearly incorrect: the Vietcong did not have helicopters, the raid is on a *North* Vietnamese village, the soldier a *South* Vietnamese (presumably trained by the Americans). The problem is partly that one *doesn't* think about it—the direct impact of the scene discourages any analytical distance—but more importantly that the perpetrator, whether American-trained or not, is still an Asian: were De Niro executing a fellow American the scene, in the context of the entire film, would read very differently. As it stands, the good, morally outraged American is pitted against the oriental Other, and nothing elsewhere in the film counters this impression. The film, of course, presents the war as a terrible thing, a trauma, but it was terrible because "our boys" suffered so much. As in almost every other Hollywood film about Vietnam (the most striking and honorable exception is *Twilight's Last Gleaming*, significantly a box office disaster), political analysis is totally repressed and the possibility that it might be regarded as a war of American aggression/imperialism never permitted to surface. (It should be added, in fairness, that the film never attempts to justify the war in political terms either and that the America that insisted on fighting it is nowhere endorsed.)

The rejection of the film on political grounds is in fact closely involved with the issue of realism and the confusions that almost invariably attend the use of that term. The film is perceived as realistic; yet the general consensus seems to be that the Vietcong did not play Russian roulette with their prisoners; therefore the film is unrealistic. That the apparent dilemma rests upon a simple confusion over meaning seems so obvious that one feels some diffidence about attempting to explicate it; however, every reader of popular film criticism knows how widespread and stubborn the confusion is. (E.H. Gombrich's *Art and Illusion* is very useful in helping to clear it up, and I am indebted to that book here.)

A work of art can, in a very general way, supply true or false information. For example, a painting entitled "Coney Island in Summer" that represented that location as totally deserted of human beings and covered with tropical vegetation would be supplying false information, while one that showed it crowded with holidaymakers and covered with amusement parks would be providing true information; whether we were misled would depend upon our prior knowledge. This elementary level of truth or falsity has nothing to do with the pictures' quality or with realism *as an art form*. The aim of realism is to give the spectator/reader/viewer the feeling that what is depicted is real whether it is or not. The success of this is likely to depend on the interplay of a number of complex factors none of which has anything to do with truth or falsity in the factual/historical/geographical sense. One of these factors is skill; a second is stylistic choice; a third is the contemporaneity of conventions. Let us briefly apply each of these to our hypothetical example:

Assuming that both painters of Coney Island wished us to believe we were looking at a real place, it is quite possible that the former, with his tropical foliage, might far surpass the skills in representation of the latter, for all his correct information: the lie might be more successfully realistic than the truth.

Let us suppose that our second artist, while continuing to provide true information about crowds, climate, flora, etc., had aims quite other than creating an illusion of the real (they might include, for example, caricature, satire, the expression of a transcendent vision, Brechtian alienation, challenging the dominant modes of representation). The first picture, in that case, for all its misleading information, might be thoroughly realistic, the second highly stylized and antirealist.

Even a cursory glance back over the past hundred years will show that yesterday's realism is today's stylization. Our notions of the realistic are very much dependent upon our familiarity with, and acceptance of, current conventions of representation—our ability to decode *automatically*. Assuming again that both our artists aimed at realism, and granting them equal skills, it is probable that we would accept the more recent painting as the more realistic. (It is a not uncommon phenomenon today that Classical Hollywood movies are perceived as stylized while TV movies are perceived as realistic.)

We can, then, characterize *The Deer Hunter* as a realistic film without this committing us to any claims about its factual veracity. We might consider substituting for the term realism the phrase "realistic effect": the distinction is not mere pedantry, the word "effect" insisting upon something which is fabricated, and thereby reminding us that we are dealing with a particular set of aesthetic/stylistic choices, not with anything that guarantees truth. It is worrying, of course, that this confusion is so endemic to our culture and that so much realist art (including *The Deer Hunter*) is to varying degrees complicit with it—that the film's richness in realistic effect should be widely misconstrued, audiences believing that they are being offered factual information rather than mythology. If it were proved tomorrow that, after all, Russian roulette was practiced by the Vietcong, this would not make *The Deer Hunter* in the least a better film than it is, nor would conclusive evidence that it wasn't in any way diminish it. That the film more widely imposes as truth a particular view of the Vietnam war is equally regrettable. The realistic effect is certainly one of the major strategies of bourgeois art in its tendency to impose ideology as truth; it is a strategy, however, that can easily be countered by education without destroying the art in question.

Rejection of *The Deer Hunter* is also strongly influenced by its historical immediacy. Critics no longer feel the need to dismiss, say, Ford's *Drums Along the Mohawk*, though it is vulnerable to precisely the same objections (false factual information, an inescapably ideological view of American history, a crudely external, biased and demeaning depiction of the Indians). The pastness of Ford's film, both in terms of the historical moment it depicts and the historical moment in which it was produced, ensures that it is readily visible as mythology and is no longer construed as socially harmful. I don't see why we should have to wait twenty years before acknowledging the stature of *The Deer Hunter*: its mythologizing is sufficiently transparent that it can easily be exposed as such today. I would add that, realist art being in question, the intensity and vividness with which the realistic effect is imagined and constructed, though it has nothing necessarily to do with factual veracity, has a great deal to do with artistic authenticity.

Adequately to analyze the means whereby realistic effect is constructed would require an essay in itself; it depends upon the complex interplay of a number of factors, of which I here list a few of the most obvious (not all have to be present in any given instance): (1) Identification with sympathetic characters, but also, more important, with commonly experienced emotions such as delight, excitement, pain, fear, rage. The orchestration of identification within a given scene can be extremely elaborate and complex. For example, the first Russian roulette sequence invites us to identify, not only with the diverse reactions of Mike, Nick and Steven, but at moments with the Vietcong leader, simply on the basis of his youth and vulnerability. (2) "Suturing": the binding of the spectator, through camera position and editing, into the dramatic situation, either with point-of-view or shot/reverse-shot figures, or simply by bringing us in so close that we are denied the possibility of contemplative distance. (3) Physicality: suggestions of physical sensation that automatically evoke an empathic response (the rat on Steven's head in the Vietcong camp, the black soldier with bandaged stumps in place of hands in the Saigon hospital). (4) Spontaneous, naturalistic acting derived from the

Method school/Actors' Studio. (5) Superfluity: the use of redundant or irrelevant detail that draws on our sense that life is not a coherent narrative and that lots of things happen simultaneously, giving a sense that this is indeed "life," not an organized fiction. The entire wedding party scene is an unusually sustained and elaborate example of this strategy.

✳ ✳ ✳

The common emphasis, whether favorable or hostile, on the realism of *The Deer Hunter* has an unfortunate corollary: it (and, even more so, *Heaven's Gate* after it) is widely regarded as lacking structure, amorphous, sprawling, undisciplined, totally under the sway of the superfluity principle. No criticism could be less justified; to offset it, it is precisely the film's formal properties that I want to insist on here. With *The Deer Hunter* and *Heaven's Gate*, Cimino has established himself decisively as one of the American cinema's great architects and as one of its most authentic formal innovators. It is the innovativeness that blinds critics to the structures he creates: the charges of formlessness rest invariably on false assumptions, rooted in the conventions of classical narrative cinema, as to what constitutes form. The traditional concept of form testifies above all to the dominance of narrative: form is dictated by content, and content means, essentially, narrative development. The filmmakers who are held to possess what Cimino and Scorsese are said to lack—a sense of structure—are those who, first and foremost, are skilled in telling a story clearly and economically (exposition of characters, relationships and situations; development and resolution of conflicts). In the work of "the masters" such as Hitchcock and Ford this is enriched and deepened by a closely integrated thematic/symbolic structure created by means of stylistics, recurrent imagery, effects of symmetry/asymmetry, etc., which is, however, still dependent upon the narrative and subordinated to its movement. Significantly, a common formula for Cimino's alleged deficiency is that he can't tell a story.

Two things should be made clear at once. I am not trying to mount another highly fashionable attack on classical narrative, and I am not advocating a theory of pure form. I do, however, want to suggest that other relationships between narrative structure and thematic/symbolic structure are possible and valid, that classical narrative does not constitute a sacrosanct set of rules. This implies not only a rethinking of what we mean by form but of what we mean by narrative. Narrative in our culture is always highly personalized: it is about characters and what happens to them. Thus, given a plot outline of *Heaven's Gate* and the project of producing from it a traditionally effective narrative, one's first concern would be to establish the triangular relationship between Kris Kristofferson, Isabelle Huppert and

Christopher Walken as early as possible (Cimino does not establish it until around the film's midpoint). Narrative, however, might equally be treated as the means of building a thematic/symbolic structure that *transcends* individual characters, reversing the traditional relationship of dependency.

A fuller development of this argument must be postponed for the discussion of *Heaven's Gate*. In *The Deer Hunter*, the relationship of narrative structure to formal structure to thematic/symbolic structure is much closer to the traditional model, though Cimino's audacity is already apparent. My description of him as an architect was not empty rhetoric: it is the film's very striking architectural quality (only loosely tied to character development) that most strongly counters—when we become aware of it—the potential coerciveness of the realistic effect, allowing us to see the film as a structure and thereby allowing a degree of distance. I want to suggest, then, that the architecture is important in its own right, as influencing the spectator's relationship to the film; it is also, however, closely related to its overall narrative progression, its thematic content, its emotional effect.

The Deer Hunter is built upon the combination of three structural principles, each simple enough in itself; both the architecture (crudely, "form") and the complexity (crudely, "content") derive from their interaction.

1. Alternation   The basic, apparently elementary, apparently symmetrical form of the film, derived from its geographical locations, is ABABA, in which A is Clairton, Pennsylvania, and B is Vietnam. One is dealing, then, with five narrative blocks:

  a. *Clairton*: the wedding, the first hunt, the eve of departure.
  b. *Vietnam*: capture, escape, Nick in Saigon.
  c. *Clairton*: Mike's return, Mike and Linda, the second hunt, Mike and Steven.
  d. *Vietnam*: Mike in Saigon, Mike and Nick, Nick's "suicide."
  e. *Clairton*: the funeral, the wake, "God Bless America."

What makes the alternation pattern striking and exceptional is the *exclusiveness* of each block—no cut backs to Clairton in the first Vietnam block, no cut backs to Vietnam (to show what is happening to Nick) in the second Clairton block, etc. The crude and simple symmetry is strongly qualified by

2. Diminution   Within each alternating series, each block is significantly shorter than the one that precedes it: the first Clairton block lasts over an hour, the last a mere ten minutes; the first Vietnam block lasts just over forty minutes, the second less than twenty. The symmetry of location is, then, countered by the asymmetry of duration. This "rough-hewn geometry" (a phrase Noel Burch uses to define Kurosawa) can be depicted in a simple diagram. That this is not form for form's sake is immediately suggested by the film's most obvious overall narrative movement: it begins with a wedding and ends with a wake. The content ("what it is about") is reflected and underlined in the formal principle of *dwindling*, from plenitude to impoverishment. The principle is further enacted in all three leading male characters: Nick loses his life, Steven his legs, Mike his sense of (and right to) charismatic authority.

3. The Crossing Over of Motifs   This third structural principle is more obviously related to meaning, to the film's thematic organization. A simple but effective example: each Vietnam block is introduced by the noise of whirring helicopter blades; the final Clairton block begins with a television newsreel showing helicopters being dumped overboard from American warships. The film is centrally concerned with the way in which the invasion of Vietnam (a country) by America is answered by the invasion of America by Vietnam (an experience, a symbol, a state of mind). Another crossing over motif supplies the inverse of this: the blasts of flame in the Clairton steel mill that (almost) open block 1 become the blasts of Mike's flamethrower that (almost) open block 2. The fire imagery is also taken up in the "inferno imagery" (Andrew Britton's phrase) of block 4—the inferno of Saigon is seen, retrospectively, as already implicit in Clairton from the film's beginning. The principle of crossing over, however, goes beyond what such relatively local examples suggest, definitively binding the film's architecture.

The first (Clairton) block is centered on the hunt and the ritual killing of the deer ("one shot"). The fact that most of the footage is devoted to Steven's wedding does not seriously challenge the significance of this as the block's dominant motif: it is introduced at the outset in the dialogue as the men leave work; taken up in the dialogue between Mike and Nick in their home ("I don't think about 'one shot' that much any more, Mike"); and the *mise-en-scène* of the hunt, with its heavenly choir and romantic low angles, itself insists (both strenuously and artificially, the strain and artifice taking on their significance by the film's end) on the weight to be attached to the scene. The first Vietnam block balances this by introducing the film's second dominant motif (at once the opposite and complement of "one shot"), the Russian roulette game: the block is composed, in fact, around the two enactments of the game, in the Vietcong makeshift camp and in the Saigon gambling den where Mike sees (and loses) Nick. The second Clairton block recapitulates the hunt, but permits the Russian roulette motif to erupt into it (the scene in the hunt where Mike, exasperated beyond endurance, presses the revolver to Stan's temple); the Bingo game, another game of chance, in the veteran's hospital further dramatizes the motif. This crossing over is then answered in the second Vietnam block by the climactic reference to "one shot" that immediately precedes Nick's suicide.

✳ ✳ ✳

This formal strength—immensely satisfying in itself as architecture, and in its organic relation to meaning—does not alone account for the richness and fascination of *The Deer Hunter*. Cimino's audacious innovativeness on the formal level is by no means incompatible with, and, in fact, is given depth and substance by, the rootedness of his art in a central Hollywood tradition. To define that tradition simply as Hollywood is inadequate: its literary antecedents far precede the invention of film, as suggested in the way Cimino's "deer hunter" echoes James Fenimore Cooper's "Deerslayer." For present purposes, however, it can be defined as the extremely complex tradition to which the work of Ford and Hawks is central, the complexity being suggested by the many ways in which those two directors, while indisputably belonging to the same tradition, can be regarded as antithetical: a tradition fundamentally concerned with the construction of images of America, with responses to the idea of America. *The Deer Hunter* can be viewed as at once the culmination of that tradition and an elegy for it: for its lost viability.

One can draw two specific parallels, the intertextuality producing a complex network of signification. Many have noted the indebtedness of the film, along with numerous other recent American movies, to *The Searchers*: here Debbie (Natalie Wood), abducted by the Comanche, becomes Nick (Christopher Walken), part traumatized, part seduced by Vietnam; in both cases the hero's task is to rescue the errant character from the alien world and restore her/him to American civilization. Immediately, the structure of parallels produces a richly suggestive structure of differences: that Nick is male and adult; that his capitulation to the alien world is of his own volition; that he has (as far as one can see) no family to be restored to; that he resists, rather than welcomes, the hero's attempt to bring him back; that he is finally restored to America as a corpse. There is an even more precise reversal: whereas in *The Searchers* we believe that Ethan/John Wayne intends to kill Debbie and he ends up abruptly saving her, in *The Deer Hunter* Mike/De Niro clearly wishes to rescue Nick and is (directly, if inadvertently) responsible for his death.

No one, as far as I know, has noted the equally strong parallels with *Rio Bravo*. Both films offer three heroes, representing varying degrees and types of fallibility, a central issue of Hawks' masterpiece being the efforts of Chance (John Wayne) to save Dude (Dean Martin) from alcoholism; Nick's defection in *The Deer Hunter* is presented as much in terms of an *addiction* (literally, to drugs, metaphorically, to the roulette game) as of deracination. Chance's vulnerability and awkwardness with women are transformed into Mike's persona of virgin knight. Where *Rio Bravo* parallels two women (the one responsible in the past for Dude's drinking and the "gambling woman" with whom Chance becomes involved—both "came in on the stage"), *The Deer Hunter* combines them in Linda (Meryl Streep), initially Nick's fiancée, subsequently Mike's lover. (The parallel here is of structural function rather than character, Linda having none of the negative connotations of the precipitator of Dude's downfall, though it is strongly implied that Nick's inability to confront Clairton after the loss of innocence represented by Vietnam is centered on an inability to confront Linda, who thereby becomes in a sense the cause of his defection, however innocently.) Similarly, Steven (John Savage) combines certain functions of *Rio Bravo*'s Colorado (Ricky Nelson) and Stumpy (Walter Brennan): he has the youth and inexperience of the former and becomes, in a far more extreme form, crippled like the latter.

The resonance created by this intricate intertextuality is centered above all on the concept of the hero: the charismatic, superior, yet essentially isolated figure who, while at best ambiguously "of" civilization, is yet ultimately responsible for its survival and stability. Cimino's conception of Mike has a significant place within the widespread and complex rethinking of the hero in the context of 70s America (the range can be suggested in the movement, not merely from Deerslayer to Deer Hunter but from Leatherstocking to Leatherface). It is illuminating to place Mike beside another modern hero incarnated by Robert De Niro, the Travis Bickle of *Taxi Driver*. For better or worse, Cimino has in abundance the quality Scorsese largely lacks: idealism and the will to believe—a rare (unique?) quality in modern Hollywood cinema, with which the knowing pseudo-innocence of a Spielberg or a Lucas should never be confused. Scorsese's intelligent skepticism produces a figure who fuses the western hero with the horror film monster in the context of urban *film noir*; Cimino's idealism produces a lament for a figure contemporary civilization has rendered obsolete but to which is still attributed a nobility and purity. If Travis Bickle derives primarily from the Wayne of *The Searchers* (the hero as near-psychopath is not an invention of the 70s), Mike relates rather to the Wayne of *Rio Bravo*, in his moral infallibility, both its grandeur and its human disadvantages. One might, however, qualify that by relating him also to earlier incarnations of the hero, antedating the tough, stoical resignation the Wayne of the 50s had come to epito-mize—to more vulnerable, less disillusioned heroes like the Cary Grant of *Only Angels Have Wings* (who also fails to keep his protegés alive and whole), or even to the Henry Fonda of Ford's pre–World War II period.

The dual derivation from Ford and Hawks explains not only the presentation of the hero but the presentation of the community to which he ambiguously relates; it also helps to explain, if not resolve, certain problems arising from it. If Clairton, Pennsylvania, relates most obviously to Fordian microcosms of Ameri-can civilization, it also relates (in the insistence on male bonding, and in the purely peripheral, quite un-Fordian position of women) to the Hawksian all-male group existing, of necessity, *outside* civilization. It must be added at once that the opposition is not that simple: Ford's microcosmic images of America fre-quently stand in a strikingly ambiguous relationship to American civilization itself. There are, on the one hand, the pioneers of *Drums Along the Mohawk* and the (daytime, Sunday morning) Tombstone of *My Darling Clementine.* On the other hand, in *Stagecoach* established civilization is already explicitly repudiated, and the potential for community the film endorses is represented by an outlaw, a prostitute, and an alcoholic doctor. When we get into the 50s, and to *Wagonmas-ter,* we reach a point in Ford's development where American civilization can be represented positively only by those expelled from it: Mormons and "show-folk." No more than that can *The Deer Hunter* be read as an endorsement of contem-porary America.

In a plausible and partially persuasive assault on the film in *Movie 27/28* ("Sideshows: Hollywood in Vietnam"), Andrew Britton compares the wedding of *The Deer Hunter* to the celebrated church-floor dance sequence in *My Darling Clementine.* The comparison seems to me useful in ways different from those Brit-ton acknowledges. His argument is, basically, that the Ford sequence represents a kind of art (that of Classical Hollywood cinema at its finest, one might say) only possible under a happy coincidence of certain (industrial, ideological, generic, aes-thetic) conditions, and that those conditions are no longer available. Fair enough. The argument can, however, be read as having unfortunate implications that Brit-ton seems not to have intended. The nature of *The Deer Hunter* is determined by a completely different set of conditions. It may be possible to argue that the condi-tions that determined the nature of *Clementine* were somehow intrinsically supe-rior, more conducive to art: the cultural moments within which a particular art form has flourished (Elizabethan London, the Vienna of Mozart and Haydn, Clas-sical Hollywood) have always been characterized by the availability of *stable* con-ventions. In contemporary Hollywood, art can scarcely be said to flourish: any sig-nificant work that emerges must be achieved despite, not because of, the general cli-mate (which includes the dominant critical climate). In such a climate minor

Male camaraderie: Christopher Walken, Robert De Niro, Chuck Aspegren, John Savage, John Cazale

The wedding party: John Cazale, Chuck Aspegren, Robert De Niro, John Savage, Rutanya Alda, Christopher Walken, Meryl Streep

talents, lacking support and incentive, drown, and major talents find it harder and harder to produce; and in such a climate we cannot expect the same *kind* of significance, the same *kind* of achievement. Behind *Clementine* is that whole complex of conventions, acting, shooting, editing (the subordination of the actors to the narrative, the celebrated Fordian "editing-in-the-camera") to which we give the name "Classical Hollywood"; behind *The Deer Hunter* is a far less defined and stable tradition of Method acting, improvisation, realistic effect and a concept of editing that "extracts" the film (Arthur Penn's phrase) from a great mass of raw material. It is not a tradition that encourages the Classical virtues of poise, lucidity, economy and precision. Neither, however is the "achieved ideological harmony" (Britton's phrase) of the *Clementine* sequence—which those virtues serve to incarnate— accessible in 70s America. Indeed, the set of conventions we label Classical Hollywood is itself the embodiment of ideological security; the set available to Cimino testifies to the collapse of that security. I am reluctant to believe that significant art is only possible within an ideologically secure culture: such a belief would drastically limit its function and its range of potentiality. (It is also a problem that the *Clementine* church-floor dance constitutes a ten-minute sequence in a notoriously uneven and unsatisfactory film, and that its "ideological harmony" is bought with the repression of all the film's problematic elements: its usefulness as a means of belittling *The Deer Hunter* is not exactly clear-cut.)

The value of the comparison seems to me to lie precisely in the way it illuminates both the conventional and ideological differences and the relationship between the two. Ford was concerned to embody a myth of an ideal America at the moment of its conception. In so far as the Clairton of *The Deer Hunter* is comparable to the Tombstone of *Clementine*, Cimino is concerned with that myth at the moment of its disintegration. The poise, dignity, and control of the *Clementine* sequence (both within the action and in the execution) are answered by the hysteria into which the Clairton wedding celebration is imminently in danger of collapsing: in place of harmony and unification, one finds incipient chaos, tension, disruption. The ominous proximity of Vietnam (the three men are to leave for the war the next day) is only one of the sources of this hysteria, albeit the decisive one, I shall single out two great poetic moments where the tension crystallizes (I use the word "poetic" in its root sense of "bringing things together").

My first example centers on the drops of wine spilt, unnoticed, on Angela's bridal dress during the ritual in which bride and groom drink from the branched wedding vessel (if no wine is spilt, their life together will be happy). Most obviously, the moment anticipates the blood of Vietnam and Steven's loss of his legs, but its connotations reach far beyond that of simple omen. For a start, it is Steven who spills the wine, by drinking too fast and tilting the vessel. His impetuosity relates to his consistently signified near-hysteria, which has its source in his split allegiance to the world of domesticity (Angela, marriage) and to the world of male camaraderie (see his resentment that the other men are going deer hunting on his wedding night). But the basis of the marriage itself is subsequently revealed as precarious in the extreme: Angela is already pregnant, but Steven is not the father (who remains unidentified), and the two have not even slept together, though the blood on the bridal dress publicly betrays her loss of virginity. The ritual (we may think of Yeats' "custom and ceremony," and of the "blood-dimmed tide" in which "the ceremony of innocence is drowned") belongs to the traditional practices that have unified the ethnic community; the blood evokes the failure of that tradition to withstand pressures from without and within. Hence the moment relates back to the little scene near the start of the film where Steven's mother visits the priest for comfort and guidance (receiving neither), and directly connects the breakdown of traditional sexual morality (Steven marrying a girl who is "not so *thin*, if you get my meaning") with Vietnam, her speech culminating in an unanswered plea that someone "explain" to her.

The connection confirms the film's place within the tradition of the western, evoking the genre's habitual projection of *uncontainable* energies on to the Indians (habitually travestied, as are *The Deer Hunter*'s Vietcong, with no political awareness that they were a people fighting not only for their independence and their right to cultural autonomy, but for their right to exist). The crucial difference can be seen, again, in comparison with Ford (not just the *Clementine* dance, but, for example, the magnificent sequence of the Halloween dance in *Drums Along the Mohawk*): in Ford the containment is secure, achieved through the elimination of incompatible elements, and threatened only by outside forces; in Cimino, the containment, much more inclusive than in Ford, is already riddled by cracks and lines of tension. Further, the *attitude* to the containment is no longer secure; the film cannot be read simply as endorsing a nostalgia for the organic community. Hence the difference between the actual dances (both in themselves and in the way they are shot and edited), in Ford highly organized, in set patterns, in Cimino improvisatory, the order at best precarious, with far greater freedom of expression—individuals choose their own movements, men dance with men, women with women, people fall over, violence erupts.

The second great poetic moment, involving the Green Beret, is built upon a direct reference to poetry: the wedding, the three "wedding guests" (though one is here the bridegroom), the "Ancient Mariner." Part of the emotional effect depends upon recognition of the allusion: the compression of the Mariner's elaborate chronicle of horrors into the succinct but eloquent "Fuck it," the fact that all three men turn away without wishing to learn, rejecting the revelation offered them. Again, the moment stands as more than omen, reflecting back on the innocence and ignorance of Clairton, on the huge banner ("Serving God and country proudly") that dominates the "wedding feast." The effect is not to endorse and romanticize the Clairton world in opposition to an as yet undefined horror outside it, so much as to comment on its insularity. The Green Beret, though he has returned to America, is no longer "of" it: totally alienated, he cannot participate, even peripherally, in the celebrations, can only retreat to the isolation of the bar's darkest corner. What he knows renders Clairton, its marriages, its traditions, its normality obsolete. In fact, the insularity of Clairton and its vulnerability to penetration from the outside are vividly established in the film's first image: the town seen huddled within the frame of a bridge that seems at once to enclose and protect it, then a huge industrial truck suddenly emerging from the foreground, charging under the bridge like a threat. The appearance at the wedding of the Green Beret at once brings to a focus such prior anticipations and itself anticipates: Nick's inability to confront Clairton and Linda after what he has seen and experienced, Steven's clinging to the protection of the veterans' hospital, Mike's reluctance to face his welcome home party, all further aspects of the theme of dwindling, are all extensions of and variations on the Ancient Mariner experience of alienation.

Andrew Britton, following Mike Westlake in *North by Northwest* 8, is clearly correct in his perception that Cimino is not much interested in the men's working-class status: what is important to him about it is presented, powerfully but very briefly, and without analysis of class structures, in the visual imagery—the inferno motif—that parallels the steel mill and Vietnam. The America of heavy industry, monopoly capitalism, and consumerism is felt from the outset as a threat to the integrity of the organic ethnic community. The point is, however, that that integrity has already deteriorated at the outset of the film: Britton's further perception that the characters are not, in what they "do or say," noticeably ethnic at once makes the point and misses it. During the wedding ceremony, Nick and Linda look clearly ill at ease and tentative in their performances with the marriage crowns; during the party, ethnic dancing rapidly gives way to racially anonymous ballroom dancing. The film establishes quite clearly the archaism of the ethnic rituals whose lingering trace continues, very tenuously, to hold the community together. The point is underlined by Nick's insistence in the Vietnam hospital that his Ukrainian surname is "American." Subsequently, the corruption of Vietnam by America (the Saigon bars and nightclubs, the prostitutes who sell themselves to American soldiers) is paralleled by the less gross, but still palpable, corruption of Clairton: the formal repetition of shots showing the Ukrainian church from the street (blocks one and three) is marked by the intrusion into the foreground of the frame of the supermarket where Linda works, with its brand name commodities and its denial of ethnic difference. The effort at the end of the film to reaffirm the sense of community is countered by our knowledge that the community is eroded beyond repair.

It is against this background of erosion that the film's presentation of the hero, the hunt, and the dominant motifs of the "one shot" and Russian roulette must be placed. The *mise-en-scène* of the hunt—grandiose landscapes, choir, hero against the skyline—is clearly a critical crux: your response to the entire film will be colored by how you read it. It seems to me further evidence of Cimino's audacity. On the one hand, it certainly cannot be taken ironically; on the other, the stylization, the break with realistic effect, is much too extreme and much too foregrounded for it simply to be read straight, the "standard emblems of romantic uplift" (Britton) being clearly placed, as it were, within quotation marks. The mode within which the sequence operates is, it seems to me, the mode of the archaic: the stylistic archaism at once embodies and places a concept of nobility and heroism that belongs to a past (perhaps a purely mythic one).

This provides the clue to the hero and the "one shot," the latter the guarantee of the hero's charismatic authority. I confess I cannot see the "curious analogy" Britton finds "between the hunt and the game of Russian roulette": we are clearly meant to make a connection, but one of opposition rather than analogy. The total control implied by the ability to kill a deer with one shot is contrasted to the total chance of Russian roulette where the bullet may be in any chamber. Britton's suggestion that Mike's drive for control is displaced on to the Vietcong is brilliant: witness the characterization of the Vietcong leader as tense, suspicious, almost hysterical, terrified—everything that Mike (apparently) isn't. At once Mike's double and Mike's opposite (Mike's control, echoing back through the whole western gunfighter/charismatic hero tradition, of Young Mr. Lincoln, Wyatt Earp, and Shane, is benevolent, the Vietcong's sadistic and destructive), he represents the impossibility of Mike's aspirations outside a limited, defined environment.

The parallel with *Rio Bravo* can be developed further. Both films are built upon the relationship between the strong, morally infallible hero and the weaker man whom he strives to save, both by example and direct intervention. In both, the director's commitment to the strong character is scarcely in question; yet the films' complexity arises partly from the way in which the weak character is used subtly to comment upon the strong one, consistently exposing the latter's limitations. Hawks admitted that *Rio Bravo* was really Dean Martin's film; a similar case can be made for suggesting that *The Deer Hunter* is really Christopher Walken's, and Cimino might be taken as confirming this by having Walken appear first in the retrospective end credits, his image summoned up by the final toast "to Nick" and the intercut shots of Mike and Linda, the two people who loved him. This is not, of course, to suggest that the film endorses Nick's capitulation to Vietnam, any more than *Rio Bravo* could be read as an endorsement of alcoholism. Yet the use of Nick to criticize Mike is consistent throughout the film. His sense of Mike's archaism is introduced near the beginning ("I don't think much about 'one shot' any more"); his sense of the presumption inherent in Mike's attitude erupts in the Vietcong camp ("Who do you think you are—God?" in response to Mike's abrupt decision that the only thing to do about Steven is to "forget him"). Finally, his suicide at the Russian Roulette table amounts to a demonstration to Mike of the irrelevance of "one shot" within a chaotic reality beyond the control of anybody.

We can now return to the crossing over of motifs and the film's architecture. Where the heroes of *Rio Bravo* and *The Searchers* succeed, Mike fails, and his failure is defined consistently in the juxtaposition of the two dominant motifs. Three scenes can be singled out.

1. *The Second Hunt.* First, Mike refrains from killing the deer, exerting his one shot control: his sense of his divine right has deserted him. Then, in the hunt, he erupts into fury at Stan and brutally forces upon him a Russian roulette game. The moment echoes the climax of *The Chase*, Calder's capitulation to mindless violence: the hero, who has always defined himself in terms of perfect (self-) control abruptly loses it, succumbing to the chaos against which he has tried to stand.

2. *The "Rescue" of Steven.* Mike's entry into the veterans' hospital to bring Steven home against his will is greeted by what sounds like a gunshot ("one shot") but proves to be the crash of a tray dropped by a nurse. The film remains noncommittal about the validity of Mike's actions—whether it is better for Steven to have to face the world or for him to remain within the security of the veterans' community. Certainly, it offers no guarantee of a positive outcome.

3. *Nick's Suicide.* That the film's architecture is no mere formalist abstraction is finally demonstrated by the way everything comes together at its climactic moment and the two dominant motifs are brought into direct confrontation, the one shot of heroic authoritarian control abruptly and with brutal irony transformed into the bullet Nick fires into his own brain from the Russian roulette gun.

The detail and tone of the film's last scene arise logically from the dual attitude it has by this point fully defined—the emotional commitment to values simultaneously perceived as obsolete. The tone has been widely misunderstood, a local failure that indicates a wider incapacity for dealing with art of any interesting degree of complexity. How one reads it is invariably presented as a simple choice between clear-cut attitudes: either the ending is affirmative or it is ironic. In fact it is neither. Its total effect depends on the organization of a number of elements that hint delicately at possibilities rather than add up to a single coherent attitude or statement (let alone "message").

1. *The Familiar Made Strange.* John's tavern has been the setting of three previous scenes (block 1, before the wedding; block 1, after the hunt; block 3, where Mike learns of Steven's return); notably, its use to close block 1 is symmetrically balanced by its use to end the film, the structure inviting us to compare the two sequences. Juxtaposed, they sum up the film's movement from plenitude to impoverishment. The final scene is haunted by the ghosts of the earlier ones, the bar that was once filled with the noise and movement of male camaraderie now hushed and subdued, spontaneity replaced by self-consciousness. The sense of strangeness is subtly confirmed by the simultaneous serving of beer and coffee, the disturbance of function and order.

2. *The Presence of Women.* The bar has previously been an exclusively male envi-

Vietnam: Robert De Niro and John Savage

ronment; the sense of strangeness in the last scene is centered on the presence of Linda and Angela. Women were also explicitly excluded from the deer hunt, and the deer hunt (at least in its symbolic "one shot" sense) has now become impossible. The inability to identify with a female viewpoint is a major weakness of Cimino's work to date (*Heaven's Gate*, despite the prominence of Isabelle Huppert's role, does not effectively contradict this). The same might, of course, be said of Scorsese, but he handles the disability much more circumspectly, perhaps because he is more aware of it. *Raging Bull* offers the female spectator a viable position, not through identification, but in its analysis of and attitude toward masculinity; *The Deer Hunter*, on the other hand, must be among the most difficult of all films for women to relate to. It is not that the film is openly or obviously misogynistic (Linda, especially, is presented as a thoroughly sympathetic character, and is invested by Meryl Streep with intelligence and dignity); rather, it is that women are marginalized without the film expressing any awareness that they are harmed by that. Nevertheless, the acceptance of the women into the male space of the tavern (and Linda drinks beer, as she did at the wedding), in the context of the breakdown of male ritual and the failure of the hero, achieves a certain resonance which the film leaves undefined.

3. *John's Bar/the Saigon Den.* It would be a long and arduous task to map the film's

whole structure of symbolic oppositions—the operation of Barthes' code of antitheses (S/Z), which also relates to Levi-Strauss' analysis of myth in terms of binary oppositions. If the film's master opposition is that of "one shot"/Russian roulette, an important subordinate (and supportive) opposition is that of Clairton bar/Saigon gambling den: both are exclusively male spaces, both places of entertainment connected to hunt and roulette game respectively, the two locations coming to dominate and epitomize the two worlds of the film. (Both Vietnam blocks juxtapose the gambling den and the Mississippi bar, with its go-go dancers and prostitution, extending the opposition.) The terms of the opposition are clear enough: the bar is the place of male togetherness, the den that of male competition and confrontation; the den is characterized by exploitation for money, the bar is run by a member of the male group (John's position, financially dependent on his friends/customers but not exploiting them for the sake of profit, closely recalls the hotel owners of Hawks' films—Dutchy in *Only Angels Have Wings*, Frenchy in *To Have and Have Not*—and their peripheral group membership); the entertainment in the bar is provided by the men for each other, a matter of conviviality and equality, while that in the den is a gladiatorial show for an audience who want blood, money, or both. In this context, the culmination of that crossing over that I have specified as one of the film's structural principles is reached in the final scene: a funeral wake, held in the bar that was earlier a place for celebration, for a man who has blown out his brains in the Saigon den.

4. "*God Bless America*": obviously the crux of the affirmation vs. irony question. The tone (and it colors the entire sequence) is in fact one of tentativeness. Dramatically, the singing develops out of John's collapse into tears as he tries to cook the omelettes; it is clear that he is weeping not just for the death of Nick, but from a much more generalized sense of loss. The song is his way of cheering himself up. It is then taken up by Linda and subsequently by the others, but the tone of the singing never becomes confident or affirmative. However, it is also plainly not ironic, and no evidence exists anywhere that the film is adopting an ironic attitude toward it. The best way to define the tone seems to be to ask exactly *what* America God is being invited to bless: at this stage of the film it can scarcely be the America that has corrupted Saigon and eroded the communal integrity of Clairton, the contemporary real America of imperialism and consumer capitalism. There are two answers, operating on different levels. First, on the level of intertextuality, the America the film defines positively is the mythic America—already riven with tensions and contradictions—of the Hawks-Ford tradition, centered on the notion of the charismatic leader-hero. Second, on the dramatic level, the only America the film has validated is that of Clairton—a community of eastern European immigrants which the dominant America has virtually destroyed. On whatever level the film is read, it is clear that if the song affirms anything, it is something already perceived as lost.

5. *Steven and Angela.* I have suggested that the film is noncommittal as to the validity of Mike's actions in returning Steven to his home. More precisely, it refuses to simplify the issue, or to suggest that there *is* such a thing as a successful resolution, preferring, again, a delicate balancing of possibilities. This is already evident in the two sequences in the veteran's hospital. From one viewpoint, the hospital is Steven's logical home where he can be part of a group with a sense of belonging; from another, there is the negative suggestion that he uses the hospital as an escape (from the sense of being a burden and from his sense of himself as castrated—the fact that he is not the father of Angela's child clearly has its importance here). At the same time, the adequacy of the feeling of community the hospital provides is seriously called into question by the use of the bingo game as its characteristic mode of entertainment. Bingo parallels Russian roulette. Both represent a surrender to chance, a refusal to be responsible for one's own destiny, the bingo game again enacting this in an innocuous (indeed, vacuous) form—a precise definition of its role in contemporary civilization.

Nothing in the final scene guarantees the couple's happiness. Again, it seems legitimate to invoke the principle of intertextuality, the reference point here being that most celebrated film of post-war recuperation (in both senses), *The Best Years of Our Lives.* The wedding that marks the culmination of Wyler's movie depends essentially on a particular notion of women, assigning them great strength so long as that strength is used in the support of men: Cathy O'Donnell's function in the film amounts to little more than that of convincing Harold Russell that he is still a man, even if he has lost his hands. No one is likely to suggest that Angela represents a positive view of women, but at least she is never reduced to *that*: her distress is her own, it is not merely for the man. The difference in tone between the Wyler and Cimino scenes can partly be accounted for in the difference between World War II and Vietnam—not merely a difference between victory and defeat, but between a war that had to be fought and one that didn't. But the difference also lies in the two films' attitude to the American notion of progress—essentially, the progress of capitalism—about which Wyler could still be affirmative, with the sense of widespread and confident popular support for such an affirmation.

Nevertheless, the refusal of affirmation and the general sense of loss and failure are qualified by two understated details. The first is when Steven, within a group shot in which the action is accorded no particular prominence, unobtrusively takes Angela's hand. The second is when Angela breaks her near-catatonic state for the first time, though all she finds to says is "It's been such a gray day."

6. *Mike/Linda/Nick.* The most problematic aspect of *The Deer Hunter*, the most difficult to get a secure purchase on, is its treatment of sexuality. Certainly, one has a strong sense that the film is blocked from doing what it wants to do (not necessarily to be equated with what Cimino wanted it to do: its logic derives from the movement of culture as much as from an individual sensibility). To put it bluntly,

it wants to define the relationship between Mike and Nick as unambiguously sexual, as well as—not instead of—spiritual, fraternal, comradely; better still, perhaps, it wants to establish the Mike/Nick/Linda triangle as bisexual (with the obvious limitation, already acknowledged, of the inability to identify with a female position). Such a project (leaving aside the question of the conscious aims and decisions of Cimino as enunciator) would have been quite impossible in 1978 and is still impossible now, given the specific historical circumstances of our culture and given the *kind* of film *The Deer Hunter* is. As soon as a film seriously raises the issue of homosexuality, it becomes precisely that—an issue—and the result is a social problem movie like *Making Love*, a movie self-consciously "about" homosexuality. The narrative of *The Deer Hunter* is posited on, largely motivated by, the love of two men for each other, but this, far from being a problem, is assumed to be unequivocally positive and beautiful; therefore, the film is compelled to permit the spectator to pretend that its sexual implications do not exist. At the same time, it leaves remarkably clear, if not always coherent or consistent, traces, so that those who wish to see may do so; they are, once again, the traces of the universal bisexuality our culture strives to repress, that is to say they are not limited to, though centered on, a single relationship.

The male love story takes clear precedence over the heterosexual romance. The phenomenon is by no means new, its periodic recurrence underlining its importance, its insistence on recognition: one might again invoke the work of Hawks— *A Girl in Every Port, The Big Sky, Rio Bravo.* (*The Big Sky* offers particularly close parallels: there, too, the women's role is essentially that of mediator between the two men.) The triangular relationship of *The Deer Hunter*, however, goes beyond the use/misuse of women in the buddy movies of the 70s; the woman is not present merely to prove that the men are not gay. The film comes as close as any to articulating her function as mediator: the men make love to her because they are barred from making love to each other; she, at the same time, is ready and able to love them both. This raises a complex issue: to argue that the film carries very strong positive overtones in relation to the acknowledgement of bisexuality is not to deny that they are achieved partly at the woman's expense. The problem belongs, absolutely, to our culture's present historical moment, and can only be resolved when the boundaries of gender construction become so blurred that men can move with ease, and without inhibition, into identification with a female position. (I put it that way deliberately: our culture's inherent sexism has always encouraged women to understand and accept the "superior" male position, while making it unnecessary and even demeaning for men to lower themselves to identifying with the female.)

Christopher Walken's persona itself mediates the cultural definitions of masculinity and femininity. His appearances in films have been diverse (he is clearly a very gifted actor, capable of a wide range of characterization), but it seems fair to say that his persona has achieved its clearest, most authentic definition in his work for Cimino and Cronenberg (*The Dead Zone*). Crucial to it is his readiness to project those properly human qualities which our culture (in the interests of the preservation of gender roles, the family, and patriarchy) chooses to label feminine: sensitivity, vulnerability, the overt display of emotions, gentleness, grace, a physical beauty divorced from any macho traits. From first to last *The Deer Hunter* realizes this more completely than any other film in which Walken has appeared: the barroom scene near the beginning, especially, draws on his background as a dancer and his grace of physical movement in Nick's spontaneous response to the song on the jukebox ("Pretty baby . . . I love you baby") within an all-male environment. The film's distinction cannot be separated from the distinction of Walken, one of the most striking and potentially subversive presences of modern American cinema.

To preserve the film's uneasy equivocation, it is essential to preserve the enigma of Mike's sexuality. His status as hero—the superiority and charisma, the mystique of the "one shot"—is intimately bound up with the connotation of chastity, the persona of virgin knight; yet he is also regarded as the possessor of superior sexual knowledge. Both sides of the contradiction are dramatized in Mike's relationship with Stan: it is Stan who reveals, in the prelude to the first deer hunt, that Mike never goes with women; it is Stan who, in the bowling alley scene, appeals to Mike for advice about the woman he has picked up (Is she beautiful? Is she intelligent?, etc.) It is also Stan who accuses Mike of being a "faggot" (a charge which Mike leaves—contemptuously? enigmatically?—unanswered). The two love scenes with Linda scarcely clarify this necessary obscurity: it is to their credit that they don't, as the only permissible clarification would be to produce Mike as unambiguously heterosexual. They are set up by Linda's suggesting that they might go to bed "to comfort each other" for the loss of Nick. In the first, Mike apparently (he may be pretending) falls asleep before Linda gets to the bed; the second, where they actually do get to make love, is entirely noncommittal, the lovemaking happening discreetly between, not within, what we are shown. It is certainly possible to read this discretion as suggesting that Mike's sexuality is something the film cannot speak.

We have seen that virtually every Hollywood film that can be read as dramatizing homosexual relationships (*Thunderbolt and Lightfoot* an honorable exception) feels the need to cover itself with a homophobic disclaimer. The use *The Deer Hunter* makes of this convention is extremely interesting. The homophobia is restricted exclusively to Stan, who is characterized above all as sexually insecure (he is incessantly preoccupied with his personal appearance and with questions as to whether he is desirable to women and whether women are desirable to him). In other words, of all the characters in the film, Stan is the only one who is presented as *threatened* by homosexuality, the other side of which is his insistence, in the safety of a public space, on dancing with Mike at the wedding.

Before the film begins, Mike and Nick have been living together in a bungalow shack that appears to have only one bedroom. What is especially interesting here is that this point, in fact virtually thrown away amid all the detail of the opening, has no narrative necessity whatever; one is licensed, then, to see its necessity as existing within a subtext.

The scene where (after the wedding, before the hunt) Mike runs down the street in front of the bridal car and strips off his clothes remains, to me, unreadable: I really have no idea what the film is trying to say at that point beyond, perhaps, connecting Mike with nature and his near-namesake the Deerslayer, Cooper's Natty Bumppo. I can accept Andrew Britton's description of the aftermath (the Mike/Nick duologue) as a "secular wedding": Nick begins by saying, about Vietnam, "Don't leave me there," then immediately emends this to "Don't leave me." But what, precisely, are we to make of Mike's stripping off his clothes? His first submission, on the eve of departure for Vietnam, to impulse, as against (self-) control? But then, to whom is this impulse directed? By what is it motivated? For whom is he stripping? One can read it, perhaps, as a protest against the entrapment in domesticity represented by marriage (Steven prevented from participating in the hunt): but such a reading easily lends itself to a further implication, the desire to return to a freer, less constricted and defined, sexuality.

The imagery offered in John's bar in the aftermath of the first deer hunt—the final image we are given of pre-Vietnam Clairton—is quite extraordinary in its suggestiveness and is the culmination of the male camaraderie already established. The men invade the bar, grab cans of beer (Nick especially prominent in this), lie on their backs, shake the beer cans, then open them so that the beer spurts out: remove the clothing, substitute real orgasms for the mock orgasms, and you have a characteristic image from a Joe Gage orgy scene. The sequence is one of the modern Hollywood cinema's most striking symbolic enactments of homosexual release, comparable to the motorbike sequence in *My Bodyguard*.

The climactic sequence of the film—that of Nick's death—is marked by Mike's twice-repeated assertion "I love you," albeit qualified the first time by "You're my friend." Nick's responses (first, to spit in Mike's face, second, to shoot himself) are perfectly consistent with a reading of the character to which I shall return.

The last shots of the film are committed, not, as the rules of classical narrative would lead one to expect, to the constitution of the surviving heterosexual couple, but to the reaffirmation of the bisexual triangle. There is no suggestion that Mike and Linda are now going to get together, indeed, the film's reticence on this point is conspicuous. Instead, following the toast to Nick, Linda looks at Mike, Mike looks at Linda, and a freeze frame on a group shot follows, succeeded immediately by the end credits which begin (unprecedentedly), not with a shot of the star of the film, but with a close-up of Nick, as the John Williams theme music returns on the guitar. The theme itself (by Williams the guitarist, not the Williams of *Star Wars* and the Boston Pops) has interesting connotations: two years before *The Deer Hunter* was released, it was popularized as a song by Cleo Laine (on the splendid

Laine/Williams album "Best Friends"), with the words "He was so beautiful." Introduced in the opening credits, the theme also dominates the Mike/Linda love scenes; its ultimate association with Nick is eloquent.

The decision to begin the end credits with Nick amounts to an admission that he, not Mike, is the true center of the film, and permits a retrospective rereading of the male love story, of Mike's status of hero, of the film's precise valuation of the Clairton community, and above all of Nick himself. The objection to this rereading is that it rests upon a hypothesis—that Nick both is *and knows himself* to be in love with Mike and that Mike reciprocates the love but can't admit it, even to himself—which the film never states: the strength of the objection, however, is undermined by the fact that the film *could not* state it. The only fair test, then, is whether the hypothesis produces a coherent reading. For the sake of clarity, I shall again tabulate the essential points.

First, in the early scene in their shared home, Nick accuses Mike of being a "control freak," specifying the "one shot" as the emblem of control. The film is quite clear that control involves control over one's emotions and over one's sexuality (Mike as virgin knight). Granted this, the whole conversation can be read as coded, concerned with the opposition between control and surrender on levels beyond the literal meaning. Nick's "I don't think about one shot that much any more" is answered by Mike's "You *have* to think about one shot—one shot is what it's all about." To this account of what the mountains, that is, nature, mean to Mike, Nick opposes an image of passivity: "I like the *trees.*" The recapitulation of this conversation during the climactic Russian roulette game, immediately prior to Nick's "suicide," confers upon it a particular retrospective significance.

Second, Nick is characterized from the outset as aware of other men's physical attractiveness or unattractiveness. One of the first intelligible lines of dialogue in the film is his "Stan—it's no use," as he sees Stan trying to beautify himself in the mirror of the factory changing room. This is taken up in his remark in the house as Mike prepares for the wedding: "You trying to look like a prince?"

Third, during the wedding party, Mike embraces, in turn, Steven and Angela; he then embraces Nick, whose response is immediately to arrange that Mike dance with Linda. The oddness of Nick's behavior is emphasized by Mike's twice-repeated, mock-incredulous, "You want me to dance?"—the virgin knight doesn't usually relax to that degree. Nick then invites the angular and somewhat horse-faced woman who earlier mistook Mike's glance at Linda for a glance at her, to dance with him. Mike then dances with Stan (watched, from the background of the shot, by Nick) before returning to Linda and suggesting they get a beer. The segment ends with Nick, still dancing with the other woman, watching them as they walk off, his face conveying a mixture of disturbance and resignation, his mouth turning down at the edges in a grimace. It is possible to read this retrospectively in terms of Nick's fear of losing Linda to Mike; it reads at the time (no suggestion of a romantic attachment to Linda having been established at that point) as a fear of losing Mike to Linda, the preceding behavior indicating his sense of being debarred from any but friendly physical contact with Mike and his use of Linda as mediator between them.

Fourth, the confusion Nick feels about Mike (he is committed to their relationship yet knows that it cannot achieve physical expression) is epitomized in his behavior in the scene where Mike strips off his clothes: after covering Mike's genitals, he turns his back on him while he dresses, then begs him "If anything happens, don't leave me over there," immediately emended to "Just don't leave me. You've gotta promise."

Fifth, the orgasmic spurting of beer in what might reasonably be called the orgy scene (the aftermath of the hunt) is actually initiated by Nick, who is shown in close shot shaking the beer cans before opening them. Subsequently, holding the can near his crotch, he shoots beer at Mike, and Mike from offscreen shoots back.

Sixth, the sequence of events in Vietnam from Nick's convalescence in the hospital to his capitulation to the world of Russian roulette offers further confirmation of the possibility of this reading. There is, first, his attempt to call home: he places the call, looks at Linda's photograph, and immediately cancels the call. The film has provided no evidence that he loves Linda (indeed, the possibilities for moments of intimacy between them at the wedding party seem systematically avoided), yet he is engaged to her: to return to Clairton is to return to Linda, not to Mike. This is followed by Nick, in the streets of Saigon, mistaking another man for Mike—a familiar enough case of wish fulfillment when there is someone we very much want to see, but in the Hollywood cinema usually associated with separated lovers (*Vertigo* is the most obvious instance). From there he goes to the Mississippi bar, where he is picked up by a young prostitute who asks what he wants to call her: he calls her "Linda," but flees abruptly from her room where her child is crying in its pen. The moment is quite adequately motivated by moral revulsion, yet, if one accepts that as sufficient explanation, the scene's narrative necessity remains unclear. From it, Nick passes straight to the gambling den, led in half against his will by another authoritative male (the Frenchman) who, like the Devil, seems to know more about what Nick wants than he does himself.

The reading I am constructing has the advantage of offering a far more precise and detailed explanation of Nick's capitulation to the world of Russian roulette than the somewhat general and commonplace Vietnam-as-trauma. We have seen that, in the film's system of symbolic oppositions, the gambling den corresponds to John's bar, as its opposite/complement and its perversion, the shooting of beer transformed into the spurting of blood. Nick, rebelling from the outset against Mike's obsession with control (one might substitute "repression"), is inevitably drawn to the world of pure chance represented by the roulette game. More important, however, it is the game Mike forced him to play in the Vietcong camp and thus from Nick's viewpoint a monstrously perverted enactment of the union he has always desired: hence his fixation on it.

Finally, every detail of Nick's behavior—every change in facial expression—during the climactic scene with Mike now makes sense. Crucial are his responses to Mike's two assertions that "I love you." The first of these, in the corridor leading to the Russian roulette room, is immediately qualified by "You're my *friend,*" whereupon Nick spits viciously in his face. The second almost saves Nick's life, then indirectly provokes his death. Confronting Nick over the roulette table, Mike repeats "I love you"—this time without qualification—and Nick suddenly appears on the verge of capitulation. Mike follows this up by talking of "the trees . . . the mountains," but this leads Nick, by association, straight back to "one shot." Mike fatally misconstrues this as a *positive* association and takes it up enthusiastically: "One shot! One shot!" Nick laughs ironically, and Mike hears the laughter but misses the irony, exclaiming "Hey!" Nick says "Yeah," detaches his hand from Mike's, and shoots himself: he has recognized that Mike offers nothing but a return to repression. (The verbal text is quite inadequate to convey the substance of this scene, and the movement of vocal inflection and facial expression is too subtle to capture even in frame enlargements; the reader is urged to look again at the film itself.)

Many critics have sensed a homosexual subtext in *The Deer Hunter* and have generally been disparaging about it; I would claim only to be the first to examine it systematically and to view it as one of the film's most positive aspects. It will be clear, however, that it is of a different order from, and much more problematic than, the homosexual subtext of *Raging Bull.* The latter pervades and indeed structures the film to the degree that one might legitimately question whether the term "subtext" is appropriate. That of *The Deer Hunter* flickers sporadically and often ambiguously (some of the instances I have listed can be satisfactorily interpreted without resorting to it), and comes into conflict with the dominant text, implying a far more critical attitude to Mike than the film explicitly defines. The conflict can be taken to represent an unresolved ambivalence in the film, a wavering between a commitment to Mike (control, repression) and a commitment to Nick (release, liberation). The wavering extends, interestingly, to the film's attitude to Clairton: it is not sufficient to see this in terms of a sentimental attachment to an idealized organic ethnic community. If, on one level, what is valued is the tradition that binds the community together (roughly corresponding to Mike and control), on another it is precisely the instability of that tradition, allowing for possibilities of change, of freedom and release.[1]

1. Raymond Williams' admirable *Marxism and Literature* (Oxford University Press, 1977) offers a very precise way of defining this tension by means of the concepts of the "residual" and the "emergent," both potentially conflicting with the "dominant," within social process.

✳ ✳ ✳

The creative methods of Scorsese and Cimino seem almost diametrically opposed. Where Scorsese starts from a small, specific, concrete subject and probes it until it reveals the widest and most radical implications, Cimino (both here and, even more obviously, in *Heaven's Gate*) starts with a grand tragic vision and fills in the details, as it were, retrospectively. If this book devotes more space to Cimino than to Scorsese, this does not imply a higher valuation of his work. Indeed, it is precisely because Cimino's work is so much more vulnerable to adverse criticism that it is necessary to defend it at length, the argument for his films becoming inevitably more complex. It must be conceded that, within the grandeur of its architecture, certain important aspects of *The Deer Hunter* remain unfocused and unrealized. The inferno imagery that connects the Clairton steel mill with the Vietnam war and the hell of Saigon is a striking rhetorical gesture that is never substantiated by any analysis of the realities of alienated labor or the relations of production under capitalism; consequently, although the film is concerned with the destruction of a certain concept of America, the internal causes of this remain very vague, the destructive forces projected on to a largely mythical Vietnam. How much weight such considerations carry in relation to acceptance or rejection of the film must depend upon the intricacies of one's aesthetic/ideological position: for Andrew Britton they define the film's failure; for me they are effectively countered (though by no means obliterated) by the impressiveness of its successes and by my sense of the engagement of a remarkable sensibility in complex and difficult material. *The Deer Hunter*'s greatness lies, perhaps, in the richness of its confusions.

HEAVEN'S GATE REOPENED

> You had the feeling you were working with Michelangelo, and he was letting you paint a stroke here.   —Kris Kristofferson on *Heaven's Gate*

Readers are probably familiar at least in outline with the history of *Heaven's Gate* so far: the disastrous simultaneous premiere in three North American cities of the original three hour forty-minute version; its immediate withdrawal from each city except New York (where it was allowed to play for a week), despite bookings for an indefinite run with advanced ticket sales; the release, several months later, of a second version edited by Cimino to a length (approximately two-and-a-half hours) specified by his producers, which played to tiny audiences and was withdrawn after a fortnight; the promise (or threat) of a ninety-minute version not edited by Cimino retitled *The Johnson County War* concentrating on action and, according to a report in *Variety*, providing a reversed sense of the original ending—the good guys win.

A few features of this astonishing debacle may be less familiar. Incredible as it seems no one at United Artists looked at the film prior to its abortive premiere. Further, Cimino insisted that the so-called original version did not fully correspond to his intentions, that he was under pressure to bring it out for the predetermined date and did not consider it ready. (If this is true, and since the running time of the second version was dictated to him, we shall never see an authentic Cimino version of the film.) Finally, American critics greeted the original version with extraordinary vituperation and ridicule, often modified but never retracted for the second version. Reviews in Britain and France contrasted notably with this reaction. It is obvious that the American response can be only partly accounted for in terms of the film's alleged deficiencies. Almost no reviewer made any attempt to examine it: instead each vied to outdo the other with sarcasm and contempt. (The only favorable account of the original version that I am aware of—a highly creditable one which has influenced this chapter—appeared in a campus newspaper of York University, Ontario, where I teach, though its author, Zachariah Cameron, was then unknown to me.)

Three factors seemingly provoked this negative response. The first concerned the much-publicized cost of the film (estimates vary from $36 to $40 million) and the hype surrounding Cimino's extravagances, juxtaposed with its failure to satisfy the demand which any TV movie hack caters to as second nature: the clear exposition of a narrative. Second, resentment combined with anxiety—resentment of the freedom granted to the relatively untested upstart Cimino on the strength of the enormous, popular, and Oscar-sanctified success of *The Deer Hunter*, which was only his second movie, and liberal anxiety about the earlier film's allegedly right-wing position. The third factor centered in dominant characteristics of the American critical establishment, wherein "the common pursuit of true judgment" is totally subordinated to the journalistic necessity of being at the forefront of the latest trend, and of being the loudest to praise or condemn whatever is fashionable according to pseudo-sophisticated bourgeois elitist taste at the time. (Such characteristics, I hasten to add, are certainly not exclusive to North America, though they flourish there in a particularly shameless and malignant form.) Clearly, Cimino's major crime is the crime within and against capitalism: not to waste money, but to waste so much. Perhaps it is useful to ask what, in this context, "waste" actually means: the expenditure would not, one feels, have been a crime if the film had been manifestly profit-making. It was not a waste to make the *Friday the 13th* movies or to make *Raiders of the Lost Ark*. In other words, this is an issue, not of morality or art, but of capitalist economics.

When the original version was shown, the hostile reaction took two forms: the objection that the narrative was so muddled that it verged on the incomprehensible, and a vague, troubled murmur about Marxist content (liberal anxiety being by no means aroused exclusively by the *right* wing). I shall return to the second point later, merely remarking for now that it is not as silly as it sounds (granted the general American paranoia about anything that could be remotely construed as Marxist) and that, rather curiously, the same murmurs have not been audible—at least, not in terms of hostile criticism—in the case of *Reds*: clearly, the principles of fashion and capitalist economics are again relevant, *Reds* being instantly perceived on both counts as a relative success.

The difficulty of the narrative does indeed constitute the film's major problem, a far more complex one than I initially recognized. I have seen the film now eight times, and the first five viewings were of the two-and-a-half-hour release version. I thought then that, although obviously very impressive, the film was open to serious objections on grounds of narrative clumsiness—that, to put it crudely, Cimino couldn't tell a story. I have come increasingly to question (without entirely abandoning) this response, though I am not sure whether this is due to my belated exposure to the original version (which is without question appreciably superior) or simply to my passing through that period of adjustment that true innovation always demands. Certainly, what looks like clumsiness in the shortened version looks far more like audacity in the original: one has the impression that Cimino's attention was focused on a great vision, a "grand design" (Kristofferson's phrase), rather than on mundane problems of telling a story. I am now not sure whether the film would gain or suffer were the major character relationships more clearly established during its first half. As it stands in both versions, we suddenly discover around the midpoint that Averill (Kristofferson) and Nate Champion (Christopher Walken) are close friends, the film having neglected up to that point to hint that they were even acquainted; Champion works for cattle baron Canton (Sam Waterston), but we never see them together until the confrontation after Ella's rape and are given no information as to what they think of each other; it is never clear exactly how or why Canton relates to Billy Irvine (John Hurt). Those who, like myself, became familiar with the shorter version first tended to assume that the ellipses must be due to cuts; but the longer version proves even *more* elliptical. There Ella (Isabelle Huppert), the central female character, doesn't appear until over a third of the way through, and her relationship with Nate (introduced quite early in the shorter version) isn't established until well beyond the midpoint.

Another way of saying that Cimino can't tell a story might be to say that *Heaven's Gate* violates some of the basic principles of classical narrative; our complaint may be simply that the story is not being told in the way to which tradition and repetition have long accustomed us. As classical narrative (perceived as ideological reinforcement) has been so much under attack during the past decade, the can-he-tell-a-story criterion would appear to have been substantially undermined, but the news has evidently not filtered down to the Kaels and Canbys. Part of the problem is, no doubt, that the film doesn't *tell* us that its narrative is going to be difficult (in the way in which, for example, a Godard movie announces this in its first few shots).

Intelligent American movies are especially vulnerable here (compare the critical and commercial failure of *Blade Runner*): the critics expect foreign films to be demanding, to make you work, whereas Hollywood films are supposed to take you by the hand and guide you safely, step by cause-and-effect step, to the final resolution, an expectation greatly encouraged by the easy indulgence most contemporary Hollywood movies offer. Whether one attributes the elliptical nature of Cimino's narrative to oversight (in the strict sense—seeing so far, one may miss what is under one's nose) or to deliberate strategy, *Heaven's Gate* seems to me one of the few authentically innovative Hollywood films (in the context of classical narrative in general, and of a cinema in particular that has always tended to build on its traditions rather than challenge them). In this respect it must be decisively distinguished from that particular brand of trendy chic, usually derived from Fellini, that passes for originality with most American critics, and of which *All That Jazz* and *The Stunt Man* are especially obnoxious instances. By using the term "authentically" I suggest that the innovativeness of Cimino's film arises from inner necessity rather than from a desire not to lag behind the latest fashion. It is absurd to suggest that the film lacks structure. Its structure is simply of an order radically different from anything to which the Hollywood cinema has conditioned us; neither does it derive from any obvious European models.[2]

Though Cimino is clearly more an intuitive than a theoretical artist, the eccentricity of his narratives can be theorized: it is not explicable solely in terms of naïveté. Especially since the rise of the novel, traditional narratives in our culture have been primarily about people and relationships; if the narrative is also about history, it is still carried forward by the evolution of individuals. In *Exodus*, for example, we are introduced to, and invited provisionally to identify with, Eva Marie Saint, and our understanding of the case for the founding of Israel is filtered through her consciousness and developed through her relationships (especially with Jill Haworth and Paul Newman) and her evolution toward commitment (she is not of course our only identification figure, but she is the central one). Crucial to this is our sense that we know all about her all the time, meet people when she meets them, change our views as she changes. More recently, and much more crudely, *Under Fire* asks us to interest ourselves *primarily* in the triangular relationship of Nick Nolte, Joanna Cassidy, and Gene Hackman, and *through* that in the struggles in Nicaragua. To delineate the precise difference between this and the method of *Heaven's Gate* is a somewhat delicate matter. After all, every scene in the film is in some sense about a character or a relationship, there is not a scene from which all the half dozen main characters are absent, and no scenes are purely concerned with mass movement or the movement of history in the manner of Eisenstein. The dif-

2. Pasolini's *Medea*, a film little known in North America, offers some striking parallels in the handling of narrative.

ference lies rather in the maintaining of a far more problematic relationship between the spectator and the individualized characters. Instead of being given the characters, as we are given Eva Marie Saint in the opening scenes of *Exodus*, we have to wait to find out about them, and their personal relationships are not granted a privileged importance. The obvious way to construct *Heaven's Gate* would have been to build the whole narrative on the Averill/Ella/Nate triangle; as it is, we don't know the triangle exists until the film is more than half over. Thus the relationship between foreground (the emotional problems of individuals) and background (the movement of history) is radically altered: the characters and their relationships continue to be important and engaging but cease to be primary, and no longer carry the narrative: instead they become components in the "grand design."

This rejection of character development as the prime means of unfolding the narrative is confirmed by a striking phenomenon of the editing of the two versions: the shorter version was arrived at not just by cutting but by transposition. Whole scenes (I consider one below) could be removed without affecting the course of the narrative; but, more significantly, passages could be lifted from one part of the film and placed in a completely different narrative context without destroying the sense (though the four-day time period of the main action, Saturday to Tuesday, is much clearer in the original version). I cite two examples: First, in the original version, Ella is introduced about a third through the film when Averill delivers her birthday present, the elegant and expensive carriage; her relationship with Nate is established long after this, when he visits the brothel, reprimands her for accepting stolen cattle as payment, finds Averill there in a drunken stupor, and takes him home before returning to spend what is left of the night with Ella. In the shorter version, this scene is split into two, the first half occurring about a half hour into the film, *before* Averill delivers the carriage. Next, the second version, the scene that introduces Nate (the shooting of Michael Kovacs) is followed almost immediately by his confrontation with the immigrant boy he catches stealing a steer, which elides with his assault on his fellow mercenary for his attitude to immigrants. In the original, these three scenes occur, widely separated, in three different parts of the film, the third following a scene of laborious communal plowing that does not appear at all in the second version.

Clearly, Cimino regards these segments as movable building-blocks: they have a necessary place in the overall design, but it is no longer the fixed place dictated by the strict cause and effect of classical narrative, the relationships between the parts being conceived as far more fluid and open. Though the film is in no obvious way self-reflexive, we are given the sense of being allowed to participate imaginatively in its construction, to use our own judgment in making connections back and forth. It is like watching a painter create an immense fresco: he may not start at top left and end at bottom right, but by the end we see how everything falls into place, how this relates to that; we may even feel that the fresco is not quite complete, that there are patches of wall left uncovered, or that, if the wall were larger, the fresco could be indefinitely extended. And, although the film is in no obvious way Brechtian, each of the components—each building block, the architectural metaphor being especially apposite to Cimino—constitutes a separate, lucid, and forceful "history lesson": about privilege, about poverty, about compromise, about being unprepared, about power, about community, about collective action, about the betrayal of the poor by a rising bourgeoisie, about the destruction of a possible alternative America by the one that is so much with us.

Consider, as a random example, the wonderful little scene (cut from the second version) in which Averill, returning to Coldwater in Ella's carriage, encounters on the road a widow and her children struggling to pull a heavy cart containing the murdered body of her husband, executed by Canton's mercenaries. The scene has no narrative necessity; it is not a link in any chain of cause and effect. Its only narrative function (a redundant one) is to reiterate Averill's quandary as marshal in a community where power and law are coming increasingly apart, his professional position committing him to the latter while his class position aligns him with the former. Consummately realized in terms of pure cinema, the scene is really about the discrepancy between the help Averill promises from his position as Marshall and his failure to offer help on an immediate, concrete level—that is, to delay his visit to Ella and help push. Everything important in the scene is conveyed, not by or even through dialogue, but in visual counterpoint to it. We can specify three precisely achieved effects: the crosscut exchange of looks between Averill and the two children; the Averill point-of-view shot of the road winding into the far distance; the final intercutting of Ella's carriage and the cart as Averill and the woman resume their journeys. That Averill is a sympathetic character (indeed, the film's nominal hero), that Ella will be delighted with her gift, and that we shall be encouraged to share in that delight in a scene of great charm, vivacity and tenderness are factors that add to rather than detract from the complex force of this concise, self-contained, practical lesson about poverty and privilege and the practical difficulties of commitment.

One can further define the particularity of the film's narrative method by reference to the codes of classical narrative enumerated by Roland Barthes in S/Z. Traditionally, at least in Western cinema, the dominant codes of narrative have been the linear ones: the proairetic (code of actions) and hermeneutic (code of enigmas), whose function it is to carry the story forward and maintain the reader/viewer's curiosity. Indeed, the tendency of much determinedly progressive, and in some respects effectively reactionary, theorizing has been to reduce classical Hollywood film to the operation of these two codes. Noel Burch's account, in his brilliant and infuriating book on Japanese cinema *To the Distant Observer*, is typical: "Each of these infrastructural signifiers had one and only one corresponding meaning. Each was concatenated in a one-to-one relationship with its immediate neighbors in the chain and, through these, with the totality of the chain as it stretched into the 'past' and 'future' of the narrative" (p. 97). Most current assaults on classical narrative, conceived as entrapping the reader/viewer in a closed ideological position, are in effect assaults on the dominance of the linear codes. Cimino audaciously downgrades them: the privileged codes in *Heaven's Gate* are the semantic (the code of implied meanings out of which the work's thematic structure is developed) and the symbolic (usually functioning in terms of oppositions, in which *Heaven's Gate* is particularly rich)—hence again the basis of an overall structure that transcends the mere what-happens-next of linear narrative.

The point can be exemplified very precisely by reference to a line of dialogue not in the original version but dubbed in for the release version, a decision that testifies eloquently to the tyranny of the linear codes. At the film's opening, before the graduation ceremony and celebrations, Averill says to Irvine "Still coming to Wyoming with me, Billy?" It is the only line in the entire Harvard sequence that explicitly points ahead to any subsequent events; it establishes immediately a coming action (journey to Wyoming) to keep the audience interested, which can be supposed to produce its own ensuing chain of actions; and it introduces a group of enigmas (Why Wyoming? Will Billy go, too? What will they do there? What will happen?) which the film, with its abrupt twenty-year time leap, will signally fail to resolve in any way the audience might anticipate. The main function of the proairetic and hermeneutic codes is to facilitate the work of reading: an action is announced, and we know it will be developed and carried to a conclusion, that it will lead to further actions; at the same time, the play of enigmas will keep us guessing what will happen, focusing our attention on events, outcomes, solutions. We attend to what is actually before us not for itself but for what it will lead to: we are continually pointed ahead, given enough hints to formulate a general sense of probable developments but never enough to give us certainty or preclude surprises.

Cimino, on the contrary, invites us first to immerse ourselves in and contemplate the action that is happening in the present (such as, during the Harvard sequences, the dance, the ritual battle) and then later (perhaps much later) to reassess it and our reactions to it in the light of subsequent actions. While the big set pieces might be taken to invite a simple surrender to the immediate creation of mood, the film as a whole will make no sense to us if our engagement is not continuously active and analytical. The line about Wyoming (though too casual and thrown away to be seriously disruptive) has the effect of distracting us from the matter in hand and insidiously reassuring us that we needn't think about it too much: the question "What am I being shown?" tends to be superseded by "What's going to happen next?" The American critics, in ridiculing Cimino's presumed ineptness at storytelling, were partly rejecting a valid and innovative rethinking of the codes and strategies of classical narrative.

A similar point can be made in relation to the frequent complaint (expressed far more vociferously by those who saw the original version, and generally linked to assertions about self-indulgence offered in terms of personal affront) that this or that sequence goes on too long. Too long, we must ask, in relation to what? The only answer can be, to the making of narrative points—that is, to the efficient operation of the proairetic/hermeneutic codes. The roller-skating scene is the ideal example, because (if one thinks of narrative in purely linear terms) it is virtually superfluous *in toto*: the action represents no necessary link in an ongoing chain, the scene neither develops/resolves any previously introduced enigmas nor establishes new ones. One might compare it and the "Blue Danube" sequence in this respect with the (justly) celebrated ball scenes in *The Magnificent Ambersons*, Minnelli's *Madame Bovary*, and *Madame De . . .* , none of which, needless to say, can be *reduced* to the operation of the linear codes, but all of which can be very precisely explicated and justified by reference to them. I wish to establish here not superiority (on either side) but difference: the linear codes have become so completely naturalized through our experience of classical literature and film that we are likely to have great difficulty in perceiving them as codes at all, but their dominance is not sacrosanct. As soon as one accepts this, the whole question of duration (how long is too long?) is automatically reopened, and criteria we take for granted can be recognized as a matter of long conditioning.

Of course, this does not in itself constitute a defense of Cimino's work, but I think it forms a basis on which a defense can be raised. If the linear narrative of the film is problematic, it nonetheless displays a marvelous feeling for essential structure—the feeling for structure that transforms linear narrative into symbolic drama. One may agree with Andrew Britton that within the big set pieces analysis is sacrificed to the creation of mood. Cimino's *mise-en-scène* is not analytical in the manner of Ford, for example, as is obvious if one compares *The Deer Hunter*'s wedding reception with the church floor dance in *My Darling Clementine* or the noncommissioned officers' ball in *Fort Apache*. The entire method of filming and editing is fundamentally different, Cimino prodigally shooting vast amounts of material from which the sequence is extracted, as against Ford's famous economy ("editing in the camera"). At times, indeed, Cimino seems to use the élan of a scene to distract the spectator from asking awkward questions. The roller-skating birthday celebration in *Heaven's Gate*, for example, generates such infectious energy that one has little chance to ask why Ella is suddenly accepted without qualification by a community that only a few minutes earlier appeared to be more than somewhat divided about her: here analysis seems not merely sacrificed but willfully obliterated. However, Cimino's big impressionist blocks never exist solely for themselves—for all the obvious delight in orchestrating movement and developing rhythms—and, in a somewhat different sense, analysis may be said to transpire *between* the set pieces: what becomes crucial is their structural relation to each other. In other words, the analysis is not offered us as passive spectators; we are encouraged to construct it, as active participants.

Before considering the film's overall architecture, however, I want as preparation to examine the Harvard prologue in some detail. In both versions it has been particularly singled out for its alleged redundancy (and may be expected to disappear altogether from *The Johnson County War*, if indeed that mutation ever materializes). It seems to me crucial to the meaning and structure of the film. There are nine points to be made:

1. The much-criticized use of Oxford for Harvard works very much to the film's advantage as soon as one begins thinking of it in terms of symbolic drama/national myth rather than of realistic historical reconstruction: it adds a nondiegetic level to the creation of Harvard as essentially an Old World, European culture, characterized by obsolete rituals, value structures, modes of comportment, and societal relations.

2. In a film generally regarded as structurally unsound, the very first shots (Averill's frantic run through the deserted college grounds to catch up with the graduation parade), underlined in the shorter version by the addition of a line of dialogue ("Late again, James?"), establish at the very outset both the defining mark of the film's central character (Averill will be "late again" in committing himself at every crucial point in the film on the political and personal levels) and one of its central thematic concerns.

3. The graduation parade marching tune (the "Battle Hymn of the Republic," also familiar as "John Brown's Body"), with its associations with the abolition of slavery, provides an important (and, in retrospect, bitterly ironic) link between the Harvard prelude and the shift to Wyoming: when Averill, after the twenty-year time lapse, gets off the train at Casper and watches its load of poverty-stricken immigrants descending from the roof, we hear a melancholy, tentative version of the same music on a solitary guitar. The link underlines the cultural clash, centered in Averill's consciousness, between the complacent, privileged Harvard culture and the economic-political realities of the nation at large. (After the Harvard scenes, the film abandons all grandiloquent music: David Mansfield's marvelously evocative score never employs more than a handful of instruments, and never attempts the grandiose musical gestures usually expected of the Hollywood epic.)

4. Cimino's use of Oxford architecture, with its narrow archways, high walls, and enclosed quadrangles, not only establishes the sense of an Old World tradition, but also emphasizes that tradition's insularity: it can flourish only in total detachment from an outside world. Harvard, based on class and privilege, becomes a dream from which the plunge into Wyoming is the rude awakening.

5. The valedictory address of the Reverend Doctor, far from being some kind of irrelevant period piece or local color adornment, establishes concerns crucial to the film's thematic development, though not in any simplistically didactic way: Cimino's method rigorously eschews any direct Author's Message, everything in the film being enacted rather than stated. The casting of Joseph Cotten is significant, the actor being primarily associated (the Welles films, *Duel in the Sun, Beyond the*

From Harvard . . .

. . . to Wyoming

Forest) with likable but ineffectual characters. On the one hand, the speech is placed retrospectively by the cultural realities Averill discovers in Wyoming, realities which render obsolete the earnest and pious injunctions to bring culture to the uncultivated. This missionary notion of high culture and of the educational responsibilities of those who have it to bring it to those who don't will give place, in the course of the film, to the awareness of a social-political situation that could be redeemed only by the communal and revolutionary action of the common people working in solidarity. On the other hand, Cimino uses the speech to reflect upon the students—bored, indifferent, clowning, impatient for the festivities, they testify to the justice of the Reverend Doctor's sense that this is not an age in which "thought and meditation" flourish. Related to Averill's habitual hesitation and delay, and central to the film's tragic vision of America, is the notion of unpreparedness, the failure of the right people to think and act in union against an exploitative and oppressive regime that knows exactly what it is doing—a concern of pressing contemporary relevance in the context of Reaganite America.

6. Much critical abuse of the "What's he doing in the movie?" type has been heaped upon John Hurt (both the actor and the character he plays): he seems so incongruous, so "out of things." This is precisely the point, though Cimino, characteristically, doesn't feel the need to spell it out. Obviously, Billy Irvine is meant to be a relatively recent immigrant (though a rich and privileged one in contrast to the starving Wyoming masses), an Englishman whose upbringing has left him hopelessly unprepared and ill-equipped for the situations in which he finds himself. The point seems so elementary that one is amazed the critics missed it, presumably because they were not told: it is the practice of classical Hollywood always to establish or confirm plot points in explicit dialogue. We are never told that Irvine is English. Nor are we told that Ella Watson is French: Cimino expects us to be able to read the evidence of their accents. Irvine's own fear of his inability to cope produces the Harvard scene's most poignant moment, a characteristic Cimino modulation: the expression on his face when, the mock-battle over, his nose bloodied, and Averill's protective arm around his shoulders, he suddenly registers that this is the last night of Harvard security. Again, we are not *told* that he is thinking this, but context, mood and *mise-en-scène* make it impossible to read it otherwise. The sense of double-edged critique established in the Reverend Doctor's speech is developed in Billy's response as class orator, which is totally cut from the second version— another building block, expendable in terms of telling the story, with its place in the grand design. Billy's wasted brilliance (a theme taken up when he sadly quotes his own past, abandoned poetry to Averill in the billiard room of the Association's club) is suggested in the speech's simultaneous vivacity, cynicism and irresponsibility: he undermines the earnest pieties of the Reverend Doctor but offers nothing in their place. Billy's place in the film's overall scheme should be clear enough: relating to both Averill and Canton, he embodies a third upper-class response to the social-

political situation, his aesthete's conscience making it impossible either to accept or effectively revolt against Canton's Fascist brutalities, so that he can only escape into nihilism and alcohol. The magnificent shot that closes part 1 of the original version eloquently expresses the sense of tragic waste: whisky flask to his lips, Irvine vanishes into the dust raised by Canton's horses.

7. The "Blue Danube." It is essential to the method of *Heaven's Gate* that the attitude to the class/wealth/privilege of Harvard culture is never spelled out for us, but only becomes evident retrospectively from the film's overall structure. Nothing in the presentation of the Harvard celebrations compels us to view them negatively or ironically: rather we are encouraged up to a point to become directly involved in them, to share in the innocent pleasures of the participants, so that the rude awakening of Wyoming shall be ours also. Hence the stylistic strategies of the "Blue Danube" sequence. Cimino's camera work and editing have a dual function: to involve us in the dance uncritically while preserving the possibility of distance and detachment. For the most part, camera movement and editing participate in and enhance the formal patterns of the dance: the sequence is edited to the music, and the choice of camera distance is consistently linked to the holdings back and rushings on of the waltz's pulse. Yet the sequence is introduced by a lengthy crane shot over the dance in long shot and high angle that invites us to survey from a distance and a height, and at the climax Cimino cuts back to a similar high-angle, long-shot position.

8. Significantly, the culture of class and wealth is also presented in terms of gender inequality. The women serve a double function: posed decoratively in the gallery of the senate chamber and subsequently within the frame of a high window they are beautiful objects to be gazed at, and they are there to look on, passively but admiringly, at the exploits of the men from whose glories they are excluded (the graduation ceremony, the mock-battle). They do not choose, they are chosen: it is Averill who negotiates the change-of-partners that secures him the woman he wants.

9. Most important of all, the Harvard prologue establishes the major unifying motifs—the dance, the battle, the circle, and the tree—on whose permutations the structure of the entire film is built. The two parts of the Harvard celebration comprise the dance and the battle. These are recapitulated, with significant variations, in the film's other two major set pieces: the roller-skating party and the final cattle baron/immigrant battle. The sequences are linked by the obvious similarities of action as well as by the motif of the circle: the dancers at Harvard circle a tree, the roller skaters a central pillar (which is also the stove that heats the hall); in the Harvard ritual battle Averill leads the attack on a group entrenched around a tree, and at the film's climax this pattern is repeated exactly. The parallels have the function of foregrounding the systematic opposition from which the essential meaning—the thematic/symbolic progress—of the film arises.

The Dances. The Harvard dance is to cultured European music (the "Blue Danube") performed by a full offscreen orchestra, and takes place amid stone-walled surroundings defined as the exclusive preserve of the wealthy and privileged. The participants are dressed in elegant formal wear that constitutes a class uniform, and their movements are also formal, dictated by the set patterns of the dance. Heterosexual relations are defined in terms of male competition and ownership; the dance celebrates the success (graduation) of a group defined as male, rich, and socially privileged. Characteristically, the class basis of all this is not analyzed or commented upon in the *mise-en-scène*; indeed, the tone of the whole sequence is nostalgic and celebratory, with the viewer invited to surrender to the visual beauty and the intoxication of music and graceful movement. Between the Harvard dance and the roller skating, however, comes the shock of the plunge into Wyoming, with its pervasive violence, poverty, bitterness, overt exploitation, and domination, its endless treks of houseless immigrants. The rude awakening (for the audience as much as for the characters) parallels the shock of *The Deer Hunter*'s plunge into Vietnam, while being quite different in meaning. (The political enormities of the earlier film are totally avoided in *Heaven's Gate*, which may indeed be read as Cimino's apology for them.)

The music for the roller-skating scene is indigenous rural American, performed by a small group of on-screen musicians on equal terms with the dancers; the sense that they are performing not so much for as with the dancers is confirmed when the young fiddle player joins the skaters. The dance takes place within "Heaven's Gate" itself (through which only the rich cannot enter)—the all-purpose community assembly hall also used for political meetings, site of the later attempt to found an embryonic democratic/cooperative society to oppose the landbarons. The participants wear a wide variety of informal functional clothing, classless in its connotations; their movements, allowing for the limitations imposed by roller skates and a crowded floor, are freely inventive and spontaneous, conforming to no predetermined patterns and expressing individual creativity within a community of equals. If the dance has a central figure and a specific function beyond pleasure, it is Ella and the celebration of her birthday: as the brothel keeper and prostitute who clearly enjoys her work (the film makes clear that she doesn't sell herself indiscriminately), she has slept with many of the men present. In the course of the film, Ella not only maintains her right to choose her customers (hence, by contrast, the horror of the rape scene), but asserts her capacity for loving two men on equal terms: it is they (Walken and Kristofferson) who impose choice on her.

The Battles. The Harvard battle is a student ritual: one group clusters in a tight circle around a tree to defend the prize, a bouquet of flowers; Averill leads the charge to smash through the circle. The class status of attackers and defenders is equal; the worst harm that befalls anyone is a bloody nose, and the attackers win

Heaven's Gate

Isabelle Huppert and Kris Kristofferson

Rollerskating

the battle. No women participate: arranged and framed as in a painting, they watch admiringly from a high window.

The final battle is desperate warfare: a struggle for survival and on the symbolic level for an American identity centered on equality and cooperation. Averill has abandoned his class to aid the oppressed, and donates the resources of his education to supervise the attack of the immigrants against their persecutors and would-be exterminators. His contribution of Roman tactics becomes an ironic realization of the Reverend Doctor's exhortation to the graduates to bring culture to the people. Engaging physically on equal terms as earlier they engaged politically, the women fight beside the men. Where the Harvard sequence culminates in Averill's triumph, here victory is abruptly frustrated in a stroke that eloquently uses the conventions of the western in order to invert their meaning as well as the whole set of historical/ideological assumptions that supports it: the U.S. cavalry rides in to the rescue, but on the wrong side.

* * *

Cimino's naïveté is not restricted to his handling of classical narrative; it extends to every level of the film and is quite inseparable from its positive qualities (actually, amid the cynicism, opportunism and weary reactionism of so much 80s Hollywood cinema, a little naïveté comes as a welcome relief). The alleged Marxist content does not progress very far beyond what is implicit in the saying of Christ to which Cimino's title refers. It might better be described as an adolescent idealism—an idealism that has the courage of its own convictions and that combines idiosyncratically with other very different qualities, such as a pervasive elegiac melancholy, a sense of irreparable loss and failure, to make the film's fusion of innocence and experience so haunting. On a personal level, this sense of loss is dramatized in the triangular relationship between Averill, Nate Champion and Ella, who loves both men and is quite prepared to go on doing so. (It is part of the film's great interest that it tentatively raises through Ella the possibility of new and less restrictive forms of sexual relationship, though it doesn't follow this through.) Cimino's mastery of emotional effect (which is never arbitrary or opportunistic, but an aspect of essential structure) is shown again in the scene of Nate's death at the hands of the cattle barons and their mercenaries. The poignancy of the scene arises from its bringing together two emblems that have accumulated rich emotional resonance through association: Nate's log cabin, which he has recently beautified with wallpaper (in fact, newspaper pages) in the hope of bringing Ella into it as his bride, and the improvised fire wagon the mercenaries use to burn it down, in fact the carriage Averill gave Ella for her birthday. The emblems evoke the moments of Ella's greatest happiness in the two men's love for her.

But the film is about loss in national as well as personal terms, its distinction lying in the way it counterpoints and connects the two. It is an elegy for a possible alternative America destroyed before it could properly exist by forces generated within, yet beyond the control of, democratic capitalism. If *Heaven's Gate* contains an embryonic Marxist content, it is in its playing down of the heroic individual and its emphasis on the communal action of the common people (here the immigrant farmers) shown groping toward the formation of a socialist democracy—the solidarity of citizens of many nationalities (tending, like Nate and Ella, to stress their belief in America by adopting "American" names) and both sexes (the women playing as active a role as the men). The central characters are all, to varying degrees, denied full heroic status in the American tradition. Billy Irvine, who has the shrewdest, most privileged awareness of what is going on, is also the most ineffectual, hopelessly compromised by his position among the powerful; Nate remains, until too late, a servant of the system, disowning his own immigrant status in the service of the established rich, his eventual rebellion more personal than political in motivation; Ella is destroyed because, as brothel owner, she tries to exploit the system without challenging it; and Averill, the film's apparent hero figure, at every point acts too late, a motif established at the very beginning of the film. Similarly, Canton is denied the status of archvillain (the unexpected casting of Sam Waterston, an excellent but not exactly charismatic actor, works beautifully): personally insignificant, his power derives solely from his wealth and class position.

The film also develops the inquiry into the validity of the individual hero that was complexly initiated in *The Deer Hunter*. I wondered how Cimino would follow up the earlier film's insight into the archaism of the individual hero: whether, indeed, in the context of American commercial cinema it could be followed up, as opposed to endlessly reiterated. The move in *Heaven's Gate* toward a concept of the people-as-hero is at once perfectly logical and totally unexpected. It is necessary, however, to stress "move toward": the film, on this level too, is not without its uncertainties and confusion. Averill delays his engagement on the side of the farmers (as he delayed proposing to Ella—again, the personal story closely parallels the political) until the battle appears to be lost; he is nonetheless still able to rally the disintegrating forces and lead them on in the final, almost triumphant charge. If this, too, proves useless, it is less because the individual hero has been effectively discredited than because the powers of monopoly capitalism are too strong.

The relationship of *Heaven's Gate* to *The Deer Hunter*, and of both to the Ford-Hawks tradition, is far from simple. The earlier film celebrates a community already on the verge of disintegration from internal tensions as much as from external pressures, the later a community in the process of forming and defining itself. While both communities function to some degree as myths of America, that of *The Deer Hunter* is shown to exist in isolation from the rest of the nation (one of the conditions both of its continuance and of its precariousness), while the question of

national identity is at stake in *Heaven's Gate*. An obvious reference point here, in relation especially to the roller-skating party, is, again, the church-floor dance in *My
Darling Clementine*. As Douglas Pye suggested in "John Ford and the Critics," the
myth of America embodied in Ford's film, while wishing to appear inclusive, in fact
depends on the tacit suppression of a number of elements in the film's overall symbolic structure (not just the Clantons, but Doc Holliday and, most significantly,
Chihuahua); the dance, while expressing energy, also contains it, repressing by exclusion what can't be safely contained. The energy expressed in the roller-skating scene
is not contained within formal dance patterns, and the only people excluded are the
repressive rich. Further, the dance is associated with sexual freedom through its
being centered on Ella, who magically fuses the opposites (Clementine, Chihuahua)
that in Ford were irreconcilable. Moreover, no sense of hierarchy exists: when (as in
Clementine) the marshal joins the dance, no one has to "sashay back" to make way
for him, the dance is not interrupted, and he becomes one of the crowd. Instead,
one has a celebration of individual skills within a community of social equals as
exemplified in the simultaneous skating and fiddle playing of Ella's young male servant (an enigmatic figure of great physical beauty, whose precise status and function
in the brothel are left tactfully undefined). Certainly, the absence of analysis makes
possible the scene's nature as wish fulfillment—a quality that seems acknowledged
by the shift, in the original but not the release version, from a full color range to sepia
monochrome; but the myth of community celebrated here remains very suggestive
and engaging in relation to the dichotomies of the western genre.

    The final comparison *Heaven's Gate* invites is with *Birth of a Nation*. I must say
immediately that despite the status of Griffith's film as classic (or museum piece—
it is of course much more than that, but its monumentalization within film culture
certainly creates barriers to any immediacy of response), I see no reason to suppose
it is the greater of the two works. I think *Heaven's Gate* rivals it, not only in sweep
and ambition, but in realization. And if *Heaven's Gate* has ideological problems,
what are we to say of *Birth of a Nation*? (Or is a museum piece somehow trans-
muted beyond ideological responsibility?) Like Griffith's film, *Heaven's Gate*
belongs in obvious respects to the epic genre: it is a vast, ambitious, extravagant
work concerned with immense issues of national identity and national destiny. It
is, however, a very unusual kind of epic. Virtually all epics, from the *Iliad* and the
Aeneid to *El Cid* and *Exodus* (and including *Birth of a Nation*), have been celebrations of achievement, and in particular national or imperialist achievement (though
they may also be centrally concerned with the cost of the achievements they celebrate). *Heaven's Gate* is an epic about failure and catastrophe, both personal and
national. It might almost have been called *Death of a Nation*, and one can readily
grasp that it is the last film that people who flock to *Star Wars*, *Raiders of the Lost
Ark* and *E. T.* would wish to see, as it offers no reassurance or comfort whatever.
Birth of a Nation celebrates an America established upon the denial of Otherness

(the Klan/blacks opposition clearly paralleling that of cavalry/Indians in the classical western), and centered on family/monogamy/purity, involving the simultaneous idealization and subordination of (white) women. *Heaven's Gate* shows the destruction of a possible alternative America (one located in the historic past, but bearing in its values striking resemblances to the radical movements of the 60s and 70s): a democracy in which Otherness is accepted and valued, in which women become the equals of men, in which sexual arrangements have at least the potential to become nonpossessive and noncoercive, and in which the family is subordinated to the collective community.

Valid objections to *Heaven's Gate* can be raised beyond its alleged deficiencies as readily accessible narrative. Particularly, Ella (not merely the Perfect Whore but the Perfect Woman, sweet, spontaneous, endlessly giving, and, in the swimming scene, an earth mother/nature goddess) is clearly a figure of adolescent male fantasy, and the idealization of the whorehouse is not free of sentimentality. Yet the very innocence of the vision, and the candor with which Cimino offers it, are inseparable from the film's energies. Cimino succeeded strikingly in communicating the idealism to Isabelle Huppert, whose performance is so responsive that the fantasy comes closer to validation than my description would give one any right to expect; in *Heaven's Gate* she is able to express a side of her personality—vital, exuberant, active—that was consistently repressed in her work for Goretta, Téchiné, Godard, etc. All this makes more appalling the rape of Ella and the slaughter of her whores at the hands of Waterston's mercenaries, in the name of a morality clearly determined by money interests (Ella accepts stolen cattle as payment). The tragic statement the film offers, while concerned with choices and failures in the distant (and largely mythical) American past, takes on particular resonance in the context of the Reagan administration, with its shameless bolstering of the rich camouflaged and given spurious validity by its "moral" crusade: the present political context makes Cimino's conception of the film, some years ago, curiously prophetic. For me, the sheer beauty of *Heaven's Gate*—expressed through, but by no means confined to, its rich, elegiac images—makes all objections secondary. It seems to me, in its original version, among the supreme achievements of the Hollywood cinema.

. . . and Beyond

14.

Day of the Dead

THE WOMAN'S NIGHTMARE

I dealt in chapter 6 with the first two films of George Romero's "living dead" trilogy; the third, *Day of the Dead* (1985), had not then been made. The following account should be read in conjunction with the earlier chapter.

It is perhaps the lingering intellectual distrust of the horror genre that has prevented George Romero's "living dead" trilogy from receiving full recognition for what it undoubtedly is: one of the most remarkable and audacious achievements of modern American cinema, and the most uncompromising critique of contemporary America (and, by extension, Western capitalist society in general) that is possible within the terms and conditions of a "popular entertainment" medium. *Day* is not merely the conclusion of the trilogy (which Romero has long planned to transform into a tetralogy, if he could raise the necessary finance); it is also its "clincher," in many respects the most remarkable of the three films. One must, therefore, begin by accounting for its generally negative critical reception and its commercial failure, especially striking given the critical and popular success of *Dawn of the Dead* (1979).

Day belongs to the 80s as surely as *Dawn* to the 70s, but its relation to its period is quite different. *Dawn* was fully compatible with certain progressive aspects of its time, the period of the great radical movements (women's liberation, the black movement, gay rights . . .) that challenged the basic ideological assumptions of the culture. *Day* represents an uncompromisingly hostile response to the 80s, both to Reaganite America and to the cinema it produced. We can now look back on *Dawn* with a certain nostalgia for the exhilaration and excitement of a past age; *Day* is if anything more relevant today than it was when it appeared, as things have only got progressively blacker and more desperate, and events are currently escalating into a world situation of which the end of life on the planet (whether through nuclear war or the pollution of the environment) seems a not unlikely outcome.

The film's resonance relates not only to the political evolution of America but to the evolution of its mainstream cinema. Since the Reaganite takeover and its increasingly reactionary sequels, Hollywood has become indeed the "Dream Factory" for which intellectuals always mistook it. Films are now financed, produced, and controlled largely by the massive corporations and conglomerates that are threatening our world with devastation in the interests of "making money"; the function of Hollywood has become simply that of "keeping people happy" and inhibiting thought. The contemporary "action" film—with its mind-numbing special effects, its computer-generated spectacle, its interminable mayhem, crashes, explosions, its reduction of what used to be characterization to expressions on actors' faces, and above all its rapid editing that allows no breathing space for reflection—exemplifies merely one dismaying aspect among many: the teen films, the gross-out comedies, the painting-by-numbers romantic comedies . . . *Day* confronted not only the false, manufactured optimism of its period but also the cinema's reinstatement of masculinism as a central issue: the Rockys, the Rambos, the Chuck Norris and Schwarzenegger movies, the popular response to feminism (accompanied by feminism's gradual absorption, suitably modified, into the dominant ideology). It was the last film a public duped into heaving a vast communal sigh of relief that radicalism was no longer necessary wanted to see. On the topic of masculinity it is absolutely unequivocal.

In my discussion of the trilogy's first two films I pointed out the triangular structure of the character-groups: in *Night of the Living Dead* (1968), zombies/besieged/sheriff's posse; in *Dawn of the Dead*, zombies/besieged/motorcycle gang. *Day* repeats the structure but with somewhat different contents. Here, each member of the central group of sympathetic, progressive characters is initially attached to one of the three major groups (zombies/scientists/military): Sarah is a scientist, her lover Miguel a soldier; John, the West Indian, flies the military helicopter; the Irishman Bill McDermott is the electronics expert. All, in other words, are connected or belong to an authority group. In the course of the film they progressively dissociate themselves, by their actions and their attitudes, from these nominal allegiances, forming an oppositional group of their own.

The increasing bleakness and desperation of the trilogy—scarcely an unreasonable response to the Reagan era, and certainly not a hysterical one (*Day* is a perfectly controlled movie)—is marked most obviously by the increasing power of the zombies. In *Night* they could still, apparently, be contained (though the film's attitude to the forces of containment remained resolutely negative and ironic); in *Dawn* they appeared to be getting the upper hand, though the surviving characters could still fly off, with the possibility that there might be somewhere safe where resistance was still feasible. In *Day* they have taken over the world, outnumbering the humans (according to calculations by Sarah's immediate superior, Dr. Logan) by 400,000 to one; the only safe place left to fly to is a desert island that may exist only in fantasy. But perhaps the most significant progression from *Dawn* to *Day* lies in the images of money: in *Dawn* it was still worth helping oneself from the mall bank, "just in case"; in *Day*, money blows about the abandoned city streets, so much meaningless paper.

It was in *Dawn* that the zombies were first defined as "us," and the definition is taken up in *Day*, though now only by the film's monstrous scientist, embodying his "scientific" view of human nature. The implications of this definition need to be carefully pondered, as it is obviously both true and false. The zombies are human beings reduced to their residual "instincts": they lack the functions that distinguish true humans, reason and emotion, the bases of human communication and human society. (The zombies throughout the trilogy never communicate, or even notice each other, except in terms of an automatic "herd" instinct, following the leader to the next food supply). The characters in all three films are valued precisely according to their potential to differentiate themselves from the zombies, their ability to demonstrate that the zombies are *not* in fact "us." Something clearly needs to be said about my use of the term "residual instincts." I am not referring here (and neither is the film, despite Dr. Logan's commitment to such essentialist notions) to some God- or nature-given human essence. Certainly one might claim the need for food as a "natural" instinct, but *Day* is quite explicit on that score: "They don't eat for nourishment." What we popularly call "instincts" are in fact the product of our conditioning, and the residual instincts represented by the zombies are those conditioned by patriarchal capitalism. Above all, they consume *for the sake of consuming* (a revelation of *Day*—it was not apparent in the earlier films); all good capitalists are conditioned to live off other people, and the zombies simply carry this to its logical and literal conclusion. But it is through "Bub," Dr. Logan's prize zombie pupil, that the theme is most fully developed. What Bub learns, through a system of punishments (beatings) and rewards (raw human flesh) that effectively parodies the basis of our educational system, is "the bare beginnings of civilized behavior": in fact, the conditioned reflex. It is Logan's thesis—his hope for the human future—that the zombies can be trained, and to prove it he trains Bub to perform precisely the actions he was trained to perform in life, saluting and firing guns, subservience and violence, obeying orders without questioning them. The full savagery of the film's irony can be gauged from the fact that Bub also responds, with the same automatism, to Beethoven's "Choral" Symphony. Indeed, Schiller's "Alle Menschen werden Bruder" takes on multiple ironic connotations in relation to all the film's major groups—soldiers, scientists, zombies; and his (already thoroughly conditioned) sexism, which verbally excludes women from the universal "brotherhood," receives its implicit answer in the trilogy's progressive emphasis on women, to which I shall return.

First, however, I want to take up a point from the only review of *Day of the Dead* I can remember reading when the film appeared, in the *Village Voice*, in which the reviewer compared the film to Hawks's splendid early 50s sci-fi movie *The Thing from Another World*, finding that Romero reverses Hawks's values: the earlier film favored the military over the scientists, *Day* favors scientists over military. This rests, I think, on a serious misreading of both films, between which there is indeed a close relationship, one much more complex than that of simple opposition or reversal. Superficially, it is true that Hawks favors his military men (the airmen of the Arctic base) over at least his leading scientist Dr. Carrington (who has major characteristics in common with Dr. Logan), but they are favored not at all for militarism but for what they embody as human beings. Hawks downplays all sense of hierarchy (along with patriotism, which scarcely interests him at all): the men, whatever their rank, become individual and equally valued members of a typical Hawksian male group. What is celebrated in them (as also in the relationship between Captain Hendry and the woman Nikki) is their capacity for spontaneous affection and mutual respect, the pleasure in contact and communication that is fundamental to any valid community; they correspond, in fact, rather closely to Romero's "good" characters, and not at all to his military men.

Romero, of course, being far more politically conscious than Hawks and working during the Reagan era, sees precisely what Hawks chose to ignore: the fact that the military is an institution, and one embodying in its extreme form the masculinism that pervades and structures the entire hierarchy of our culture. If *Day* as a whole must be read as a response to Reaganite America, its presentation of "masculinity" in its military characters is specifically a response to Reaganite cinema, the Rocky/Rambo syndrome. *Day* presents this in sexual terms (the overvaluation of the phallus, the obsession with "size") and in more general terms of aggression and domination. As there is nothing subtle about the phenomenon, so there is nothing subtle about the presentation: masculinity, here, is rendered as caricature, grotesque and gross, the implication being that there is nothing more to be said about it. Is this presentation, in fact, any more gross than the general celebration of masculinity in the films of so many of Romero's contemporaries? What Romero captures, magnificently, is the *hysteria* of contemporary masculinity, the very excesses of which testify to an anxiety, a terror. In *Day*, the grossness of the characters is answered, appropriately, by the grossness of their deaths: dismemberment and evisceration as the ultimate castration. The militarist mentality, and what it produces, gets its ironic comment when Bub, having shot Captain Rhodes (the group's gung-ho military leader), dutifully salutes him as he is literally torn apart by the zombies.

That the film favors the scientists is, however, another misconception. It is true that Sarah, its most positive figure, is a scientist, just as Nikki in *The Thing* was associated with the scientists' group (though in the subordinate role of secretary). Yet in both films the woman is valued partly for the way in which she dissociates her-

Day of the Dead

(right)
Bub (Howard
Sherman) learns to
shave

(below)
Captain Rhodes
(Joseph Pilato) tries
(unsuccessfully) to
intimidate Sarah
(Lori Cardille)

self from the values science embodies. "Science" in *Day* is "Dr. Frankenstein," and it is revealed as yet another symbolic extension of masculinist ideology. If what distinguishes the human beings from the zombies is their potential for reason and emotion, then the science of Dr. Logan represents the overvaluation of a certain kind of rationality at the expense of other distinctively human qualities. The film is not exactly antiscience; neither, despite its reputation, was *The Thing*. In Hawks's film the monster is finally destroyed by the functional use of scientific knowledge; in *Day*, technology and knowledge provide the means of escape, in the form of the helicopter and John's ability to fly it. Both films make a similar distinction between knowledge placed at the service of human beings and knowledge as a means to power and domination: if "masculinity" as constructed within our culture has led to war, imperialism, the arms race, it has equally led to the domination—and destruction—of nature. Rationality has traditionally been claimed by men as an essentially male attribute, and as the justification for their power; women are fobbed off with "female intuition" as compensation. One can certainly argue that it is men who are the greater losers. The "rational," from this point of view, is what the conscious mind works out for itself without assistance, while the "intuitive" is what the conscious mind comes to understand when it permits itself to remain in touch with the subconscious and with the emotional levels of human psychic activity. Dr. Logan's science is rational in this limited and limiting sense, its results disgusting, dehumanizing, and ultimately useless (the film presents him as increasingly bloodsoaked as the action progresses). On the other hand, there is nothing *irrational* about the decisions and actions of the positive characters: like the sympathetic characters of *The Thing*, they simply permit their reason to remain in touch with actual human needs.

Central to the trilogy's progress is the development throughout the three films of the female protagonists. Barbara in *Night* becomes virtually catatonic early on and remains so throughout the action, a parody of female passivity and helplessness; Fran in *Dawn* is at first thoroughly complicit in the established structures of heterosexuality, then learns gradually to assert herself and extricate herself from them. In *Day* the woman has become, quite unambiguously, the positive center around whom the entire film is structured. Strikingly androgynous in character, she combines without strain the best of those qualities our culture has traditionally separated out as "masculine" and "feminine": strong, decisive, and resourceful, she is also tender and caring, and shows no desire to dominate. As a scientist, she wants to understand what has produced the zombies so that the process might be reversed; Logan wants to control the zombies, turning them into his slaves and the proof of his theories. Initially antagonistic, Sarah progressively associates herself with the two men who have opted out of the military-versus-scientist conflict; she effectively learns, in fact, to abandon any attempt to save American civilization, which the film characterizes as a waste of time. Her lover, Miguel, is the least masculine of the

Day of the Dead

The zombies in need of sustenance

The death of Miguel (Antone DiLeo)

soldiers, tormented indeed (partly under the goads of the other men) by the failure of his masculinity, and provoking disasters by his attempts to reassert it.

The film begins and ends with Sarah awakening from a nightmare of being assaulted by the zombies: the overtones of rape link the zombies to the military, who repeatedly threaten her with exactly that. This formal device produces complicated narrative ambiguities. We are given no clear sense of where the final nightmare begins (the zombies are inside the helicopter, and attack Sarah as she climbs in): it is possible to read the entire film as the woman's nightmare, with the exception of the brief coda where Sarah wakes up on the beach of a tropical island, the two men fishing nearby (though, paradoxically, that ending validates the nightmare's reality). However, the abruptness and implausibility of this "happy ending" (a striking example of what Sirk called the "emergency exit") encourages an opposite reading: the body of the film is the reality, the epilogue a wish-fulfillment fantasy (perhaps Sarah's fantasy as she dies, perhaps simply the filmmaker's ironic commentary—the island image forms part of the décor of John's room in the underground shelter). Romero allows us a tentative and qualified optimism if we wish: the final image relates back to John's solution, that they fly away to a desert island and have babies who will be reared without ever even having to know that the whole legacy of American culture existed. ("Teach them never to come here and dig those records out"—the records of "the top five hundred companies, the defense department budget, the negatives of all your favorite movies"—effectively, the records of the economic/political base and the ideological superstructure of American capitalism: "This is a great big fourteen-mile tombstone with an epitaph on it that nobody's going to bother to read.") "Qualified" optimism at best: the zombies have taken over the entire world and, while they can't reproduce, they appear not to die unless deliberately slaughtered; and the notion of flying away to a desert island is established, near the film's beginning, as a form of hedonistic escapism. The ambiguity renders even this limited hope for any human future tentative and dubious, and we are permitted no hope whatever for American (Western capitalist, masculinist) civilization. It was an extraordinary film to come upon in the midst of the *Rockys*, the *Rambos*, the *Back to the Futures*, that dominated the era; it still seems extraordinary today

To me it is a matter of some urgency (if one retains any faith in the power of art to effect change) that *Day of the Dead* receive at last the attention and respect it deserves. It is if anything more important today than it was when it was made. If not quite about the end of *the* world, it is clearly about the end of *ours*, which it now seems that little short of a universal miracle can prevent.

15.

On and Around
My Best Friend's Wedding

I want to discuss *My Best Friend's Wedding* (1997) in relation to three associated topics: its relation to classic screwball comedy and the other recent attempts to rethink that genre in contemporary terms; its auteurist relationship with *Muriel's Wedding* (1994); and the current widespread use of gay characters in contemporary comedies. As this chapter will accordingly be more "around" than "on," I had better begin by saying plainly that I love the film: if not "profound" or in any of the more obvious ways "groundbreaking," it seems to me a flawless and progressive example of its genre, giving continuous delight over many re-viewings.

SCREWBALL ANCIENT AND MODERN

We all recognize certain films as "screwball," yet the term requires definition; the simplest way to define it is to situate it between the "romantic" comedy and the "crazy" or "slapstick" comedy, as it clearly relates to both while remaining distinct from either, its distinctness arising perhaps from the ways in which it borrows and combines elements from each. McCarey provides the ideal touchstones, as he produced outstanding examples of all three categories: *Duck Soup*, the ideal crazy comedy; *Love Affair* or its remake *An Affair to Remember*, the ideal romantic; and *The Awful Truth*, among the greatest screwballs.

At the heart of both "screwball" and "romantic" is the romantic couple, generally absent from or marginal to "crazy." (Although Chaplin and Lloyd always had romantic "interests," their films are celebrated primarily for the comedians' performances, set pieces, and skills; although Laurel and Hardy might at a stretch be seen as a romantic couple, the stretch would be a very long one; and I don't think anyone would label the various courtships of Groucho and Margaret Dumont "romantic" exactly.) This is why the distinction is not always clear-cut. A rough but sufficiently accurate way of putting it might suggest that the romantic comedy is primarily *about* the construction of the ideal romantic couple, while the screwball comedy is primarily about liberation (and the couple it constructs is often very short of the romantic ideal—see, for example, *Bringing Up Baby* or *The Lady Eve*— or *Too Many Husbands*, which audaciously constructs a threesome): the overthrow of social convention, of bourgeois notions of respectability, of traditional gender roles. (The resolution of *My Best Friend's Wedding* is already clearly in view and might be claimed as the genre's logical "happy end," which has only in very recent years become possible within the constraints of Hollywood cinema.) This is precisely where "screwball" links to "crazy"—to the anarchy of the Marx Brothers, or the (often inadvertent) destruction of social norms, homes, and property in Laurel and Hardy: plausibility is much less an issue in "screwball" than in "romantic." *The Awful Truth* might be taken as the perfect midpoint between the two, "crazy" and "romantic" held meticulously in balance.

The most interesting aspect of this movement toward liberation, the overthrow of norms, is the recurrent emphasis in screwball (the theme, one might claim, of the best screwballs) on the emancipation and empowerment of women. Hence *The Awful Truth* is essentially about (in Andrew Britton's words) "the chastisement of male presumption"[1] and the progress of the couple toward equality. The most extreme instance—hence the closest of all the screwballs to "crazy"—is of course *Bringing Up Baby*, single-mindedly concerned with Cary Grant's liberation at the merciless hands of Katharine Hepburn, and culminating with faultless logic in that still potent image of the overthrow of patriarchy, the collapse of the dinosaur skeleton into "nothing but a heap of old bones," to misquote Hepburn from earlier in the film. Other notable examples: *The Lady Eve*, *Two-Faced Woman* (the original version, not the bowdlerized horror currently available on video—see Richard Lippe on this in *CineAction* 35), and (on a lower level of achievement) *Theodora Goes Wild* and *Too Many Husbands*, in which Jean Arthur, despite having been compelled by the patriarchal legal system to choose between Fred MacMurray and Melvyn Douglas, ends up keeping them both. From this viewpoint, these films are more progressive, subversive, and potentially revolutionary than almost anything Hollywood is turning out today. This becomes particularly clear when one considers a more recent attempt at screwball that most obviously corresponds to the classic model: *Forces of Nature* (1999), where the model is patently *Bringing Up Baby*. The film was generally attacked (reasonably enough) for its ineptness and the actors' total lack of chemistry or charisma, but its real crime is the betrayal of its Hawksian forerunner: instead of

1. "Cary Grant : Comedy and Male Desire" (CineAction 7).

progressing toward liberation, its characters simply learn to be older and wiser, a condition which presumably renders liberation superfluous.

Screwball comedies are no longer concerned with women's empowerment, following the widespread social assumption that women don't need to be empowered any more, they've won all their battles and they're empowered quite sufficiently, thank you. Meanwhile, I open my newspaper every morning to read about all the battered, raped and/or murdered women who have been battered, raped, and murdered by men, most commonly their husbands or male lovers; about all the single mothers struggling in poverty, driven up to or over the brink of homelessness; the closing of women's shelters and of day care centers following the withdrawal of government funding; the struggles of women to secure tenured positions or promotion in universities, and their struggle everywhere to secure equal pay for equal work; their virtual exclusion from the upper echelons of male-controlled capitalism, unless they are committed to supporting the further empowerment of men; or, conversely, the enormously greater number of female secretaries, servants, housecleaners than male. The only contemporary screwball comedy to treat this subject responsibly has been generally ignored: *The Associate* (1996), flawed by faulty construction and indifferent direction but distinguished by splendid performances by Whoopi Goldberg and Dianne Wiest. The film's attack on the subordination and exploitation of women (and of blacks) within the overwhelmingly white-male-dominated structures of our financial institutions and corporations is crude but devastating.

Yet, if the great underlying subject of classic screwball has now been declared officially obsolete by the current capitalist/patriarchal conspiracy, the genre itself has, by a process of mutation, at its best replaced it with other concerns apparently distinct from it yet clearly relevant to it: the assault on the traditional bastions of marriage, family, biological parentage, sexuality, and gender. If the problems of women are now officially "solved," then the problems that are so intimately and intricately involved in women's continuing oppression—indeed, they form its basis—are now being exposed to criticism as never before. I have particularly in mind *Flirting with Disaster* (1996), *The Daytrippers* (1996), and *My Best Friend's Wedding*.

Our civilization has come a long way since the great days of screwball—a long way toward potential and perhaps imminent cataclysm: we have had World War II, the threat of nuclear annihilation, and the devastation of the environment by the joint (if contending) forces of advanced capitalism—not only in the countries of the West but now also in former Soviet Russia and even in Communist China—with the apparently insatiable greed of those who believe that the possession of vast hoards of money by a few justifies the social misery of millions and the possible end of life on the planet. Accordingly, civilization's basic structures—social, political, ideological—and the structures of social/sexual organization that are at once their product and sustenance are provoking increasingly greater anxiety, discontent, disturbance: it cannot be stressed too often (as so few appear to listen) that there *is* a clear and logical connection between the patriarchal nuclear family and the dominant socioeconomic/ political structures. Given capitalism's continuing power, especially its power to keep its populations in a condition of chronic mystification through the media it essentially controls, this disturbance crystallizes into fully conscious opposition only among a small minority; but the inchoate *sense* of dissatisfaction is by now virtually all-pervasive, especially among the younger generations. Because the dissatisfaction can't be consciously formulated, it expresses itself only in cynicism and impotent forms of rebellion. Yet the disillusionment with our traditional, fundamental institutions—marriage and family, the organization of gender and sexuality—is discernible everywhere. It structures the best contemporary screwball comedies as surely as the empowerment of women structured the classics of the 1930s and 40s.

The most complete and rigorous working through of this is clearly *The Daytrippers*, perhaps the most shockingly neglected American film of the past decade, little known, seldom screened, currently accessible only on a "formatted to fit your TV screen" video and a DVD that does nothing to remedy this. Never screwball, and by its end no longer even a comedy, it nonetheless has an archetypal screwball premise and narrative structure: wife, after tender and affectionate early morning scene with husband, sees him off to his office, then finds (while doing the housework) a love note signed "Sandy" under the bed. Distraught, she enlists the aid of her mother, who in turn enlists father, younger sister, and younger sister's fiancé for a trip into the city to confront the errant husband *en masse*. One can even imagine how this might have been cast, in the heyday of screwball in its more conservative "family" mode: William Powell as the husband, Myrna Loy or Irene Dunne as the wife, Mary Boland and Charlie Ruggles as the parents, Ann Rutherford as the younger sister . . . There would have been a series of hilarious misadventures; the husband, finally tracked down, would explain that "it was all a mistake"; and familial and conjugal solidarity would be restored, confirmed by the promise of the younger couple's imminent wedding. *The Daytrippers* systematically reverses this pattern: the journey, starting in early morning, ending in very late night, is a steady progress into darkness and disintegration. By the end, both the marriage and the engagement have broken up, the family has fallen irremediably apart, and the two sisters walk off together into the night. As usual with American narrative movies, all this allows itself to be read in purely individual terms (*this* particular marriage, *this* family, etc.), but it in no way forbids a symbolic reading, as a "fable for our time" (the family is clearly presented as "typical"). Perhaps the reason why it is the most radical of current screwball (or screwball-derived) comedies is because it is the furthest from its models, in tone and narrative progression.

My Best Friend's Wedding is obviously more lightweight, truer to the screwball spirit. But beneath its more frivolous, less openly subversive, surface it relates clearly enough to the same tendencies.

WHAT My Best Friend's Wedding HAS IN COMMON WITH Muriel's

Muriel's Wedding was both written and directed by P. J. Hogan; on My Best Friend's Wedding he has only the director's credit. I have no information on why exactly he was invited to Hollywood (though obviously the critical and popular success of the Australian film had a great deal to do with it), or on how he came to direct the film he did: was it his choice (from a range of possible screenplays or subjects offered), was it chosen for him as some kind of specialist in weddings, to what extent did he control or contribute to the evolution of the final screenplay? If the finished screenplay was simply handed to him with a "Direct this," then we are dealing with a most remarkable coincidence: despite their enormous differences (in tone, milieu, characterization), the structures of the two films reveal striking similarities. The differences can be accounted for by the change in national and social milieu and the different possibilities offered by the American and Australian cinemas and their very divergent inflections of the comic genre. At risk of treading upon sensitive nationalist toes, I have to say that most of the Australian films (or films set and shot in Australia) I've seen come across as terrible warnings: "Never, never emigrate to Australia. Don't even contemplate it. At best you'll be screamed at and victimized, and at worst forcibly sodomized by Donald Pleasance." (Let me add that I could say much the same about the cinema of my own home country, England.) The contrast between the sophistication and nuance of My Best Friend's Wedding and the in-your-face crudity of its predecessor are impossible to account for in terms simply of authorial sensibility—though in the case of the American film this must be attributed to the influence of genre rather than to anything discernible in the contemporary Hollywood scene.

The trajectory common to both films can be summed up as follows: a woman becomes obsessed (for quite different reasons) with a particular wedding, real or fantasized (her own purely hypothetical one—Muriel/Toni Collette—and that of the man she has suddenly realized she loves—Julianne or "Jules"/Julia Roberts). In both cases, though, the woman wants the wedding to be her own—for Muriel it is a status symbol that will at last gain her some respect; for Jules the means of possessing the man she loves, colored by the even more ignoble desire to get her own way, her behavior at times suggesting that of the little girl who stamps her foot and cries "I want it!!! I want it!!!" Each female protagonist is obsessed with a particular song that offers her a fantasy image of herself: Abba's "Dancing Queen" for Muriel, "Just the Way You Look Tonight" for Jules; and in both films the song returns in the final sequences as a signifier of her liberation from obsession. In both films the woman's obsessiveness drives her increasingly into selfish and irresponsible behavior that takes no account of other people's feelings and which she ultimately recognizes as a betrayal of her own finer ones. The wedding brings disillusionment and with it liberation: she begins to look at herself and examine her behavior, and to free herself of her obsession. Most remarkable is the congruence of the endings: both films end with the heroine reunited with the character who has come to represent her conscience, but who also, significantly, is an outsider-figure, set apart by a marked "difference," with whom she appears to be cementing a permanent relationship but whom she cannot possibly marry, and whose personal situation (crippled, gay) places both in a position where they can view the social milieu, its traditions and behavior patterns, objectively and critically. One might say that they are presented as the most admirable characters of their respective films precisely *because* they can't marry— can't, that is, participate in their culture's central principle of organization.

The films share an extremely jaundiced view of weddings and their function, and beyond that, implicitly, of marriage. This is expressed quite blatantly in *Muriel*, and is somewhat gentler and more circumspect in *Best Friend*, where the tone is established at the outset by that charming, hilarious, satirical credit sequence. Our confidence in the Dermot Mulroney/Cameron Diaz marriage is subtly but thoroughly undermined: the pair are obviously mismatched, their interests totally incompatible (reminiscent, in fact, of Stewart and Kelly in *Rear Window!*) in the archetypal manner of our culture, (male) adventurer versus (female) settler. Jules is able to undermine their apparent stability at first serious attempt, the instant quarrel she negotiates only resolved by the woman's instant and total capitulation to the man's needs. And the central sequence on the sightseeing launch makes it clear that the prospective groom's attachment to Jules remains considerably more than friendly and can be reignited quite easily. In view of this the film's final celebration of the traditional couple, as they depart for their honeymoon with the aid of romantic music, slow motion, confetti, and sudden gushing fountains, must be read as part-ironic, part an aspect of the film's generosity, a tribute to the essential niceness and excellent intentions of its characters: the effect might be summed up as "You haven't a hope but we wish you well."

PERFORMANCE/STRUCTURE

Though generally liked, *My Best Friend's Wedding* has not received anything like the recognition it deserves. It is one of the great American comedies, comparable in its perfection with the finest "classic" screwballs, perfectly written, perfectly cast, perfectly acted, perfectly directed. I have watched it at least half a dozen times, replaying whole sequences for the sheer pleasure of the nuances of timing and the ensemble playing. It is continuously *alive*, down to the smallest detail: when one has watched (for example) the scene in the karaoke bar, or the sequence of the eve-of-wedding luncheon party, a few times, one suddenly begins to notice the extras: there is no "dead" space on the screen; every visible extra in the crowded bar or restaurant is caught up in the overall performance. The four principals are beyond

My Best Friend's Wedding: Director and star discuss a scene praise. If Roberts and Rupert Everett strike one most immediately, that is because they have the showiest roles; but their performances are matched by those of Diaz and Mulroney.

The film is built upon a dual structure: the shifting and evolving relationships between Julianne and the two men in her life, Michael (Mulroney) and George (Everett). Both relationships are introduced, with great economy, at the outset: Julianne, a prestigious food columnist and critic, is dining out with George, her editor (the "date" combines work and pleasure, as she is reviewing the restaurant); during the meal she checks her messages on her cell phone and receives the urgent communication from Michael (she is to call him back, any time, even in the middle of the night) that precipitates the entire action. Michael is her "best friend," with whom she once had a brief romantic fling; when they broke it off they swore to marry each other if they hadn't found a partner by the age of twenty-eight. Both will be twenty-eight within weeks; it is George who initially puts into her head the notion that a wedding with her "best friend" is on the horizon.

The film plays throughout on the "best friend" motif. When Kimmy (Diaz) asks Julianne to be her maid of honor, she adds: "This means I have four days to make you my best friend" (Julianne has the same four days to break up the wedding). At the ballpark, when Michael first begins to see Julianne in a new light, he asks her: "What did you do with my best friend?" At the tailor's, when Michael is being fitted for his suit, Julianne introduces George as "my good friend . . . my *best* friend these days." George has already replaced Michael as Julianne's best friend; at the film's extraordinary conclusion he will also replace him as Julianne's groom, the wedding of Michael and Kimmy becoming also that of George and Julianne, giving the film's title a final twist.

The nature of the relationship between Julianne and George is gradually defined through their scenes together: a mutual dependency that is neither romantic nor sexual, hence free of the demands, restrictions, and jealousies of "traditional" love relationships. If an overtone of male dominance remains, it is one that Julianne can reject whenever she wishes: professionally he is her editor (though neither the film nor the character makes anything of that), personally her wise adviser—not so much because, as a man, he knows better, but because, as a *gay* man, he can view from the outside the social conventions and behavior patterns from which Julianne has never quite emancipated herself. His concern for her (because he senses that she is going to behave badly, in ways of which she will be ashamed) never expresses itself as even remotely bullying or dictatorial, and it is always balanced by his fear of losing her: Michael's instant jealousy when he believes Julianne and George are lovers is balanced by George's sense of loss when he believes she will be absorbed in a traditional marriage. If he is her "best friend," it is clear that she is also his; if this is not what one normally thinks of as a "love" relationship, perhaps our definition of love needs rethinking.

My Best Friend's Wedding

The innocent bride (Cameron Diaz, *right*) and her maid of (dis)honor (Julia Roberts)

(*Below*)
A startled George (Rupert Everett, *right*, with Julia Roberts and Dermot Mulroney) learns that he is suddenly Julianne's fiancé

The film takes over from *Muriel's Wedding* the use of a song associated with the heroine and becoming a marker of her development, but it develops this device far more elaborately and satisfyingly. There are, in fact, *two* songs involved, one associated with Julianne's relationship with Michael, the other connected to her relationship with George. "Just the Way You Look Tonight" is introduced in the sequence of Julianne's first serious (and almost successful) attempt to break up Michael's relationship with Kimmy—the restaurant scene where Kimmy, at Julianne's instigation, asks Michael to work for her father in an office job for six months, enabling *her* to fulfill certain life choices (finishing college, beginning her own career in architecture) instead of sacrificing everything for *him*: he arrives for lunch singing it to Julianne, as a memory of their romantic fling. He sings it to her again on the sight-seeing launch and they dance together, publicly, yet seemingly completely unaware of the presence of outsiders. He has by this time admitted that he felt "crazy jealous" of George, and his revived attraction to Julianne has become very evident; it's the moment that convinces her of her *right* to break up the marriage, which can't possibly be a happy one, the couple being hopelessly incompatible and Michael still being romantically attached to *her*, releasing her from her last promptings of conscience or consideration for others, enabling her meanest and most reprehensible action. George's song, introduced at the eve-of-wedding luncheon, is Burt Bacharach's "I Say a Little Prayer for You" ("Forever, and ever, you stay in my heart/ . . . Forever, and ever, we never will part"). George introduces it in relation to his account (hilarious, and totally fictitious) of his first meeting with Julianne, and it is immediately taken up, first by the two bridesmaids, then by the entire assembly: it's important that it becomes a public song, symbolically uniting the supposed couple with an outside world, while the Michael/Julianne song is strictly personal and hermetic, shutting the world out.

In the final scenes the two songs are juxtaposed, representing the choice that Julianne must make. In her obligatory "maid of honor" speech at the wedding reception, Julianne publicly acknowledges the ugly and psychopathic nature of her behavior, then confers the song she shared with Michael upon the new couple, as her wedding gift, "until you find your own song." It is her way of relinquishing her obsession, and with it the past. After the couple leaves for the honeymoon, the reception continues. Julianne is alone among the crowd. Her cell-phone rings: George of course. But George is there, at another table, and he presents her with what is effectively *his* wedding gift to her: "I say a little prayer . . . " We are then given an entirely new variation on an old convention (a convention that will be repeated, shopworn and totally unconvincing, in its original form, at the end of Roberts's subsequent *Notting Hill*): the public proposal. George advances toward her across the floor, making it clear that what he is offering is a permanent relationship: "And though you quite correctly sense that he is—gay, like most devastatingly handsome single men of his age . . . There won't be marriage. There won't be sex. But, by God, there'll be dancing." Earlier in the film Michael had protested to her at the ballpark (her dancing with the best man at the reception being in question) that "You can't dance. When did you learn how to dance?" Their dance together on the launch was slow, tentative, private; her dance with George is abandoned and ecstatic, a dance of liberation. The film closes on "Together, forever . . . " The film thus fulfills the traditional Hollywood obligation to progress toward the "construction of the couple," but it is no longer the "construction of the *heterosexual* couple."

As with *The Daytrippers*, it is a simple matter to relate *My Best Friend's Wedding* to classic screwball: indeed, it directly evokes *Bringing Up Baby*, which was also about a woman determined at all costs to prevent a man from marrying his fiancée within a short period of time. In the 30s, Katharine Hepburn would have played the Julia Roberts role and the ending would have been a foregone conclusion: the prospective bride would have been revealed as either an idiot bimbo or a calculating bitch, hence jettisoned without the least discomfort for either the other characters or for the audience—the groom would have realized his terrible mistake, Hepburn would have replaced the bride at the altar in a breathless last-minute upheaval, and the wedding would have formed a triumphant conclusion. That is precisely how I "knew" the film would end the first time I saw it, though I was increasingly disturbed by the question of how it would manage to jettison Cameron Diaz without doing itself irreparable damage: her character was simply too sweet, too lovable, too vulnerable, too sincerely in love. Another source of disturbance was that the Cary Grant role seemed somehow to have become split between Dermot Mulroney and Rupert Everett.

GAYS IN 90S COMEDY: PROBLEM OR SOLUTION?

What above all distinguishes *My Best Friend's Wedding* from classic screwball is something that couldn't have happened in any mainstream film prior to the 60s, and didn't in fact happen before the 80s: the inclusion of a character who is not only openly gay but is represented positively and attractively. Rupert Everett's George is very different from the grotesques and lost souls who first represented gays when the taboo on explicit gay representation was lifted in the 60s (*Boys in the Band, Staircase, The Killing of Sister George* . . .): in every aspect but the sexual he is an ideal partner for Jules. Recent films are beginning to suggest that the right-wing dread of the "gay lifestyle" is not without foundation: what is feared is not merely that, were gayness viewed positively, virtually everyone would immediately become homosexual, but rather that gay relationships might become a model for a new, freer, alternative "normality." It is not, when you think about it, in the least surprising that the collapse of confidence in the traditional norms would be accompanied by the sudden emergence of images of attractive gay men leading apparently happy and productive lives. The apparently open arms with which gays have suddenly been welcomed in recent Hollywood cinema have not yet opened indiscriminately: gays have been mainly restricted to comedy, where there is less need to show sexual acts or even expressions of love. The gay love story is a genre so far restricted to small films aimed at gay audiences (*Making Love* was generally ridiculed by gays on its appearance, but its audacity seems now proven by the fact that it has still, twenty years later, had no sequel). Hollywood remains rather wary of gay couples, though they are beginning to appear in some surprising places (*Big Daddy, Go*). The most radical use of gay characters is once again in *The Daytrippers*, where the final breakdown of the marriage and the dissolution of the family coincides with—is indeed precipitated by—the discovery not only that the husband *has* indeed been unfaithful, but with another man: on the symbolic level, the co-incidence of the collapse of norms with the production of a gay relationship is eloquent.

A favorite (and logical) role for gays in the new Hollywood comedy was quickly discovered: make the gay character the heroine's best friend (*The Object of My Affection, Blast from the Past*) and the problems are solved, the potential embarrassment of the more repressed and inhibited members of the audience averted. *My Best Friend's Wedding* seizes on this and brilliantly turns its limitations to advantage: the film's use of the Everett character is exemplary in its intelligence. George's maturity, considerateness, tact are intimately connected to the gayness that sets him apart from the social norms, permitting him a wise distance from the practices and conventions in which those around him are entangled. He is able to talk to Jules in a way that would be impossible for a heterosexual man, offering her always an intimacy that is the closer for being nonsexual. Hence the film's remarkable culmination, its "happy end" which becomes the securer alternative to the marital union which Jules has renounced, in its way an alternative "marriage": George's public speech to her, at the wedding reception for her "best friend" and the woman of his choice, constitutes a veritable proposal, the commitment to a relationship that will be permanent but nonexclusive, built upon much sounder foundations than romantic love or sexual attraction. As a friend of mine once wisely said to me, "You should live with friends, not with lovers." The film leaves us with the question of which man *is* now her best friend, and whose wedding is this anyway?

The implications of all this are far-reaching. I omitted—in my rough list of what, in gay life, the Hollywood cinema continues to suppress or skirt rather uneasily around—the question of *sexual freedom*. This is why *My Best Friend's Wedding* can tell us little or nothing about George's sex life. There is one brief scene which may offer a clue, the scene where Julianne, desperate, calls up in the middle of George's dinner party to beg him to come to her aid. George is at the head of the table, as host; to his left and right are two presumably straight couples; at the other end (where traditionally the wife would sit) is a bald-headed man, briefly glimpsed:

are we to take him as George's lover? As another friend? There is no clue other than his position at the formal table. The right talks of "the gay lifestyle," but in fact gay life comprehends many distinct lifestyles. There is reason to believe that the original model for gay couples, imitated from the only obvious available model and imitating traditional marriage—ostensible monogamy, with "cheating" (horrible word, horrible concept!) on the side, with the resulting rows, growing tension, and constant suspicions—is gradually dying out. More gay couples are accepting the natural polygamy of (most?) human beings and ceasing to regard sexual behavior outside the relationship as "infidelity" (another horrible word, as commonly used) since the couple remains, essentially, faithful to each other. But to "live with friends, not with lovers" would remove any lingering residues of the past, the jealousies, tensions, and quarrels. The very notion of "the couple" need no longer have the status it still retains: why not three, or four, or more, and what would it matter if the relationships were sexual or not? It would not of course be necessary to share the same living space (there is no suggestion in the film that Julianne and George will live together).

And what would be the consequences if such practices spread to the heterosexual world?

Surely, for many, the release from all the strains of traditional marriage-and-family would entail, above all, a vast sigh of relief. Freedom of choice: you could, if that was what you wanted, have sex with only one person for the rest of your life (so long as you didn't insist that he/she do the same) or with a hundred thousand. You would still, if you wished, and if you found the right person(s), have permanent or semipermanent relationships, and they would be built upon the very strong bonds of common interests and compatibility, not on the quicksands of sexual desire and "romantic love," both of which seem to fade rather quickly. How many couples, gay or straight, do *you* know who still have passionate sex (rather than sex-as-duty or sex-as-routine) after ten years of living together?

All that remains is the question of children: how they would be conceived and born? how they would be raised? And, really, all that needs to be discarded is our culture's obsession with biological parentage, which is merely a form of possessiveness and pride (one of the seven deadly sins!). Our entire culture conspires to suggest to children, almost from birth, that it is a matter of enormous and far-reaching importance who are their fathers and mothers. Yet, within our civilization, by far the largest portion of neurosis (with its concomitants of inhibition, repression, anxiety, generally stunted potential, and in the more extreme cases far more disastrous results) develops within the traditional family, passed on from generation to generation. Speaking personally, I certainly include myself in this, but I also include virtually everyone else with whom I have come into close contact throughout my life. The damage is irreparable: *Why* do we want it to continue? There would be no problem in producing and raising children within the various possible versions of social organization I have outlined: surely, today, we can dispense with antiquated notions about "bastards" and "children born out of wedlock"? A child should be free to relate, on a primary basis, to people other than her/his biological parents; should, in fact, have a similar freedom of choice to that of adults. And sex would fulfill its evolutionary trajectory, its growth through the millennia from mere reproductive agency to its ultimate destiny: the sharing of pleasure, affection, and intimacy among human beings.

16.

Teens, Parties, and Rollercoasters

A GENRE OF THE 90s

PARTY TIME: OR, CAN'T HARDLY WAIT FOR THAT AMERICAN PIE

The first question is, I suppose, Why? Why bother, when everyone knows these films are trash? ("Everyone" being the journalist critics, always eager to express their superiority and make themselves look like intellectuals.) First, I must confess, personal enjoyment: yes, I actually *enjoy* these films, or at least some of them (and that "some of them" immediately suggests that there are discriminations to be made, despite the films' apparent indistinguishability, even their titles being confusing). At least the films are about characters (or, anyway, "types") who are more or less recognizable as related to human beings, and are not made primarily by computers (though one may suspect that some of the screenplays were), as opposed to the dominant genres of Hollywood movies today, which consist mainly of special effects and computer-generated explosions. But am I, at the age of seventy-one, hence doubtless on or beyond the verge of senility, merely reliving my youth? (No, my youth was not remotely like that; I was pathologically withdrawn, already gay, riddled with guilt and self-disgust). Fantasizing, then, about the youth I never had? Possibly: I *do* find something seductive in the films' extrovert energy, and perhaps somewhere in me is an alternative self who wishes he could have enjoyed raunchy all-night house parties, especially when they include the destruction of the bourgeois home. But there is a more intellectually defensible reason for my interest.

My central predilection has always been Hollywood, though essentially the classical period (roughly 1930–1960, from the coming of sound to the dominance of television and the beginning of the takeover by corporations). It's a question of which you value more highly, communal art or personal art. All the richest periods of artistic achievement—Renaissance Italy, the Elizabethan drama, the Vienna of Haydn and Mozart—have been instances of communality: the availability of established genres, the constant interaction and exchange among artists, the sense of *belonging* to the culture, of being supported by it, of speaking to and for a wide audience that cuts across all divisions of class and gender. Compare the isolation of the modern artist, the emphasis on self-expression, "originality," novelty, the audience dwindled to a small elite. But art that is mere "self-expression" tends to become increasingly impoverished and uninteresting. With Fellini, for example, self-expression reached its apotheosis in *8 ½*, which fully deserves its established position as a modern masterpiece; everything since seems variously (and comparatively) thin, repetitive, strained. Bergman's work, which once seemed to me the peak of cinematic achievement, has come to satisfy me less and less. His personal psychodramas in which the characters (aspects of the artist's psyche?) appear totally isolated from all social realities, stripped of all social/political context, and in which ideological despair is mistaken for "the human condition," come to seem increasingly limited in their interest, while the great films of Hawks, Ford, Hitchcock, McCarey, Preminger, Ophuls, Cukor, Sturges (Preston!), Mann (Anthony!), Ray, Sirk . . . retain their amazing freshness and vitality today. Aside from Ophuls (who returned to Europe), none of these directors survived the collapse of the Classical Hollywood system in the 60s, though some continued making films. One could list with ease 300 films from the classical period that remain of great interest, of which about a third can be claimed as masterpieces; because of the existence of shared conventions, genres, forms, shooting methods, stars, even certain works by otherwise quite undistinguished directors retain their vitality and resonance. One would be hard-pressed, I think, to find a comparable tally in the last 30-year period.

Genre cinema today—deprived of the sustaining base of the star/studio system, replaced by a set of businessmen sitting around a conference table asking "Well, what made the most money last year?" and constructing a "package" resembling it as closely as possible but going a little further—obviously survives only in an extremely debased and impoverished form. The great Hollywood movies were genre pictures; the nearest to great movies in Hollywood since the early 60s, when related to a genre at all (e.g., *Bonnie and Clyde*), are inflected toward the European "art" movie (Penn, early Altman, Scorsese). Largely, the notion of an evolving genre, inflected in various ways by directors and stars, has been replaced by sequels, imitations, and remakes. In discussing 90s high school movies, I shall not (I warn you now) be unearthing any neglected masterpieces, and very little where one can discern the personal touch, the distinctive enunciation, the creative commitment, of a Ford, a Hawks, or a Preminger. This group of films is in no way comparable in quality to the screwball comedies of the late 30s/40s, the *films noirs* of the 40s/50s, the domestic melodramas of the same period, or the continuously evolving western. The films share, however, a certain generalized sense of energy, a sense of "having fun" (which Hawks always claimed as the basis of *his* filmmaking), and, as I intimated above, there are distinctions to be made.

There are in fact two viewpoints from which one might interest oneself in a group of films of this nature: the artistic (using the word somewhat loosely) and the sociopolitical. The former will in this case obviously yield the less profit, yet one should expect such a body of work to be of *some* creative interest simply because it resembles, in certain respects if not in others, the kind of communal generic work seen at its highpoint in the classical period. In happier, less cynical working conditions a major figure might have developed out of it, as Bach or Haydn grew out of an already established set of conventions and syntax. This hasn't happened and is not likely to do so, Hollywood having evolved precisely into what it was always accused of being by shortsighted modernist intellectuals—a factory.

The latter viewpoint is clearly the more productive. The films have been commercially very successful (though today the cycle has lost steam and appears to be in danger of losing its audience with it): a great many young people rushed to see them and enjoy them. That in itself should suggest their importance. Do they *reflect* dominant trends in our culture? Is this what high school students today are like, is this how they behave, are these their values? Or do the films offer seductive fantasies of how young people would *like* things to be? Do the films encourage the behavior patterns they dramatize? Are they encouraging irresponsibility in an entire generation? Given the films' popularity, can one distinguish any positive, progressive aspects in their treatment of today's teenagers? Such questions are seldom raised or discussed by our journalist reviewers, who find it usually sufficient simply to express their superiority to the films and the behavior they depict. The older generation typically raises its jaundiced eyebrows in distaste and deplores their possible effect on the young (though at the same time implying that they don't have any because they are, after all, "just entertainment").

For me, the two approaches are not really separable. On the whole, the better films are the more progressive. This should surprise no one: progressiveness (the desire to "say something") is typically accompanied by a somewhat greater creative interest, an *aliveness*, whether in the narrative, the writing, or the realization. The rule is not absolute, and the films under discussion provide one (but only one) striking exception, to which I shall return.

The films within a generic cycle will, by definition, share a certain number of specific concerns, thematics, narrative patterns, motifs, character relations, iconography, etc. I've organized what follows under nine headings, which I mean to represent the underlying thematic structure on which the individual films perform a number of variations:

1. and 2. These belong together, as the most basic: I see them as the structuring presence and structuring absence of the cycle as a whole—respectively, sex and education.
3. Literary sources. Rather surprisingly, six films are relevant here.
4. Parents: presence or absence, relative importance.
5. Gender issues: how do the films reflect the changes in male/female relationships, the changes in attitude, since the women's movement of the 60s and 70s?
6. Race. To what extent do the films recognize, characterize, integrate persons of color?
7. Class. Is class an issue at all? Or is its reality denied (as so commonly in American culture, in "the land of equal opportunity")?
8. Politics. Do the films show any awareness of wider issues outside the characters' immediate preoccupations?
9. Sexual orientation. Are gays even acknowledged? If so, how are they represented?

Before I work through this list I think I should get out of the way the one exception I noted above to the general sense that the more lively films artistically are also the most progressive. When asked to name the greatest French novelist, André Gide famously replied, "Victor Hugo, *hélas.*" If asked to name the best, overall, of the high school cycle, I would feel compelled to say "*American Pie, hélas.*" It strikes me as one of those rare films where "everything came together": one has the impression that the actors really enjoyed themselves, that there was a constant sense of fun and pleasure in the making of the film, a communal creative engagement more pronounced than in any of the other films. And the film benefits enormously from the presence in the cast of both Jason Biggs and Chris Klein, two of the most engaging and likable of young contemporary male stars. The film is very funny, but also very *sweet,* generous to its characters and with a sort of seductive innocence. It also has a rare supportive father who actually *encourages* his son's interest in sex, much to the latter's embarrassment. From the viewpoint of giving pleasure it is perhaps the best film in the cycle (its chief competitors being *Can't Hardly Wait* and *Bring It On*). BUT: the women (though never degraded) are generally subordinated to the men; there isn't a single memorable black or Asian presence (an absence very unusual in the cycle as a whole); politics is never even a marginal issue; and the very possibility of gayness is totally suppressed.[1]

---

1. Since this was written, *American Pie 2* has given us an extended sequence involving a pair of (apparent) lesbians who compel the boys to kiss each other, with the suggestion that they might learn to enjoy it. But the "lesbians" are not lesbians and the scene has no sequel.

The following list is incomplete; it represents the films I have seen (and in many cases saw again when planning this chapter); most of them are referred to in what follows:

Major Forerunners

Porky's (1981)
Fast Times at Ridgemont High (1982)
Heathers (1989)

The 1990s

Dazed and Confused (1993)
Clueless (1995)
Can't Hardly Wait (1998)
American Pie (1999)
She's All That (1999)
Ten Things I Hate About You (1999)
Cruel Intentions (1999)
Whatever It Takes (2000)
Get Over It (2001)

There are also two films that can be read as, to some extent, critiques of the cycle, and I deal with these separately at the end: *Bring It On* (2000) and *Not Another Teen Movie* (2002). To these I shall also add two very interesting Canadian films, probably not released outside Canada (they were barely released within it, though they are available on video and/or DVD for anyone with the patience to search):

Kitchen Party (1997)
Rollercoaster (1999)

Note: *Fast Times at Ridgemont High* anticipates almost everything in the later films and must be seen as the cycle's origin and archetype; it also remains, in my opinion, easily the best of the "typical" films. The word "typical" automatically excludes the other two highly distinguished works, *Dazed and Confused* and *Heathers*, both completely different in tone from all the rest, far darker and more disturbing (when I described the former in an article as a "horror" movie, I received a message from its director Richard Linklater congratulating me on being the first to notice his intentions!).

1. Sex, the Structuring Presence   Sex is at once the films' primary source of energy and the source of the older generation's discomfiture. Yet is it surprising that our culture is currently sex-obsessed? When I grew up the word itself could not be spoken, unless it was used purely to distinguish between men and women and had no reference to any actual physical activity; it was, in D. H. Lawrence's memorable phrase, "the dirty little secret." The contemporary obsession, though perhaps disproportionate, is understandable and inevitable, the opening of long-closed floodgates. We still have a long way to go. Lawrence tried to purge the sexual terminology of its "dirty" associations by using the words in their correct senses, but we only have to listen to everyday conversations to see how little he succeeded, the words still being used as "obscenities." In a sexually healthy culture, "Fuck you" wouldn't be an insult but a simple question, to which the answer would be either "Yes, please" or "No, thank you."

Typically, the films have twin plots which develop side by side: they might be summed up as "getting laid" and "falling in love," apparently two quite distinct pursuits (*Can't Hardly Wait* and *American Pie* are the definitive instances). The films are in fact extremely conservative, for all their determination to shock: the ideal remains true love and monogamy; the women are divided into "nice girls" (usually virgins) and "bitches," depending upon whether they attach themselves to the central male character or dump him; notions of sexual freedom or "free love" are never offered as desirable alternatives to the traditional forms of sexual organization. See, as exemplary, the construction of the "good couple" in *American Pie, Can't Hardly Wait,* and *She's All That*: in all three the relationship has not been consummated at the film's end. The "double standard," despite all the advances of Women's Lib, remains supreme: the boys' charisma is enhanced by "getting laid," but sexually active girls are generally put down and punished.

"Graduation" is a central issue in most of the films, which are set in the final year of high school and typically end on or around graduation day. *American Pie* and *Can't Hardly Wait* are linked by more than their temporal proximity (one year apart). The last third of *Pie* takes place during the graduation party, as does virtually the whole of *Can't . . .* (aside from a few minutes at the beginning and end and one magical sequence in the middle), both parties taking place in private houses rather than at end-of-school proms, etc. It becomes a question of just what the students are graduating from and to: education or sex? Do you graduate by passing your exams (never given more than passing mention) or by "getting laid" or "falling in love"? Which brings me to . . .

2. Education, the Structuring Absence   It comes of course as no surprise to find that neither the characters nor the films express the least interest in education, although, in view of the fact that the characters presumably spend a major part of their lives outside their screen time in the classroom studying something apart from how to

She's All That: Freddie Prinze Jr. with the obligatory "black content"

get laid, this might logically be considered something of an anomaly. What *is* interesting is that the characters, although forced to spend great stretches of their lives doing things in which they appear to have no interest whatever, never complain. Remarkably few of the films have scenes set in classrooms, and when they do it is either to have the class interrupted, to show notes irrelevant to the lesson being passed surreptitiously, or to show that there are teachers unreasonable enough to get annoyed when it becomes obvious that their students' minds are elsewhere. It never occurs to the characters or to the films to *attack* the system—the organization of education within our culture. The implication is that it is somehow a necessary (if inexplicable) chore, to be endured but never challenged. The point is basically a political one: an attack on our education system (in which human beings are forced at all ages to study things in which they have no interest) would inevitably imply an attack on capitalism itself, since capitalism demands that any genuine and intrinsically valuable education be replaced by career training. Under capitalism, children grow up in an environment in which their elders' interest in knowledge has already been deadened by education, alienated labor, and the media, so that the child's natural curiosity about things is stunted more or less from birth. A film that dared say such things could not possibly be made within mainstream commercial cinema and would be far too disturbing to pass for the casual entertainment capitalism requires to distract its victims from any dangerous and subversive suspicions that they may not after all be living in the best of all possible worlds.

The films do occasionally make vague gestures toward the notion that education will have to be taken more seriously when the students pass on to university, a suggestion that the (closely related) movies set in universities do little to substantiate. *Road Trip* is of particular interest here. Its leading character will not graduate unless he gets a B+ in the course he is taking on Greek philosophy, for a paper on Plato's *Republic*. But, when he should be spending the crucial weekend in last-minute cramming, a far more important issue supervenes: he must travel over long stretches of America to intercept an incriminating video sent in error to the woman to whom he is engaged. But all is not lost. One of the guys traveling with him turns out to know all about Plato, and fills him in on exactly what he need say on the way home. That moment has great resonance for me. Many is the time I have been approached at the start of a course by a student who asks: "What do I have to do to get a B+ on your course?" The question is asked quite innocently, without the least awareness of how deeply offensive it is. Such a question— and the attitude to learning it implies, and that *Road Trip* casually dramatizes—is, however, thoroughly encouraged, if not actually initiated, by our educational system, which breeds precisely that kind of cynicism. ("Our" here means North America and Britain; I am not familiar with how things are in continental Europe.) As the films unwittingly witness, the modern university is merely an extension of our school system, and far more interested in career training than in learning for its own sake, for what, as a fully human being, one might get from it, or for the future of the culture. The fundamental crime of the modern university is to tie courses to grades: the system enforces the *compulsory* education of high school, compelling students (though now adults) to take courses in which they have no interest whatever, with teachers they may despise, simply to get a B+. A form of prostitution, in fact, "Doing something you don't want to do, for money." Capitalism might be defined as institutionalized prostitution, and our universities are now its servants.

My own experience in a British university fifty years ago was very different. There was no connection between courses and grades. Taking a course did not involve writing essays; you took it because you were interested in the subject matter or impressed by the teacher (who would not even have your name on a list). When I started as a naive freshman, I attended about a dozen courses a week during my first month because I assumed it was what I should be doing; by my third month I was attending perhaps three, spending the rest of my time far more profitably reading books, listening to music, going to movies, discussing everything I read, saw, or heard with my friends, writing an essay a fortnight to discuss with my personal supervisor (still with no grade attached). That university system was

Road Trip: The decline of the American university

far from perfect, allowing tenured professors to continue giving the same lectures year after year from the same notes to almost empty lecture-rooms, and leaving one's fate dependent upon the end-of-year examinations. But compared with what we have today it seems to me almost paradisal. One could really study for learning's sake, for interest's sake, for the development of mind and spirit, and not only within the immediate framework of one's "subject" or of academic demands. Music and film have been a vital part of my education, but I wasn't officially "taking" either. Everything I studied I studied because I wanted to, and I had all the time in the world for it, uninterrupted by useless, tedious courses in which I had no interest. As for people who weren't really interested in studying at all but were there only to delay entry into the workforce, or because it was expected of a "gentleman," they seldom lasted beyond the first-year exams. There are plenty of training colleges available. The true university doesn't exist any more, greatly to the impoverishment of our culture. My own university education, by the way, was paid for entirely by the British government; I was never subjected to the anxieties contingent upon student loans, nor did I have to take part-time jobs, because I was given a grant to cover my living expenses, above and beyond tuition fees etc., most of which went to the purchase of records, a major part of my education in rarely performed (at that time) twentieth-century music. Without it I might never have discovered Nielsen's symphonies or the later works of Stravinsky, both of which have been important in my life, and both are essential to any education in the arts.

To say that academic standards have fallen would be an understatement: they have collapsed completely, to the extent that, if one receives a really good essay in an undergraduate course, one immediately suspects that it has been plagiarized. It is becoming increasingly common for courses to be graded on "tests," sometimes requiring answers of just a few sentences, culled from "required reading" texts— presumably the current means of encouraging original thinking. Those old fuddy-duddies like myself who demand essays are frequently rewarded with partly incomprehensible attempts by students for whom English is a second language— not, of course, the student's fault (and the intermittent glimmers of comprehensibility sometimes suggest that this might, given a command of the language, be one of the most interesting students in the class), but how is one to grade a paper one can't understand? The simple suggestion that students should not be allowed into courses demanding essay-writing before they have mastered the language is frowned upon as "racist." I vividly remember, however, one essay on which I wrote something to the effect that "I really cannot pass this because it is incomprehensible. I respect your problems as a foreign student, but it is unwise to enroll in a course that requires essays until you have mastered English." When it was handed back I was confronted by its author, a very angry young Caucasian Canadian who believed I was being deliberately insulting or sarcastic . . . More recently, I received a letter from an old friend who went through university with me and, like me, became a professor, also (like me) retired, in which he suggested that, as things are going, the time would soon arrive when a student would be given an A+ for answering correctly the question: "Name one character in *Hamlet*." But for how much longer will Shakespeare even be studied? The university curriculum has been, we are told, "expanded," to "keep up with the times," and the expansions are taking over. The Canadian university in which I taught for twenty years is currently erecting a whole new building to house its "Business School," in which students will, presumably, be initiated into the sacred mysteries of corporate capitalism and taught how to cooperate in the destruction of the planet. The college within that university to which I was attached (the "Adult Education" college, predominantly night school) has, since my retirement, "progressively" disbanded its film studies program (together with most other arts courses), but it is offering a course in "Performance Skills," open to anyone concerned with his/her future career: roughly, how to speak, how to behave, if you're, say, a nurse who would like to be promoted. The last thing any *real* university would cut back must be its Arts program, to which all other programs should be subordinate. It is only through training in the Arts that the crucial process of learning can take place: the process whereby we can learn simultaneously to *think* and *feel*, the process of becoming fully human. The Arts are the true heart of any healthy culture. We are in danger of losing our heart, of becoming a race of half-humans, deprived of depth and substance. F. R. Leavis called the university (potentially at least) the "creative center of culture"; it is rapidly degenerating into the anti-creative center of capitalism.

We can no longer look for help to the universities.

So much for the structuring presence and absence; the rest of my headings apply less consistently, their presence or absence flitting in and out from film to film.

3. Literary Adaptations   Given the generally humble aspirations of these films ("making money" is a humble aspiration, though most of us are forced to make it our chief one), it seems curious that their makers seek a spurious intellectual prestige by adapting plots sanctified by past highly respected literary works. What is the rationale? Respectability? Hardly: the films otherwise court its opposite. A sense that "It worked before so it will work again"? Mere laziness? I'm not sure. But some of the screenplays have a certain freshness and sophistication, and one would like to believe that the references derive from a degree of ambition to construct a resonance, however compromised by the supposed demands of the cycle's supposed audience, many of whom would, I think, be willing to be carried much further than the films are willing to take them.

For the record, the borrowings are: *Clueless* / *Emma*; *Ten Things I Hate About You* / *The Taming of the Shrew*; *Whatever It Takes* / *Cyrano de Bergerac*; *She's All That* / *Pygmalion*; *Cruel Intentions* / *Les Liaisons Dangereuses*; *Get Over It* / *A Midsummer Night's Dream*.

Just to complicate matters, one might add that *Ten Things I Hate About You* and *She's All That* have almost the same plot, although adapted from completely different sources (but, intriguingly, made the same year): roughly, a bet—the man must woo an apparently recalcitrant and hostile woman and persuade her to be his partner at the graduation prom.

4. Parents/home   Most of the films seem reluctant to suggest that all these high school students actually come from somewhere, that they have a specific background. The mother's presence is particularly negligible, by far the most important mother being the dead one of *She's All That*, continuing to exert her influence on the heroine, and on the whole beneficially. Fathers are generally obstructive and a nuisance (in my experience a reasonable supposition). *She's All That* is especially interesting here too, as it produces two contrasted fathers, negative and positive, respectively upper- and working-class, the hero's and the heroine's. Aside from the comic father (Eugene Levy) of *American Pie*, the working-class father of *She's All That* (which will emerge, by the way, as one of the most progressive of the films, if not necessarily one of the "best") is the only supportive father in the entire cycle, even ultimately constructing the *mise-en-scène* for the central couple's union.

5. Gender The films in general manage to acknowledge that women are now (in theory) on equal terms with men, asserting themselves and making choices, where before choice was a male prerogative. Yet the films remain resolutely male-centered, the main action (the "plot") invariably initiated by the males. The nearest exception is *Clueless* (adapted from a novel by a woman, directed by a woman), in which the active female character's motivation is to find a suitable male partner for her protégée. There are, however, two films in which the central thematic impetus is provided by a mutual education between male and female (*Ten Things I Hate About You* and *She's All That*), and in the latter it is the male who more requires educating.

6. Race Almost all the films scrupulously include black or Asian characters—but *never* in leading roles or as objects of desire for the white characters, male or female (there is no miscegenation in high schools, outside the admirable *Zebrahead* [1992], which I have not included here because it is so untypical, belonging more to the "social problem movie" than to the high school movie, in which social problems generally don't exist). Blacks are used mainly in supportive roles, friends of the white male lead, which at once establishes his lack of prejudice, his openness to difference, his generosity, and asserts his *superiority*: he has the main role, he "gets the girl," there is never any suggestion that *he* might fall in love with a black or Asian woman or, conversely, that the (white) woman he loves, whether "bitch" or "nice girl," will be sexually interested in a male from another ethnic group. The kind of genteel hypocrisy going on here—blacks and other ethnic groups are *just great*, we've nothing against them, but *of course* we couldn't possibly be attracted to them—is among the more contemptible and retrograde aspects of this group of films, though reviewers never seem to notice it or find it worth comment.

7. Class Is class an issue at all? Officially, it doesn't exist in America, even though there are millionaires and homeless people living in the same cities, but that's just what you deserve, because everyone is born equal. The one intelligently supportive father, the heroine's in *She's All That*, structurally paralleled with the hero's problematic and oppressive father, is less concerned with his offspring's "success" than with her happiness and fulfillment, presented as quite distinct goals, and he is also the only working-class father in the entire cycle.

8. Politics In the majority of the films one has the impression that the characters, obsessed with "getting laid" or with finding the ideal love, have no interest in politics (national, global, or sexual) or political action. The most prominent exception is Laney (Rachael Leigh Cook) in *She's All That*. One feels, at times, that the films' defining characteristic, their raison d'être within the grotesque present phase of capitalist culture, where even the future existence of life on the planet is at stake, is indeed the *suppression* of political thought. What, after all, might happen if all these young people suddenly ceased to be preoccupied with "getting laid" as life's ultimate goal? The current Emperor of the World (and President of the United States) might find the idea quite worrying, if his obviously severely limited imagination can stretch that far.

9. Sexual Orientation   The changing social attitude to gays and lesbians has been one of the most striking (and one of the very few encouraging) features of the last decade: nowadays, one scarcely encounters an adult comedy without at least one gay character. But where did they all go to school? Of the *American* films listed, only two (*Clueless* and *Can't Hardly Wait*) have the guts to raise the issue of gayness at all, the former marginally, the latter very confusingly. (*Get Over It*, the most recent of the cycle and easily the worst, has Martin Short as a drama teacher, embarrassingly still doing the kind of insulting gay stereotype that one thought went out when the 90s began.) Interestingly, both of the Canadian films listed raise the issue prominently and responsibly, together with that other subject totally excluded from the American films, teen suicide, but their whole tone is utterly different. The problem seems to be, How do you raise it in the context of high school (given, for example, the horrifyingly high percentage of gay teen suicides and the fact that high schools are notoriously still a stronghold of homophobia) without destroying the general sense of euphoric comedy? Elton, in Amy Heckerling's generally delightful movie (named simultaneously after the Reverend Elton in Jane Austen's novel and Elton John!), is never permitted a boyfriend and seems to have very little intercourse of any kind with anyone except the heroine. *Can't Hardly Wait* introduces an ambiguous gay subplot more centrally, to the film's credit, but sends out such mixed messages that it's virtually impossible to unravel what the film is actually saying. But it is at least *possible* to read the character of Mike (the high school's leading jock/ladykiller), when he is taunted as being a "fag," as realizing that he is actually gay, although living in a state of total denial. The film lacks any *positive* attitude to gayness (except perhaps in its magical one quiet moment, the "Barry Manilow" scene with the "angel," away from the noise of the party) and throws around the word "fag" somewhat indiscrimately, but at least it shows some awareness that there is an issue there.

Leaving aside *Dazed and Confused* and *Clueless* (both highly idiosyncratic and personal films by directors who had already distinguished themselves), I would single out *American Pie* (for all-round excellence), *Can't Hardly Wait* (for its energy, its inventiveness, its uniformly marvelous performances from an ensemble cast, the unpredictability—a rare virtue in these films—of certain of its plot developments),

Ten Things I Hate About You: Tamer Patrick Verona (Heath Ledger, *left*) confronts Shrew Kat Stratford (Julia Stiles, *right*), under the watchful eye of their "dysfunctional guidance counselor" (Allison Janney)

and *She's All That* (for its progressiveness, but especially for its last ten minutes); indeed, *She's All That* goes just a little further than its near-contemporary mirror-reflection *Ten Things I Hate About You*, which also deserves commendation, besides introducing two young actors who have since become prominent (Julia Stiles, Heath Ledger). *American Pie* can be left to fend for itself, its virtues being obvious and straightforward; I have a few more words on the other two.

Can't Hardly Wait offers a fascinating comparison with the Canadian *Kitchen Party*, the first feature of Gary Burns, both films taking place within about fifteen hours and mostly occupied by graduation parties, the parties located in the homes of parents (who are of course absent) and culminating in the desecration of the parental bourgeois home. Both films include one distanced, intelligent young woman who positions herself outside the celebratory festivities. The similarities highlight the extreme differences. The exuberance of the American movie is totally lacking in the Canadian, whose tone is far more serious and (for want of a better word) "realistic"—bourgeois life (which the American films implicitly celebrate, even if its strictures are an occasional nuisance) is here narrow, repressive, and generally stultifying. The desecration of the home is merely funny in *Can't Hardly Wait*, and there is no payoff with, for example, the return of the parents, whereas the climactic (and final) moment of *Kitchen Party* has the son (threatened with being denied university if there is a single spot on the bourgeois carpet, hence the film's title) deliberately opening a bottle of beer in the deserted living room as he hears his parents returning, and pouring out its contents as they enter—the film's moment of liberation, which makes me burst into tears every time I see it. The film also includes one character who *may* be gay, and who locks himself in a car and contemplates suicide for a long stretch of the running time. Parents play a far larger part than in any of the American films, Burns intercutting scenes of the kids' party with scenes of the parents' party in another location (it must be said that he seems more at ease directing the younger generation). The American films merely *assume* that there is an unbridgeable gulf between the generations; *Kitchen Party deals* with this as an essential aspect of the subject matter. Predictably, the film was a commercial disaster, since adults have no interest in teen movies and teens (apparently) have no interest in films that fail to indulge them. I apologize to readers outside Canada for writing about a film they will probably never have a chance to see, but there is no better way of suggesting the limitations within which the American films operate. *Kitchen Party* is an excellent movie that deserves universal distribution; it repays repeated viewings more than any of the American films. It is, quite simply, more intelligent (though less "clever").

The distinction of *Can't Hardly Wait* (for which two directors, one female, one male, share the credits—Deborah Kaplan and Harry Elfont, who have since collaborated on the well-received but quite dreadful *Josie and the Pussycats*) lies partly in its almost nonstop energy (somewhat exhausting until one learns to adjust) and the uniformly splendid performances by a superb ensemble cast of young actors who seem mostly to have disappeared from the Big Screen, but more in its creative use of the formulas, arousing certain expectations then surprising us by negating them. Structurally, the film is built upon the construction (actual or potential) of three partially interacting couples, only one of which is signaled as such from the outset: Preston (Ethan Embry) and Amanda (Jennifer Love Hewitt); Kenny (Seth Green) and Denise (Lauren Ambrose); Mike (Peter Facinelli) and William (Charlie Korsmo). At the start, Preston is established as the "serious" lover, Kenny as the one whose ambition is to "get laid." Initially, Preston is paired with Denise, but as her friend; their conversation establishes his crush on Amanda, the most popular girl in the school, to whom he has never dared to speak but to whom he has now written a letter expressing his love which he intends to give her at the party. Expectation: he will learn to abandon his adolescent romanticism and accept Denise as his right mate. Actual ending: after numerous mishaps, complications, and misunderstandings, Amanda gets the letter, is touched by it, and the couple end up together.

Kenny's aim is strikingly *un*romantic: he is desperate to lose his virginity (an issue much elaborated upon in *American Pie* the following year). Expectation: after various obligatory comic mishaps he will get his wish and prove his manhood. Actual resolution: On the point of realizing his ambition, while practicing positions from the

Kama Sutra, he gets accidentally locked in the bathroom with Denise, whom he dumped in junior high because she was too serious and not conventionally attractive, not *prestigious* enough; after working through their mutual antagonisms they recognize their genuine attraction to each other and make love on the washroom floor, but not very successfully—Kenny becomes aware of his own inexperience and the (marginally) more experienced Denise is quite frank with him about his inadequacy. By the film's end they have established a tentative on-again, off-again relationship.

The Mike / William subplot is the most intriguing, but the filmmakers seem (understandably, in the context and with the expected audience) somewhat scared of developing it: the implications are clear enough, but not so clear that homophobic teenagers will feel forced to confront them. At the outset it is established that the two young men have been enemies throughout school, Mike (school stud, sports hero, lover of the almost iconic Amanda) using William (the intellectual, the "geek," the "nerd") as a butt for cruel jokes. William, with the assistance of two of his pals, sets up his revenge: lured out to the pool house, Mike will be leapt upon, chloroformed, stripped, and placed very publicly in a compromising position with another male. Expectation: the plot will succeed, Mike will be humiliated, the geeks will triumph (a teen comedy is obliged to offer satisfactions to *all* potential members of its audience). Actual outcome: Mike is publicly humiliated by Amanda when (somewhat drunk) he attempts to reestablish his relationship with her, expecting her gratitude. When she strips him of all his pretensions, one of the young women in the audience yells out "Fag!" and he staggers off in terror. William, still pursuing his own revenge, follows him into another room and tries to lure him out to the bathhouse, but stops abruptly when he finds Mike in a state of collapse. Mike tells him he has been called a "fag," staggers over to him, puts his arms around his neck, and apologizes for his past behavior. To William's mixed delight and dismay the action becomes a prolonged embrace; the song on the soundtrack (diegetically, the music playing for the party, hence just "accidentally" occurring at this moment of the film) has the words "I'll make love to you / Like you want me to / And I'll hold you tight . . . " (but it is easy to ignore, as similar songs have been playing almost throughout the film). William's response is at most ambiguous, but it seems primarily readable as his delight that the school hero has revealed his vulnerability and is now miraculously his friend. At this moment (conveniently?!) the police raid the party. William helps his drunken friend (potential lover?) outside, inevitably to the poolhouse at the back, where his two inept cronies (who have both lost their flashlights) immediately chloroform them both, strip them and leave them apparently amorously entwined.

The resolution again does not insist upon a gay subtext but allows anyone who wants to to find one without great difficulty. We learn that Mike has saved William from certain disgrace (with his parents as well as the arresting cops) by claiming that the whole chloroform plot was his, to compromise William. The Mike of the film's first half would never be capable of such a gesture. Their final confrontation the next morning (the almost proverbial "cold light of dawn") is especially interesting. In a cafe, Mike is going through his habitual macho routines with his pals when William appears, in the evident expectation that their new relationship will be continued; Mike rejects and humiliates him. But this is followed by the *American Graffitti*-inspired printed end-statement about the caharacters' future lives (one allotted to each of the three "couples"). Mike's tells us that he has become overweight, taken to drink, and lost both his prestige and his job (as "groundsman") because of "incriminating polaroids." It is left to the viewers' discretion to guess just what these photographs may reveal. Are they the photographs from the party, or from some subsequent indiscretion?

Although *She's All That* has no gay characters, it does at least acknowledge the gay presence in schools, and in a very positive (if decidedly unobtrusive) way: as preparations are made for the school's graduation prom, we see a number of different groups carrying placards supporting Laney (Rachael Leigh Cook, the "Eliza Dolittle" character) as Prom Queen, a student directing them as to where the placards are to be placed. To one group he says: "Gay Students? Over there." It is the only film of the entire group that acknowledges that such an organization might exist. Further, the moment is followed immediately by another placard announcing that Laney is "The Pro-choice Choice." Not only does the film have (uniquely) a thoroughly politicized heroine (who is also an artist), it also suggests that her popularity as Prom Queen rests upon the support of politically active, progressive groups of students. She also has the support of the film as a whole, which is clearly thoroughly behind her.

It's a pity the film isn't better: the plot is too obvious, and (perhaps because we all know what's going to happen) is perfunctorily worked out; Laney is so obviously attractive from the start (all she needs is a bit of makeup and a better hairdo). The "bitch" character (anyone who dumps Freddie Prinze Jr. *must* be bad) is treated with the usual brutality for being sexually active. But one criterion for judging these films is, Do they ever surprise us?—and the last ten minutes of the film contain a series of surprises:

1. Contrary to all the narrative odds, Laney is *not* elected Prom Queen (she loses to the "bitch," and the film actually calls into question what being a Prom Queen amounts to anyway).
2. The black presence, unusually strong throughout the film (while still there to "support" the white characters), becomes almost the dominant element in the celebrations.
3. Perhaps the greatest surprise of all, though not a political one: there is a terrific dance number, wonderfully choreographed and executed, almost worthy of Minnelli or Kelly / Donen.
4. Freddie Prinze Jr. frantically rushes around the city trying to find the hotel

where Laney is supposedly being raped; he fails, and it turns out that she was perfectly able to take care of herself, thank you, with the help of a blast-gun that destroys her rapist's hearing in one ear.

5. She does not relinquish anything; her commitment to art is confirmed; her would-be transformer has (unlike Professor Higgins) learned more from her than she has from him, and he accepts this unproblematically.

Not Another Teen Movie and Bring It On

One is always forewarned when a cycle is reaching its end: the "spoofs" begin. Just as *Scary Movie* marked (thanks to heaven!) the demise of the teen horror movies, so *Not Another Teen Movie* marks that of the high school comedy. One greets the former with a sigh of relief, the latter with no more than mild regret. The two cycles belong together, the "teenie-kill pic" dramatizing the guilt aroused by the unquestioned, supposedly "liberated" sexuality of the school films, in which guilt is totally repressed.

The first rule of an effective parody is that it must be more sophisticated than its object, its aim being to criticize through satire. *Not Another Teen Movie* is much *less* sophisticated than even the worst of the films it parodies. It demands an extensive knowledge of the cycle, with extended references to *American Pie, Can't Hardly Wait* (with "clones" standing in for Chris Klein, Seth Green, Jennifer Love Hewitt, etc.), prominent ones to *Bring It On* and *Ten Things I Hate About You,* and back glances to *Porky's* and *Fast Times* with a final *hommage* to *Pretty in Pink* (one wonders how many of the current teen audience have seen it), complete with a cameo appearance from Molly Ringwald. But its chief source of misplaced pillaging is *She's All That* (which at least the film acknowledges): it takes us doggedly through the film's plot and especially its last fifteen minutes, without the least recognition that the latter, at least, neither deserves nor responds to parody. It never establishes a tone or a stance or the least critical judgment, spraying its scattershot indiscriminately over the cycle's best and worst features and never betraying the least sign of intelligence. I didn't laugh once, and here I seem to be in tune with contemporary teen audiences: it bombed out at the box office.

Bring It On is another matter altogether. It looks as if it was made with the express aim of correcting the major imbalances, suppressions, and omissions of the cycle as a whole—the subordination of women, the marginalization of blacks, the almost total absence of gays—though Peyton Reed, in the Director's Commentary on the DVD, never describes this as his conscious intention. Being single-mindedly concerned with cheerleading (which it promotes quite seriously as an art form), with a number of stunningly choreographed and executed sequences influenced (we have Reed's word for it) by Busby Berkeley and Bob Fosse, it does no more for education. It also has a wonderfully charismatic leading couple (Kirsten Dunst and Jesse Bradford) who play together beautifully, often in whole scenes without dialogue (the teethbrushing scene is a marvel of subtle interplay).

Women   *Bring It On* is not the only female-centered teen comedy (*Fast Times at Ridgemont High* and *Clueless*, both by Amy Heckerling, are clear forerunners), but it is easily the most strongly female-dominated, the men relegated to the back row of cheerleaders or reduced to spectators. There is a strong emphasis on female bonding and group solidarity, the main plot is female-driven, and the spectacle displays and celebrates the women's activeness and energy, never reducing them to mere objects-for-the-gaze or immobilizing them in passive and exotic Berkeley-style patterns.

Blacks   The plot involves the unfriendly rivalry of two cheerleading teams participating in the national competition, one white, one all black. After considerable well-motivated hostility, Dunst discovers that the black team doesn't have the money necessary to enter. Partly from grudging admiration, but also from a desire to have them in the competition to beat, Dunst persuades her father (who is in "big business") to sign a generous check for them. Reed reveals in his commentary that in the original screenplay the check was accepted; in his revised version the leader of the black team tears it up, rejecting charity from wealthy whites, and team members raise the money themselves through their own talents. They also win the competition (the Dunst team in second place), and the two leaders are left forming a tentative and cautious friendship.

Gays   A gay male cheerleader has a fairly prominent role ("a very well-adjusted gay high school student, very comfortable with his homosexuality"—Reed) and is permitted roughly the same screen time and the same dignity as his heterosexual buddy. The real surprise is that he is even allowed a tentative "date," encountering near the end of the film a student from a rival team, with instant mutual attraction and promise of further meetings. The scene is played very charmingly, and there is nothing like it in any of the other films in the cycle. Within the genre's limitations (which it stretches but never quite bursts beyond), it is a splendid film.[2]

THE PARTY'S OVER: SCOTT SMITH'S *Rollercoaster*

Even in Canada, Canadian films (unless directed by David Cronenberg, or Atom Egoyan in his later works) are categorized instantly as "small," and I think we

2. I wish to thank Michael McKegney for drawing my attention to this film.

should ask ourselves exactly what this conveys, and by what criterion smallness or bigness can be gauged. The answer is clear: "small" here has nothing whatever to do with subject matter, quality, or ambition; it has to do exclusively with money and is yet another proof of our insidious and all-pervasive corruption by capitalist values.

I wonder how many people reading this chapter have even heard of *Rollercoaster* (or, perhaps, are expecting a critical exploration of the 1977 Sensurround movie of the same title, a disaster film in every sense, in which case I shall disappoint them). Scott Smith's film is, in the common usage, "small": its budget was not exactly enormous, and I assume its cast of six (uniformly marvelous) actors were each paid somewhat less than the $10 million nowadays taken for granted by major Hollywood stars, though they give performances as good, if not better. And the film is "merely" about teenagers, our culture's disenfranchised, disenchanted, and desperate members, and (more specifically) about teen suicide: a "small" subject? I have to suppose it is, for most people. We read brief references to it in the newspapers, but nothing is ever done so presumably no one cares, it not occurring to them that these same teenagers (the ones who survive) represent the future of our culture. But then, does anyone care about that either?

Rollercoaster is a great movie, but its pleasures and disturbances will be spoiled for you if you haven't seen the film before you read what follows. It is available (although not all stores bother to stock it) on both VHS and DVD in a really splendid widescreen transfer. The DVD includes a very useful Director's Commentary and an intermittently illuminating commentary by the teenage actors.

I missed *Rollercoaster* in the Toronto Film Festival (2000) but attended its theatrical opening on its first day. I was the only person in the auditorium. It ran, I believe, for one week. Since then I have watched the DVD five times, seeing more on each viewing, partly thanks to certain insights derived from the commentaries. The film is not in any obvious way "difficult," but it is rich in significant detail (a gesture here, an expression there, a throwaway line of dialogue, a camera movement, a particular use of décor). I liked the film straight away, but I attribute my initial underestimation to precisely those preconceptions about Canadian cinema that I have attacked: I suppose my attitude could have been summed up as "very good for a small Canadian movie." So I have not avoided contamination; consequently I missed things I should have picked up on from the start. My renewed interest in the film developed out of my engagement with the American high school comedies. While noting their total refusal to confront certain crucial problems involving teenagers today (gayness, teen suicide, the frequent connection between the two), I thought suddenly of *Kitchen Party* and *Rollercoaster*, to both of which these issues are central. (One must now add *Ginger Snaps*, which had not then appeared, but which takes as its starting point the projected joint suicide of two sisters. It seems to me inferior—less "thought through"—than the two earlier films.) The Hollywood films belong, as a group, quite blatantly to that favorite and essential capitalist strategy of "making us all think we're happy"; the Canadian films are oppositional and, whatever the filmmakers' conscious intentions, can stand as a critique of their jolly American relatives. The closest American equivalent is Larry Clark's *Kids*, to which *Rollercoaster* seems to me vastly superior on every level.

Structure   The film's intricate overall structure is built upon a set of interlocking structures:

1. *The 24-hour time scheme.* The film starts in early morning, ends in the next early morning. The effect is not mere symmetry: the "next" morning is "the morning after," when everything has changed, and where there are glimmers of fresh hope following tragedy.

2. *Weather.* Shooting restrictions for this ultra-low-budget (but by no means "small") film, shot entirely on location and outdoors, were extremely tight. That one scene—and one scene only—takes place in the rain, with all its connotations of simultaneous sorrow and purification, was apparently (to judge from the commentaries) fortuitous. It just happens that it's the film's pivotal scene, to which everything leads up and from which everything follows.

3. *Progression A.* The rides in the amusement park (within or just outside which the entire film, up to the last shot, takes place). For the first third of the film everything is shut down, static, the kids climbing on a motionless rollercoaster; in the middle section (as things start moving dramatically) the machines are turned on; when night falls, the kids turn on all the lights, start all the rides, and the park becomes a wonderland, a celebration of life (albeit a partially ironic one, in which suicide is still an option).

4. *Progression B.* Dramatically, the film builds up to and then beyond two parallel crises (Chloe's, Stick's), the two linked by *disclosure*, the revelation of what was previously unspoken.

5. *Paradox.* The most likely of the characters to commit suicide is the one who emerges strengthened; the one who seems least likely is the one who goes through with it.

Source   Smith reveals in his commentary that the source of the film was a true story. Four teenagers decided to commit suicide together, as life appeared to hold nothing for them. But, when it came to the point, they found they'd run out of beer. So they drove off to a liquor store, came back, drank all the beer . . . and committed suicide. This story is told in the film by Stick, in one of its many extraordinary shots. He is standing (long shot) on the highest reach of the stationary rollercoaster, addressing his suicidal friends (with one of whom he is, potentially at least, in love). In the background is a mountain, with clouds around its peak, strongly suggesting the smoke from a latent, but about to erupt, volcano. I have been haunted by that image ever since I took serious interest in the film—by its fusion of visual beauty, precariousness, and imminent disaster. There are many such beautiful moments in the film, marking it as the work of an artist with an instinctive understanding of cinema; if this single image stands out, it is because of its duration and the lack of movement, suggestive of a contemplative pause in the film's otherwise swift forward momentum.

Location and Cinematography   Having made the decision to shoot virtually the entire film within an out-of-season amusement park, Smith makes dazzlingly inventive use of its potential, both visual and dramatic. Nothing is faked, there are no back projections or studio sets, the camera is up there on the rides with the kids, whether the rollercoaster and the other machines are static or in motion. The contrast with current Hollywood "action" movies couldn't be stronger, their computer-generated unreality mercilessly exposed. The meager reviews of the film I read (polite, condescending) showed no sign of recognition of the nature or quality of Smith's achievement. The climactic sequences, where, at nightfall, the kids turn on all the amusement park lights in a celebration of life that is partly real, partly (in the context of darkness and imminent death) ironic and valedictory, are at once exhilarating and painful. The use throughout of the various machines and other amusement park décor is consistently intelligent, never merely "colorful," always dramatically justified: the "Zipper" in which Ben is tricked and trapped, the bumper cars in which the characters' diverse tensions are released, the rollercoaster from which Darrin will throw himself, the hidden video "eyes" that watch from various adornments.

Stick's Progress

It is perhaps unfair to single out Brendan Fletcher's performance from a cast that contains no weaknesses and, under Smith's direction, plays faultlessly as an ensemble. (One gathers from the DVD's cast commentary, in which all six actors join, that Smith got them involved as a group before shooting started, and that they have remained friends ever since.) But Fletcher has the showiest role and plays the character who undergoes the most development; if anyone can be said to dominate the film it is he.

The subtleties with which Stick's progress is charted may not be apparent to the casual viewer, or perhaps to anyone on first viewing. Hollywood has habituated us to the careful spelling out of plot points, seldom allowing them to be made purely visually but indeed often underlining them in the dialogue. With Stick this is impossible: the gayness which he denies to himself as much as to the world can be "spoken" only through inadvertent physical behavior, and especially through his insistent physical contact with Darrin (Kett Turton), mainly a matter of those "playful" punches that easily pass for "normal" masculine behavior among teenage boys. (Smith points out in his commentary how he tried as often as possible to connect Stick and Darrin in two-shots, one of which he describes as the "lovers on the beach" shot). This inexplicitness serves an important function: the film becomes a cunning trap for homophobic teenagers in the audience, for whom Stick, throughout the film's first two-thirds, is the most obvious identification figure, the most seemingly extrovert, the most active, the rowdiest. When the park attendant Ben (the film's only adult character) traps Stick in the washroom and sexually molests him, it is possible to read, carelessly, Stick's reactions merely as a sort of paralyzed horror, Ben thereby becoming, at that point, the film's representative of homosexuality. The tables are then turned, the trap sprung, by Stick's subsequent revelation (the beginning of his self-acceptance).

If, however, we attend to the details of Fletcher's remarkable performance, the stages of Stick's progress become clear: (1) his constant "playful" provocation, and constant awareness, of Darrin, never entirely rejected; (2) the extremely complex reaction to Ben's molestation as rendered by the actor's face, where horror mingles with desire (in the cast commentary the actors describe him as "torn"); (3) his pathetic attempt at self-denial in abruptly "feeling up" Chloe, in whom he has previously shown not the least sign of sexual interest; (4) his crucial speech to Justin (Darrin's younger brother), when Justin describes Ben as a "fag" ("No. *I'm* a fag. *He* fucks kids"), in the scene Smith describes as the film's "little window of hope"; and (5) the climactic revelation of his desire, in the game in which everyone has to lie, saying the opposite of the truth ("I *hate* you, Darrin. I fucking hate you"—Darrin understands perfectly and turns aside).

Does this contribute to Darrin's suicide? As with Stick, Smith refuses to spell things out for us, but the context suggests the possibility, adding to the film's poignance and complexity. Its underlying assumption seems to be that these teenagers (including the barely teenage Justin) are at an age where sexuality has not been finally "fixed," where there is still the possibility of flux. Darrin's fondness for Stick is evident throughout the film (to the point where one could almost substitute "attraction to" for "fondness for"). And Darrin has already had to face Chloe's revelations (which parallel Stick's): that she has been sexually promiscuous, that Darrin may not be the father of her child, and that in any case the child (the pretext for the joint suicide—Chloe's "We're not going to bring our baby into this world") has already been aborted. The film's sensitivity to the confusions and fears of teenagers struggling to make sense of a harsh and hostile environment and of their places within it strikes me as a rare and valuable quality, totally lacking in the corresponding American teen comedies.

The film's delicacy and inexplicitness is summed up in the last scene, a single-take extreme long shot. Outside the amusement park at last, the four survivors drive off. Then the car pulls up, and we see Justin get out and set off on his own, up a steep bank to the main highway. The car drives on, leaving the foreground empty, but then backs up and stops again. Stick gets out and follows Justin. The boy (apparently about thirteen) has earlier shown a mature sensitivity toward Stick, responding to his "It will be hard on you without Darrin" with "It'll be hard on *you*." Clearly, Stick has replaced Darrin as "elder brother," and his following Justin is an acknowledgment of responsibilty accepted; there is also the possibility that Justin may grow up gay, hinted at in his readiness to accept Stick. The "little window of hope" (which refers to the possibility of supportive, positive human relations within a cruel and uncaring world) has opened a little further.

17.

Hollywood Today
IS AN OPPOSITIONAL
CINEMA POSSIBLE?

The immediate—and obvious—question: Was it ever? I suggested in the new prologue to this edition that certain films made during the classical period can be read as, at least potentially, "radical" or "subversive," but were they at the time? The answer is, almost certainly not—neither by audiences nor by reviewers, and in most cases probably not even by their directors. The explanation lies above all in genre and its conventions. I take as exemplary three films that I regard as masterpieces (I in fact included them in my latest list for the international critics' poll *Sight and Sound* organizes and publishes every decade in choosing the "10 Best Films of All Time"): *Rio Bravo, Rally 'Round the Flag, Boys!*, and *The Reckless Moment*.

In its day, and perhaps even now, many critics have regarded *Rio Bravo* as a right-wing response to the "liberal" *High Noon*; today it is easier to read it as an early assault (translated into the mythic terms of the classical western) on corporate capitalism (represented by the Burdetts) by a group of heroes whose values have nothing to do with money or greed—thereby highlighting not only capitalism's manifest inequities and iniquities but also its dehumanizing effect on its practitioners. It is likely that general audiences of the time (1959) saw it as neither: it was "just a western." *Rally 'Round the Flag, Boys!* was even easier to cope with and render safe: it was a (very late) screwball comedy, hence, by definition, not to be taken seriously. What was the social/political force of these films when they appeared? Probably zero. One cannot, of course, estimate their unconscious effect, but there is no indication whatever that they led to any social change. It is also not just possible but probable that their makers were completely unaware of their potentially explosive content. If McCarey, especially, had understood the content of his own best films he would probably have felt compelled to denounce himself, along with certain of his colleagues, to the McCarthy era's Un-American Activities tribunal (see the essay on McCarey's work in *Sexual Politics and Narrative Film*).

The Reckless Moment is a somewhat different case: it is built upon the interaction between two genres whose potentially radical content was always closer to the surface (the woman's melodrama, *film noir*), and it was directed by an outsider, a European émigré marginally associated with Bertolt Brecht, who was a far more conscious artist (more conscious than Hawks or McCarey of *being* an artist), not just a "popular entertainer." The film—having throughout its length provided a meticulously detailed analysis of the repressions, the subjugated tensions, the resentments and frustrations on which the patriarchal nuclear family is constructed—seems to offer in its final scene a characteristic generic escape route: the disruptions are removed, order is restored, the family members gather in the entrance hall of their domestic prison for the absent father's phone call from Berlin—the classic "happy end." But one can take it so only if one is totally impervious to the art of *mise-en-scène*. Ophuls shows us that the patriarchal family is not merely restored but reproduced, the whole sorry mess repeating itself: the rebellious daughter in her mother's fur coat, the rebellious son in a neat, respectable suit, the black maid relegated once again, after her shortlived prominence, to the background of the image, the camera finally descending to show the mother, as she mouths her Christmas platitudes, behind the prison bars of the banisters. One will find no equivalent in *The Deep End*, the recent remake.

But if these films had no discernible social effect when they appeared, what, then, was/is their use? My answer is that they are of inestimable value to us today, not just for the manifold pleasures of their realization by directors of genius, but for their insights into the profound unease and dissatisfaction with the structures of Western capitalist civilization which they so clearly dramatize, our culture's Collective Unconscious. All those tensions that finally erupted in the great radical movements of the 60s/70s are already demonstrably *there*. They just hadn't been recognized for what they were.

Crucial to these works (including, to a great extent, *The Reckless Moment*) was the relative lack of self-consciousness. Hawks, for example, could become, intermittently, a great artist: the circumstances of Classical Hollywood permitted it, even encouraged it, without the least awareness of doing so. *Only Angels Have Wings* and *Rio Bravo* can be read as offering a complete and satisfying (if primitive) philosophy of human existence, developed spontaneously and organically out of a whole complex of interlocking factors (genre, writers, actors, cinematographers), while Hawks himself appeared to believe that he was just "having fun." That kind of unself-consciousness, a prerequisite of full, free-flowing creativity, is no longer possible. Today, a filmmaker of ambition cannot be simply the central controlling and organizing factor within a spontaneously evolving work: he is "making a statement." Consequently, although surrounded by actors and technicians, he works in terrible isolation: the statement must be *his*, it must be consciously intended, it cannot simply evolve. There is a sense in which even art as closely and densely "worked" as the greatest plays of Shakespeare developed out of communal experience (genre, conventions, preexisting forms and materials, a sense of cultural belonging). The possibility still existed, to an extent, in the 1980s and early 90s— witness the greatest achievements of that period, *Raging Bull, Heaven's Gate*, the "living dead" trilogy. All are marked to an extent by a degree of self-consciousness quite alien to Hawks or McCarey, but all retain a sense of free-flowing creativity, a spontaneity, a readiness to take chances, to try anything and see if it works.

Fifty years from now, circa 2053, will critics be discerning comparable radical impulses in today's Hollywood movies? It's possible, I suppose, but it seems unlikely. For a start, we have become far more self-conscious, hence more wary, more on our guard. Films may have become more "daring" in terms of sexual explicitness and extreme violence, but such things have nothing to do with social/political subversion and our internal censors will warn us against anything more dangerous than the spectacle of crashing cars and exploding buildings, created with the aid of the latest technology. The grotesquely reactionary period we live in is not far enough removed from the upheavals of radical feminism, black power, gay rights, to have lost awareness of them; their partial cooption into the mainstream does not entirely remove their potential threat. Filmmakers are now largely under the control of vast capitalist enterprises whose aim seems to be distraction, not disturbance. And, with the now increasingly patent devastation of the planet, environmentalism is likely to grow in force and supporters. But the majority, as yet, remain in the state of stupefied mystification that corporate capitalism requires for its continuance: Shock us, make us laugh, but please, please, don't encourage us to think.

The past few years have not been entirely devoid of movies critical of American institutions. Two recent ones come to mind, *Spy Game* (the CIA) and *Training Day* (the police), both raising questions of corruption and morality, professional duty/personal loyalty. They have certain features in common: each juxtaposes an experienced older man (Robert Redford, Denzel Washington) with a young novice (Brad Pitt, Ethan Hawke), with the advantage of a duo of intelligent and gifted male stars, giving each film a certain distinction. Both are flawed (*Spy Game* far more seriously) by two of the prevalent diseases of contemporary Hollywood filmmaking, respectively overediting and the apparent inability of the current action thriller simply to end. The point of hysterical overediting appears to be that it offers speed, thrills, excitement; it chief effect is to permit the spectator no opportunity for thought. The very real moral questions that *Spy Game* raises concerning CIA ethics are drowned in a welter of images that dazzle the eye and numb the intellect, and a film that should have encouraged serious reflection ends by annihilating it. It needed a Preminger; it got Tony Scott.

Training Day is altogether more impressive—an audacious, outspoken, and disturbing examination of pervasive corruption within the American police system. At the height of *film noir* in the 40s it would have come as no great surprise, but in the contemporary context it stands out like an exemplary sore thumb . . . until its last ten minutes. Is there really a demand today, at the "final" climax of an action or horror movie, for a whole series of endings in which either the hero or the monster survives what appears to be certain death, to come up for yet another bout of violence? It wasn't necessary to the original *Frankenstein*, for example, or its first two sequels, but in *Hollow Man* Kevin Bacon has to be rekilled *ad nauseam*, post-absurdity and beyond tedium, and in *Training Day* Ethan Hawke has to survive a comparable series of apparently lethal disasters before, inevitably, "good" can triumph over "evil" (yes, there are problems with the police but one good man can overcome them . . .).

I end by offering brief accounts of two contemporary filmmakers of variable distinction who might be considered "oppositional," one who has attempted to operate within the mainstream, one who has located himself firmly outside it.

THE STRANGE CASE OF DAVID FINCHER

Within the contemporary Hollywood mainstream, David Fincher's films stand out as, to say the least, an anomaly. Their most immediately obvious quality is their darkness and drabness: colors tend to be muted, reduced to a narrow range of grays and browns; their tone ranges from the overwhelming pessimism and despair of *Seven* (1995) to the caustic, brutal near-nihilism of *Fight Club* (1999). Whatever one feels about the films' success or lack thereof, they cannot be accused of providing the mere mindless distractions that characterize most of the current Hollywood fare. Even the more conventional *Panic Room* (what Hitchcock used to call a "run for cover" movie, a built-in commercial success after *Fight Club*'s spectacular audacities) is recognizable as a Fincher movie from its drab lighting and narrow tonal range.

Seven, the most completely achieved of Fincher's films to date, stands somewhat apart from my current concerns, its engagement with the contemporary social/political realities swallowed up in what comes across as a form of existential despair about "the human condition." Richard Dyer, in his meticulously detailed, brilliant, and perhaps definitive BFI Modern Classics monograph, sums it up: "The film is a single-minded elaboration on a feeling that the world is beyond both redemption and remedy." On the other hand, *Alien 3*, *The Game*, and *Fight Club* form a kind of loose, uneasy, and unstable trilogy about the ravages of corporate capitalism.

Alien 3 (1992), besides being the darkest, most disturbing, and most coherent of the four *Alien* movies so far, is easily the most successful and least compromised of this trilogy, and this is surely because it's primarily and unapologetically a genre movie, "just entertainment" about good guys and bad guys, and can therefore get away with anything; the cost of this is that it is forced to waste much of its time (throughout the middle section) providing (very efficiently) the kind of shocks, suspense, and thrills that audiences for the *Alien* films expect. (Significantly, it appears to be the least popular of the four.) Only in its final third does it really play its hand, cards down.

The film's ultimate villain is not the alien but "the Company" (corporate capitalism in miniature). Its audacity can be gauged from its choice of opposition: not just Sigourney Weaver (intelligent and formidable as she is), but the earth's worst criminals, the multi-rapists and serial killers who populate the tiny planet that has been converted into a maximum security prison to which they can be deported, the strategy being to suggest that the evil represented by the Company is far worse, since it places the entire human race in jeopardy. The film's ending approaches sublimity. The confrontation between Ripley (the new alien in her womb) and the head of the Company (Lance Henriksen) on the platform above the vast vat of molten ore opposes human emotion, human conscience, to the naked greed for power: with the alien as its weapon, the Company can achieve world domination or the annihilation of human life on the planet. Ripley's self-sacrifice transforms her into a veritable Christ figure, giving her life to save humanity.

From the sublime to the ridiculous. *The Game* (1997) is a genre movie *manqué*, a disaster that might have been a near-masterpiece. If you forget its last ten minutes ever happened, you have a fascinating update of *film noir*. All the major ingredients are there: the nocturnal city, with menace lurking around every corner, an atmosphere of all-pervasive deception and treachery; the protagonist/victim struggling, first, to make sense of what is happening to him and, subsequently, just to survive; the ambiguous woman, who may be his loyal supporter but may equally be the archetypal *femme fatale*; the villains (who could be anyone or everyone) motivated solely by the greed for possession; no one to be trusted, not even the protagonist's younger brother. The absolutely logical and topical updating lies in making the ultimate villain "big business" itself, the protagonist the millionaire head of a corporation in a dog-eat-dog world, the macabre twist that he is lured to his destruction by being led to believe he is participating in an elaborate game, gradually revealed as deadly, the stakes his wealth, his position, his identity, and ultimately his life.

The film should have been a magnificent "fable for our time." Our credulity may be strained at times (could even the wealthiest, most powerful amalgamation of businessmen organize a "game" on this scale, utilizing the resources of an entire city?), but here generic convention saves the day: *film noir* has accustomed us to the extremes of paranoid reality/fantasy, and the extra step we are invited to take is easily accomplished by a "willing suspension of disbelief."

Yet all this promise goes for nothing. I know of no other film that is so completely destroyed by a trick "happy ending." Even the notorious "It was only a dream" ending of Lang's *Woman in the Window* can be justified by a close look at its opening scenes, and the film's essential meaning remains undamaged. But the revelation of Fincher's film (it really *was* only a game) does irreparable harm on all levels. It isn't merely a matter of plausibility (though credulity is no longer strained, it is totally shattered, the entire film becoming patently ridiculous). The far more serious damage lies in its self-betrayal. Far from defining the world of corporate capitalism as a monstrous extension of the *noir* vision, it now tells us that everyone was basically benevolent, that the "game" (in which Michael Douglas might have been killed half a dozen times) was just a kind of jolly romp to turn him into a better human being. He used to be a nasty capitalist tycoon, now he's going to be a nice one. Yes, it's as banal as that . . .

I don't find *Fight Club* a success on any level, but one can say, positively, that it at least represents some kind of disturbance within the all-pervasive distractions of contemporary Hollywood—an intervention both incoherent and irresponsible, but an intervention nonetheless. Its chief interest is that it ever got made at all. It could not, as it stands, have been made after September 11, 2001, because it can be read (with some difficulty) as condoning terrorism. It can also be read, with only a little less difficulty, as denouncing it. In the last resort it appears to be unreadable, like its obvious forerunner, Bergman's *Persona*.

Persona, equally the forerunner of David Lynch's *Mulholland Dr.* (2001), has proven a disastrous model, largely because what is imitated is (infallibly it seems) its worst part. The abrupt rejection, around two-thirds to three quarters through each of the three films, of a more-or-less coherent narrative with carefully defined characters, the collapse into "anything goes" pseudo-avant-gardism, is in each case taken by the filmmaker as an invitation (from himself, to himself) for indulging his own personal obsessions. This is nowhere more obvious than with Bergman himself (as I discuss at length in the essay on *Persona* in *Sexual Politics and Narrative Film*), but both Fincher and Lynch use it as a self-authorized license to irresponsibility: the move to some (undefinable) "other level of reality" gives them the freedom to get away with anything.

Fight Club differs from *Persona* in that its narrative (we suddenly discover) was unstable from the outset: whereas in *Persona* (and in *Mulholland Dr.*) the two women are (fictionally) "real" until the breakdown moment (which in Lynch's film *may* imply that everything we thought was real was a dream), Tyler Durden/Brad Pitt has never existed except as the (nameless) narrator's (Edward Norton) *alter ego* or "demon" self, the self he would unconsciously like to be but isn't. Otherwise the parallel holds: there is even the equivalent (in both films a kind of tremor before

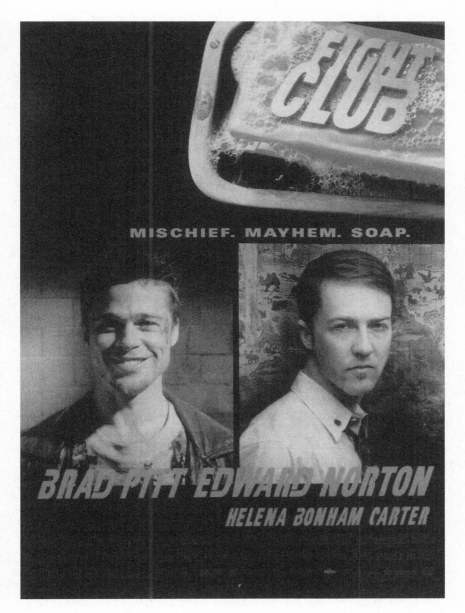

Fight Club: The original poster

the earthquake) of *Persona's* projector-breakdown: the sudden instability of the camera when Norton begins to doubt Pitt. In *Fight Club* the "earthquake"—the moment when the reality level definitively changes—is the car crash, in which we may well believe that "both" men were killed, it being difficult to imagine anyone surviving more or less unscathed. Before it, the narrative (given the expectations of extremely stretched plausibility to which the contemporary action cinema has accustomed us) can just about be accepted as plausible; after it, it cannot. The car crash is closely followed by the scene where Norton (who may or may not be dead) wanders downstairs in the building he has been occupying to find that the previously modest "fight club" has suddenly transformed itself into a vast terrorist organization, manufacturing weapons of destruction in his own cellar. This in its turn is followed by the scene in which Tyler Durden reveals that he has no independent existence but is simply Norton's hidden self, summoned up to do all the things Norton would never dare.

Norton (a sort of modern "Everyman" character, a reading underlined by his namelessness) has (we deduce) summoned up Tyler out of his disgust and disillusionment with contemporary civilization and his own position within the business world, the world that Tyler exists to (literally) blow up. It's a wonderful and audacious concept: one may speculate that Fincher wanted to make the film as a correction to *The Game*. But the film's potentially explosive force is largely dissipated in its confusions. There seem to be two (quite incompatible) ways of reading the ending, partly depending on whether you see the narrator or Tyler Durden as the film's "hero":

1. Terrorism is not pretty, but it's the only way to overthrow corporate capitalism, therefore it must be accepted—hence the narrator has been merely cowardly in rejecting his "other" self and trying to prevent the cataclysm. The support for this is partly the satisfaction the film offers its audience in watching the final collapse of the buildings as the explosives go off, Tyler having made it clear that the primary targets are the headquarters of the major credit card companies: all credit card debts will be wiped out, a fantasy that must surely appeal to the vast majority of the film's spectators. But this reading is further supported by the fact that, during the final stretches, *everyone* in a subordinate position (including restaurant workers and even the police) appears to have become a member of the underground organization: it is a popular movement, a people's revolution.

2. Corporate capitalism is a great evil but terrorism (the only challenge to it the film offers or even hints at) is brutish, wasteful, ugly, and purely negative: the narrator was right to denounce his *alter ego*. (We may note that Tyler himself has named the revolution "Project Mayhem," although he also claims, impossibly, that no actual people will be harmed in the explosions.) This reading is supported by Fincher himself in his audio commentary on the DVD, where he compares

Fight Club: Infectious waste

Tyler's assembly of fight club initiates to the Nuremberg Rally; and in the actors' audio commentary there is a concerted effort by everyone to suggest that the members of Fight Club are fascists and morons. As membership, by the film's climax, seems to include most of the working class, this verdict may strike us as somewhat sweeping.

I find both these available readings politically irresponsible, and the unresolvable clash between them, together with the film's failure to suggest that there might be a positive alternative in the form of organized political protest, simply repeats the despairing cynicism of *The Game* in a different form. Ultimately, the film panders to that section of the public (unfortunately a large one) that requires a further dose of impotent desperation to prevent it from starting a *real* political revolution. *Fight Club* raises the question of whether it is possible to make a radical movie in Hollywood today, and answers it, by implication, in the negative.

JIM JARMUSCH: POET OF ALIENATION

> "America is a big melting-pot . . . When you bring it to the boil, all the scum rises
> to the top." —John Lurie in *Down by Law* (1986)

Excluding his first, which I have never had a chance to see, Jim Jarmusch has written and directed six fictional films, which fall neatly and chronologically into three pairs:

1. Two films in black-and-white (the only ones prior to *Dead Man*), studies in urban alienation and attempted escape, built upon the uneasy friendship between two men and an outsider (in *Stranger Than Paradise* a young woman, in *Down by Law* Roberto Benigni).
2. Two multiple-narrative films, taking place during a single day or night: three overlapping stories (*Mystery Train*) set mainly in the same rundown hotel; five stories taking place in different parts of the world (*Night on Earth*).
3. Two films within what would normally be regarded (if this wasn't Jarmusch) as an "action" genre: a western (*Dead Man*) and a samurai movie (*Ghost Dog*), in both of which the "hero," signified as doomed from the outset, is shot down at the end.

I have always enjoyed Jarmusch's films, in a casual sort of way, but it had never occurred to me to write about him until I saw *Dead Man* (1995), and there I doubted my ability: I didn't feel sufficient contact, our sensibilities seemed too remote. I still have difficulty entering the Jarmusch world (seductive as it is to an outsider), and what follows is necessarily tentative. But in the context I have set up, some attempt seems unavoidable: he is one of the only contemporary American filmmakers of consistent and distinguished achievement who has dared to say a resounding No! to contemporary America. I am careful to say "American" filmmaker, not "Hollywood," his one apparent flirtation with mainstream cinema, *Night on Earth* (1991), culminating—if I have understood correctly—in his emphatic rejection of it. Instead, he has reached out repeatedly to compatibly idiosyncratic European "arthouse" filmmakers, aligning himself with their work (Claire Denis in France, the Kaurismakis in Finland, both acknowledged in *Night on Earth* in the Paris and Helsinki episodes by his use of actors associated with them), as well as to less-than-"respectable" American individualists (he made a documentary about Samuel Fuller). Reseeing the films today, in their chronological sequence, has greatly increased my affection for them and (with certain reservations) my commitment to them. It is probably impossible today for anyone to make an even halfway commercial movie that shouts, in some positive sense, "Revolution!" as loudly as its lungs can bear, so one must celebrate the films that seem (whether deliberately or not) to imply its necessity.

Jarmusch's male characters are both like and unlike the wanderer of the traditional western: like, because they too are inveterate wanderers; unlike, because the westerner either is escaping from something in his past or is a man with a mission, frequently revenge, sometimes, like Shane, in the service of the good but vulnerable. Jarmusch's wanderers are essentially motiveless: they wander simply because they are totally alienated from the culture through which they move, which is invariably even stranger than they are themselves. There is only one character in all the films whom we see in a fixed residence, and the "home" is a rooftop populated mainly by carrier pigeons, the domicile a rough shack erected beside the cages: the black samurai (Forest Whitaker) of *Ghost Dog*. Even he, in his chosen profession, is traditionally a wanderer, and without *personal* motivation, paid for hire by a "master" whose "retainer" he has elected to become, killing people because he is instructed to. Otherwise, Jarmusch's characters (the men, and most of the women) are seen in cheap, temporary, barely furnished apartments (the first two films); in prison (the middle section of *Down by Law*); in decrepit hotels (*Mystery Train*); in taxis, as drivers or passengers (*Night on Earth*); or astray in the western wilderness (*Dead Man*). Typically, they inhabit a barren world, a world without a past, without traditions, without a cultural history; they come from nowhere and have nowhere to go.

In the two early films these alienated wanderers are all we are allowed of identification figures, and identification is extremely problematic (though one suspects that Jarmusch identifies with them to an extent, whilst presenting them ironically). They never seem aware or intelligent enough to fight or protest; their alienation is passively accepted, as a fact of modern existence. Women, on the other hand (though, after *Stranger Than Paradise*, they seldom figure very prominently, the two multinarrative films providing the chief exceptions), are the settlers, though as unlike the heroines of John Ford as it is possible to get: they appear to have accepted the civilization as it is and are making the most of it, which makes them quite impossible identification figures in the Jarmusch world. The exception here is Eva (Eszter Balint) of *Stranger Than Paradise*, the only woman in a Jarmusch film who seems privileged and valued above the men (who treat her abominably); there is no comparable figure in the later films, though Winona Ryder and, especially, Beatrice Dalle in *Night on Earth* both come close. Eva stands up to men without making demands on them (which *these* men could never meet), and becomes the film's emotional center as well as its center of intelligence. Insofar as we are allowed to identify with anyone in the film, it is with her. But, especially in the early works, Jarmusch's stylistic decisions preclude identification rigorously: no point-of-view shots, no use of that old Hollywood standby the shot/reverse-shot pattern. This stylistic rigor is relaxed slightly in the multinarrative films but returns in full force in *Dead Man*. One guesses that Godard was an influence on the first two films, which are replete with the alienation devices that Godard learned from Bertolt Brecht.

Ghost Dog: "Ghost Dog" studies and practices "The Way of the Samurai"

The ironic stance of the first two films is . . . not lost . . . but partially and intermittently submerged until you get to *Dead Man*. *Night on Earth* can be read as a
turning (back) point, even a moment of hesitation. Each episode is built upon a
confrontation between the cab driver and his/her passenger(s). The first four are all
essentially duologues; the first three are constructed upon two people learning to
understand and respect each other, despite differences of class, nationality, and
color/handicap (respectively). We may not, first time around, notice (I didn't) that
the episodes, as they move east, become progressively pessimistic about human contact. The first (Los Angeles: Winona Ryder/Gena Rowlands) is surely the nearest
Jarmusch has come to "feel good," both women strengthened by their mutual
understanding; the second (New York: Armin Muller-Stahl/Giancarlo Esposito)
ends with the two men liking each other but with no real understanding; the third
(Paris: Isaach De Bankolé/Béatrice Dalle)[1] culminates in a kind of deadlock
between them, their sense of (and affection for) each other becoming clear only
after they have separated. The fourth episode (Rome: Roberto Benigni/Paolo Bona-
celli) is misleading because it is so hilarious, yet here there is no mutual understanding at all: one character dies of a heart attack brought on by the other's monologue, and we are left with a dead body propped up on a bench in the darkness. This
paves the way for the final sequence (Helsinki), where contact is minimal, the ending totally desolate. It was as if Jarmusch was tempted by the lure of the mainstream
but made the film as a vehicle for the expression of his rejection of it.

Dead Men

Jarmusch's two most recent films at time of writing are both centered on protagonists who are announced as "dead" from the outset: a few minutes into *Dead Man*,
the train fireman tells William Blake (Johnny Depp), whom he has never met
before, that he has seen him drifting in a boat on the river, which is where Blake will
die at the film's end ("You think to yourself; Why is it that the landscape is moving
but the boat is still?"); *Ghost Dog* (1999) begins with a quotation from *The Book of
the Samurai*: "Every day without fail one should consider oneself as dead." The two
characters are linked because, unlike their predecessors, they have rejected the purely
passive role of the alienated wanderer, Depp by accepting a job (which turns out not
to exist) in the far West, Whitaker, more positively, by forging an artificial identity
for himself as a modern samurai. Their decisions make of them totally isolated figures (Depp inadvertently, Whitaker from deliberate choice), doomed to destruc-

---

1. The two stars are familiar to admirers of Claire Denis, in whose films they appear regularly: no one will forget De Bankolé, an icon of impregnable dignity, in the title role of
Chocolat. Denis is credited as assistant director on *Down by Law*.

tion. In certain respects Jarmusch's early films suggest lingering fragments of the hippie movement so intelligently analyzed by Arthur Penn in *Alice's Restaurant*, admirable but ineffectual, the movement's force undermined by its isolation, worn away by pressures both internal and external, so that there is no longer the least sense of community or belonging that gave it what precarious strengths it had. The stance continues into *Dead Man*, but suddenly becomes far more potent, the disdain for mainstream culture transformed into a bleak, icily controlled rage. It is among the most impressive American films of the past ten years, a work of startling originality and integrity. Insofar as it evokes any previous film it is perhaps Godard's *Les Carabiniers*: there is a similar pervasive grim humor at which it is quite impossible to laugh, and (like Godard's remarkable film) it evokes and pays homage to silent cinema in the starkness of its black-and-white photography, the stylistic journey back in time corresponding to the film's backward itinerary into the American past.

The film also resembles *Les Carabiniers* in its stylistic fusion of apparent opposites, realism and extreme stylization. Today, the use of black-and-white photography is already a form of stylization (when it was the norm it was experienced as "realistic"). In *Dead Man* its distancing effect is intensified by the precise framing of iconic images, the deliberate, unhurried editing (the editing style already an affront to contemporary Hollywood). Yet, just as while watching *Les Carabiniers* we get the feeling that this is what war is really like (its tedium, its arbitrariness, its degradation, as well as its violence and horror), so here we feel (without having been there) that we are seeing the Old West as it really was, brutish, debased, squalid, degenerate before it could even begin to become civilized. One may reflect, as one emerges, that the idealism of a Ford, the stoic heroism of a Hawks, were probably there too, in occasional patches, yet those directors' "natural" styles (the shooting/editing patterns to which Hollywood accustomed us) seem a deception beside what Jarmusch shows us with his schematism and stylization. The strategy is beautifully established in the film's opening sequence, William Blake's journey by train into the wilderness, constructed upon alternating series of shots: medium close-ups of Blake, becoming increasingly worried, insecure, and alienated; static shots of the succession of men who sit opposite him (from dignified, well-dressed townsman to rough trapper), the "moving" shots (but the train is moving, not the camera) of landscapes that become progressively wilder, culminating in the wigwams of an Indian tribe. The precise sequence is:

1st passenger: elderly, dignified, civilized
1st landscape: young fir trees (a plantation?)
2nd passenger: unshaven, cowboy hat, wife beside him
3rd passenger (off to one side): woman (mid-30s?), modest, smiling at Blake coyly (widow in need of a new husband?)
2nd landscape: woods, ruined covered wagon (abandoned)

3rd landscape: rocky, barren mountains

4th passenger: elderly, bearded trapper-type, wearing skins, long (but clean) hair

4th landscape: flat, barren desert, outcrops of rock

(We see the fireman, stoking the fire, as train enters tunnel.)

5th passenger(s): hunters, fur hats, rifles

5th landscape: wigwams, but half-demolished, no sign of habitation

6th passenger: unkempt, wearing skins, long, shaggy, dirty-looking hair, almost crazy expression.

(The culminating image is of a number of such men firing frantically out of the train windows to kill buffalo and add to the destruction of Indian civilization.)

The protagonists of *Dead Man* and *Ghost Dog* are doomed for quite different reasons. Ghost Dog himself has made a deliberate choice, distinguishing himself from the chaos, formlessness, and confusion of contemporary America: the perverse adoption of a set of codes that made sense within a different culture in a different age but here are arbitrary and artificial. It is, in its way, heroic even while its morality and sense are questionable (it involves killing people when ordered by a local Mafia associate); his downfall stems from his refusal to kill an "innocent," drug-addled young woman, even though she is a witness to other killings. We never know exactly why William Blake has chosen to go West (because of an unhappy love affair?—but the curiously visionary train fireman dismisses this as inadequate motivation). Unlike Ghost Dog, he wanders innocently into trouble, completely out of his depth, learning to make choices only when they are forced on him, killing to survive (and he barely survives the squalid, primitive town before losing himself in the wilderness).

Ford, in *My Darling Clementine* (1946), attempted a clear distinction between the daytime Tombstone (civilization, order, people going to an unbuilt church, "sweet-smelling" hair oil and "the scent of the desert flowers," the dance on the church floor centered upon "our new marshal and his lady fair") and the nighttime (darkness, violence, drunkenness, the "Clanton" world). Jarmusch, in 1995, can give us only the nighttime version, even during the day. The most conspicuous sights that William Blake passes on his initial walk through the streets of Machine are half-finished coffins and buffalo skulls, human misery (a woman, who looks too old to be the baby's mother, rocking a cradle), male faces of suspicion and hostility, a man getting his cock sucked in public by a prostitute (and instantly drawing a gun when he sees Blake watching): recognizable as the genesis and basis of the "civilization" we are shown in *Stranger Than Paradise* and *Down by Law*, as if there were direct continuity. Ford also saw early American civilization as turning a "wilderness" into a "garden." In *Dead Man*, the only approach to a garden is suggested by the paper roses of the young woman Blake assists when she is thrown into the gutter by one of the town's male citizens. "When I get the money," she tells him, "I'd like to make them out of cloth." When they are in bed, and he asks her why she keeps a gun under her pillow, she replies simply, "Because this is America." Our final image of the town is of the paper roses lying in the gutter. That would appear to be about all Jarmusch—an intelligent and profoundly honest artist—can offer us in terms of "positives."

The structure of the film allows, very clearly, for the construction of a very different "positive" in the form of Indian culture—the culture that the British, in both the United States and Canada, effectively destroyed. I know nothing about the working of Jarmusch's mind, but I cannot help wondering whether, for perhaps one second, the possibility of presenting this passed through it. After all, a number of American filmmakers, with good intentions, varying degrees of intelligence, and (predictable) unsuccess, have attempted such a thing: Ford in *Cheyenne Autumn*, Fuller in *Run of the Arrow*, Penn in *Little Big Man*, Kostner in *Dances with Wolves*. The possibility is there, in the film, in the figure of the Indian who saves Blake's life, but Jarmusch refuses its temptations from the outset. He has clearly understood that for an American to glorify Indian culture (as "innocent," "natural," "unspoiled," etc.) is either hypocritical, sentimental, or both (and in any case quite useless today, whether to Native Americans or whites). Hence Jarmusch's Indian is "Nobody" (the massively iconic Gary Farmer), an outcast from both the tribes (unspecified) that produced his mixed parentage. This gives him a certain advantage (when asked by the first group of three possible killers who else is "out there," Blake can reply, quite truthfully if not exactly honestly, "Nobody," and get all three swiftly shot to death). But this is in itself at best a mixed blessing: the first three are not the hired gunmen, are in fact quite innocent of malice, merely stupid and blundering. Nobody is, in fact, one more of Jarmusch's alienated dropouts, a person without an identity, and even he is not permitted to survive the movie.

The other "positive" value the film seems to offer also emerges from Nobody: the Indian's passionate commitment to the poems of William Blake (whom he assumes the film's William Blake to be). He quotes: "Every night and every morn / Some to misery are born ./ Every morn and every night / Some are born to sweet delight. / Some are born to sweet delight, / Some are born to endless night . . . "—the last line addressed very pointedly to Blake, the personification of America's future. But, within Jarmusch's America, past and present, *none* is born to sweet delight. Ultimately, in his films, endless night seems all that's left.

The film's latter half, as the action moves further from white civilization into the wilderness, seems, indeed, to move beyond any level of social criticism to a level of philosophy (which will mean more to those who belive in "absolutes" and "eternal truths" than it does to me). The commentary on American civilization continues, with the sequence centered on the corrupt and hypocritical trading post official

(Alfred Molina), but this seems partly to give way to a sense that human life is in itself irredeemable, the sense of some fundamental sickness at the very roots of existence. I feel very tentative about this, but I feel Jarmusch here to be hovering on the brink, indecisive as to which way to step. The issue is not resolved in *Ghost Dog*, which (fascinating and estimable as it is) takes us no further.

The following books and articles are either referred to or quoted in the text.

Barthes, Roland. *Mythologies*. London: Jonathan Cape, 1972.

——. *S/Z: An Essay*. New York: Hill and Wang, 1974.

Bellour, Raymond. "Hitchcock, the Enunciator." *Camera Obscura* 2 (Fall 1977): 69–94.

Berger, John. *Ways of Seeing*. London: Pelican, 1972.

Britton, Andrew. "Blissing Out: The Politics of Reaganite Entertainment." *Movie* 31–32.

——. "*Mandingo*. *Movie* 22: 1–22.

——. "Sexuality and Power, or, the Two Others." *Framework* 6 (Autumn 1977): 7–11; and 7–8 (Spring 1978): 5–11.

——. "Sideshows: Hollywood in Vietnam." *Movie* 27–28: 2–23.

Brown, Norman O. *Life Against Death: The Psychoanalytical Meaning of History*. Middletown: Wesleyan University Press, 1959.

Burch, Noel. *To the Distant Observer: Form and Meaning in the Japanese Cinema*. Berkeley: University of California Press, 1979.

Burstyn, Varda. "Masculine Dominance and the State," published in *The Socialist Register* (1983), 45–89. London: Merlin Press.

——. *The Rites of Men: Manhood, Politics, and the Culture of Sport*. Toronto: University of Toronto Press, 1999.

Coveney, Peter. *The Image of Childhood*. London: Peregrine, 1967.

Dyer, Richard. *Seven*. London: British Film Institute, 1999.

Freud, Sigmund. *Case Histories II*. London: Pelican Freud Library, vol. 9.

——. *On Sexuality*. London: Pelican Freud Library, vol. 7.

Gombrich, E. H. *Art and Illusion*. Washington, D.C.: National Gallery of Art, 1959.

Hardy, Robin. Review of *Cruising*. *Body Politic* (March 1980).

Horowitz, Gad. *Repression: Basic and Surplus Repression in Psychoanalytic Theory: Freud, Reich, Marcuse*. Toronto: University of Toronto Press, 1977.

Johnston, Claire, ed. *The Work of Dorothy Arzner: Towards a Feminist Cinema*. London: BFI, 1975.

Leavis, F. R. *English Literature in Our Time and the University*. London: Chatto and Windus, 1967.

Lippe, Richard. "*New York, New York* and the Hollywood Musical." *Movie* 31–32.

Marcuse, Herbert. *Eros and Civilization: A Philosophical Inquiry into Freud.* Boston: Beacon Press, 1955.

Mulvey, Laura. "Visual Pleasure and Narrative Cinema." *Screen* 16.3 (Autumn 1975): 6–18.

Pye, Douglas. "Genre and History." *Movie* 25: 1–11.

——. "Genre and Movies." *Movie* 20: 29–43.

——. "John Ford and the Critics." *Movie* 22: 43–52.

Rossiter, A. P. *Angel with Horns.* Edited by Graham Storey. London: Longmans, 1961.

Schneider, Michael. *Neurosis and Civilization: A Marxist/Freudian Synthesis.* New York: Seabury Press, 1975.

NOTE: Titles are in italics. An asterisk indicates titles of works other than films. Initial articles (e.g., *The, La, Les, Une*) are ignored in sorting.